The Bar and the Old Bailey,
1750–1850

STUDIES IN LEGAL HISTORY

Published by the University of North Carolina Press in
association with the American Society for Legal History

Thomas A. Green and Hendrik Hartog, editors

THE BAR

and the

OLD BAILEY,

1750–1850

ALLYSON N. MAY

The University of North Carolina Press

Chapel Hill and London

© 2003 The University of North Carolina Press
All rights reserved

Manufactured in the United States of America
Set in Janson by Tseng Information Systems, Inc.

⊗ The paper in this book meets the guidelines for permanence
and durability of the Committee on Production Guidelines
for Book Longevity of the Council on Library Resources.

Library of Congress Cataloging-in-Publication Data
May, Allyson N. (Allyson Nancy), 1961–
The bar and the Old Bailey, 1750–1850 / Allyson N. May.
p. cm. — (Studies in legal history)
Includes bibliographical references and index.
ISBN 0-8078-2806-8 (cloth : alk. paper)
1. Great Britain. Central Criminal Court—History. 2. Criminal justice,
Administration of—Great Britain—History. 3. Criminal procedure—Great Britain—
History. 4. Trial practice—Great Britain—History. I. Title. II. Series.
KD8289.M38 2003
345.42′05—dc21
2003008353

cloth 07 06 05 04 03   5 4 3 2 1

To John and Anne,
Nicole, Sean, and Coco,
past and present zoo

Contents

Tables and Illustrations

Acknowledgments

I would like to thank the staff at Microtext and Interlibrary Loans, Robarts Library, University of Toronto; the York University Law Library; the British Library; the Greater London Record Office; the Guildhall Library; the Public Record Office; the Supreme Court Library (Bench); and Ian Murray, former archivist of the Inner Temple, for their assistance in the course of my research. Given the nature of the project, the bulk of my time was divided between two further institutions; thus I am particularly grateful to the archivists and searchroom attendants at the Corporation of London Records Office (CLRO) and to the librarians and staff at Lincoln's Inn Library. Thanks to Jim Sewell, Juliet Bankes, Vivienne Aldous, Hugo Deadman, Sophie Bridges, Philip Gale, Elizabeth Scudder, Larry Francis, and Tim Harvey at the CLRO, and to Guy Holborn, Catherine McArdle, Frances Bellis, Roland Nedd, and the resourceful library assistant who pried a jammed disc from my laptop with a letter opener at Lincoln's Inn. Guy's research into biographical sources for lawyers greatly facilitated the initial stages of this project. Thanks also to Jenny Ramkalawon at the British Museum (Prints and Drawings) for her help. I am grateful to the British Museum, the Harvard Law Library, and the Corporation of London Records Office for allowing me to reproduce the illustrations in this book.

I thank the University of Toronto and the Social Sciences and Humanities Research Council of Canada for funding the Ph.D. in which this study originated, and the Centre of Criminology, University of Toronto, for facilities provided when I was a graduate student. I also thank the Peter Wall Institute for Advanced Studies at the University of British Columbia for appointing me a Visiting Junior Scholar in 1998. Apart from the generous funding, the international and interdisciplinary nature of this program was truly invigorating.

Donna Andrew, Victor Bailey, John Beattie, Simon Devereaux, Tom Green, Guy Holborn, Joanna Innes, John Langbein, Randy McGowen, and Andrea McKenzie read and commented on various drafts of this work. Their feedback was much appreciated, and I hope I have put it to good use. Chapters—or portions thereof—were also presented at meetings of the American Society for Legal History, the Canadian Law and Society Association, the North American Conference on British Studies, the Toronto Legal History Group, and the Yale Legal History Forum. Any outstanding errors are of course my sole responsibility. I am especially grateful to John Beattie, who supervised my doctoral dissertation on the Old Bailey bar, and Tom Green, series editor for Studies in Legal History, both of whom have provided long-term support and encouragement.

I thank the Huntley-Nisson clan at Marden Hill, Hertfordshire—Colin and Tove, Mutti, Karin White, and Lars—for their unfailing hospitality over the course of my research trips. Thanks as well to Charles Grench, Amanda McMillan, Paula Wald, and Aimee Bollenbach of the University of North Carolina Press, and to my copyeditor, Mary Reid.

Finally, I thank my family, to whom this book is dedicated.

The Bar and the Old Bailey, 1750–1850

Introduction

The Bar and the Old Bailey chronicles the history of the English criminal trial and the emergence of a criminal bar from the mid-eighteenth century, when the employment of counsel in felony trials was rare and the activities of defense counsel restricted, to the mid-nineteenth, by which time adversarial procedure in the criminal courts had been accepted and professional standards of conduct formulated. It is in large part a study of the transformation of the criminal trial from a private altercation between victim and accused into a contest between paid advocates. But while its subject might be described as the rise of advocacy in the criminal courts, the focus, as the title indicates, is on the advocates. What follows is also a history of the development of the criminal trial and a criminal bar in a particular place: metropolitan London. In the late eighteenth and early nineteenth centuries there was significant variation in the mechanics of lawyers' participation in criminal trials—the proportions of trials in which counsel were employed, whether their presence was divided equally between the prosecution and the defense, the way in which counsel for the prosecution opened his case— among the assize circuits and between the circuits and the Old Bailey, London's principal criminal court. That variation renders the present history London history. Many of the issues discussed, however, have a much broader significance, for the "special problems of the metropolis" would shape the development of English trial procedure.[1]

Traditionally, felony trials consisted of a confrontation between victim and accused. England had no system of public prosecution, and although lawyers were permitted to raise points of law on behalf of the accused, they were prohibited from speaking to the facts. The first change in this scenario was restricted to trials of high treason. Perversions of justice occasioned by politically motivated prosecutions in the late seventeenth century led to the enactment of the Treason Trials Act of 1696. Persons accused of high treason, who met inevitably with a lawyer-driven prosecution, were granted by this statute the right to full legal representation. While no such change was legislated for trials of felony until the nineteenth century, informal, ad hoc developments resulted in the entry of defense counsel over a century earlier.[2]

The introduction of lawyers into criminal proceedings was the result not of any deliberate intent on the part either of the state or the legal profession to refashion the felony trial as a professional contest; it was instead rooted in particular historical circumstances, prominent among which were commercial expansion and rising fears about crime, especially in metropolitan London. These circumstances are reviewed in Chapter 1, which opens with a description of London as it existed, geographically and socially, when we can begin to identify early criminal practitioners. Chapter 1 further establishes the context of "the coming of the lawyers"[3] by surveying the contemporary administration of criminal justice in the metropolis before introducing the counsel practicing at the Old Bailey in the period 1750–80.

A prototypical Old Bailey barrister had emerged in the person of William Davy in the middle of the eighteenth century, and by the 1780s a small bar was attached to London's criminal courts. It was controversial from its inception, and fact and fiction soon blurred where this bar was concerned. The stereotype of the "Old Bailey hack" became a fixture of the nineteenth-century legal professional literature, and it has been reproduced in modern studies of both the bar and the criminal trial. Thus J. R. Lewis reports that according to "the commonly held view" of the Old Bailey, "the ruffianism of the prisoners is now and then surpassed by the ruffianism of the advocates"; Raymond Cocks that the Old Bailey "was regarded as a forum for dishonest hacks"; and David Bentley that, into the 1840s, the Old Bailey bar, "notorious for its touting, bullying of witnesses and rudeness to the bench, was an open disgrace," while David Cairns complains of the "low standards of advocacy" typical of the Old Bailey.[4] Behind the stereotypes and stereotypical behavior, however, lie real barristers. Chapters 2 through 4 identify the counsel who practiced at the Old Bailey from the 1780s into the 1830s, outline their legal practice, and consider their role in the criminal trial in the era preceding the Prisoners' Counsel Act of 1836.

In seeking the explanation for the rise of adversarialism we must look to the motivations and interests of a number of actors: prosecutors, defendants, the bench, and the state each contributed to the development of adversarial procedure in the Old Bailey courtroom. But the motives of counsel themselves have also to be considered. Chapter 2 explores the reasons for the attachment of Old Bailey counsel to London's criminal courts, in the process considering their political affiliations and their views on crime and punishment. The emergence of an Old Bailey bar coincided with mounting criticism of England's penal code, which prescribed death by hanging as the punishment for most serious crimes.

Practice at the Old Bailey was not exclusive; it formed part of a broader "metropolitan practice," a subject taken up in Chapter 3. Members of London's criminal bar tended not to succeed in the high courts of justice found in Westminster Hall, but they appeared regularly in the customary and petty courts of metropolitan London. Their careers were distinct from those of other colleagues at the bar, but the distinction was one of professional venue rather than specialization of law, for in the various metropolitan courts they handled a wide variety of civil cases. Chapter 3 thus affords a glimpse at a level of professional practice rarely discussed in histories of the bar.

Within metropolitan practice City connections proved particularly important. While the "stars" of the Old Bailey—William Garrow in the 1780s, Charles Phillips in the 1820s and 1830s—possessed a flair for advocacy and a talent for cross-examination that ensured success in the criminal courts, some of their colleagues probably owed their attendance to an association forged early in their careers with the City of London. The City's "common pleaders," barristers who purchased monopolies of practice in its petty civil courts, were occasionally provided by the City solicitor with a brief for a criminal prosecution. This City connection becomes an important theme of the book, as it had significant consequences for justice in early-nineteenth-century London.

Where Chapter 3 establishes the broad parameters of Old Bailey counsels' legal practice, Chapter 4 focuses on the role they played specifically in the criminal courts, from pretrial procedure through to their influence on sentencing. Full-fledged adversarial process lay in the future. The majority of felony trials took place without counsel engaged for either the prosecution or the defense, and even in the small proportion of trials involving counsel on both sides, the professional contest in this period was an uneven one. The limited participation of defense counsel nonetheless altered the dynamic of the trial in fundamental ways. Whereas the focus in the early modern criminal trial had been on the accused's response to the charges laid and the evidence presented against him, defense counsel redirected attention to the strengths and weaknesses of the case presented by the prosecution. The trial became a test of the prosecution evidence.[5] The eighteenth-century introduction of counsel into trials of felony also constituted the thin end of the wedge of professional adversarialism.

Chapter 5 pauses to consider public and professional reaction to the participation of counsel in criminal trials and, more specifically, to the phenomenon of an Old Bailey bar. It explores the reputation of individual barristers and the development of the generic stereotype, the "Old Bailey hack." It also distinguishes between lay and professional concerns about advocacy in the criminal courts.

The subject of reputation continues in Chapter 6, which follows the promotion of certain Old Bailey counsel to the bench of that court by virtue of their appointment to the offices of recorder and common serjeant of London. This development alone justifies a study of London's criminal lawyers, for the City's judges wielded considerable power and influence. Hundreds of criminal cases were tried annually at the Old Bailey in the late eighteenth century, thousands in the early nineteenth century. By the 1830s the City judges presided over the majority of these trials. Moreover, until 1837 the recorder reported to the king and cabinet on all capital convictions in London. Those reports provided the basis for the decisions made as to who would hang and who would be reprieved.

Chapters 7 and 8 return to the felony trial and the role of counsel within it, describing the second stage in the transformation of the trial: the changes effected by the Prisoners' Counsel Act of 1836. These chapters take the story to the middle of the nineteenth century and address issues of national rather than local significance.

The parliamentary history of the Prisoners' Counsel Act has been described elsewhere;[6] Chapter 7 thus focuses on the positions taken by barristers practicing at the Old Bailey and the legal profession more generally during debate over prisoners' counsel. At the heart of this debate lay profound disagreement over the relationship between truth and advocacy. By 1836 a limited participation of counsel in felony trials had long been taken for granted and acknowledged as useful. Few would argue that legislative sanction should not be bestowed on existing arrangements, and a provision entitling the accused to copies of the depositions sworn against him, which he had traditionally been denied, met with broad support. The controversy was occasioned by a further innovation: not only would the Prisoners' Counsel Act grant to those accused of felony the right to counsel, it would also allow defense counsel to fully assume his client's defense, that is, to address the jury on his client's behalf. At issue was whether professional advocacy would promote or impede discovery of the truth.

The participation of counsel in late-eighteenth- and early-nineteenth-century criminal trials did much to drive the trial in the direction of a professional contest. The bar, however, had never consciously been working to achieve this end. Many of its members, including prominent Old

Bailey counsel, were vehemently opposed to implementation of the Prisoners' Counsel Act, and while the reasons for their resistance were various, mistrust of professional advocacy was prominent among them. In the 1830s strong doubts about the utility of advocacy in the criminal courts were entertained within the bar as well as without.

Because the bar had resisted implementation of the Prisoners' Counsel Act, professional justifications for the changes it imposed derived after the fact of change. Theoretical engagement with the new form of trial dates from the 1840s. This engagement, and the development of rules of professional conduct for defense counsel, is explored in Chapter 8. The issue of public opinion is also taken up, as the English public, relatively mute in the discussions preceding the Prisoners' Counsel Act, subsequently found its voice.

Over the course of the 1840s the bar and the public engaged in a sustained debate over the rights of the accused, the proper role of defense counsel, the duty owed to a (potentially guilty) client, the problems posed by a confession of guilt, and, more generally, the morality of advocacy, especially as it pertained to the criminal trial. These issues had inevitably to be resolved once the Prisoners' Counsel Act was in place, but their determination would be provoked in large part by a controversy involving London's leading criminal counsel, Charles Phillips, arising from a murder trial heard at the Old Bailey in June 1840. This particular murder, the victim of which belonged to one of England's most prominent political families, had from the initial reports attracted intense public interest. The decisions arrived at by the bar with respect to the duties of defense counsel would thus be reached in the full glare of publicity.

During debate over the Prisoners' Counsel Act in the 1820s and 1830s, attention had centered largely on the protection of innocence. Allowing defense counsel to comment on the evidence, the reformers argued, would facilitate determination of the truth of the charge against the accused. It would prevent wrongful convictions and encourage rightful ones. The *Courvoisier* trial of 1840 diverted the debate from "truth" to "justice," for at midtrial the accused admitted to his counsel that he had committed the murder but refused to change his plea to guilty. There were no agreed-upon rules of conduct to guide Phillips in these circumstances, and his decision to continue with the defense occasioned both public outrage and considerable soul-searching within the legal profession. Chapter 8 examines the public and professional response to Phillips's conduct of Courvoisier's defense and the bar's elaboration and acceptance of a distinction between legal and moral guilt.

As described in the Conclusion, at the point at which this study ends many important developments in the history of adversarial trial procedure lay in the future. Theory and practice had not converged by the middle of the nineteenth century; for practical reasons, that is, criminal trials had not routinely assumed the form of a professional contest. Yet by 1850 a criminal bar was an established fact, and the criminal trial had undergone a dramatic theoretical revision. For good or ill, the foundations of the modern form of Anglo-American criminal trial had been laid.

CHAPTER ONE

London, Crime,
and Criminal Justice

The Eighteenth-Century Metropolis

In 1750 England's great metropolis comprised both the City of London, a medieval creation whose origins can be traced back to a Roman city established on the north bank of the Thames in the second century A.D.,[1] and Westminster, which lies two miles west on the river. By the eighteenth century the City had become both a mercantile stronghold and the financial center of England, while Westminster, originally the site of an eighth-century Benedictine abbey, was the center of both the royal court and Parliament. London and Westminster retained separate identities for the purposes of municipal government, but the physical distance which divided them had long since been built up, the Strand running into Fleet Street, so that "geographically they had become one."[2] Buildings had likewise grown up on land whose administration, including the administration of criminal justice, lay with the county of Middlesex.

Eighteenth-century London would appear small to the modern observer: in 1750 the area to the north of Bloomsbury Square was still undeveloped; to the west Chelsea and Fulham were the sites of market gardens; to the east the former village of Whitechapel had become part of London, but Stepney had not yet been swallowed up. South of the Thames there was less development still: the bulk of metropolitan London lay on the river's north shore. At the south end of London Bridge—until Westminster Bridge opened in November 1750 the city's sole bridge—lay the borough of Southwark, east of which some commercial ribbon development was taking place. Very little building was to be found opposite Westminster in the mid-eighteenth century. Nevertheless, metropolitan London had become the largest city in Europe, and for contemporaries it was a place of rapid expansion and change.[3] The construction of the "New Road" (now the Marylebone, Euston, and Pentonville Roads) in 1756–57 stimulated development in

[7]

the north, while Westminster Bridge and a third bridge, Blackfriars, completed in 1769, allowed further development south of the river. The second half of the eighteenth century witnessed continued growth. By the 1760s the villages of Hammersmith, Chelsea, Paddington, Marylebone, and St. Pancras were being steadily drawn into the metropolis, and by the 1790s some early development had begun in Camden Town. Even the older parts of London looked new. Four-fifths of the City had been destroyed in the Great Fire of London (1666); in the process of rebuilding, the City within the walls retained its narrow, twisting lanes, but the gabled, half-timbered houses and lattice windows of the medieval and Elizabethan period were replaced by sash-windowed brick.[4] Wren's domed cathedral had arisen on the site of the medieval St. Paul's, while to the west the palaces which had once lined the Strand were gone and in their place stood glass-fronted shops.

The growth of "opulent, enlarg'd, and still increasing" London[5] in the first half of the eighteenth century owed as much, if not more, to increasing wealth as it did to population. The population of metropolitan London in 1700 has been estimated at 575,000; by 1750 it was 675,000, and by the end of the century it had reached 900,000. This growth in numbers owed primarily to immigration rather than natural increase: a contemporary estimated in 1757 that two-thirds of London's adult population had been born elsewhere.[6] London's potent "brew of government, trade and industry"[7] attracted immigrants from within and without England and from every social class. Thomas Gisborne wrote of its attraction for the "upper and middle ranks of society": "Business, interest, curiosity, the love of pleasure, the desire for knowledge, the thirst for change, ambition to be deemed polite, occasion a continual influx into the metropolis from every corner of the Kingdom."[8] The center of conspicuous consumption, London attracted those whose social aspirations went beyond a mere ambition to be deemed polite, those who aspired to live in the "bon ton."[9] It also drew thousands of young Englishmen and women of the laboring classes in search of work. Irish immigrants likewise arrived in search of employment, while continental migrants included Huguenots fleeing persecution in France at the end of the seventeenth century and, from the 1750s, Polish and German Jews similarly in search of a safe haven.[10]

The majority of Londoners lived outside the City proper. In 1750 the intramural population was roughly 87,000, but London's inhabitants had long since overflowed the walls built by the Romans, rebuilt in the medieval period, and now a memory—although the six gates which had once controlled access were not torn down until 1760, a few years after the last decayed houses and shops on London Bridge were demolished. Migrants in search of work gravitated toward adjoining districts, and many of those entitled to the City's freedom were choosing to live farther afield. Affluent merchants had begun to move west in the reign of Charles II, and this process was accelerated by the rebuilding which took place after the fire. In the eighteenth century the West End became the more fashionable residential area, attracting not only London's commercial wealth and the politicians (who naturally sought proximity to the seat of government) but aristocrats as well. England's landed elite spent their winters in town, and the aristocracy had begun to migrate west from their former haunts—Covent Garden, Leicester Fields, Soho Square—in the early part of the century, to concentrate in the parishes of St. James's and St. George's and north of Piccadilly.[11] The polarization between the East End and the West was well established by midcentury: polite society quitted the courts, lanes, and alleys typical of sixteenth, seventeenth, and early eighteenth-century London for the elegant new squares being built in the West End.

The bar, the upper branch of England's legal profession, and the judiciary lagged behind in the westward migration of the well-to-do. Throughout the eighteenth century both bench and bar tended to remain near their professional institutions, the Inns of Court—the Inner and Middle Temple, Lincoln's Inn, and Gray's Inn—which lay just within and immediately without the City's borders.[12] Traditionally a barrister's chambers had provided both living accommodation and legal office, and into the nineteenth century young, unmarried barristers lived in as well as worked from their Inn. Once married they sought larger quarters—chambers typically consisted of no more than three or four small rooms—but remained in the same area. Addresses in Chancery Lane and Lincoln's Inn Fields were common; Bedford Row, just west of Gray's Inn, was thickly populated with legal counsel by the 1780s;[13] and the new suburb of Bloomsbury, designed to meet the needs of the professional classes, likewise proved popular. Where the bar is concerned, westward migration dates from the second half of the nineteenth century.[14]

Although the Inns of Court provided a young man with a "genteel" address, they also offered close proximity to less respectable neighborhoods.[15] This diversity was typical of central London. Samuel Johnson, who famously claimed that a man who was tired of London was tired of life, commented that the intellectual man could not help but be struck with the metropolis "as comprehending the whole of human life in all its variety."[16] The "full tide of human existence" was to be found at Charing Cross.[17] This full tide encompassed not only those aspiring to the good life but also legions of the poor, divided by Daniel Defoe earlier in the century into two classes:

the merely poor, those who "fare hard," and "the *miserable*, that really pinch and suffer want,"[18] those who in the nineteenth century would be classified as the "residuum." Against Cowper's portrait of "opulent" London must be placed that of William Blake: "I wander thro' each charter'd street, / Near where the charter'd Thames does flow / And mark in every face I meet, / Marks of weakness, marks of woe."[19]

As Dorothy George described, London's poor lived primarily in insalubrious and dangerous areas, notably in the interstices at the borders of municipal authority, such as the maze of lanes and alleys surrounding Chick Lane and Field Lane, or Turnmill Street and Cow Cross, where authority was divided among parishes of the City of London and the county of Middlesex.[20] The older parts of the metropolis—"the courts off Holborn and Gray's Inn Lane, the rookeries of St. Giles and some dreadful places off Great Queen Street and Long Acre"—had generally become dangerous areas in which to live, as were many of the courts and lanes off Fleet Street and the Strand, those surrounding Haymarket, St. James's Market, and Covent Garden, and the older parts of Westminster. To the east of the City, "East Smithfield, Houndsditch, parts of Shoreditch and Whitechapel, Rosemary Lane (Rag Fair), Petticoat Lane, Ratcliffe Highway were dangerous neighbourhoods," as was Southwark, south of the river.[21] In fact, much of central London was riddled with neighborhoods of bad character, in which the honest poor and the criminal were forced to rub shoulders.

While the poverty-stricken were often blamed for their own distress, the nature of employment in the capital was frequently the root cause. Writing about London's poor in 1753, the Methodist preacher John Wesley commented indignantly that he had found in the city's cellars and garrets "not one of them unemployed who was able to crawl about the room. So wickedly, devilishly false is that common objection, they are poor only because they are idle."[22] Irregular and uncertain employment was the lot of many of London's migrants: "The dominating impression of life in eighteenth-century London, from the standpoint of the individual," wrote George, "is one of uncertainty and insecurity."[23] The metropolis might offer a reasonably secure living to those engaged in neither trade nor manufacture—a group which included lawyers—but those whose living depended on tradeable services inhabited a completely different world.[24] Much of their work depended heavily on the social season, which affected not only providers of domestic and local services but those employed in the textile and clothing industries and, higher up the social scale, those involved in the luxury trades serving the West End: jewelers, furniture makers (Chippendale opened workshops in Long Acre around 1745), and coachmakers, among many others.[25] Work on the river likewise depended on seasonal flows of trade. Many of London's inhabitants thus routinely experienced long periods of unemployment. In 1750 1,000 of 2,400 houses in Spitalfields, a suburb to the east of the City inhabited largely by silk weavers, were not required to pay the poor rates levied on well-to-do householders, as they were occupied by "journeymen weavers and other artificers and labourers" unable to support themselves or their families without resort to credit.[26] The situation worsened in the succeeding decades as downswings in trade led to further unemployment and riots in the streets.

Credit was not available to everyone in times of dearth. Magistrate Saunders Welch estimated that some twenty persons a week died indirectly of starvation in London, and the *London Magazine* reported with horror in 1763 that a prospective purchaser being shown over an "empty" house found in one of its rooms the semi-naked corpses of three emaciated women: whatever meager clothing they had possessed had apparently been stolen. Three other women were sheltering in the same house, two of them on the verge of the same fate.[27] Poor relief in the metropolis was organized at the parish level, responsibility shared among the parishes of the City of London, the City of Westminster, and a further fifty or so metropolitan parishes, and the system was stretched to its limits. Technically, to be eligible for relief the petitioner had to prove that he or she belonged to a particular parish. Some of the metropolitan parishes bent the rules and granted temporary or casual relief to nonsettled supplicants,[28] but many of London's poor were shunted from one jurisdiction to another by officials keen to avoid the expense of keeping them. In the City, lawyers benefited from the process: "passing the pauper" provided a steady, if modest, source of income for barristers employed in what were known as settlement cases.[29]

Crime and Criminal Justice

If poverty was a persistent problem in the metropolis, so too was crime. London was acquiring the reputation of a dangerous city, and it was increasingly a fearful one. The *London Magazine* reported in 1748 that "not only pickpockets but streetrobbers and highwaymen, are grown to a great pitch of insolence at this time, robbing in gangs, defying authority"; Horace Walpole wrote in the following year that "one is forced to travel, even at noon, as if one were going to battle."[30] Experts agreed. Henry Fielding, the novelist and Bow Street magistrate, warned in 1751 that London's streets would soon be "impassible without the utmost Hazard."[31] Metropolitan London's highways and byways were policed by part-time parish constables and watchmen, whose job it was to maintain public and moral order and to prevent crime by surveillance — especially during the night. Detective functions and the duty and capacity "to discover, arrest and prosecute" criminals did not, in 1750, form part of their responsibilities, although Fielding's "Bow Street runners" did undertake investigative work.[32]

Fielding laid the blame for increasing crime rates in part on London's very prosperity. Luxury was no longer confined to palaces: "[T]he eyes are feasted with show, and the ears with musick. . . . [G]luttony and drunkenness are allured by every kind of dainty. . . . [T]he finest women are exposed to view. . . . [T]he meanest person can dress himself clean, may in some degree mix with his betters, and thus perhaps satisfy his vanity as well as his love of pleasure." Luxury confined to the upper classes did little damage, but when it descended downward to "the tradesman, the mechanic, and the labourer" it was "most evidently the parent of theft and robbery."[33] Fielding also pointed to "that poison called *Gin*" — the subject of Hogarth's famous print, "Gin Lane" — which he suspected to be "the principal sustenance (if it may be so called) of more than an hundred thousand people" in the metropolis. Drunkenness, he argued, was a frequent cause of crime, leading to robbery and murder.[34] But, as contemporaries had recognized from the end of the previous century, crime rates were also affected by war and peace.[35] Public alarm and what have been described as "moral panics" occurred in the years of peace separating a series of wars, discernible after the conclusion of the War of Austrian Succession in 1748 as it would be again at the end of the Seven Years' War in 1756, when the war with America ended in 1781, and, in the nineteenth century, at the conclusion of the Napoleonic wars. Whenever the forces were "demobbed" an increase in criminal activity was assumed, and marked increases in prosecution occurred in the intervals of peace, particularly in the early 1750s and the 1780s. Reports of outrages — especially gang activity — proliferated, and widespread discussion of both the failure of the criminal justice system to deter and what was seen as the moral degeneracy of the nation ensued. The government undertook various initiatives to combat the problem, offering rewards for conviction and enhancing the severity of an already harsh criminal law.[36]

Whether stimulated by drink, fueled by envy, or exacerbated by the economic pressures of peace, crime in the eighteenth century was considered the result of moral failure. The criminal was thought to proceed from the minor crimes of childhood, such as idleness, lying, and petty theft, to debauchery in youth, which typically led to crimes involving drink, gambling, and women, to more serious property crimes and ultimately, perhaps, to murder, ending his career at the gallows. Hogarth's *Industry and Idleness* series, which contrasted the respective careers of Francis Goodchild and Tom Idle, famously depicted this trajectory in 1747. The records of the courts, however, reveal an obvious connection between poverty and property crime and tacit contemporary acknowledgment of this fact.

Well into the nineteenth century anyone convicted of a serious offense, including various forms of theft, faced the possibility of death by hanging, and public executions were a fact of late-eighteenth- and early-nineteenth-century life. But in practice England's criminal law was less severe than it appeared on the statute book. Offenders who were apprehended might never be tried, let alone executed, for English criminal justice depended on private prosecution. Even if a legal prosecution did ensue there were various ways in which the execution of an offender could be avoided: the exercise of discretion was available at virtually every stage of criminal proceedings.[37] The grand jury, the body of men who sat to determine whether the charge brought before the magistrate merited further action, might not return a "true bill," in which case the matter would not proceed to trial.[38] In cases that did come to trial juries sometimes delivered a "partial verdict" and convicted on a lesser, noncapital charge.[39] And even those convicted of a capital crime were not necessarily hanged. A few felonies retained a legal fiction known as "benefit of clergy," which allowed a capital convict to be branded on the hand and discharged for a first offense,[40] and a branding iron is mentioned in an inventory of the Old Bailey's fittings in the 1780s.[41] But in the eighteenth century it was the pardon system which operated to ensure that many of those who were sentenced to death were never actually executed.[42] At the conclusion of each Old Bailey session the recorder, the City's chief legal officer and Old Bailey judge, reported to the king and cabinet on all capital cases tried, and at a meeting which came to be known as the "recorder's report" it was ultimately determined who would hang and who would be spared.[43] Convicts themselves could also petition personally for mercy. Outright pardons were used to correct jury error, where it was felt that the accused had been wrongly convicted. There was no court of appeal. More frequently, however, pardons substituted the lesser punishment of transportation—to America before the Revolution, to Australia after 1787—where the circumstances of the crime and the character of the offender were thought to warrant it. Increasing dissatisfaction with the official alternatives of hanging or branding and releasing convicted offenders had resulted in the adoption of this secondary punishment in 1718.[44]

The administration of criminal justice in the eighteenth century was thus underpinned by the dual premises of terror and mercy. The real possibility of death by hanging was thought to deter criminals: public executions and the occasional display of gibbetted corpses served as dire warnings of the consequences of crime. But the harshness of the "Bloody Code" was tempered by the king's mercy, the exercise of which was believed to strengthen the bonds of loyalty between the sovereign and his subjects.[45] In the result, a significant gap existed between capital convictions and actual executions. In London it could not have been otherwise, for if every felon convicted at the Old Bailey had been hanged, their numbers would have been such as to create public revulsion and to destroy any legitimacy the law possessed. Application of the capital sanction was deliberately manipulated, and in choosing whom to hang, whom to transport, and whom to pardon the authorities walked a fine line. Sufficient and appropriate examples had to be executed, yet the numbers must not be such as to destroy public faith in the criminal justice system.

Administering Justice in London

By virtue of its size, eighteenth-century London posed considerable problems for the administration of criminal justice, straining a system designed for rural communities rather than the metropolitan conurbation. The strain was felt at every level of the system, from policing through the magistracy to trial and punishment. Crime, criminals, and the criminal justice system were thus topics which increasingly occupied the attention of private individuals, local officials, and the state.

The complex system by which justice was administered in metropolitan London reflected the city's diverse origins. Elsewhere in England the superior court judges, normally based in Westminster Hall,[46] rode out on circuit twice a year to administer the king's justice in what came to be known as the assizes. London, however, and the contiguous county of Middlesex fell outside this system of itinerant justice. There were no assizes for either jurisdiction. Nisi prius trials—civil cases in which there were factual issues to be determined, thus requiring a jury—were presided over by three judges of the common law bench, while criminal trials were held by virtue of commissions of the peace, of gaol delivery, and of oyer and terminer. Local justices of the peace, that is, were given authority "to enquire into, hear and determine" minor criminal offenses, while high court judges were empowered to try those held in gaol awaiting their arrival and to hear and determine any criminal cases brought before them. Separate commissions of oyer and terminer were issued for London and Middlesex, but the two jurisdictions shared a gaol: Newgate, the prison adjacent to the Old Bailey. Middlesex prisoners were transferred to Newgate the night before the sessions began and, like City prisoners (some of whom may also have originally been detained elsewhere), were delivered at the gaol delivery of this prison.

English criminal law made a distinction between crimes which were perceived as so heinous that the perpetrator's very life was forfeit (felonies) and those not thought sufficiently serious to warrant the death penalty (misdemeanors).[47] The distinction had consequences at various stages in criminal procedure, dictating where the trial would be heard and by whom, as well as the punishment attached to a conviction. Misdemeanors were tried by lay magistrates, while capital felonies were (usually) tried before two of the high court judges; the prescribed penalty for a convicted felon was death by hanging, while a range of lesser forms of punishment applied to those convicted of misdemeanors.

In metropolitan London the less serious criminal offenses were heard before the magistrates of the sessions of the peace. Precisely who served as magistrate again varied among the different jurisdictions of the metropolis. Within the City the twenty-six men elected for life to its executive council, the Court of Aldermen, were by 1741 required to sit as magistrates as part of their administrative duties.[48] The lord mayor, elected from within the Court of Aldermen to serve an annual term, was the leading magistrate. In the county of Middlesex magistrates were nominated by the lord lieutenant. Westminster had neither corporate status nor a lord mayor and aldermen; Middlesex justices thus sat on the Westminster bench.[49]

Elsewhere in England magistrates were men of property, drawn from the landed gentry; in urban Middlesex, however, it was difficult to find their equivalents, and Middlesex and Westminster justices of the peace consequently tended to be men of lower social standing than their provincial or City counterparts. Deservedly or not, they were frequently accused of being "trading justices," whose primary interest lay in collecting the fees of their office.[50] By the middle of the eighteenth century, however, metropolitan London had effectively acquired a stipendiary magistrate. Traditionally the office carried no salary, but Sir Thomas de Veil, who became a Middlesex magistrate in 1728, received both compensation and expenses from the central government; his successors at Bow Street, Henry Fielding (1748–54) and Fielding's half-brother John (1754–80), were likewise paid by the state. By 1780 the salary was openly acknowledged and the Bow Street magistrate recognized as the senior magistrate in metropolitan London.[51]

In theory, the metropolis was relieved by the presence of the Court of King's Bench in Westminster Hall from the obligation of holding quarter sessions of the peace, but few criminal cases were actually tried in that court, and the pressure of numbers meant that within metropolitan London "quarterly" sessions had in fact to be convened eight rather than four times a year. Sessions of the peace were held in three separate locations: at the Guildhall in the City of London, out of term at Westminster Hall in the City and Liberty of Westminster, and at the Clerkenwell Sessions House in Middlesex, Hicks' Hall, located in the vicinity of Smithfield market.[52] By the 1770s Hicks' Hall was in a state of grievous disrepair, and a new sessions house was constructed on Clerkenwell Green at the end of the century.[53]

Quarter sessions business included the administration of local government as well as minor criminal matters: the magistrates made orders respecting the poor law, wage and price regulations, and public works and had the power to grant or withhold licenses for taverns, hawkers, and fairs. While some sessions business had no connection with crime, in the eyes of contemporaries the licensing of taverns was closely tied to levels of criminal activity, and the metropolitan magistrates were continuously urged by the press to be more strict in ensuring that existing licensees did not abuse their privileges—that their taverns were not open all night or on the Sabbath—and to refrain from issuing licenses for new establishments. Drunkenness was believed to contribute to moral decay, and many taverns were less than respectable, the haunts of prostitutes and thieves.

Felonies in London were tried at the court commonly known as the Old Bailey; minor property crimes tried elsewhere in the country at the sessions of the peace were also usually left for the judges who sat at this court.[54] The bench found at the Old Bailey was itself unique, consisting of a combination of high court judges and City officials. While the judges of the superior courts attended in rotation, as they did elsewhere in the country on circuit, the City had been granted a degree of control over criminal jurisdiction within its boundaries by Henry I. The Old Bailey was thus nominally presided over by the lord mayor. The mayor's name had been included in gaol commissions from the Middle Ages, and a charter of 1327 declared him ex officio a justice of gaol delivery.[55] Into the second half of the eighteenth century, it seems that the lord mayor occasionally tried minor cases.[56] The recorder and senior aldermen had also traditionally been included in the commissions of the peace and oyer and terminer, and Edward IV's first charter to London (1462) confirmed that practice. Charters of 1638 and 1692 increased the number of aldermen to be included in the commission, and in 1741 George II had constituted all of them justices. Business could not proceed unless at least one of the City's aldermen was present on the bench, and in the eighteenth century they too may occasionally have presided over trials of minor crimes. The recorder routinely served as a judge, and from 1790 the common serjeant, a legal officer elected by the City's lower chamber of government, the Court of Common Council, was also required to act in that capacity. In the early nineteenth century the City would create a third civic judge.[57] The City thus retained its special privileges with respect to the administration of criminal justice despite changing demographic realities. As the metropolis expanded, Middlesex prisoners constituted "an increasingly large proportion of the Old Bailey calendar."[58] Newgate, however, lay within the City's boundaries, and Middlesex magistrates were not included in the gaol delivery commission.[59]

The Old Bailey sessions, like the sessions of the peace, were held eight times a year, convened in the periods which fell between the four law terms at Westminster and the assize circuits (when the judges of the superior courts would be otherwise engaged)—thus, typically, in January, February, April, May, June, August, October, and December. The metropolis was once again unique in that there was no formal separation between the sessions of the peace and those of oyer and terminer and gaol delivery: sessions of the peace in the City and in Middlesex were held at the same time as the Old Bailey sessions, and the records of both courts were kept together.[60] The Old Bailey had no grand jury—the body of men responsible for scrutinizing the bills of indictment presented by the local magistrates and pronouncing them "true," in which instance the cause went forward to trial by the petty jury, or "not found," in which case the prisoner was allowed to go free—of its own. It was supplied instead with bills provided by the grand juries of the three administrative units it served: Westminster, Middlesex, and London. The London grand jury, the same body of men assembled at the Guildhall for the sessions of the peace, was sworn in again at the Old Bailey on the opening day of the sessions. The Middlesex grand jury, charged at Hicks' Hall at the beginning of the sessions of the peace, presented the majority of bills, forwarding them to the Old Bailey from the Clerkenwell Sessions House.[61]

The Old Bailey Courthouse

The first courtroom built on the site of the present-day Old Bailey, which takes its name from the street that runs from Ludgate Hill to Holborn, was erected in 1539, although prisoners had been tried within the adjacent gaol, Newgate, or in neighboring premises, from the end of the twelfth century. Newgate, of Roman origin, was one of the ancient gates leading into the walled City of London; like Ludgate and Cripplegate it was also used as a prison by both the City of London and the county of Middlesex. The keeper of the gaol reported to the sheriffs of those two jurisdictions. One of the reasons expressed for the necessity of a separate justice hall had been the danger of infection inherent in trying cases within Newgate itself: "[M]oche peryll and daungyer hath chauncyd to the Justyces and other worshipful cominers attendyng upon the Justyces for delyveraunce of the Kynges gaole," noted London's Court of Common Council.[62] The design of the original court reflected the same fear: a print published in the early eighteenth century shows that one side remained open to the elements to allow fresh air to circulate.[63]

The justice hall in use at the Old Bailey in 1750 was described in the early eighteenth century as

> a fair and stately building, very commodious . . . having large Galleries on both sides or ends, for the reception of Spectators. The Court Room being advanced by Stone Steps from the Ground, with Rails and Bannisters inclosed from the yard before it. And the *Bail Dock*, which fronts the Court, where the Prisoners are kept until brought to their Trials, is also inclosed. Over the Court Room is a stately Dining Room, sustained by ten Stone Pillars. . . . There be fair Lodging Rooms and other Conveniences, on either side of the Court. It standeth backwards, so that it hath no Front towards the Street, only the Gateway leading into the yard before the House, which is spacious.[64]

By the 1760s the sessions house no longer appeared commodious or stately, and George Dance, the architect employed by the City in 1767 to reconstruct Newgate Prison, was also instructed to report on it.[65] If properly repaired, he said, the existing courthouse might last another thirty or forty years, but much of it he considered "totally useless." Dance's report detailed the accommodation required. Aside from the Justice Hall and the clerk of arraigns's room, considerable space was devoted to parlors, dining rooms, and withdrawing rooms for various City officials,[66] testimony to what would increasingly be felt as an unseemly admixture of hanging and transportation with the guzzling and swilling of the City's elite.[67] The new sessions house, which opened in October 1774, contained an elegant dining room for the lord mayor, with kitchens, butler's pantries, china closets, and wine vaults to serve it. The courtroom shared the first floor with parlors for the lord mayor and sheriffs of London; there was also a dining room for the swordbearer, which seated twenty-five, a drawing room for the same official, and a separate room for the lord mayor's clerks.[68] The City swordbearer had by custom lived in the sessions house until 1757, when, having complained about the state of repair of the building, he was awarded an allowance to live elsewhere. No apartments were provided for the swordbearer in the new sessions house, but the incumbent was allotted the gallery and entitled to charge a fee for admission.[69] City officials continued to profit from admission fees to the Old Bailey well into the nineteenth century.[70]

Rooms directly related to the administration of justice included the grand jury room and an indictment office, and for the first time a room was set aside for the use of witnesses, who formerly had the choice of standing in the open air in the yard or retiring to a local public house until they were called. In the new courtroom, lit by brass chandeliers, the bench followed a D-shaped curve. Above it were mounted the sword of justice and, from 1786, the king's arms; immediately below was a horseshoe-shaped table covered in green baize and reserved for counsel, whose presence was clearly antici-pated. A row of brass hooks was mounted on the rear wall to hold their gowns and wigs. Adjacent to the courtroom was a small closet equipped with inkstands and reference works: recent acts of Parliament, the *Statutes at Large*, Coke's *Institutes*, Foster's *Crown Law*, and Hale's *Pleas of the Crown*, plus six testaments and a "Hebrew bible."[71] A housekeeper and servants lived in, charged with taking care of the City's furniture and keeping the various apartments clean and in good order, while other City officials were responsible for fumigating the courts with "Nosegays and Strewings and Vinegar" morning and night during the sessions (a ventilator was also in-stalled in the ceiling in an attempt to draw off stink and infection), making sure that the cisterns of the water closets were supplied with water, providing the bench, counsel, and jury with paper, and placing the statute and other books on the court table before the sessions opened and returning them to the library each night.[72]

Trial at the Old Bailey

In 1750 the transmission of the dreaded gaol fever from Newgate to the courthouse famously killed the lord mayor, Sir Samuel Pennant, two judges (Baron Clark of the Exchequer and Sir Thomas Abney, judge of the Court of Common Pleas), an alderman, an undersheriff, several jurymen, and, according to one source, "some of the counsel."[73] Typically, the coun-sel remain unnamed. At that time the participation of lawyers in crimi-nal trials was still relatively rare, for the early modern criminal trial was far removed from the professional adversarial contest found in the Anglo-American world today.[74] Although criminal prosecutions were carried on in the name of the king, there was no system of public prosecution. The state's involvement in prosecution was extremely limited: law officers of the Crown prosecuted those accused of treason, and in the eighteenth century they be-came increasingly involved in coining and forgery cases. Murder occasioned another exception: homicide was a serious breach of the king's peace, and any violent or suspicious death was from the Middle Ages investigated by the coroner, who convened a jury to assist him. The coroner was empowered to bind over witnesses and suspects to appear at the next assizes, to imprison anyone suspected of homicide, and to take depositions.[75] As Langbein notes, the coroner system "was the closest English approximation to Continental-style public prosecution by an investigating officer."[76] But in the overwhelming majority of criminal prosecutions the state played no role at all. Victims of crime bore the chief responsibility for bringing offenders to justice: a victim's pursuit and apprehension of a suspected felon and his willingness to take that person before a local magistrate were crucial to prosecution. There were obviously disadvantages to a system of private prosecution. It did not deal adequately with public offenses, crimes in which no one had received special injury and for which no one would step forward to claim special satisfaction, and the financial burden borne by the private prosecutor must also have barred many victims of crime from seeking legal redress. Public prosecution, however, was viewed by the English as a potential threat to their constitutional liberties.[77] English criminal justice was thus rooted in private prosecution, and while there was no rule forbidding private prosecutors to engage counsel, they did not do so until the opening decades of the eighteenth century. At midcentury the presence of counsel for the prosecution was still rare.[78]

Just as the victim was largely responsible for the prosecution of a felony, the accused bore the responsibility for conducting his or her defense. Although defendants were not allowed to testify on oath before 1898,[79] their unsworn response to the charges laid was a fundamental determinant of the outcome of a trial. Lawyers were expressly and consistently forbidden to speak to the facts for the defense in felony trials. They could in theory be called upon to argue a point of law.[80] But legal assistance in answering the charges was thought to be unnecessary; there was even the suggestion that it might tend to obscure rather than promote a true determination of guilt or innocence: "[I]f counsel learned should plead [the defendant's] plea for him, and defend him, it may be that they would be so covert in their speeches, and so shadow the matter with words, and so attenuate the proofs and evidence, that it would be hard, or long to have the truth appear."[81] The defendant's unrehearsed reaction to the accusations made against him in court was believed essential to a determination of their truth, as William Hawkins, the author of an early-eighteenth-century treatise on Crown law, explained:

> [G]enerally every one of Common Understanding may as properly speak to a Matter of Fact, as if he were the best Lawyer. . . . [I]t requires no manner of Skill to make a plain and honest Defence, which in Cases of this Kind is always the best, the Simplicity and Innocence,

artless and ingenuous Behaviour of one whose Conscience acquits him, having something in it more moving and convincing than the highest Eloquence of Persons speaking in a Cause not their own. . . . [O]n the other Side, the very Speech, Gesture and Countenance, and Manner of Defence of those who are guilty, when they speak for themselves, may often help to disclose the Truth, which probably would not so well be discovered from the artificial Defence of others speaking for them.[82]

All the professional assistance required by a defendant was provided by the judge, who had a duty to ensure that nothing was "urged against him contrary to law,"[83] to ensure, that is, that "the prisoner" (as the accused was usually referred to in this period) was not subjected to illegal procedure, and that he or she was given the benefit of any technical loopholes—such as those afforded by an error in the indictment—legally available. In no way did the judge act as the accused's advocate.[84]

Before the eighteenth century the felony trial thus consisted of an amateur "altercation"[85] between the victim of the crime, or another private individual acting on that person's behalf, and the accused. It was, to use Langbein's phrase, a "contest of citizen equals."[86] In this form of trial the judge examined and cross-examined the victim/prosecutor, the accused, and any witnesses brought forward, while jurors were free to interrupt with questions of their own. The report in the printed Old Bailey Sessions Papers (OBSP)[87] of the trial of John Hughs for robbery (1751) provides a good example of the judge's role in the traditional form of the criminal trial. William Lawrence, the prosecutor, testified that Hughs had struck him from behind in Harp-alley and twice more when he turned to face his attacker, who then ran off with Lawrence's hat. When Lawrence had finished telling the tale the judge interrogated him as to whether Hughs had said anything to him, which way Hughs went, the name of the man who had stopped him, whether it was light or dark at the time, whether he was certain Hughs was the man who had attacked him, whether Lawrence was sober at the time of the attack, and what Hughs had used to strike him with. The judge put similar questions to the witness who had stopped Hughs in his flight.[88] In this form of trial the prisoner was also given the opportunity to question his accuser and witnesses and to answer the evidence given against him. He was entitled to present both material witnesses (witnesses to the facts) and those who could testify to his general character and reputation, although he could not compel such witnesses to appear. The prosecutor's witnesses, in contrast, were bound over by a magistrate to appear in court. In practice, the overwhelming majority of defense witnesses testified solely to character.[89]

At opposite ends of the spectrum of criminal activity very different forms of trial prevailed. In trials of treason, the Crown was represented by the highest-ranking counsel in the land: the attorney- and solicitor general. A person accused of being a traitor invariably met with a lawyer-driven prosecution, while forbidden himself, until the end of the seventeenth century, to engage counsel. In the wake of notorious perversions of justice perpetrated by late Stuart judges—in particular, the treason trials arising from the Popish Plot (1678), the Rye House Plot (1683), and Monmouth's Rebellion (1685)—the restriction was lifted by the Treason Trials Act of 1696. This statute addressed the previous imbalance in favor of the state and provided some protection against the political abuse of criminal process by partisan judges.[90] As John Beattie argues, "It flowed from the Revolution of 1689 as a means of redressing a wrong the now-dominant Whig political class had suffered in the previous decade—the use of charges of treason to destroy political opponents."[91] By the eighteenth century both the prosecution and defense of persons accused of treason were entrusted to lawyers, and the trial took the form of a professional contest.

At the lower end of the spectrum, a professional contest had for centuries been permitted for trials of misdemeanors. While a person accused of committing a felony was denied counsel, someone charged with a lesser offense was entitled to employ a lawyer to conduct his or her defense. The explanation offered for this perplexing discrepancy is that misdemeanor was a catchall category of offenses, including civil as well as criminal infractions of the law. Many misdemeanors involved property issues, and a lawyer's assistance was traditionally thought necessary where such issues were involved.[92] Why civil and criminal matters should originally have been placed in this same legal category remains unexplained.

As in trials of felony, the victim of a misdemeanor was responsible for any prosecution that ensued. The number of victims who chose to employ counsel and the percentage of defendants who engaged a barrister to protect their interests has never been the object of close inquiry, largely owing to the fact that trials of misdemeanor were less likely to be reported. It is clear that by the end of the eighteenth century barristers routinely attended the sessions at which misdemeanors were tried;[93] exactly when they began to do so, and in what proportion of the total trials heard they appeared, remains unknown at present. A person charged with a minor crime may or may not have been faced with a lawyer-driven prosecution and may or may not himself have chosen to employ legal counsel.

At the beginning of the eighteenth century, then, the form taken in a particular criminal trial depended in part on the nature of the charge. Treason trials had become professional contests; felony trials had not; trials of misdemeanor may have done so. If the defendant was accused of treason he was legally entitled to make his full defense by counsel; if he was accused of a misdemeanor he had the same privilege. But if the offense charged was murder, arson, rape, or a wide range of property offenses, the accused was required to make his own defense. By 1750, however, this picture had altered. According to the strict letter of the law, the prohibition against defense counsel in felony trials remained in effect, but by the mid-1730s the bench had taken the "epochal decision" to permit their presence.[94]

"The Coming of the Lawyers"

The entry of lawyers into criminal proceedings has a highly complex history. It was the indirect result of government activity, developments in policing, commercial expansion, and public concern over crime rates, among other things. It owed above all to new prosecutorial initiatives. Lawyers entered criminal proceedings on the side of the prosecution rather than the defense, and the first to be employed came from the lower branch of the legal profession. Solicitors or attorneys, that is, were engaged to prepare prosecution cases before barristers were employed to conduct those cases in court.[95]

In the early eighteenth century solicitors became involved in the investigation of criminal cases, gathering the evidence which would be presented at trial and formulating the charges laid. And while a few individuals chose to engage solicitors to perform these functions, the main impetus seems to have come from institutional prosecutors: the Royal Mint, the Bank of England, the Post Office, and the Treasury, all of whom engaged their own officers to prosecute criminal cases on their behalf.[96] The solicitor to the Mint prosecuted coinage offenses (clipping and counterfeiting); the solicitor to the Bank of England prosecuted forgery of its bank notes;[97] the solicitor to the Post Office prosecuted theft from the mails. Increasing commercial sophistication thus contributed to the entry of the lawyers into the criminal trial. As Langbein explains, coining and counterfeiting were precisely the types of public crimes that did not victimize particular persons and which private subjects were unlikely to prosecute, while forgery and embezzlement were complicated crimes to prove, requiring both extensive preparation and legal skill. The solicitors attached to the Mint, the Bank, and the Post Office expended considerable energy in investigating crime, gathering evidence to present at trial, identifying and preparing witnesses. They also financed investigations, subsidizing Bow Street's force of constables "on a case-by-case basis," for instance.[98]

But complicated commercial transactions were not the sole impetus for the coming of the lawyers. Political concerns and fears about violent crime also played a role. In the eighteenth century the Treasury solicitor was entrusted with the broad responsibility of advancing the Crown's interest in criminal prosecution. Sedition, as might be expected, was his chief preoccupation. John Beattie has recently described how secretaries of state, in particular the secretary for the Northern Department, and undersecretaries likewise became engaged in criminal prosecution.[99] In the early years of the Hanoverian succession the central government, sensitive to potential threats to the new regime, not only paid the costs of prosecuting coiners, rioters, and the printers and publishers of seditious material but also "organized and co-ordinated" many of the prosecutions itself.[100] After 1724 a new system arose whereby the Treasury paid private citizens to prosecute riot and sedition, and official views of what kind of offenses threatened the state and public order became increasingly elastic, even extending—albeit rarely—to rape, murder, and violent property offenses. The attorney general, for instance, was instructed to prosecute George Smith and three other men for the murder of Anne Bristol in 1723, and the Treasury solicitor prepared the case for trial.[101]

The "episodic" interventions[102] of the state into criminal prosecution are intimately tied to metropolitan London, for it was a perceived increase in violent crime in that city, the seat of national government, that prompted the Whig government's actions. "By the mid-1720s," the undersecretaries of state "seem to have been expecting to pay for the prosecution of at least some felonies at the Old Bailey," including robbery and burglary.[103] They also developed contacts with the Middlesex and Westminster benches. As Beattie indicates, the engagement of solicitors in ordinary criminal prosecutions in the first half of the eighteenth century remained the exception rather than the rule. But the government's willingness to pay costs "perhaps established a pattern";[104] moreover, the utility of professional pretrial preparation had been demonstrated. When "the central authorities wanted to strengthen a criminal prosecution, they did it by sending in the lawyers."[105] Their example perhaps encouraged private prosecutors to do the same.

An institutional solicitor was also attached to the Corporation of the City of London. The office of City solicitor dates from 1544, and the duties of its incumbent were various. Many of the prosecution briefs at the Guildhall sessions of the peace were distributed by the City solicitor, who was required to prosecute persons presented by the inquests of the twenty-six wards of the City for offenses, nuisances, and actions that affected their inhabitants. These included regrating, selling bad meat or fish or adulterated flour, and the use of false weights, balances, or measures. The solicitor prosecuted charges of keeping a disorderly house and indictments for nuisances such as erecting a building for the boiling and manufacturing of soap or establishing a slaughterhouse in a residential district. He was also required to prosecute anyone who assaulted the City's officers in the execution of their duty; offenders whom any of its magistrates thought deserving of prosecution, when no public funds were available for the purpose; and cases where the injured party was unable to prosecute and the "delinquent" would otherwise escape justice.[106] The City solicitor was thus empowered to undertake the investigation and preparation of routine criminal cases, in effect acting as a public prosecutor. Before the mid-eighteenth century he seems only to have intervened in cases in which City property or interests were directly involved,[107] but the City solicitor would subsequently be called upon by London's aldermen to prosecute violent crimes involving ordinary citizens.[108]

By the middle of the eighteenth century solicitors for the prosecution were an established fact where corporate or institutional prosecutors were concerned, and individual prosecutors may occasionally have employed them. At least some defendants would also have engaged a solicitor by this date. There was no rule forbidding such assistance: the proscription with respect to counsel applied only in court, and there is evidence in both the *State Trials* and the OBSP for the first half of the eighteenth century that defendants in trials for felony as well as treason employed solicitors.[109] The historical record is sketchy, however, and does not permit determination either of when defendants began to employ solicitors or how often they did so.

When they were employed, the activities of solicitors took place prior to the trial itself. Solicitors could not appear in court, for by the eighteenth century audience at trial was reserved for the bar. In the seventeenth century solicitors, it seems, were permitted to appear before the bench at quarter sessions,[110] and Langbein has identified at least one instance in the early 1700s of a solicitor being allowed to conduct his client's defense at the Surrey assizes.[111] Generally, however, solicitors remained behind the scenes. But as the eighteenth century progressed they were increasingly likely to employ a barrister to present the cases they had so carefully investigated and prepared. Barristers thus came to be "instructed" by means of a brief which typically summarized the indictment, provided a short statement of the charges, and listed various factual propositions along with the witnesses to be called to prove them.[112]

Prosecution counsel at the Old Bailey can first be detected, in very small numbers, in the 1710s and 1720s, and counsel for the defense followed in

the early 1730s.[113] No statutory change had been made permitting defense
counsel: persons accused of felony did not win the legislative right to representation by counsel until 1836.[114] But a change in judicial practice allowed
barristers a limited role in the criminal trial, that is, they were permitted
to examine and cross-examine witnesses, although forbidden to address the
jury.[115] Defense counsel were not to make opening or closing speeches; they
could not reply directly to the charges laid. This prohibition protected the
traditional form of the trial, characterized by Langbein as "the accused
speaks": "The logic of the early modern criminal trial was to pressure the
accused to speak, either to clear himself or to hang himself."[116] While the
introduction of defense counsel would ultimately silence the accused, in
the eighteenth century they continued to "serve as an informational re-
source for the court."[117]

James Fitzjames Stephen identified the decision to allow defense counsel
a limited role as the "most remarkable change" in the history of the English
criminal trial.[118] Determining the reasons for it is an exercise in speculation, for no explicit statement was ever made by the judiciary. As Langbein
points out, it may even be misleading to refer to a "decision": the change
more likely came about in a piecemeal fashion, the result of individual exer-
cises of judicial discretion rather than a collegiate determination to change
the rules. In 1741, during a case tried in Bristol, a barrister described existing
practice as he saw it. Objecting to the accused's desire to have his counsel
cross-examine a main witness, the barrister said:

> This, I apprehend, is a matter purely in the discretion of the Court,
> and what can neither in this or any other court of criminal justice be
> demanded as a right. The judges, I apprehend, act as they see fit on
> these occasions, and few of them (as far as I have observed) walk by
> one and the same rule in this particular: some have gone so far, as to
> give leave for counsel to examine and cross-examine witnesses; others
> have bid the counsel propose their questions to the Court; and others
> again have directed that the prisoner should put his own questions: the
> method of practice in this point, is very variable and uncertain; but this
> we certainly know, that by the settled rule of law the prisoner is allowed
> no other counsel but the Court in matters of fact, and ought either to
> ask his own questions of the witnesses, or else propose them himself to
> the court.[119]

At the Old Bailey a year later, reference was made by a barrister appearing
for the defense in a murder trial to "the Course of the Court," whereby he
was forbidden to comment on the prosecutor's evidence, but he claimed to

be allowed to introduce the defense case providing he refrained from any such comment.[120] Inconsistencies in practice support the view that judicial retreat from the ban on defense counsel occurred on "court-by-court basis."

One development which may have influenced the judges' decision was a change in the substantive law of forgery. In 1729 forging private financial instruments, a crime traditionally classified as a misdemeanor, was made a felony. This reclassification removed the accused's right to counsel. As forgery cases typically posed complicated questions of both fact and law, and involved complex proofs with respect to the identity and circulation of the note forged, the signatures involved, and the acceptance of the note by the victim, the new prohibition against counsel imposed significant hardship on the accused. This situation may have been perceived as particularly unfair, given that forgery cases tended to be prosecuted by counsel. The victim of forgery was typically a bank or merchant, who routinely employed both solicitors and barristers to prosecute on their behalf. Thus from 1729 defendants in forgery cases appeared at a very real disadvantage. That such defendants were normally of a higher social class than petty thieves may also have inclined the bench to sympathy.[121]

The retreat more generally from the rule preventing legal counsel from speaking to issues of fact in the criminal courtroom has been attributed to a new imbalance found there.[122] The engagement of lawyers for the prosecution in a felony trial skewed the contest. Some accused would meet with a professionally prepared prosecution, and in these circumstances it seemed unfair to deny them counsel, particularly if the prosecutor was a powerful institution like the Bank of England. The government's efforts to stimulate prosecution by offering monetary rewards on conviction likewise placed the accused at a disadvantage. Rewards had been offered periodically during the seventeenth century, and after 1689 statutory rewards for the conviction of offenders became a fixture in the administration of criminal justice.[123] Other rewards were offered by proclamation, for crimes such as murder or highway robbery. In 1749, as earlier in the century, a £100 reward was offered for the conviction of street robbers in London; the Treasury's total expenditure for statutory and other rewards in that year was £600, and that expenditure would subsequently increase. Designed to secure the conviction of dangerous offenders, the reward system also stimulated false or malicious prosecutions. There were a number of prominent scandals in the first half of the eighteenth century, chief among them those involving Jonathan Wild, John Waller, and the Macdaniel gang. Wild, a receiver of stolen goods who, in the early years of the reign of George I routinely mediated the return of these goods for a fee, also informed on thieves and profited from the rewards, styling himself the "thief-taker general."[124] Waller similarly brought false prosecutions for monetary gain; he died in the pillory at the hands of the brother of one of his victims in 1732.[125] Macdaniel, for his part, was a "thief-maker" whose corrupt activities were exposed in 1754.[126]

The Macdaniel scandal, as Langbein indicates, placed the reward system "under a cloud of doubt from which it never recovered."[127] The system was not abandoned, however. Parliamentary rewards, known colloquially as "blood money," were offered until 1818.[128] And while Stephen Landsman argues that thief-taking was less of an issue after the middle of the eighteenth century,[129] the evidence of *The Times* suggests otherwise. That paper, founded in 1785 as the *Universal Register*, returned repeatedly to the problems posed to justice by those who lied under oath. In 1785 it commented, "Perjury is a crime from whence a hundred others originate, affecting the dearest interests of society, and ought therefore to be punished with rigour."[130] Perjury trials were reported in some detail; earlier in the same year, for example, *The Times* reported the trial at the Guildhall of a constable indicted for perjury committed in an Old Bailey trial of highway robbery, in which two men had been convicted. Harvey, the constable in question, had claimed one of the men had fled from him and been pursued. This lie enabled the constable to share in the £80 reward received by the prosecutors. Recalling the conviction of thief-takers several years earlier, *The Times* commented, "Conviction-rewards, rather create, than amend the evils, which they were intended to prevent."[131] The following year the paper reported with exasperation, "The crime of perjury has increased, is increasing, and ought to be diminished; at present it is dangerous for an honest man to make an affidavit in a Court of Law, it being the practice of the swindling tribe, when fined or prosecuted, to overpower him with a train of suborned witnesses, and outswear him by numbers."[132] The physical evidence of the Old Bailey courtroom testifies to the same concern. Three passages of Scripture warning against perjury were inscribed in gold lettering on the wall above the bench:

> If a false witness shall rise up against any man to testify against him that which is wrong, then shall ye do unto him as he had thought to do unto his brother. — *Deut.* c. xix. v. 16
> A false witness shall not be unpunished, but he that speaketh lies, shall perish. — *Prov.* c. xix. v. 9
> Ye shall not swear by my name falsely, neither shalt thou profane the name of thy God. — *Lev.* c. xix. v. 12.[133]

The Waller scandal, and another made public a few months later (Bartholomew Harnet's false prosecution of William Holms for highway robbery), doubtless contributed to the judiciary's decision to allow defense counsel into the courtroom in the early 1730s, and "questioning the reliability of prosecution evidence in reward-driven prosecutions" would become a staple of their work.[134] But rewards were not the only prosecutorial initiative to cause problems. The Crown witness system for generating accomplice testimony, which operated in close conjunction with the reward system from the early eighteenth century, likewise offered material incentives to perjury, in this instance immunity from prosecution in return for testimony against a former confederate.[135] Judicial tolerance of the presence of defense counsel (and occasionally of their unruly behavior) must owe in large part to recognition of the fact that counsel, through cross-examination, were much more likely than an unrepresented layman to expose the perjured testimony and deliberate perversions of the truth that plagued the eighteenth-century justice system.

The Bar at the Old Bailey

When barristers began to appear in criminal cases on a regular basis is difficult to determine. During the Lancaster assizes of 1758, Mansfield, the lord chief justice, reported, "[T]he Crown side almost as good to the Bar as the other. I had an enormous Gaol and the cases such that I think I had not a single tryal without council on both sides."[136] Based on the evidence of the OBSP, the extent of the participation of counsel in criminal cases was more limited in London until the 1780s. Beattie's sampling of counsel at the Old Bailey showed an upper limit of roughly 3 percent of prosecutors and 6 percent of defendants as having been represented by counsel in the middle of the eighteenth century; Landsman's figures are slightly higher, but both agree that no substantial increase in the presence of counsel occurred before the 1780s.[137] Beattie concludes that the increase observable from that decade cannot be accounted for by changes in reporting alone, and there is a variety of evidence to suggest that he is correct. As discussed in Chapter 2, contemporary acknowledgment of an Old Bailey bar—as opposed to individuals who occasionally appeared in that court—dates from the early 1790s.

The eighteenth-century English bar as a whole was small, "a close, centralized body" of men whose numbers are thought not to have exceeded six hundred "at any time."[138] Fewer than four thousand men were called to the bar over the course of the century, averaging roughly forty per year. A decline in bar calls had been evident from the late seventeenth century, and by the 1760s the aggregate of calls was a mere twenty-five per year, although a period of recovery followed.[139] The number of barristers with a working practice was smaller still. David Lemmings, emphasizing that his figures are

best seen as an indication of the relative size rather than absolute limits of
the practicing bar, has calculated that the Westminster courts—in particular, the Courts of Common Pleas, King's Bench, and Chancery—"provided
work for between 250 and 400 barristers over the course of any one year"
in the eighteenth century. His study of the rule and minute books for the
various courts revealed a decline in the size of the practicing bar from "mod-
erately high levels" in the opening decades to a low of 255 in 1770, again
followed by a modest recovery.[140]

Few of these barristers appeared at the Old Bailey in the mid-eighteenth
century, and of those who can be identified, some remain very shadowy figures indeed. The limited evidence of both the OBSP and the manuscript sessions papers housed in the Corporation of London Record Office indicates
that a Mr. Lucas and a Mr. Stow attended at the Old Bailey sessions from the
1750s through the 1770s. Lucas's name appears not only in Dudley Ryder's
Old Bailey diary[141] but in settlement papers, suggesting a type of legal practice common to his successors.[142] If the "Lucas" identified by Lemmings
as one of the leaders in practice on the plea side of the Court of King's
Bench in the 1770s is the same man, however, he achieved greater success
than most members of the Old Bailey's bar.[143] "Mr. Stow" was presumably
John Aylett Stow, called to the bar of the Inner Temple in 1743. Having only
semi-materialized, Lucas and Stow fade from the record entirely by the end
of the 1770s.

More visible are Serjeants Glynn and Hayward, Robert Graham, Henry
Howorth, and Edward Bearcroft, who appeared at the Old Bailey from the
mid-1740s into the early 1780s.[144] With the possible exception of Howorth,
none of these men could be characterized as "Old Bailey barristers," nor indeed would they have appreciated such a label. As recorder of London (1772–
79) Glynn would eventually sit as a judge in that court. Graham's legal practice lay chiefly in the Court of Chancery; he subsequently became a baron
of the Exchequer and a privy councillor.[145] Bearcroft was one of the best-
known barristers of his day. Like Howorth he was made a King's Counsel
in his mid-thirties, having established an extensive King's Bench practice. In
the same year (1772) he lost the recordership of London to Glynn by a
single vote.[146] Howorth, "a gentleman of high reputation at the bar,"[147] possessed of "fulness, power, argument, and fine voice,"[148] appeared in a number of high-profile criminal trials, including those of Margaret Rudd and
Dr. Dodd, both forgery cases.[149] His obituary in the *Gentleman's Magazine*
described him as "one of the first crown lawyers in practice,"[150] and David
Lemmings has suggested that Howorth may have been the leading counsel
at the Old Bailey in the 1770s.[151] Whether he had routinely attended at that

court before becoming a King's Counsel, however, is impossible to determine. His promising career in the Court of King's Bench was cut short when
he drowned in a boating accident in 1783.[152] Had he lived, one contemporary
commented, Howorth "must have made a great figure in his profession."[153]
Mansfield was said to have deeply regretted his death.[154]

Of the early criminal practitioners who can be identified, William Davy
stands out as the prototype of the Old Bailey barrister who would emerge
in the 1780s.[155] Davy's social origins were humble: he had been an Exeter
grocer and/or druggist as well as a bankrupt in the King's Bench prison before entering the Inner Temple in 1741. The assessment made of his abilities
as a lawyer was that which would be applied to criminal practitioners generally: "Davy's reputation for knowledge did not stand high, but he was an
acknowledged master of the art of cross-examination."[156] He knew little law
but was said to possess a "strong natural understanding." His professional
manners earned him the nickname "Bull Davy."[157] From the earliest days of
their appearance barristers at the Old Bailey had occasionally to be reproved
by the bench for their conduct in court, and Davy—who became a serjeant-
at-law in 1754—was no exception. An exchange between the serjeant and his
brother, Serjeant Impey,[158] during a murder trial in 1769 met with a rebuke
from Justice Gould: "We are trying two men here for murder; let us do it
with all gravity." Gould continued, however, to disallow the leading question which had provoked Davy's irritation.[159] Serjeant Davy generally had
little difficulty in standing up to the bench. In a dispute over a point of law
Mansfield once said to him, "If this be law, Sir, I must burn all my books, I
see." "Your Lordship had better read them first," was the serjeant's retort.[160]
Davy is also reputed to have informed Mansfield, when the judge announced
his intention to sit on Good Friday owing to the volume of business, that he
would be the first since Pontius Pilate to do so.[161] Serjeant Davy's relations
with the lower branch of the legal profession likewise proved stormy. When,
in 1766, he publicly attributed "19 out of 20" mistakes made in the management of causes to "the ignorance of attorneys," an angry Society for Gentlemen Practisers retaliated by sending the serjeant to professional Coventry,
denying him briefs until he obliged them with a written apology.[162]

Serjeant Davy's posthumous reputation, however, is not solely for bullish
manners. He was also remembered for his eloquence. Some nineteenth-
century commentators believed that it was the criminal courts which best afforded the opportunity for a "display of oratory." If, wrote William Forsyth
in his history of advocacy, we wish "to know the highest kind of eloquence
in this country, in former times, we must turn to our old divines,—to Hall,
Taylor, Barrow, and Leighton, in whose works we possess some of the no-

blest thoughts which have ever been conceived by man, clothed and adorned in a profusion of the richest imagery." Among the lawyers, he claimed, eloquence had been almost unknown until the late eighteenth century. Forsyth attributed its absence in part to the technicality of English law but also to the fact that advocates had been barred from appearing in trials of treason and felony.[163] An article published in the *New Monthly Magazine* in 1825 made the same point: "The feeble growth or total absence of eloquence, before Lord Erskine, is a standing contumely against the English Bar." Surprisingly, the example of "something . . . which may be called elaborate and avowed oratory" provided by the magazine was taken not from one of Thomas Erskine's famous speeches but from a speech made by Davy during the trial of Elizabeth Canning for perjury:

> Of all the crimes (says he) the human heart can conceive, perjury is the most impious and detestable. But the guilt of this person is so transcendent as to defy aggravation. To call upon the God of truth, in the most solemn form, and on the most awful occasion, to attest a falsehood—to imprecate the vengeance of Heaven upon her guilty head—to prostitute the law of the land to the vilest purpose—to triumph in the destruction of an innocent fellow-creature—to commit a murder with the sword of justice—and then, having stript her own heart of all humanity, to insinuate herself, by all the arts of hypocrisy into the compassion of others—such is the peculiar sin of this person, not yet twenty years of age![164]

While Davy was long remembered within the legal profession (an anecdote relating to his sense of humor appeared in the *Law Times* in 1856),[165] the extent of his practice, or that of his colleagues, at the Old Bailey remains unknown. As described in the next chapter, however, when he died in 1780 a regular bar at that court was beginning to emerge.

CHAPTER TWO

The Emergence of a
Criminal Bar in London

In 1843 the *Law Times* commented, the "Criminal Bar is yet in its infancy." The law had by that date been altered to allow prisoners a full defense by counsel, and this change had in turn, the paper argued, afforded the opportunity for the true practice of advocacy in the criminal courts. "Anciently," the author continued, "counsel were limited to cross-examination; a bully to browbeat a witness best served the turn, and an ignorant man with a brazen face was never placed in a position by which his ignorance could be betrayed. But the appeal to the jury is now the one great defensive weapon; juries cannot tolerate a bully, and, however uneducated themselves, they like to be talked to by an educated man and a gentleman. Perforce the Old Bailey bully has been thrust aside to give place to men who can win the attention of juries by their bearing and keep it by their eloquence."[1]

By the 1840s the Old Bailey barrister had "passed into a proverb," and it had become difficult "to sever . . . the real Old Bailey Barrister from the imaginary pictures of him painted in novels and farces."[2] It is equally difficult to sever real-life criminal practitioners from the representations found of them in the nineteenth-century periodical press, and those representations are similarly misleading. The author of this particular article, for instance, boasts that he has never entered the doors of the Old Bailey, and his account of the Crown court's bar, replete with prejudice, grossly misrepresents the work of that bar in the late eighteenth and early nineteenth centuries, where its "infancy" is properly located.

A blanket dismissal of Old Bailey barristers as disreputable thugs and bar-bullies contributes nothing to our understanding of the development of advocacy in the criminal courts. The activities of these counsel, described in Chapter 4, did much to alleviate the problems created by the government's reward system and to further the cause of justice. But it would also be a mistake to see the early members of the Old Bailey bar as political radicals defending the liberties of Englishmen. The emergence of that bar owed little, if anything, to political beliefs.[3]

An Old Bailey Bar

A brief notice published in the *Jurist* in 1845 reporting the death of John Adolphus described him as "the father of the Old Bailey Bar."[4] But when Adolphus began to practice at the Old Bailey in the early nineteenth century a small group of barristers had been attached to London's chief criminal court for over twenty years. Evidence of the existence of a late-eighteenth-century Old Bailey bar comes primarily from two sources: the Old Bailey Sessions Papers, pamphlet accounts of trials heard at the Old Bailey,[5] and the *Law List*, a professional directory published from 1775.[6] For the 1780s we must rely on the OBSP alone: the legal professional press was virtually non-existent,[7] and the *Law List* did not identify London's criminal bar until the 1790s (even then, the identification was oblique). The OBSP, however, began to name counsel from 1783, with sufficient consistency to permit the identification of regular practitioners.[8] And from 1793 the *Law List* identified counsel who routinely attended the metropolitan sessions, which included those held at the Old Bailey, just as it listed the barristers attached to the various circuits. Occasional references in the nineteenth-century legal periodical press confirm that by the 1790s a "powerful bar" had been established at the London and Middlesex sessions.[9]

It would be wrong to overstate the extent of lawyers' participation in criminal trials in London, or to claim that professional adversarialism predominated at the Old Bailey by the turn of the nineteenth century. It clearly did not. While the presence of counsel appears to have expanded rapidly between 1780 and 1800, the evidence of the OBSP suggests that the majority of trials took place without counsel, and the percentage in which barristers appeared on both sides was very small indeed. Excluding cases originating in the Gordon riots, just under 4 percent of prosecutors and just over 7 percent of defendants were represented by counsel in 1780; those figures had risen to approximately 21 and 28 percent, respectively, by 1800.[10] The statistical record with respect to legal representation shows little change between 1800 and 1830: on average, the OBSP suggest that roughly 70 percent of trials at the Old Bailey in the first three decades of the nineteenth century took place without any counsel at all, and well under 10 percent were professional contests.

While the level of employment of criminal counsel in London thus re-

TABLE I
Counsel at the Old Bailey, 1805–1830

Year	Number	No Counsel		Prosecuting Counsel		Defense Counsel		Both	
		N	%	N	%	N	%	N	%
1805	729	468	64.2	160	22.0	187	25.7	87	12.0
1810	900	711	79.0	54	6.0	116	12.9	27	3.0
1820*	1,539	1,206	78.4	165	10.7	227	14.8	76	5.0
1825	1,806	1,308	72.4	156	8.6	445	25.2	99	5.5
1830	2,127	1,484	70.0	187	8.8	587	27.7	128	6.0

Source: OBSP.
*1815 omitted due to erratic reporting of counsel

mained relatively low, by the latter decades of the eighteenth century the benefits of employing counsel had nonetheless been recognized. As described in the previous chapter, institutional prosecutors had from the beginning of the century chosen to engage first solicitors to prepare their cases and then barristers to present them in court. By 1790 merchants, manufacturers, and shopkeepers too were increasingly inclined to hire counsel to prosecute those who stole from them.[11] The accused, for their part, naturally welcomed the professional assistance tolerated by the bench, where they could afford it: the potential impact of defense counsel on the progress and outcome of the trial was evident from midcentury. And by the 1780s a small number of counsel had attached themselves to London's criminal sessions. Although they neither attended solely at the Old Bailey nor practiced criminal law exclusively, over the succeeding decades these men would increasingly become identified as members of an Old Bailey bar.[12]

The bar found at the Old Bailey in the late eighteenth century formed a very small proportion of the total practicing bar.[13] In 1790, for example, 424 barristers were named in Browne's annual *Law List*, 309 of whom have been identified as being employed in the superior courts in that year;[14] six more did not appear at Westminster but were named in the OBSP, bringing the total to 315. Only ten barristers, just over 3 percent of the total, appeared regularly at the Old Bailey in the same year. Over the subsequent decades the number of barristers who chose to practice in metropolitan London's criminal courts increased to more than twenty in any given year. The highest numbers recorded are for the first decade of the nineteenth century, when the figures are consistently in the thirties. Since the bar as a whole continued to expand dramatically throughout this period, however, the number of barristers who chose an Old Bailey practice remained proportionately small, in fact decreasing as a percentage of the total bar.[15]

John Silvester

As in other courts, practice at the Old Bailey was concentrated in the hands of a very few individuals, and sometimes dominated by a single man: in the 1780s the Old Bailey and William Garrow[16] would become virtually synonymous. Before Garrow's arrival, however, a barrister named John Silvester appears to have led practice in that court. And although he was by no means Garrow's equal as an advocate, Silvester's career at the Old Bailey merits careful scrutiny. In many ways his legal practice as a whole was more typical of future Old Bailey barristers; moreover, his connection with that court continued throughout his professional life. Silvester was eventually raised from the bar to the bench of the Old Bailey, where he served as judge by virtue of his tenure in the office of common serjeant (1790–1803) and recorder of London (1803–22).[17]

Like many of his contemporaries at the Old Bailey, Silvester was London born. The son of a physician, he received his early education at the Merchant Taylors' school — where, according to one hagiographic account of his life, he "early distinguished himself by his general demeanour, correct deportment, and close application."[18] As a student he appeared in various theatrical productions, which may have provided him with a form of preparation for his subsequent career. At age eighteen Silvester went up to Oxford, and two years later he entered the Middle Temple; he was called to the bar in 1771, the same year in which he received a bachelor of civil law degree from St. John's College. As discussed in Chapter 3, a newly called barrister had to choose both a circuit to travel and in which of the superior courts he would attempt to find business. Silvester chose to travel the Home circuit, and in deciding among the Westminster courts he again chose the most popular option, the Court of King's Bench. Like many barristers, however, he failed to make a name for himself either on circuit or in Westminster Hall.[19] John Silvester's legal practice as a whole is best described as a metropolitan practice, and his professional success would owe in large part to a link forged early in his career with the City of London. Three years after his call Silvester purchased, at the not insignificant cost of £1,000, what was known as a City common pleadership.[20] By doing so he ensured constant practice in two of the petty courts of London, the Lord Mayor's and Sheriffs' Courts, and a share in prosecution briefs at the Old Bailey drawn up by the City solicitor.

Both the Lord Mayor's and Sheriffs' Courts were medieval in origin. Their continued existence testifies in part to a jealousy of the common law and veneration of local customs but reflects as well a need for prompt and affordable justice: where debts or damages to be recovered were relatively small, an alternative to bringing a suit in the superior courts could be found in one of these local tribunals, where the costs incurred would be lower and judgment received more quickly than at Westminster.[21] The Court of the Sheriffs of London and Middlesex, empowered to hear trials of debt, case, trespass, account, covenant, and customary actions, was the more ancient institution. Until 1852 two distinct courts were held by the individual sheriffs in the Giltspur Street and Poultry Compters, although the judges attached to each court could act for either. Both courts sat two days a week: Wednesdays and Fridays for Giltspur, Thursdays and Saturdays for the Poultry Compter. The jurisdiction of the Sheriffs' Court overlapped considerably with that of the Mayor's Court, but the latter proved ultimately the victor in terms of the share of business: by 1844 the Sheriffs' Court was described as the most impotent court of the City of London.[22]

The Lord Mayor's Court, however, was far from impotent. Open every day except holidays from 10 A.M. until 4 P.M. at an office over the Royal Exchange, it was held at the Guildhall roughly eight times a year, presided over by the recorder, although the mayor and aldermen were nominally its judges. A court of both law and equity, the Lord Mayor's Court had authority concurrent with that of the Westminster courts over all personal and mixed actions arising within the City and Liberties of London: actions of debt, detinue, covenant, assumpsit, ejectment, trespass, apprenticeship, and penal actions. Actions could be removed by habeas corpus or certiorari into a superior court if the debt was greater than £5. The court heard appeals from inferior courts, including (apparently illegally) the Sheriffs' Court,[23] while its own judgments could be reversed by a special court of commission, with final appeal to the House of Lords.[24] On the equity side, the Mayor's Court heard bills for general relief, fraud and duress, and matters of account; it also had exclusive jurisdiction over suits involving the custody and education of the City's orphans. Proceedings were similar to those of the Court of Chancery, but again judgment was received more quickly and at a lower cost. This court had sole jurisdiction in cases involving the custom of London. Customary actions included suits of married women engaged in trade, defamation, market overt, the supervision of apprentices, and most notably, foreign attachment, which provided the means to apply the property of an absent debtor (foreign merchant) to the payment of his debt. Merchant cases were fundamental to the foundation and development of the

Mayor's Court, and the process of foreign attachment was very important to London's commercial community.[25]

In purchasing a common pleadership Silvester acquired entry into a closed shop, for practice in the City's courts was restricted to four pleaders, each of whom bought a life interest in the office: other barristers could only be employed if one of the common pleaders were engaged as well. Silvester may also owe his entry into the Old Bailey to the City connection, for, as described in Chapter 1, the City of London, when instructed by an alderman acting in his capacity as magistrate, undertook the prosecution of certain offenders. The corporation prosecuted where the City's property had been stolen or its officers wounded or killed, but also where a victim with no formal City tie was too poor or was otherwise incapacitated to undertake a prosecution and it was clearly in the public interest that prosecution should be pursued. In the eighteenth century the vast majority of City prosecutions appear to have been for nuisances or crimes which directly affected the City's property or officers, but the City occasionally intervened on behalf of vulnerable inhabitants, prosecuting, for example, on behalf of Esther Dormant, a spinster who had been detained for twelve hours, beaten, and humiliated by a man named Dean, and on behalf of another single woman, Ann Slater, who had been viciously bitten on the face.[26] In such cases the City solicitor drew up a brief, which was assigned to one, or more usually two or three, of the City's pleaders.[27] From the late eighteenth century well into the nineteenth there would be a consistent overlap between the City common pleaders and the bar found at the Old Bailey: by the late 1790s (Silvester sold his pleadership in 1790 on being elected common serjeant) all four pleaders were listed as attending the London, Middlesex, and Westminster sessions and were named in the OBSP.[28]

The City's briefs account for but a tiny fraction of the trials heard at any given session. The majority of cases tried at the Old Bailey originated in Middlesex, and even within London most prosecutions lay with private individuals. But from the mid-eighteenth century, City briefs provided certain counsel with an entry at the Old Bailey. Once there, depending on their talents, they attracted further business. By 1783 John Silvester had established a considerable criminal practice. Somewhat unusually, he appeared more often for the prosecution than for the defense. Most Old Bailey counsel tended to be employed primarily for the defense in the early years of their careers, with the balance between defense and prosecution briefs gradually evening out as their reputations became established (see Table 2). In the final year of his Old Bailey practice, however, Silvester prosecuted in just under 91 percent of the cases in which he was employed.[29] (A contemporary

TABLE 2
Proportions of Prosecution/Defense Work,
Jerome William Knapp, 1787–1810

Year	Total Cases	Prosecution		Defense	
		N	%	N	%
1787	2	0	0.00	2	100.00
1788	5	1	20.00	4	80.00
1789	24	9	37.50	15	62.50
1790	22	1	4.55	21	95.45
1791	16	4	25.00	12	75.00
1792	16	5	31.25	11	68.75
1793	70	27	38.57	43	61.43
1794	94	28	29.79	66	70.21
1795	83	24	28.92	59	71.08
1796	89	19	21.35	70	78.65
1797	78	28	35.90	50	64.10
1798	95	30	31.58	65	68.42
1799	79	34	43.04	45	56.96
1800	115	58	50.43	57	49.57
1801	135	73	54.07	62	45.93
1802	83	31	37.35	52	62.65
1803	85	35	41.18	50	58.82
1804	103	55	53.40	48	46.60
1805	113	75	66.37	38	33.63
1806	82	45	54.88	37	45.12
1807	89	46	51.69	43	48.31
1808	85	48	56.47	37	43.53
1809	76	40	52.63	36	47.39
1810	43	16	37.21	27	62.79
Total	1,682	732	43.52	950	56.48

commented that his professional income derived "from the groans of the gallows.")[30] The high proportion of prosecution work may be explained in part by Silvester's City attachment, and his personal inclinations may also have affected the character of his criminal practice. John Silvester was a Tory more concerned with the maintenance of law and order than with the rights of prisoners. But professional competition was probably the determining factor. In 1783 Silvester was named in the OBSP as appearing for the prosecution and the defense in roughly equal proportions, in ten and eleven cases, respectively; the following year the gap began to widen, and by 1785 he appeared for the prosecution twice as often as for the defense (forty-four cases versus twenty-two). Seventeen eighty-three was the year in which Silvester had been joined at the Old Bailey by a young barrister for whom he was no match and by whom he was soon eclipsed: William Garrow.

William Garrow

William Garrow was fifteen years Silvester's junior, and his legal career would follow a very different trajectory. Born in Middlesex in 1760, Garrow received his early education at the school kept by his father, the Reverend David Garrow, and was subsequently articled to a Cheapside attorney named Southouse. Recognizing the young man's talents, the attorney recommended that his pupil train as a barrister; Garrow thus entered Lincoln's Inn in 1778 and was called to the bar in November 1783. The Old Bailey had by that date become, like the Crown side on circuit, a venue in which a young barrister could call attention to himself, and Garrow had prepared carefully for his debut. As a student he had attended assiduously at the Old Bailey,[31] and by the time of his call he had already achieved distinction as a public speaker through debating societies.[32] Like Silvester, Garrow did not confine his practice to the criminal courts but also traveled the Home circuit, then led by the brilliant Thomas Erskine,[33] where he managed "in the ordinary run of cases" to acquire a substantial share of business and was soon to be found employed either as junior counsel to Erskine or opposing him.[34] Garrow's talents as an advocate also enabled him to enjoy greater success in Westminster Hall than Silvester had been able to achieve:[35] this barrister had no need to purchase a monopoly of practice in the City's courts. At the Old Bailey Garrow established himself almost immediately after his call by his conduct in the trial of Henry Aickles,[36] and he dominated business in that court for the remainder of the decade. In 1785 he was identified as counsel for the defense in a hundred Old Bailey cases; in 1786, he was employed in 116 of the 182 cases in which counsel were named.[37] All told, Garrow appeared in "at least a thousand cases" during the period 1783–93.[38] His success alone, in fact, accounts in large part for the marked increase in the employment of barristers at the Old Bailey in the 1780s. Defendants were not merely increasingly inclined to hire counsel, they overwhelmingly opted to employ this particular barrister.

London's premier criminal counsel was generally acknowledged to be ignorant of the law. John Campbell[39] described Garrow as "wholly uneducated" and claimed that he "had never read anything except a brief and a newspaper,"[40] while Henry Brougham[41] commented in a memoir published in both the *Law Review* and the *Law Times*, "There have probably been few

William Garrow, leader in practice at the Old Bailey in the 1780s
(Harvard Law Art Collection)

more ignorant men in the profession than this celebrated leader. To law, or anything like law, he made no pretence. . . . [W]ith so slender a provision of law, his ignorance of all beside, of all that constitutes science, or learning, or indeed general information, nay even ordinary information, was perfect."[42] Garrow's professional success owed to an extraordinary talent in the exami-

nation and cross-examination of witnesses. These activities, in the era preceding the Prisoners' Counsel Act, constituted the extent of advocacy for
the defense, and they were essential to a successful prosecution. A shy man
in private, particularly where women were concerned, Garrow was entirely
self-possessed in the performance of his professional duties.[43] He had an un-
canny ability to coax or bully the truth from the most recalcitrant witness,
destroying or annihilating adverse ones by means, according to Brougham,
of a verbal net which tightened until it became a noose.[44] This talent was
not universally admired (critics claimed he was overly and unnecessarily hostile),[45] but it was important in an age in which perjured testimony posed
a threat to justice. Brougham also drew attention to Garrow's forte in examination in chief, to his remarkable ability to acquire, seemingly without
effort, a perfect knowledge of the facts and, through skillful questioning,
to elicit a clear story that carefully steered away from any potentially dam-
aging information. "No description," Brougham wrote, "can give the reader
an adequate idea of this eminent practitioner's powers in thus dealing with
his witnesses."[46]

Silvester too had been dismissed as ignorant: "[H]e knows that which is
soon learned,—Crown-practice; and that he does know any thing is saying
a great deal, for no person who hears him speak or converse would imagine it."[47] But where Silvester was condemned as "vulgar and ineloquent,"[48]
Garrow possessed a "fine voice," a "powerful voice," and a "most distinct articulation" together with "a great flow of words,"[49] a flow which caught the
attention of the shorthand reporter at the Old Bailey on numerous occasions.[50] Opinion varied as to Garrow's choice of language, some finding it
"plain . . . but well strung together" and others "correct and elegant," while
critics sneered at what they called his "Billingsgate speech."[51] But Campbell
remembered "the effect of a most beautiful voice which no one could hear
and not listen to irrespective of the sentiments it conveyed."[52] It was also
claimed that Garrow was "not only an advocate, but an actor," who, when
silent, "did not cease addressing the jury by the change in his features."[53] As
Brougham concluded, "Mr. Garrow was a great, a very great advocate."[54]

The Old Bailey in the 1780s and 1790s

Although Garrow was clearly the star of the Old Bailey in the 1780s, he
was not the only barrister attached to that court. Joining him at the green
baize table reserved for the bar, apart from Silvester, were William Fielding, son of the magistrate and novelist; Richard Peatt, James Agar, George
Lethieullier Schoen, and John Chetwood. With the possible exception of

Fielding, these men operated so much in Garrow's shadow as to be practically invisible to posterity. Fielding's career, although less distinguished than that of his father, was similarly tied to criminal justice. He attended at the Old Bailey not by virtue of any City connection but as part of a more general attendance at the metropolitan sessions which, like the provincial quarter sessions, offered a point of entry into legal practice for recently called barristers. A contemporary of Silvester, Fielding may have shared a lead in Old Bailey business in the 1770s. In 1785 the *Morning Chronicle* reported, "Mr. Fielding and Mr. Garrow may be said to have all the Old Bailey business in their own hands. At the late sessions it was clearly obvious, that the other gentlemen of the tie attended had very little opportunity of opening their mouths, except at dinner."[55] But Fielding too fell by the wayside once Garrow arrived on the scene. His eclipse was attributed in part by one critic to sheer indolence: being "too lazy" to do all the business offered to him, Fielding "turned it over" to his younger colleague.[56] When he left Old Bailey practice in 1808 it was to sit as a Westminster magistrate.

Even less is known about the remainder of the Old Bailey's bar in the 1780s. According to the combined evidence of the OBSP and the *Law List*, Peatt and Agar practiced at the Old Bailey for twenty-five and sixteen years, respectively, but they are little remembered. Schoen obviously struggled to earn a living. Called to the bar in 1784, he attended at the Old Bailey until 1795 but was named in the OBSP only forty-five times during that period. His practice at Westminster Hall was slim, and he was never recorded by the *Law List* as traveling on circuit or attaching himself to a quarter sessions outside London. Schoen's professional income must have been meager in the extreme, and he eventually abandoned the law for holy orders, becoming rector of Crick, Northamptonshire, in 1801, a post he retained until his death in 1829.[57] Both Agar and Chetwood combined Old Bailey practice with practice in the Marshalsea and Palace Court, a minor royal court in which, as in the Lord Mayor's and Sheriffs' Courts, business was restricted to counsel who purchased their positions for life.[58] In the company of such men Garrow shone like a beacon, and he virtually monopolized practice at the Old Bailey from 1784 until he was made a King's Counsel (KC) in 1792. After that date his talents were largely reserved for the government, although he occasionally appeared for the defense.[59]

While the extent to which Garrow dominated the Old Bailey courtroom in the 1780s is obvious from the OBSP, the size and character of London's criminal bar as a whole during that decade is less easy to determine. Only in the 1790s, when the *Law List* began to include a list of sessions counsel in metropolitan London, does a more comprehensive picture of the bar at the Old Bailey emerge. That bar encompassed a broad range of individuals, many of whom were associated with London's criminal courts only briefly and whose careers were therefore not always reflected in the Sessions Papers. The twenty-eight counsel listed by Browne for the year 1795, for example, included John Bayley, the future justice of the Court of King's Bench; John Bell, who went on to become a leader in Chancery; Isaac Espinasse, best remembered for his *Digest of the Actions and Trials at Nisi Prius* (1791); Simon Fraser, who became a member of Parliament (MP) for Inverness-shire in the following year; and Thomas Leach, now known for his *Cases in Crown Law* (1789-1815).[60] None of these men practiced at the Old Bailey for more than a few years. Of similar duration was the attendance of a number of less successful barristers: Charles Cowper (1795; he died young), John France (1795), Richard Gardner (1793-97), Robert Keating (1795), George-Rowland Minshull (1793-95), Charles Moore (1795), John Venner (1793-95), and John Wentworth (1793-97) do not appear to have distinguished themselves professionally at the Old Bailey or elsewhere. Robert Dower, named once in the OBSP in 1788 and listed in the *Law List* in 1795, likewise seems to have failed at the bar.[61]

The 1795 list of course includes barristers whose association with the Old Bailey was more lasting. Agar, Fielding, Peatt, and Schoen were still in regular attendance, and John Silvester, by this date common serjeant of London, was also listed as counsel, although the City of London had determined that its legal officer should not practice at the Old Bailey.[62] When Philip Keys began his criminal practice is unknown. He too was of an older generation, called to the bar in 1768, and attached as well to the Borough Court of Southwark and the Court of Record at Whitechapel.[63] Keys disappears from the record after 1795. Among the younger generation were Jerome William Knapp and Robert Pooley, both of whom practiced at the Old Bailey from their respective calls to the bar (1787 and 1793) until their deaths (in 1815 and 1816).

Of the remaining counsel listed in 1795, Jonathan Raine had begun to attend London's criminal sessions in 1793 and would continue his association with the Old Bailey until 1803, when he embarked on a career in politics.[64] Others remained involved in the administration of criminal justice after leaving the Old Bailey: Randle Jackson, like Raine, practiced criminal law in London from 1793 to 1803 (he was also counsel for the East India Company) and ended his career as a Surrey magistrate;[65] John Baker Sellon, who according to the *Law List* spent four or five years at the Old Bailey in the mid-1790s (he was never named in the OBSP), abandoned his leadership of the Norfolk circuit due to increasing deafness but served as a magistrate at Union Hall Police Court (1814) and Hatton Garden Police Court (1819–34);[66] Francis Const, who practiced in London's criminal courts from 1790, became chairman of the Middlesex magistrates and Westminster sessions (1819–32).[67] Newman Knowlys, called in 1782, would, like Silvester, proceed from Old Bailey barrister to common serjeant and then recorder of London.[68] John Gurney also stands out among the younger generation: his father (Joseph) and grandfather (Thomas) were both noted government shorthand writers; his son Russell served as recorder of London.[69] Gurney was called to the bar in 1793, made a KC in 1816, and practiced at the Old Bailey into the 1830s, when he became a puisne baron of the Exchequer. He was employed as junior counsel for the defense in the trials of Hardy, Horne Tooke, and Thelwall for high treason in the 1790s; in 1820 he secured the conviction of two of the Cato Street conspirators.[70] By that date Gurney had become one of the leaders in practice in the King's Bench and "the acknowledged head" of the Home circuit.[71]

This mix of counsel—the successful and the failures, the long-term and the fleeting—was to be typical of the bar found at the Old Bailey. However, as barristers came and went business was consistently dominated by two or three individuals. After Garrow's departure, and until the arrival of Charles Phillips in the 1820s, leadership was shared by advocates of less stature, men who would spend much of their professional careers at the Old Bailey and the Clerkenwell Sessions House. In the 1790s the Old Bailey virtually belonged to two men: Newman Knowlys and Jerome William Knapp. In 1793, for example, Knowlys was named in the OBSP eighty-seven times and Knapp seventy, while their nearest competitors, Peatt and Fielding, were each named fewer than twenty times.

Newman Knowlys's career path was identical to that of John Silvester: Old Bailey barrister and City common pleader in the 1780s and 1790s, common serjeant of London (1803–22), and recorder of London (1822–33). Like Silvester, Knowlys married a widow and had no children of his own; like Silvester, he would come to be reviled as a reactionary in the nineteenth century. Knowlys attracted consistent censure in the press as recorder and was forced to resign after nearly having hanged a convict who had been granted a reprieve.[72] In the 1790s, however, Knowlys, then in his thirties, was in demand as an Old Bailey counsel. His only real rival was Knapp.

Thanks to the efforts of a nephew-in-law with a keen interest in genealogy, Knapp's personal life is much less opaque than that of his contemporaries.[73] Jerome William Knapp was a Londoner by birth,[74] and legal connections abounded within the family: his father was a barrister, his elder brother, Thomas George, an attorney; his sister Mary Ann married Serjeant

Best, later Lord Wynford. Relations between the Bests and the Knapps appear to have been close, as members of these families repeatedly stood as godparents to each other's children. Knapp had married in 1791, four years after his call to the bar, at the age of twenty-nine; a daughter, Eleanor, was born in 1792, and two sons followed: Jerome William (1803) and Edmund (1805). All three children were christened at St. George's, Queen Square —the church in which William Garrow was married—and Robert Pooley stood sponsor at one baptism.[75] Much less information survives of Knapp's professional life. In the courtroom he demonstrated none of Garrow's charisma, nor did he share his predecessor's talent for rhetorical flourish. Thus, despite being in constant business, he made no professional splash, and editorial comment on his abilities appears to be nonexistent. Yet if he failed to attract praise, Knapp likewise avoided censure. Unlike many Old Bailey barristers he did not suffer from a hot temper, and his steady if unspectacular competence must have been appreciated by clients.[76]

The Early Nineteenth Century

In the early nineteenth century leadership among Old Bailey counsel became still more diffuse. By the time Knowlys was elected common serjeant in 1803, John Gurney and an Irishman named Peter Alley, both of whom began to practice in the 1790s, had enlarged their share of business. John Adolphus arrived on the scene in 1807, somewhat older than most newcomers—he was pushing forty—for he had abandoned an earlier career as an attorney.[77] Adolphus found a sparring partner not only in Alley but in Thomas Andrews, called to the bar in 1803. Described as a man of "athletic proportions" and a "John Bull-ish" expression, Andrews, like Garrow, possessed a "fine strong sonorous voice" and "great fluency and readiness of expression." He appeared to greatest advantage when addressing a jury.[78] William Bolland[79] and William Brodrick complete the list of men contemporaries recognized as the Old Bailey's chief practitioners in the first two decades of the nineteenth century. Bolland was said to be a "contemporary in good practice" rather than a serious rival of Alley and Adolphus.[80] Like Silvester and Knowlys he combined Old Bailey practice with a City common pleadership, but Bolland was ultimately more successful, ending his career as a puisne baron of the Exchequer. His performance on the bench was undistinguished: nineteenth-century biographers admitted that his earlier career "had not led him to that abstruse learning which is so necessary for a judge."[81] But where Gurney was remembered for his severity,[82] Bolland was described in one obituary as a "painstaking and careful judge . . . an amiable and honourable man," and Foss commented that he was "one of the most popular men of his time," pleasant, kind, and benevolent.[83] Brodrick too won posthumous praise, and he is one of the few members of the Old Bailey bar whose courtroom manners did not attract public censure.[84]

Very different descriptions survive of Adolphus and Alley, who during their lives received greater press attention. Their bad tempers and aggressive advocacy not infrequently led to altercations which spilled out of the courtroom, to the despair of the bar as well as the entertainment of the public.[85] John Adolphus was damned by one contemporary as "nearly a great man,"[86] while Campbell reported he "was never sufficiently imbued with legal principles to succeed in appearing to understand them and, after various efforts of great pretension, he sank down into a second-rate Old Bailey counsel."[87] "Second-rate" must be taken here as the legal profession's characterization of any practice at the Old Bailey rather than the share Adolphus acquired of it. He was said to have had a good grasp of the criminal law but was described as a "man of acute and apprehensive rather than of great or powerful faculties"; his "capacity was clear" but not of "the greatest comprehension, or of highest order."[88] His "voice was clear, mellow, and flexible, though not of much compass; he had neither fancy nor imagination, nor were his argumentative powers of the highest order; but the clearness of his statements, the happy disposition of his topics, and the felicity of his epithets, were the objects alike of wonder and hopeless imitation."[89] Unfortunately Adolphus was "often rash and hasty," his defect being "insufficient command of temper."[90] He was accused in one instance of sticking his tongue out at a colleague. Even Adolphus's admirers admitted that in his early days at the Old Bailey the barrister had "on some few occasions transgressed the rules of good temper and good breeding."[91] His method of acquiring business was compared to the behavior of the wolf in a fable: "The ermine, the beaver and the wolf set out to make their way together in search of fortune. They came to a deep ditch, full of mud and venemous reptiles. The ermine drew back, afraid to soil her fur. The beaver said he was a good architect, and would build a bridge over the ditch if they would wait a few months. The wolf leaped in, and, though splashed by the dirt and stung by the vermin, arrived at the other side, and shaking himself, exclaimed to his companions, 'Learn from me how people make their way.' "[92] But when Adolphus died in 1845 the *Morning Chronicle* concluded its obituary with the comment, "An erroneous idea has spread abroad that he was a man of a coarse and rugged nature. Nothing can be farther from the truth. He had to deal with men of coarse and brutal manners; and an eager, excitable nature, and a warm temper, often led him to retort in the strain in which he had been attacked; but treat him as a gentleman, and no man was more courteous or kindly in his practice."[93]

Peter Alley's reputation was much the same. Alley "devoted himself almost exclusively to criminal matters." A posthumous memoir acknowledged that he possessed many of the qualifications requisite for a good advocate—Alley was "zealous, industrious, bold, and impassioned"—but he had a volatile temper, and his "constitutional vehemence" was said to impede his powers of reasoning.[94] Like Garrow and Davy before him, Alley was accused of abusive cross-examinations, a style "sure to be popular within the gaol, the residents of which knew . . . that their prosecutors would be roughly handled."[95] Less notorious was Charles Ewan Law, the second son of Lord Ellenborough, called to the bar in 1817. A man of meager professional abilities, Law followed in the footsteps of Silvester and Knowlys, combining Old Bailey practice with a City common pleadership and then being elected common serjeant (1830–33) and recorder (1833–50) of London.[96]

It would be difficult to say which of these early-nineteenth-century Old Bailey barristers was the more successful, which the undisputed leader of London's criminal bar. With the arrival of Charles Phillips in the 1820s, however, the picture changed dramatically. Not since the 1780s had a single man so dominated Old Bailey practice: between 1825 and 1834 Phillips was named in the OBSP in over 2,300 cases, more than double the number of his closest competitors.[97] He was, as Henry Brougham acknowledged, not merely the leader "but really everything" at the Old Bailey from the mid-1820s until he left the bar in 1842.[98]

Like Alley, Phillips was an Irishman, and by the time of his call to the English bar he had already established a reputation as an orator, being famous on the Connaught circuit for "criminal conversation" cases (civil suits in which a husband sued the seducer of his wife for damages). His was not a style that appealed to everyone. Characterized by Coleridge as a "tropophrenitic distemper," a "vertiginous *Waltz* of stultification and Derangement," a "Masquerade-in-Bedlam" style,[99] Phillips's florid oratory was more popular with juries and the public than with the bar.[100] His "flowery, unsubstantial" pleading in Ireland in the 1810s, it was said, would not be "suffered in the English Courts," where it was "necessary to keep to the point of proof,"[101] and the poems and speeches he published in the middle of that decade were condemned in the *Quarterly Review* for their "ridiculous exaggeration" and lack of "common sense."[102] Phillips conceded that the editors were partially correct, but he pointed to national differences, claiming he would proceed differently if at the English bar.[103] In England, however, he continued to attract abuse from within the legal profession. "Counsellor

TABLE 3
Leadership at the Old Bailey, 1783–1834

Leaders*	Number of Cases during				
	Garrow Leadership, 1783–92	Knowlys/ Knapp Leadership, 1793–1803	Knapp/Alley/ Gurney Leadership, 1804–15	Adolphus/ Alley Leadership, 1816–24	Phillips Leadership, 1825–34
Silvester	368	—	—	—	—
Fielding	112	166	42	—	—
Garrow	879	72	24	—	—
Chetwood	40	—	—	—	—
Peatt	135	40	5	—	—
Knowlys	270	1,002	—	—	—
Knapp	85	1,006	768	—	—
Alley	—	666	646	411	162
Const	—	149	33	—	—
Gurney	—	409	633	24	40
Adolphus	—	—	84	535	585
Andrews	—	—	49	471	179
Arabin	—	—	92	151	—
Bolland	—	—	87	179	104
Brodrick	—	—	—	279	269
Law	—	—	—	332	206
Phillips	—	—	—	175	2,362
Prendergast	—	—	—	103	130
Barry	—	—	—	—	586
Creswell	—	—	—	—	156
Clarkson	—	—	—	—	835
Churchill	—	—	—	—	196
Bodkin	—	—	—	—	327
Lee	—	—	—	—	304
Doane	—	—	—	—	195

*Arranged chronologically by appearance in OBSP

O'Garnish," an impulsive and nervous man, one critic claimed, was "occasionally far too demonstrative, both in his speech and in his gestures, which were thorough pantomime."[104] In a poetical review of the bar published in the 1820s Phillips was encouraged to "Halt—and discreetly, while it yet is time, / Reduce to common sense thy strains sublime, / Restrain thy fancy, and reform thy style, / Or hie thee homeward to thy 'Emerald Isle.'"[105]

Phillips, like Garrow, possessed an attractive speaking voice: his strong Irish accent "was of the pleasing, insinuating kind."[106] In his theatricality too he was perhaps not far removed from Garrow, but Phillips was a product of his own times, a man of Dickensian sensibilities rather than eighteenth-century ones—although Dickens, who detested Phillips, would not have welcomed the comparison.[107] James Mackintosh[108] damned Phillips's style as "pitiful to the last degree" and said that "he ought by common consent to be driven from the bar."[109]

Like many Old Bailey barristers Phillips was not well known outside that court. It was argued in his defense that if he had wanted it, he could have obtained "the highest honours of his profession" and that the only thing which held him back was a lack of ambition, but John Campbell offered a different explanation: "Nothing could have prevented him from attaining to great eminence, except a head which not only was not 'a head for law', but into which no law could be crammed, and which repelled all legal definitions and distinctions."[110] Another barrister commented similarly that Phillips was "utterly guiltless of any knowledge of the very first principles of Law."[111] A modicum of law at the very least was required to succeed in the civil courts, and thus it is no surprise that Phillips signally failed at Westminster Hall. Having "laid himself open to a merciless attack" by Brougham in one of his early appearances in the King's Bench, he "collapsed under the punishment" and rarely appeared in the civil courts again.[112] Even on circuit his business lay chiefly on the Crown side. Brougham, however, subsequently became a good friend.[113]

The advent of Phillips meant that his contemporaries at the Old Bailey were, like those of Garrow, relegated to the shadows. In 1830, by which time Phillips had secured the vast majority of business, twenty-three barristers were identified in the *Law List* as attached to the London, Middlesex, and Westminster sessions, most of them little known. Of the "old-timers," Adolphus, Agar, Alley, and John Curwood, who had begun to practice at the Old Bailey in the late 1790s, were still practicing (Agar was not named in the OBSP for that year, and Curwood's name is omitted in the *Law List*). Curwood, like Knapp, appears to have been well known to contemporaries but ultimately left little professional trace. Unlike Adolphus, he had no loving daughter to publish reminiscences of his career, and at the Old Bailey he was no doubt overshadowed, first by Adolphus and Alley and then by Phillips. As a criminal lawyer, however, he was described as "among the first, if not the first, in his profession."[114] His obituary in the *Law Times* was headed, "John Curwood, Esq. The Old Bailey Barrister"; it recorded a career in the criminal courts that spanned more than thirty years.[115] Brodrick, in his final year of practice in 1830—he died on 12 October—was named in the OBSP that year in only a handful of cases, having given up a regular attendance at the Old

Bailey.[116] Younger barristers included another Irishman, John Hovenden Alley, whose Old Bailey career, if unspectacular, was of considerable duration (1816–38); Martin Charles Burney, called in 1828 and named in the *Law List* as attending the metropolitan sessions until 1841; Frederick Augustus Carrington, who practiced there between 1825 and 1842; John Henry Blencowe Churchill, a friend of Adolphus[117] (1827–42); George Evans, sessions counsel, 1827–46 (he was never listed as attached specifically to the Central Criminal Court); Samuel Fish (1825–42); and Charles Heaton (1829–40). William Glover's sessions career was brief (1830–31). John Sympson Jessop, who had practiced at the metropolitan sessions in the opening decade of the nineteenth century (1807–8), returned in 1819 and continued his association until 1840. Like George Evans he was never listed under Central Criminal Court counsel. Francis Valentine Lee had been a regular from 1820, and in 1830 he captured a respectable amount of Old Bailey business, employed for the defense in more than a hundred cases (Phillips was named for the defense in over two hundred cases in that year) and appearing for the prosecution in a further dozen or so trials. Lee remained attached to the Central Criminal Court until 1840; he died suddenly in 1846, in his early forties, leaving "a widow and a numerous family to mourn his early loss."[118] Thomas Radford's connection with the metropolitan sessions was of shorter duration (1828–32) and less successful (he was not named in the OBSP). John Smith attended the metropolitan sessions from 1827 to 1842, Thomas Stirling from 1820 to 1842.[119] John Mirehouse, who had been called to the bar in 1817, was first named as attached to the London, Middlesex, and Westminster sessions in 1830. His name is found in the OBSP only once that year. Mirehouse followed the same career path of Silvester, Knowlys, and Law, however, combining Old Bailey practice with a City common pleadership (1823) and eventually being elected common serjeant of London (1833).[120]

In 1830 Joseph Payne had been practicing at the Old Bailey for six years, an association that would continue until he was made deputy assistant judge of the Middlesex sessions in 1858. Payne was described by a contemporary as "a constant *attaché* of the Central Criminal Court . . . seldom engaged elsewhere."[121] Although his practice was "confined to the smaller class of cases — principally defences," he was both "respected and beloved" among the legal profession as "the most simple, guileless, pure-minded creature that was ever thrust before the public," a man who devoted his time and money to charity when not in court.[122] In greater business throughout the 1830s, although by no means genuine rivals of Phillips, were William Bodkin, Michael Prendergast, and, in particular, William Clarkson. Phillips, Clarkson, Adolphus, Alley, and Bodkin were often bracketed by contemporaries as the chief Old Bailey counsel in the mid- to late 1830s.[123] Bodkin, who like Payne ended his career on the bench of the Clerkenwell Sessions House,[124] was remembered as an able advocate, pleasant companion, and popular man. Serjeant Robinson reported that he was "a clever, bland, courteous man of the world,"[125] "too respectable to be either the author or the victim of many jests."[126] Michael Prendergast, in contrast, appears to have been something of a character. Physically unkempt and absentminded, he once drew out in court a hunk of cold buttered toast instead of the "single greasy sheet" of instructions he was looking for. Anyone, claimed Serjeant Ballantine, who saw for the first time

> that curious-looking figure usually seated at the corner of the barrister's bench . . . might be inclined to ask, What is it? Upon minute investigation might be discovered, encased in clothes far too large for him, the gaunt figure of a very unclean-looking man. . . . Slovenly as his dress was, his mind was more so: with a greater fund of general knowledge than most people, it seemed mixed so inextricably in his brain that it was next to useless. He rarely had any but the smallest cases from the dirtiest of clients, and whilst one of them was being tried would not unfrequently sit in a state of abstraction, out of which an unhappy clerk had to wake him. He possessed, however, much power at times, and great independence.[127]

This caricature notwithstanding, Prendergast had the reputation of an extremely capable advocate, and he was one of the few Old Bailey barristers to obtain the rank of Queen's Counsel. He too had connections with the City of London and was elected a judge of the Sheriffs' Court in 1856.[128]

William Clarkson was another kettle of fish altogether. Called to the bar in 1823, Clarkson became the closest thing Phillips had to a rival, although he was routinely named in fewer than half the number of cases.[129] Clarkson was no amiable eccentric, he was not particularly clever, and no one would ever accuse him of being courteous. Aggressive in court, he was singularly lacking in charm and possessed little of the milk of human kindness. Clarkson frightened people with his "rough and domineering manner," including a Surrey magistrate before whom he once appeared. Sir Richard Frederick was attempting to remind Clarkson of the respect due to the bench when he was warned by a fellow magistrate: "[T]his is Mr Clarkson, the Old Bailey counsel. He will not stand badgering from you or from any of us; so take care." Sir Richard stopped his address: "I beg your pardon, sir; I was not aware that you were the *notorious* Mr. Clarkson. Pray continue."[130] Serjeant Robinson described Clarkson as "a rough, bluff, testy personage, who never seemed to sympathise with people in general or with anyone in particular."[131] "Clarkson's was a very corrosive style of oratory, and he was generally said to be much fonder of his specie than his species. He could shed a tear or two on occasion, but he did not keep them well under command. He generally exhibited emotion in the wrong place; sometimes long after everyone else had finished."[132] Serjeant Ballantine remarked shortly that he could not recall any circumstances of Clarkson's private life or professional career that could be recorded to that gentleman's advantage.[133]

Politics and the Old Bailey Barrister

Identifying counsel who practiced at the Old Bailey is a much easier task than explaining the emergence of a bar at that court or accounting for the apparent increase in the participation of counsel in felony trials in the 1780s. Searching for an explanation, some historians have pointed to the larger political environment of the period. John Beattie suggests a connection between the rise of counsel at the Old Bailey and contemporary concerns about a variety of threats "to the rights and liberties of Englishmen"—the behavior of the government in America, corruption in Parliament at home—and a more general desire for reform of the relations between government and people.[134] The timing is certainly suggestive. The rejection of a paternalistic ideology according to which the judge offered the best protection of a prisoner's rights during trial can be seen to mirror increasing dissatisfaction with "virtual" political representation. On the evidence of the OBSP, legal representation (albeit restricted) for prisoners at the Old Bailey increased noticeably at the close of the American Revolution, while the right to a full legal defense was granted four years after the parliamentary Reform Act of 1832. Looking at the composition of the Old Bailey's bench, David Lemmings also suggests that the radical political inclinations of the eighteenth-century recorders John Glynn and James Adair might logically have inclined them to be more willing to tolerate the presence of defense counsel.[135] While London's recorder presided (in theory at least) over only the less serious trials, these were admittedly the most numerous cases.[136] Even if Lemmings is correct, however, we have still to consider the motives of the counsel who appeared before the court.

The bar as a whole in the eighteenth century was not noted for progressive tendencies. While Holmes and Speck argue for the existence of "a natural Whig bias in the lay professions"—within which they included lawyers—from the late seventeenth century,[137] Lemmings's analysis of voting patterns among barrister MPs in the early eighteenth century reveals that the majority "exhibited an abiding attachment to Toryism."[138] This conservatism continued throughout the century: in the 1790s lawyers generally were remarkable for their conservative opinions and had little sympathy for revolutionary ideas, whether political or pertaining to the criminal law. The English barrister in the late eighteenth century was typically an unrebellious creature, more inclined to defend the status quo "against the influence of modern liberal heresies" than to promote reform.[139] There were of course notable exceptions, chief among them Thomas Erskine. Erskine, the defender of Paine, of Hardy, Horne Tooke, and Thelwall, has, as Wesley Pue comments, been accorded "pride of place in the struggle to promote . . . 'justice and liberty.'"[140]

In attempting to account for the rise of counsel at the Old Bailey historians have naturally considered whether it owed to a liberal impulse on the part of the lawyers themselves. Thus John Beattie questions whether Garrow's defense work in the 1780s "betoken[ed] a political stance, a Whig view that a corrupt government threatened to overturn liberty at home as it had in America, and that the defense of the constitution could be carried on in the criminal courts as well as in Parliament?"[141] Following Beattie, Pue suggests the possibility of links between "lawyers, political liberalism, and particular forms of trial" in eighteenth- and nineteenth-century England.[142] Lemmings speaks more directly of an apparent "subculture of 'liberal' barristers associated with the Old Bailey and the city of London."[143] The problem is that—as Beattie and Pue point out—we have no real proof of liberalism among the counsel who can be identified at the Old Bailey in the 1780s. While political affiliation can be determined for only a minority of Old Bailey barristers, their number includes Tories as well as Whigs, and there was an essential conservatism even among the Whigs. Garrow was indeed a Whig in his youth. He joined the Whig Club in 1784, a year after his call to the bar, and he was Charles James Fox's "jaw master general" at the bar of the House of Commons during the Westminster election scrutiny.[144] John Gurney as a young man had likewise belonged to the Whig Club and the Friends of the People.[145] "In early life Mr. Gurney was nearly a rebel," wrote another Old Bailey counsel, "but it will be more polite to describe him as having been a very advanced Liberal; as, however, he progressed in the profession, the vivifying light of Toryism began to affect his senses."[146] The politics of their youth may have influenced the decisions of these barristers to practice criminal law.[147] John Silvester and Newman Knowlys, however, cannot by any stretch of the imagination be considered liberals,[148] and it would be a mistake to assume that the Old Bailey's courtroom was peppered with lesser Erskines. Among the counsel found at the Old Bailey in the late eighteenth century the sole radical is Stewart Kyd, and he spent only a year (1793) at that court. A friend of Hardy and Horne Tooke, Kyd joined the Society for Constitutional Information in 1792; with Hardy, Tooke, and ten others he was committed to the Tower in 1794 on a charge of high treason, but he was subsequently discharged.

In the early nineteenth century prominent Old Bailey counsel were again as likely to be Tories as Whigs. While Peter Alley's politics were said to be of an "extremely liberal nature" and had occasioned his departure from Ireland,[149] his rival John Adolphus was a Tory. In a history of England published shortly before he took up Old Bailey practice, Adolphus defended the conservative administrations of the late eighteenth century: "[F]ar from thinking that the aims of successive administrations have been directed to overthrow the liberties and constitution of the country; I am persuaded that liberty has been better understood, and more effectively and practically promoted during this period, than in any which preceded, and that the affairs of government have always been honestly, although sometimes imprudently, and in the conspicuous instance of the American war, unsuccessfully administered."[150] "There is no disputing," wrote one of Adolphus's early biographers, that his *History of England* "is the work of a violent partisan, a Tory of the old school, who thought George the Third honest, and Queen Charlotte handsome. . . . He believed Pitt to be entirely honest, and Fox a rogue."[151] The London Corresponding Society, an artisan-based organization devoted to political reform, was dismissed by Adolphus as a collection of "miserable brawlers."[152] His political views did not prevent him from defending the Cato Street conspirators in 1820, but he expressed astonishment at being asked to do so.[153] Charles Ewan Law was likewise a Tory, and he sat as Tory MP for Cambridge for roughly the same period he served as recorder of London.[154] Despite (or perhaps because of) an extensive Old Bailey practice, Law appears to have doubted the necessity of counsel in criminal trials.[155] Charles Phillips's political views were more liberal but focused on Irish concerns: Phillips was heavily involved in the agitation for Roman Catholic relief,[156] and his correspondence with Henry Brougham reveals a continued advocacy of Daniel O'Connell, the Irish political leader.[157]

The Old Bailey Bar and the Capital Code

When the first generation of the Old Bailey bar—Silvester and Garrow, Knowlys and Knapp—began their practice, death by hanging was the prescribed punishment for serious crimes, and in the 1780s and 1790s large numbers of convicts were routinely executed at the close of each of the

Old Bailey sessions.[158] What London's criminal practitioners thought of England's sanguinary criminal law is difficult to determine. No evidence appears to have survived of Knapp's opinions, while those expressed by Silvester, Knowlys, and Garrow date from periods subsequent to their Old Bailey practice. On the strength of the information available I would argue —cautiously—that the leaders in Old Bailey practice in the closing decades of the eighteenth century accepted the "Bloody Code" rather than desired its reform.

Silvester and Knowlys's opinions on reforms contemplated in the criminal law were sought in 1811, at which time they were recorder and common serjeant of London, respectively, and thus sitting as judges at the Old Bailey.[159] A few years earlier (1808) Samuel Romilly had procured the repeal of capital punishment for privately stealing from the person without violence (i.e., picking pockets); one of his opponents, Colonel William Frankland, argued that further reductions in the application of the death penalty should not be considered unless those involved in the administration of criminal justice could recommend them. London's recorder and common serjeant were asked to consider the effects of the 1808 reform and whether it would be advisable to remove capital punishment from shoplifting, stealing from ships in canals and navigable rivers, and stealing from a dwelling house where no breaking or burglary occurred, as bills then before the House proposed to do.[160] Silvester responded unequivocally that he believed the removal of capital punishment from privately stealing from the person had resulted in an increase in both the number of offenders and convictions for the crime. Knowlys was more cautious; he had not observed "any beneficial effect as yet" from the repeal. When pressed to comment on whether the number of pickpockets had increased or decreased, however, he said they had "very much" increased in number, that the offenders had become more numerous and were "more united in groups," and that they carried on their activities "more systematically and with greater boldness." Both men advised strongly against any further removal of the death penalty from the statute book, although Silvester conceded that some alteration of the amount of the value of articles stolen "might deserve some consideration." Knowlys was more severe: "[I]n the present depraved state of the domestic and other servants in the metropolis, I cannot possibly conceive any measure more big with mischief to every private housekeeper, and to every tradesman, than the lessening the severity of the 12th Anne, stat. 1, c. 7."[161]

Garrow's views on the criminal law likewise date from the early nineteenth century. As attorney or solicitor general throughout most of Romilly's campaign to reduce the scope of the death penalty,[162] Garrow consistently opposed reform of the criminal law, and his opposition was grounded in a belief in discretionary punishment. He argued that discretion rested safely in the hands of the English jury, the judiciary, and the Crown, claiming that in thirty years' experience with the administration of criminal justice he had not met with six instances in which he would have differed from the jury's verdict.[163] He further argued that well-supported appeals for mercy were never made in vain. Upholding the royal pardon, he asserted that "the anxiety of the royal mind on all occasions to render judgment in mercy was well known."[164] He also believed that a discretionary system provided the flexibility necessary to justice. A man or woman in dire poverty who had clearly stolen to provide food for his or her children could be dealt with leniently, while "deep-laid conspiracies" or systematic corruption would meet with well-deserved severity.[165] Hardened criminals represented a significant threat to the security of society and required the "utmost rigour" of the law.[166] Garrow even opposed Romilly's attempts to ameliorate the aggravated death penalty accorded to those convicted of high treason. He conceded the virtue of proportion in punishment, but in the spirit of the anonymous author of *Hanging, Not Punishment Enough* (1701) rather than that of Beccaria.[167] Different crimes were marked with varying signs of reproach and disgrace: "Ought a greater disgrace to be attached to the murder of the meanest subject than to the murder of a virtuous King?" he asked.[168] Persons accused of high treason were entitled to a copy of the indictment against them and of the panel of jurors; they had also the right to compel witnesses to testify in their favor, and the right to a full defense by counsel. Given these "indulgences," if a person were convicted of treason the full weight of the law should be brought to bear upon him. The question before the House, Garrow said, was not "whether we are to make a new law but whether we are to repeal an old law." If asked "whether, if a law were now for the first time to be enacted to fix the punishment of high treason, I should consent to a law declaring that the offender 'be dragged to the gallows; that he be hanged by the neck and then cut down alive; that his entrails be taken out and burned while he is yet alive; and that his body be divided into four parts,'" Garrow was sure it was unnecessary to say that he would be one of the last men to sanction such a law. But, he continued, "does it therefore follow that I should consent to alter the law which has been established for centuries?" The "safeguards" and "ancient landmarks," the "bulwarks of the Constitution" should not hastily be removed.[169]

Garrow's opposition to Romilly reveals a firm belief in the unwritten eighteenth-century criminal code. The law as it existed on paper did not tell the whole story: while the potential punishment for high treason was terrible in the extreme, testifying to the heinous nature of the crime, the threat need never be fulfilled. By the nineteenth century, if not before, Garrow clearly believed that terror operated beneficially to deter criminals; equally he believed that discretionary mercy ensured that justice might truly be served.

One barrister's experience of justice at the Old Bailey did result in a long-term personal campaign for reform. As the illegitimate son of the Earl of Sandwich and Martha Ray, a singer and famous beauty shot dead by a Norfolk rector, Basil Montagu had a more colorful background than most of his Old Bailey colleagues, and from his days as a law student he had acquired close connections with the literary world, being on intimate terms with Wordsworth, Coleridge, and William Hazlitt, among others. Montagu first met Wordsworth in 1793, through the radical William Godwin. Both men were twenty-three years of age at the time, and committed radicals, although the course of the French Revolution would subsequently alter their views.[170] Montagu's literary friends would themselves touch on the subject of criminal justice: one of Wordsworth's earliest published poems, "The Convict," which appeared in the *Morning Post* in 1797, argued in favor of transportation and against execution; Coleridge launched a passionate attack in the *Courier* on the sentence of a young woman ordered to be whipped for stealing six loaves of bread, urging that the practice be removed from the criminal code on grounds both of humanity and utility, as the shame induced by such a punishment would only destroy the "moral identity" of the victim.[171] Sharing the sensibilities of his literary friends, and unlike them constantly reminded of the severity of the criminal law, Montagu was unsuited to Old Bailey practice. A certain constitutional toughness was required to succeed in the criminal courts at this point in history, when a barrister's failure in court could result in the execution of his client. Visible reminders of such failures had also to be faced: John Campbell noted in his diary that one of his clients "was hung in chains near Stourbridge"; Campbell passed him "always in travelling from Worcester."[172]

Called to the bar in 1798, Montagu was not named in the OBSP beyond 1802, and his subsequent legal career would lie in Chancery and bankruptcy law.[173] As a contemporary noted, Montagu's attendance at the criminal courts had been rooted in "a desire to save the lives of the culprits."[174] His efforts to this end were soon redirected as he waged a sustained pamphlet war against capital punishment. In 1809 he founded, with William Allen, the Society for the Diffusion of Knowledge upon the Punishment of Death and the Improvement of Prison Discipline.[175] His pamphlets reproduced and annotated parliamentary debates on capital punishment as well as collecting the opinions of a diverse range of individuals.[176] In his various publications Montagu condemned a system that operated in a "confusion of remissness and severity" according to laws made without any consideration for proportion between crime and punishment.[177] He also abhorred barbarous displays involving punishment of the body, relating with particular horror the circumstances in which John Williams's body was interred. Williams was arrested for the infamous Ratcliffe Highway murders of 1811, in which two families were murdered at night in their homes, provoking widespread public anxiety.[178] He hanged himself in his cell in the prison of Cold Bath Fields, but not to be cheated of spectacle, the authorities had his body transported on a cart to the crossroads where, as a suicide, he would be buried with a stake through his heart. In a carefully composed tableau his corpse was displayed on an inclined plane, with the alleged murder weapons—a maul and chisel—positioned on either side of his head. The white handkerchief he had used to hang himself was around his neck, and the stake to be driven through his heart and the iron crow used for driving it were placed above his head. The procession, attended by the high constable and beadle of the parish of St. George, stopped briefly outside the sites of the murders before proceeding to the crossroads, where a grave, deliberately too short, had been dug. There the body was dropped and the stake driven through it, "amidst the shouts and vociferous execrations of the multitude." This "disgraceful outrage," Montagu wrote, was "an insult to public feeling."[179]

Montagu attributed what would be a lifelong interest in dismantling the "Bloody Code" to two occurrences early in his career at the bar. The first involved a visit, as a student, to Newgate. On entering the prison he was immediately aware of being alone amidst "brutal ignorance and hardened vice," and when, surrounded by felons, he sought the protection of a less "ferocious"-looking inmate, he discovered the man was charged with murder.[180] The second defining experience occurred a few years after his call to the bar, when he had been asked to seek a pardon for two men due to be executed on the following morning for sheep stealing. Montagu succeeded in obtaining a reprieve of one week to enable the authorities to inquire into new circumstances. Not wanting to excite "improper expectation," when he visited the condemned men he told them that it was better that they should have another week in which to make their peace with the Almighty. The reaction of one of the men in question—"Oh God, a week is a long time to live!"—was not what he had anticipated.[181] Thirty years later he wrote that he had been unable to forget either experience and that together they had convinced him that the criminal law must be changed. James Mackintosh, with whom Montagu rode on circuit, had also played a role in the formation of his opinion. It was Mackintosh who taught him that it was not the death of the sinner which should be desired, "but rather that he should turn from his wickedness and live." "This piece of gold," Montagu said, "I worked into various forms, to circulate it through society; I published it again and again."[182]

In both his desire for reform of the capital code and his efforts to promote it, Basil Montagu appears to have been the exception rather than the rule among the members of the bar at the Old Bailey at the turn of the nineteenth century. There is no evidence of reforming zeal among his companions, most of whom remained silent on the issue. The only other member of the Old Bailey bar to become actively involved in the campaign to abolish the death penalty was Charles Phillips, and, like Montagu, Phillips took up the cause after leaving criminal practice—in his case, some twelve years after he had left the Old Bailey.

When Phillips arrived in England in the 1820s the death penalty was beginning to lose its central role in the administration of criminal justice, and during Robert Peel's tenure at the Home Office the criminal law came under close scrutiny. Benefit of clergy was abolished, and the entire law relating to theft was consolidated, eliminating the distinction between grand and petty larceny and increasing to £5 the amount beyond which stealing from a dwelling house became a capital offense. Peel also supervised a Gaol Act (1823) that embraced the philosophy of the penitentiary.[183] Prison was on its way to becoming the primary punishment for serious crimes, although transportation continued to be an option until the middle of the nineteenth century.[184] Compared with those of his predecessors at the Old Bailey, relatively few of Phillips's convicted clients would be hanged, and by the time he retired from criminal practice in 1842 the death penalty was by and large reserved for convicted murderers. In the 1840s, however, a campaign for its entire abolition emerged, and Charles Phillips was among those who wanted to expunge it from the statute book altogether. It was little excuse, he said, to argue (as Garrow had) that England's cruel and sanguinary laws were not of the present generation's making, for their retention was equally barbarous. He also believed it was "unwise and unsafe to depend on the constitutional temperament" of those who sat on the bench and in the jury box, for there had been instances of "calamitous errors."[185] At the same time, Phillips disapproved of partial verdicts, believing that they served to degrade justice.[186] Romilly consequently attracted his praise as "one of those men . . . whom Providence occasionally sends on earth to mitigate the misery of his fellow creatures . . . great and good . . . a profound lawyer, a learned jurist, a wise and humane legislator."[187]

Phillips's tract on the death penalty, which first appeared in 1856, is emotional and sentimental, littered with italics, block capitals, and exclamation marks: "Death, death on the gallows — death for five shillings, and this in a civilized — a Christian land!" he exclaimed. In Dickensian fashion he cited the execution of Mary Jones, convicted of stealing food for her children, who rode to the gallows with a baby sucking at her breast.[188] Beneath the melodrama, however, was a clearly argued rationale for his views on punishment, one based on a combination of Christian morality and practical concerns. Phillips repudiated entirely the pre-reform system of criminal administration. Capital punishment was neither civilized nor Christian;[189] moreover, it did not achieve the desired ends. Making examples of selected criminals through public hangings merely brutalized spectators rather than striking terror into their hearts. Echoing Beccaria, he argued that punishment should be both moderate and certain.[190] The convicted murderer should meet not with the noose but with certain, incommutable, and perpetual incarceration within a prison appropriated exclusively to murderers, one built in a secluded location to isolate the inmates entirely from life. Here they would be subjected to the silent system one day per month, as well as on the anniversary of the crime. Dramatic to the end, Phillips recommended that the prison be sited on a visible but secluded elevation, with a black flag waving from its summit and at its foot inscribed: "The Grave of the Murderers."[191] Some found his solution overly severe, but Phillips responded that it was intended to be severe; he wrote not in "sickly sentiment" but in "a spirit of utmost sternness": "Good men and simple men are easily deceived into humane recommendations, and society is constantly imperilled by the 'felonious piety' of a counterfeit repentence."[192]

These various views on capital punishment span more than fifty years, and the differences in the opinions expressed owe in part to generational change. Phillips belongs to the nineteenth century and not to the eighteenth. The reform movement had gathered considerable momentum by the time he began his criminal practice, and although abolition of the death penalty for murder would not be achieved within his lifetime — or that of his children — he was not alone in the 1850s in advocating this final repeal. The first generation of Old Bailey barristers, however, do not appear to have contributed to the reform movement, and Montagu's efforts were untypical of the next. Where punishment was concerned, the bar attached to the Old Bailey evinced few radical tendencies.

Conclusion

In attempting to explain the emergence of a bar at the Old Bailey we should not lose sight of the fact that we are dealing with a London phenomenon. Whether representation by counsel increased noticeably on the circuits in the 1780s remains to be determined. A distinction must also be made between the personnel who undertook criminal work in London and those who handled Crown cases in the provinces. Garrow and other members of the bar found at the Old Bailey also traveled on circuit,[193] but there they shared Crown cases with junior members of the wider bar. On circuit, criminal practice had become an accepted part of a recently called barrister's workload by the third quarter of the eighteenth century, if not before. Thus Twiss reported that John Scott (later Lord Eldon), called to the bar in 1776, had little business on first attending the Northern circuit *except that which is usually entrusted to mere beginners* — the defence of prisoners indicted for petty felonies."[194] James Mackintosh, called in 1795, similarly accepted criminal briefs on the Norfolk circuit in 1800,[195] while John Campbell indicated to his brother that he expected to attend both at the Old Bailey and the Court of King's Bench in his first year of practice. Campbell undertook Crown cases on the Home circuit and at the Gloucester sessions from 1806 to 1819.[196] In 1812 he announced his intention to become "a sort of village Garrow" at the Monmouth quarter sessions; in 1813 he referred to himself as "decidedly the second man in the Crown court."[197] Campbell gave up criminal work when he first applied to become a King's Counsel, commenting: "I now mind Crown business very little. I have not had a client hanged for many a day. I get into the *civil* line, which is more *genteel* and more profitable."[198]

While criminal practice on circuit remains to be explored, at the Old Bailey we have clear evidence of two developments in the 1780s: an increase in the number of cases in which counsel were employed and the emergence of a bar attached to that court. As argued above, the increase in numbers owes much to the appearance of a single barrister: William Garrow. Garrow's attendance alone altered the statistics of representation. But the choice of a small number of barristers to attend regularly at the metropolitan sessions, just as counsel attached themselves to quarter sessions outside London, may also have promoted the increased participation of counsel in felony trials at the Old Bailey. Lawyers, that is, may have become visible in London's criminal courts in a way they had not been before. Their presence in court served to remind potential clients of the possibility of employing counsel, and Garrow's spectacular success and celebrity must have provided highly effective advertising. His success, moreover, probably inspired other barristers to attempt to follow in his footsteps.

The emergence of a criminal bar in London depended first on gradual changes in prosecutorial behavior, on the decision, that is, of the City, of various national institutions, and, by the late eighteenth century, of shopkeepers and merchants, to hire lawyers to conduct prosecutions. It further depended on judicial tolerance of defense counsel, a tolerance which had been established some fifty years earlier, and which, in all likelihood, owed to concern over the problems introduced by the central government's attempts to encourage private prosecution. A political atmosphere in which paternalism was under attack may also have contributed to the rise of counsel at the end of the eighteenth century. When we consider the motives of the barristers themselves, however, the limited evidence of their political affiliations suggests that London's nascent criminal bar was not particularly "rights-oriented." Individual liberals there may have been, but there was no liberal subculture at the Old Bailey. The political conservatism of key Old Bailey barristers, together with the fact that Crown cases on circuit are routinely cited in legal biography as the preserve of "junior" members of the bar, suggests that the practical considerations of acquiring employment and building a professional reputation impelled the lawyers' participation in trials of felony.

CHAPTER THREE

Constructing a Career

Earning a living at the bar in the late eighteenth and early nineteenth centuries was no easy task.[1] In the first two or three years after their call barristers struggled to acquire the necessary connections without "hugging" attorneys and waited for a chance to distinguish themselves in court— a difficult undertaking when, as junior barristers, they were restricted to opening pleadings and cross-examining unimportant witnesses. Many abandoned their chosen profession after discovering that "there must be so much labour, so much subserviency, so much accident to secure success."[2]

Competition for briefs was fierce, and building a legal practice typically involved attendance at a variety of courts, among which the Old Bailey had become one possibility. Changes in prosecutorial behavior in the early eighteenth century and the subsequent decision of the bench to allow the limited participation of defense counsel had created new employment opportunities for the bar. London's criminal barristers, however, did not practice exclusively at the Old Bailey. As described in the previous chapter, some owed their attachment to that court to connections with the City of London. John Silvester and other of the City's common pleaders, when not employed in the criminal courts, enjoyed a monopoly of civil practice in the customary courts of London. But even those without City connections did not restrict themselves to criminal law, and it is equally doubtful that the counsel who would come to be known as "Old Bailey barristers" embarked on their careers with that goal in mind. Professionally speaking, criminal practice was not prestigious; in fact, the very opposite was true.[3] Most of the barristers employed at the Old Bailey would have hoped eventually to relinquish their criminal briefs for civil ones, to carve out for themselves a niche in the superior courts. A few succeeded: William Garrow, for example, became a KC in 1793, which precluded him from regular Old Bailey attendance, and there is no evidence to suggest that he regretted his professional elevation. Other barristers, if they failed to establish themselves in Westminster Hall, constructed a composite practice that combined an attachment to the Old Bailey with employment in a wide range of petty tribunals.

Assizes and Quarter Sessions

The newly called barrister[4] was faced with immediate decisions to make about which courts to attend and which circuit to travel. Most barristers routinely traveled one of the six circuits made twice a year by the high court judges: the Home, Midland, Norfolk, Oxford, Western, and Northern (the Northern circuit took place only once a year).[5] The Home circuit was the most popular and the most crowded, being the cheapest to travel and never involving more than a day's journey—usually by post-chaise—from London.[6] Married barristers, or their wives, were also said to prefer it. In 1807 the cost was estimated to be five guineas per county.[7] The 500-mile Western circuit, by contrast, could not be traveled for less than £150 a year, while the Northern circuit, farthest from London (it involved a 650-mile round trip), was even more expensive. In choosing a circuit, however, barristers weighed the expense against personal connections. Relatives, neighbors, and acquaintances were all potential sources of civil work,[8] and a barrister from one of the northern counties might possess sufficient connections to compensate for the cost of the journey. Most Old Bailey barristers were southerners, many from metropolitan London, but the few born in the north chose the Northern rather than the Home circuit.[9] Barristers of Irish or Scottish birth, who had no connections on any circuit, had to position themselves carefully. Charles Phillips chose the Oxford circuit, where he assumed and retained the lead as prisoners' counsel; Peter Alley does not appear to have traveled on circuit at all. The success of Old Bailey barristers on circuit varied. Garrow "was easily the first in business" on the Home circuit in 1807; John Gurney was said to be equally successful, and Thomas Andrews was held to be a "leading member" of the Midland circuit. William Fielding, in contrast, had little or no circuit business as he neared the close of his career. He was very popular with the younger barristers, however, who appreciated his songs and anecdotes.[10]

Most barristers also attended a quarter sessions that fell geographically within the desired circuit. Here the inexperienced barrister could demonstrate his abilities, promoting his chances of acquiring assize briefs. Professional etiquette dictated that King's Counsel, serjeants, and barristers with patents of precedence[11] did not attend the sessions. In their absence junior counsel enjoyed the opportunity of addressing juries for the first time and acquired both the experience and "habits of self-possession" which would enable them to succeed elsewhere.[12] Most Old Bailey barristers chose sessions within the Home counties, and Kent was particularly popular.[13] John Adolphus described Gurney's choice of the Kent sessions as "merely introductory to the home circuit"; roughly ten years later he chose the same sessions and circuit himself. Over half of the 145 barristers who practiced at the Old Bailey for a year or more between 1783 and the creation of the Central Criminal Court in 1834 (82, or 56.6 percent) also attended quarter sessions outside the metropolis at some point in their careers. Quarter sessions briefs, apart from serving as a point of professional entry, also provided a useful supplement to income. Not every barrister achieved a level of success that allowed him to drop such work.

Within the metropolis Old Bailey barristers routinely attended the London, Middlesex, and Westminster sessions, and it was this broad attachment, rather than an association exclusively with the Old Bailey, that was recorded in the *Law List*. At the sessions they not only practiced criminal law but were equally well versed in "parochial" law. The poor law was acknowledged to be a source of great profit to barristers at the sessions, both in London and in the provinces.[14] Elizabethan in origin, it had by the late eighteenth century become a voluminous and complex code, the consequence of what one contemporary complained of as "ad scititious acts of Parliament, altering and butchering" the original legislation.[15] Much of the civil practice at the sessions consisted of poor law appeals involving intricate points of law: "[A] great deal of money was spent in ridiculous contests between parishes in relation to the support of paupers."[16] Counsel were routinely engaged on both sides in settlement appeals, which originated in the removal of a pauper from a parish in which she had become, or was likely to become, chargeable, and where she was deemed not to belong, to the parish of her last legal settlement.[17] The parish on the receiving end frequently considered itself aggrieved, and on a successful appeal the pauper was passed back. Counsel also appeared in vagrancy cases, which involved the removal of a person apprehended in a particular parish as a "Rogue and Vagabond, wandering abroad, lodging in the open air; and not giving a good account of himself or herself," or "wandering abroad and begging," again to the parish of last legal settlement. While advocates of Garrow's stature had little need to spend time assisting metropolitan parishes in passing their poor among themselves, Silvester's name, as well as those of other Old Bailey counsel, appears regularly on briefs for settlement and vagrancy cases from the 1770s.[18]

Licensing issues also proved lucrative. On the "great field day" at the

Middlesex sessions when applications for music and dancing licenses were heard, almost every member of the bar had the chance of picking up a brief or two. New licenses were hotly contested.[19] The granting of spirit licenses was also frequently opposed, as already licensed publicans rushed to prove that no new establishments were necessary.[20] Spirit licenses named the conditions to be adhered to in order to retain them, and many licensed victualers found themselves again before the quarter sessions to answer complaints. One publican was prosecuted at the London sessions for allowing his customers to play unlawful card games, to "tipple and drink" during the hours of divine service, and generally to make noise and riot.[21] Such prosecutions were not unrelated to crime, and complaints were commonly made in the late eighteenth century that London's magistrates were failing to pay sufficient attention to liquor licensing: an "unlimited number of ale-houses [are] suffered to be kept open day and night, without order or regulation; where tippling, gambling, and all kinds of vice, are not only permitted but encouraged, where thieves and prostitutes are harboured and protected."[22] Magistrates were also entreated to pay more diligent attention to vagrancy and to clear the streets of beggars.

Westminster Hall

While circuit and sessions work were a key part of most legal practices, to succeed at Westminster Hall, the home of England's superior courts of common law (King's Bench, Common Pleas, and Exchequer) and equity (Chancery),[23] was the ambition of every practicing barrister. As at the Old Bailey and on circuit, however, business in the superior courts was dominated by a handful of practitioners, and entry among their ranks was exceedingly difficult.[24] While there is no means of assessing a given barrister's Westminster caseload, the rule and minute books for each court, which record the motions made by counsel, can be used to determine comparative success. Several motions might be made in the course of a single cause, but barristers were paid by appearance and counting motions therefore provides a reasonably reliable method of gauging the extent of a barrister's business.[25] The evidence of the rule books indicates that there was little overlap in the late eighteenth and early nineteenth centuries between the bar found at Westminster and those barristers who attended the London, Middlesex, and Westminster sessions.[26] A barrister who chose to practice at the Middlesex sessions had in fact an immediate problem with attendance in the King's Bench, as they competed in term time.[27]

Few Old Bailey barristers had any success in the Court of Chancery: in

1790, for example, only Francis Const, Stewart Kyd, and William Leach appeared there at all. Chancery practice tended to be fairly exclusive. Most
members of the bar, before their call, chose to specialize in either the special pleading requisite for common law practice or equity draftsmanship in
preparation for a career in Chancery.[28] The majority of Old Bailey barristers were named in the *Law List* as special pleaders. Only a handful styled
themselves as equity draftsmen, and an even smaller number chose to study
both. Of these men John Bell, whose attachment to the metropolitan sessions appears to have been limited to the year 1795, succeeded in establishing
a solid Chancery practice, to which he eventually confined himself. Lord
Eldon described Bell as the best lawyer at the equity bar, despite the fact
that he could "neither speak, walk, nor write."[29] Bell's strong Westmorland
accent, coupled with a stammer, effectively precluded him from any success at the Old Bailey, should he have been so professionally perverse as to
prefer it.

Practice in the Court of Common Pleas was restricted to the order of the
serjeants-at-law, which prevented the majority of Old Bailey counsel from
appearing there, although a few, from William Davy in the eighteenth century to William Ballantine[30] in the nineteenth, did assume the coif—the distinctive cap worn by serjeants—later in their careers. Serjeants-at-law had
once been the leaders of the bar, and admission to their numbers had depended on professional excellence. But the fortunes of the office were linked
with those of the Court of Common Pleas, and the eclipse of that court by
the Court of King's Bench made the monopoly of practice less prestigious
and less lucrative.[31] By 1670 it had been determined that King's Counsel had
precedence over all but the King's Ancient Serjeant, and from that date barristers naturally preferred the silk gown of the KC to the serjeant's coif. On
circuit, however, a serjeantship provided precedence over junior counsel,
and until 1830 the coif allowed a barrister displaced on circuit to take refuge
in the Common Pleas.[32] Some remnants of the office's former status also
lingered: one Old Bailey barrister, William St. Julien Arabin, whose abilities
and reputation were never such as to win him a KC, thought that a serjeantcy
would provide him with a little added dignity when he was appointed deputy
to the recorder and common serjeant in 1824.[33]

The number of cases tried in the Court of Exchequer was again comparatively low, for business among the Westminster courts was not evenly
distributed.[34] In 1790, 1815, and 1830 Old Bailey barristers usually averaged
fewer than five and always fewer than ten motions per year in this court.[35]

The bulk of the cases heard in Westminster Hall were decided in the plea
side of the Court of King's Bench, and practice in that court was conse-

quently held to be the "high road" of the legal profession and the surest
route to professional eminence.[36] By the 1790s, however, there was an "increasing gulf" between the leaders and more ordinary mortals.[37] The recently called barrister's experience at Westminster was flippantly described
by John Campbell in 1807: "My court is the King's Bench. This I attend
regularly day by day, going to the others only on special occasions. It is the
pleasantest lounge in the world. I am very well acquainted with the young
barristers, and am on a very desirable footing with them. Here we assemble
and talk over the news of the day. When these topics fail us we criticize the
leaders, quiz the judges, and abuse the profession."[38] For most young barristers, however, a briefless attendance at Westminster was a source of genuine
despair rather than a "pleasant lounge," particularly if they had been so rash
as to marry early.[39]

With a few exceptions—notably Garrow and Gurney—Old Bailey barristers failed to travel the legal profession's "high road" with any degree of
success. At the end of the 1780s roughly 250 barristers practiced in the plea
side of the Court of King's Bench, but fewer than 30 appeared with any
regularity. Garrow was among the regulars, making 279 motions in 1789.
This total still left him far behind the leader, however: over 800 motions
were recorded for William Baldwin in the same year.[40] In the early nineteenth century Jerome William Knapp's business was respectable, if it did
not place him among the leaders, and the records of the court demonstrate
an increase over the course of his career. In 1815, the year of Knapp's death,
just under 300 barristers were named in the plea side rule book; only 30 of
them were named 100 or more times. Knapp made a total of 72 motions in
that year. His younger colleague, Gurney, was more successful, being named
in the rule book 231 times. The remainder of the Old Bailey bar achieved
much more limited success. The rule book testifies to contemporary opinion with respect to Silvester and Knowlys, who were said to be little known
in the superior courts. Peter Alley's appearances in the King's Bench were
likewise virtually nonexistent, and while Adolphus began with a splash and
was at the beginning of his career expected to rival Erskine, both public expectations and his King's Bench practice quickly declined.[41] His sparring
partner, Thomas Andrews, enjoyed greater success, although Andrews's colleagues commented that he was less skillful in executing practice than he was
in obtaining it.[42] William Brodrick, however, eventually left off Old Bailey
practice to concentrate on civil work in the superior courts. Phillips rarely
appeared in the superior courts after his early humiliation.

Old Bailey barristers might be expected to have assumed the leadership
on the Crown side of the King's Bench, but this was not in fact the case.

Garrow's success there in the eighteenth century was exceptional, and in the King's Bench he competed not with his colleagues at the Old Bailey but with Bearcroft and Erskine, Mingay and Baldwin.[43] Gurney's competitors on the Crown side in 1815 were similarly James Scarlett[44] and other leaders of the Westminster bar. The names of most Old Bailey barristers are found in the rule book for that year, but they appear infrequently.[45] In 1830 Phillips, by then well established at the Old Bailey, was recorded as having made only two motions on the Crown side of King's Bench.[46] Even where Crown cases were concerned, the Westminster bar and the bar at the Old Bailey remained essentially distinct.

The Metropolitan Courts

For the majority of the profession, constructing a legal practice inevitably entailed employment in a variety of tribunals. At a level below the practice of stars such as Garrow (and later Phillips), the Old Bailey seems by the 1770s to have become part of a more general metropolitan practice, one which extended beyond the metropolitan quarter sessions. The seat of England's superior and ecclesiastical courts, metropolitan London was also home to a wide variety of ancient petty courts which, if conferring no professional prestige on the barristers associated with them, nonetheless proved useful to Londoners seeking to recover small debts or to pursue specific actions. Aside from the Lord Mayor's and Sheriffs' Courts, discussed in Chapter 2, the City courts enumerated in the *Law List* in 1801 included the Court of Husting, the Court of Requests, the Chamberlain's Court, the Court of Orphans, the Pie Poudre Court, the Court of Conservancy, and the Court of the Tower of London. The Court of Husting, which predated the Sheriffs' Court, had long since been overshadowed by it. The Chamberlain's Court was established to admit to the freedom of the City qualified persons and to determine disputes between masters and apprentices, while the Court of Orphans was held before the lord mayor and aldermen as guardians of the children of deceased freemen younger than twenty-one years of age. Pie Poudre Court was reserved for the immediate administration of justice with respect to disputes arising between buyers and sellers at the ancient Bartholomew Fair; the jurisdiction of the Court of Conservancy was restricted to "Abuses relative to the Fishing on the River Thames . . . from Staines *West* to Yenfleet *East*," and that of the Court of the Tower of London was limited geographically to the verge of the City, within which it could try actions of debt, trespass, and assault. The city of Westminster, urban Middlesex, and the borough of Southwark contained a similar variety of ancient petty courts.[47]

Given the restricted jurisdictions of these courts, the extent of business in most of them is likely to have been limited. Some of the metropolitan courts, however, provided business for the counsel routinely found at the Old Bailey. Chief among the City's tribunals were the Lord Mayor's and Sheriffs' Courts, and the combination of metropolitan sessions practice and a common pleadership evident in the career of John Silvester continued into the middle of the nineteenth century. Counsel who combined Old Bailey practice with a pleadership included Newman Knowlys, John Vaillant, Henry Revell Reynolds, William Watson, William Bolland, William St. Julien Arabin, Charles Ewan Law, John Mirehouse, Edward Bullock, and Archer Ryland.[48] Law would, like Silvester and Knowlys before him, proceed from City common pleader to common serjeant and finally recorder of London; both Mirehouse and Bullock reached the serjeantcy, and Arabin too would later sit on the bench at the Old Bailey, as the "third civic judge," given the title of commissioner and responsibility for acting as a deputy of the recorder and common serjeant. Vaillant and Prendergast both became judges of the Sheriffs' Court.[49] A strong connection between the Old Bailey's bar and bench and the City of London is thus evident from the late eighteenth century.

Overlap with Old Bailey counsel is also found in the Court of Record at Whitechapel, the Borough Court of Southwark, and the Marshalsea and Palace Court. The Whitechapel court, which sat every Thursday, was useful for recovering debts between forty shillings and £5; its proceedings were described as "short and easy to the Suitors."[50] Actions initiated in it could not be removed into any of the superior courts. Philip Keys was counsel in this court, and John Silvester served as its steward from the mid-1770s until 1822. The Borough Court of Record, an ancient prescriptive court for civil pleas, had cognizance of all personal actions at common law within the lord mayor's jurisdiction at Southwark.[51] There were no limitations as to the value or amounts involved. Costs to the plaintiff ranged from £7 to £12, while the cost of a defense was around £7. Business was said to be very slight until the late 1820s, when an unexpected increase occurred.[52] Two counsel were appointed to this court by the judge or steward, and from the 1790s the stewardship of the court was held by former Old Bailey barristers: John Silvester, Newman Knowlys, and Charles Ewan Law. Silvester combined it with the office of recorder, a circumstance which was apparently uncommon before his time. Knowlys was appointed to both offices and kept the stewardship after being forced to resign as recorder; Law subsequently possessed both offices.[53]

The Marshalsea and Palace Court has a more complex history.[54] The Court of the Marshalsea of the King's House was another medieval creation, instituted to administer justice in cases involving domestic servants of the Crown occurring within the verge (twelve miles) of the court. It was presided over by a steward and marshal. By the beginning of the seventeenth century the court's jurisdiction had become uncertain; James I established a separate Court of the Verge of the King's Palace, held before the same judges and retaining the restriction of place (twelve miles within Whitehall). Its jurisdiction included all personal actions arising within this boundary. Doubts subsequently arose about the jurisdiction of the new court, and it was replaced in 1630 by the Palace Court, which heard personal pleas and actions arising within twelve miles of the Palace of Westminster that did not fall within the jurisdiction of the City of London or other liberties. Both the Marshalsea and the Palace Court lapsed during the Interregnum, but following the Restoration the Palace Court was reestablished; from 1664 it was known as the Palace Court or Marshalsea. According to the *Law List* the Palace Court was "chiefly useful in affording an easy and expeditious jurisdiction for the recovery of Debts under Ten Pounds,"[55] although it could hear pleas of action for any debt upwards of forty shillings. It also had jurisdiction in personal actions such as trespass and assault. Proceedings were almost identical to those of the Court of King's Bench, to which cases of importance were usually removed. Common costs on a verdict for the plaintiff were said to be between £5 and £6, and the plaintiff was entitled to his costs in this court upon obtaining a verdict "even for the smallest sum" in actions of trespass or assault. And because the court sat every week (on Fridays, in Southwark during the eighteenth century and then in Great Scotland Yard), without vacation, the plaintiff could avoid delay: judgment was usually to be had within three to four weeks. Judges, apart from the lord steward of the household and the knight marshal, included a steward and deputy steward, prothonotary and deputy prothonotary. As in the Lord Mayor's and Sheriffs' Courts, practice in the Palace Court was restricted to counsel who purchased their positions for life (with a power of alienation). The fees charged to clients were low, counsel receiving a mere five shillings per appearance, but again the monopoly presumably ensured steady business.[56] Three Old Bailey counsel were attached to the Palace Court for extended periods of time: John Chetwood (1750–83), James Agar (1792–1820), and Benjamin Hart (1805–20). Others—George Watlington, Robert Beville, Pinkston French, and John Jessop—held pleaderships for a year or so.[57] Former members of the bar at the Old Bailey were also found on the bench of the Palace Court in the early nineteenth century: Henry Revell Reynolds served as its deputy steward from 1815 to 1821; George Long occupied the same position from 1826.

Other Employment

Old Bailey practice was combined not only with practice in other courts but with other positions. Jerome William Knapp, for instance, served as clerk of the arraigns on the Home circuit. Clerk of the arraigns was again a purchased position, and Knapp's father had bought the office in 1754; opinion varies as to whether he paid £5,000 or £2,000 for it. On the elder Knapp's death in 1792 the clerkship passed to William Gould, but the actual work was shared between two deputies, Jerome William and his brother Thomas George Knapp.[58]

Other barristers supplemented their earnings with a commission in bankruptcy,[59] granted by the lord chancellor under the great seal. The commissioners chosen exercised the chancellor's power over the persons and property of bankrupts. Briefly, the procedure was as follows.[60] A creditor applying for recovery of moneys owed made an affidavit of "the truth and reality of his debt" before a master in Chancery; the sworn affidavit was then carried to the Bankruptcy Office, where the party suing for the commission entered into a bond with the lord chancellor to prove his debt and to prove the person a bankrupt. Once the bond was executed the clerk of bankrupts filled out a petition in the name of the person making the affidavit and forwarded it with the affidavit and bond to the lord chancellor. If the commission was granted, a private meeting of three commissioners was summoned to open it, after which they examined the truth of the debt, of the trading, and of the act of bankruptcy. If the commissioners were satisfied that the party involved was a bankrupt, a warrant was executed to seize his effects and summon him to surrender, and a notice of the declaration of bankruptcy was published in the *London Gazette*. Public meetings of the commissioners, the bankrupt, and creditors were held at the Guildhall, where creditors pressed their claims and assignees were chosen. The commissioners received fees at various stages of these proceedings: £3 for opening a commission, £3 for executing assignment of the bankrupt's effects, £3 for signing the certificate declaring that the bankrupt had made full disclosure, and so forth. A statute of George II[61] limited the fees a commissioner could take for each inventory, but this restriction was evaded by short meetings and successive adjournments: "[A] skilful commissioner," claimed Holdsworth, "could arrange thirty meetings in a morning."[62]

Bankruptcy commissioners presided over undoubtedly corrupt proceedings. The commissions were divided into lists, each of which acted independently. Precedent was without binding force. The meetings were chaotic, with a number of suitors assembled at one time competing for attention from "either young men who might be competent, but who were certainly inexperienced, or old men who were experienced, but incompetent."[63] Basil Montagu, who received a commission from Erskine in 1806, was so disgusted by bankruptcy procedure that he set out to reform it, just as his brief experience as counsel at the Old Bailey led him to conduct a sustained campaign for reform of the criminal law.[64] While the system remained in effect, however, bankruptcy commissions were "considered a most desirable thing for a young barrister. The pecuniary emoluments depend very much upon personal exertion — the pay is according to the number of attendances you give. By diligence in the office a man may make from 150*l.*, to 200*l.* a year."[65] Among the bar found at the Old Bailey, James Trebeck held a commission from 1799 to the creation of the New Bankruptcy Court in 1832, Henry Revell Reynolds from 1805 until 1830, and Charles Ewan Law from 1821 to 1829, when he became a King's Counsel.[66]

Some members of the Old Bailey's bar found employment in a related area, at the Court for Insolvent Debtors, created in 1813. Prior to the 1860s the law of bankruptcy applied only to "traders." Anyone not fitting the legislative definition of trader was dealt with by the law of insolvency, and while insolvent traders could be discharged from their liabilities by bankruptcy, other insolvent debtors were subject to the long-established "remedy" of imprisonment.[67] Some alleviation of the debtor's lot was provided for in the eighteenth century by a series of statutes that discharged persons imprisoned for debts incurred before certain specified dates, and in 1808 an act was passed allowing anyone who had been imprisoned for a year for a debt of less than £20 to be discharged — although not made free of the debt.[68] But many debtors had no redress until the establishment of the new court, which was empowered to hear prisoners' petitions for release, regardless of the amount of the debt. The prisoner applied to either the Fleet or the Marshalsea, London's chief debtors' prisons, for help from the Insolvent Debtors' Court. He was required to remain in prison for two months while a schedule of his debts was prepared and had to agree to surrender any property he possessed. Until 1820 the Insolvent Court was held in the Guildhall, but from that date it was housed in a building in Portugal Street. These were the premises made famous in Dickens's *Pickwick Papers*:

> In a lofty room, ill-lighted and worse ventilated, situate in Portugal Street, Lincoln's Inn Fields, there sit nearly the whole year round, one, two, three or four gentlemen in wigs. . . . There is a box of barristers at their right hand; there is an inclosure of insolvent debtors on their left; and there is an inclined plane of most especially dirty faces

in their front. These gentlemen are the Commissioners of the Insolvent Debtors' Court, and the place in which they sit, is the Insolvent Court itself. It is, and has been, time out of mind, the remarkable fate of the Court to be, somehow or other, held and understood, by the general consent of all the destitute shabby-genteel people in London, as their common resort, and place of daily refuge. It is always full. The steams of beer and spirits perpetually ascend to the ceiling, and, being condensed by the heat, roll down the walls like rain. . . . A casual visitor might suppose this place to be a Temple dedicated to the Genius of Seediness. There is not a messenger or process-server attached to it, who wears a coat that was made for him; not a tolerably fresh, or wholesome-looking man in the whole establishment. . . . The very barristers' wigs are ill-powdered, and their curls lack crispness.[69]

Allowing for artistic license, it may be surmised that the reputation of the Insolvent Debtors' Court was almost on par with that of the Old Bailey. The court, in fact, quickly became a cause for scandal, as the procedure for discharging insolvent debtors provided a method for habitual fraud. Dishonest operators regularly defaulted on debts, accepting the two months' imprisonment and even referring to prison itself as a "college" where further tricks of their disreputable trade could be acquired. But while the constitution and jurisdiction of the Insolvent Debtors' Court were frequently amended, the court itself was not abolished until 1861, when the law of bankruptcy was extended to nontraders. And in the fifty-odd years of its existence the Insolvent Court provided employment for various members of the Old Bailey's bar, including Henry Barry, Robert Cresswell, and Edward Sandford. Charles Phillips would end his career as an insolvent commissioner; Henry Revell Reynolds was chief commissioner of the court from 1820 until his death in 1853.

Reynolds's career provides a good early-nineteenth-century example of metropolitan practice. Reynolds was born in Bedford Row; called to the bar in 1798, he practiced at the London, Middlesex, and Westminster sessions for the first twenty years of the nineteenth century. He was named in the OBSP 174 times during those years, appearing for the prosecution in 63 percent of these cases. His practice at Westminster was negligible, but in 1801 he was appointed a City common pleader, which guaranteed him business in the Lord Mayor's and Sheriffs' Courts and a share in City prosecutions at the Guildhall and the Old Bailey. In 1806 he obtained a commission in bankruptcy; he was also deputy steward of the Marshalsea and Palace Court from 1815 until 1821. The last thirty years of his career were spent as the chief commissioner of London's Insolvent Debtors' Court (1820–53). The career paths of many Old Bailey barristers were equally contained by metropolitan boundaries.

Preparing for Criminal Practice

By the second half of the eighteenth century metropolitan practice, like practice on the assize circuits, encompassed criminal as well as civil law. At that time and into the nineteenth century preparation for employment at the Old Bailey or in any other criminal court was a matter of individual initiative, for legal education as a whole placed a heavy onus on the student. Students reading for the bar entered one of the four Inns of Court, where they would remain for a specified number of terms. After June 1762 the possession of a master of arts or bachelor of laws degree from either Oxford or Cambridge reduced the residency requirements of the Inns of Court from five to three years, and this privilege was extended to the University of Dublin in 1793. Whatever knowledge students acquired during their terms in residence was the result of their own effort: the old system of readings and moots, disrupted by the Civil War in the seventeenth century, had never been reestablished, and, a few failed experiments notwithstanding, lectures and exams lay far in the future.[70] Advice provided in the 1760s, when Silvester was a student, indicated that the law student "must take Care to read Something of the Law every Day (save *Sundays* or the like)."[71] Choice of reading matter was relatively limited: prior to the nineteenth century treatises did not occupy a prominent position in either legal literature or education, and they were few in number.[72] Coke's *Institutes of the Laws of England* (1644), consisting of commentary on an earlier text (Littleton's *New Tenures* [ca. 1450–60]), commentary on some of the older statutes, a discussion of criminal law, and an exposition of the courts, remained a standard text — although by 1792 "the quaintness of the phrases, the blackness of the letter, [and] the want of connection in the topics" were said to drive many a student from the law.[73] Blackstone's *Commentaries on the Law of England*, published between 1765 and 1769, provided a marked contrast, containing "method as well as law." The student was advised to obtain a copy interleaved with blank paper for notes and updating and to use Blackstone's text as the "cornerstone" of a commonplace book, one which would be arranged theoretically rather than by the alphabetical format under which the older abridgments of the law had been compiled.[74]

Standard works on Crown practice included Hawkins's *Treatise on the Pleas of the Crown* (1716) and Hale's posthumously published *History of the Pleas of the Crown* (1736). Geoffrey Gilbert's *Law of Evidence* (1754) was considered "the best treatise on this important subject" into the 1790s. Henry Bathurst's *Theory of Evidence* (1761) and Francis Buller's *Introduction to the Law Relative to Trials at Nisi Prius* (1772) were very similar in content, while John Morgan's *Essay on Evidence* (1789) was based on the 1777 edition of Gilbert. Gilbert's treatise, written sometime before his death in 1726 and published posthumously, would have been of limited value to criminal practitioners of the late eighteenth century. The text concentrated heavily on the written evidence found in civil trials and the hierarchy to be accorded to its various categories: record versus nonrecord, statutes, sealed and unsealed instruments, proving copies where originals had been lost, proving prior verdicts and depositions, and so forth. With respect to unwritten evidence, most of Gilbert's commentary concerned the rules disqualifying persons from testifying on the ground of interest; he touched only briefly on burdens of proof, presumptions, and hearsay evidence, and cross-examination received scarcely any attention at all.[75]

In the early nineteenth century two important new texts appeared: Thomas Peake's *Compendium of the Law of Evidence* (1801) and S. M. Phillips's *Treatise on the Law of Evidence* (1814). Joseph Chitty's *Practical Treatise on the Criminal Law*, published in 1816, was superseded by W. O. Russell's *Treatise on Felonies and Misdemeanours* (1819) and the first edition of J. F. Archbold, *Pleading and Evidence in Criminal Cases* (1822). Various members of the Old Bailey's bar made small and generally less than impressive additions to this literature. Robert Beville, who practiced briefly at the Old Bailey (1799–1803), published a slim and ill-received volume, *On the Law of Homicide and Larceny* (1799); Leonard MacNally similarly published a treatise entitled *The Rules of Evidence in Pleas of the Crown* (1802).[76] Legislative changes to the criminal law in the 1820s were described by Frederick Carrington in *A Supplement to all the Treatises on the Criminal Law* (1826). This text also covered the various points of surgery and chemistry which had become relevant to criminal trials, considering the symptoms, appearances, and tests related to poisons, wounds and bruises, drowning, infanticide, rape, burns, and insanity. It is clear that barristers armed themselves with a modicum of medical knowledge before attempting to examine or cross-examine physicians or surgeons. Knapp, for instance, in a case tried in 1800, referred several times to medical texts, while John Campbell wrote to his father in 1814, "I wish you had heard me examining the surgeon about the arteries, the muscles, etc. The night before I went to a surgeon's, and he showed me a prepared subject, and gave me a lecture on anatomy an hour long."[77]

Students and barristers alike must have benefited from greatly improved reports of cases heard at Westminster Hall, such as Durnford and East's

Term Reports (King's Bench, 1785–1800), which reached new standards of accuracy and timeliness, publishing recent decisions on a regular basis.[78] Criminal practitioners would have found the various editions of Leach's *Cases in Crown Law* useful, and Old Bailey counsel pored over the OBSP as well: many of the bound volumes held at Lincoln's Inn contain scribbled pencil notes, underscorings, and pointing fingers drawn in the margins, as well as inked-in cross-references to Leach,[79] while Garrow annotated various trials in the copy of the Sessions Papers now held by the University of Chicago's Law Library, commenting on and explaining his own interventions, correcting the shorthand reporter, and generally marking cases for future reference.[80]

Textbooks and case reports, however, were not the sole or even the primary source of instruction. Law students were expected to attend the courts and learn from observation. John Adolphus was first attracted to criminal practice by attending court: "I cannot describe the effect produced on my mind by the first hearing an impassioned address, quick taunt, convincing reply, and above all, the *viva voce* examination of witnesses, and the comments on their evidence. . . . From the day that I first heard a cause tried, I was early and constant in my attendance."[81] The student interested in criminal law could attend the Crown side of King's Bench at Westminster and of course at the Old Bailey, as Garrow did. The public gallery was typically filled by law students during "remarkable trials." Student needs, however, were only grudgingly taken into consideration by the City. A portion of the gallery at the old sessions house had been specifically reserved for law students, but by the 1770s they had lost their space. In designing the new sessions house Dance was instructed to erect a students' gallery, but after viewing the new premises in February 1777 the Corporation of London's Committee for Rebuilding Newgate appropriated it for themselves, declaring that the students had no legal right to it.[82] From this date law students were accommodated at ground level: as "a matter of favour," they were permitted to use "the space of ground in the Court Room adjoining the Middlesex jury seats."[83] When plans for a second courtroom were drawn up in 1823 a box of benches reserved for law students again lay in the court itself, rather than in the gallery, located immediately to the left of the prisoner in the dock and behind the witness stand.[84]

Speaking ability was crucial to a successful criminal practice, and many students tested and developed their oratorical skills in debating societies and speaking clubs.[85] Coachmakers' Hall, the Westminster Forum, and the great room in Spring Gardens were among the most famous of the debating clubs in the eighteenth century, while more modest establishments like the Mitre

Tavern in Fleet Street and the King's Arms in the Poultry were also popular.[86] By the turn of the nineteenth century Coachmakers' Hall and other societies of its type—conducted by a speculator and open to the public for a shilling—were gone or in decline, owing in part to government suppression of public assembly and free speech in the 1790s. They were replaced by institutions such as "the Academical," an "extremely respectable" society whose membership was restricted to those with a university degree. Adolphus, who like Garrow had not attended university, made his debut at the Athenians, a "club more miscellaneous in its composition"[87] located in Fleet Street, in 1790. He was said as well to have "distinguished himself both at Merchant Taylors'-hall, the British Forum, and the Eccentrics."[88] Later in his career he practiced his oratory in addresses delivered at the hustings in election campaigns.[89]

Acquiring Criminal Business

How barristers acquired business in the criminal courts remains something of a mystery. Although the division of labor between barristers and attorneys was well established by the late eighteenth century,[90] there was an exception allowing a prisoner in the dock to personally instruct counsel to defend him, described as "a privilege belonging to the accused" rather than a "right pertaining to the Bar."[91] At the Old Bailey the barrister himself might volunteer his services. Garrow, for instance, intervened as amicus curiae in the case of *R. v. Pearson*.[92] In the same year Knapp's services were volunteered by the presiding judge, Lord Kenyon, in a murder trial: "Will any gentleman at the bar have the goodness to ask a few questions for [the defendants], as they are foreigners? Will you, Mr. Knapp?"[93] One unhappy defendant in a case of theft found himself without counsel, asking, "Is counsellor Fielding in court, I was told that the bill was thrown out." Fielding was not, but Silvester immediately announced, "I will take it up for him," and proceeded to subject the prosecutor to an aggressive cross-examination.[94] In such circumstances the barrister obviously worked without written instructions from an attorney. On the evidence of a debate which arose in the professional press in the 1840s, it also seems probable that prosecutors too sometimes approached counsel directly, without employing an attorney as intermediary, seeking, no doubt, to minimize their legal costs.[95]

How often criminal barristers accepted cases directly from lay clients we have no means of determining. It would seem reasonable to assume that the leaders in Old Bailey practice were routinely briefed by a small number of reputable attorneys. These would include the solicitors attached to the Bank of England, the Mint, the Post Office, and various branches of the government. Attorneys in private practice, unfortunately, are virtually invisible until the turn of the nineteenth century. A few names appear in cases reported in *The Times* in the 1780s, and more rarely still in the OBSP: Mr. Platel, Mr. Jonas, Mr. Heslop, Mr. Carden.[96] The extent of these gentlemen's criminal practice is unknown. But by 1800 the attorney who would dominate defense work in the opening decades of the nineteenth century had established his legal practice.[97] The son of a Spitalfields weaver, James Harmer was apprenticed to an unidentified attorney in 1792 and later transferred to Fletcher and Wright. By 1799 he was practicing on his own from an office in Hatton Garden, his business lying chiefly in the criminal courts. Harmer estimated in 1819 that he represented roughly a hundred people a year, and that in his twenty years' practice he had represented over two thousand clients.[98] He was described by one Old Bailey counsel as possessing an "immense reputation" "amongst the classes whose natural destination was the Old Bailey."[99] Charles Phillips also held Harmer in high esteem: "[H]e is a worthy & clever man," Phillips wrote to Brougham.[100]

By the mid-1830s defense work was said to be shared chiefly between Harmer and the more recently established partnership of Lewis and Lewis. James Graham Lewis, admitted attorney in 1829, set up practice with his brother George in Ely Place, Holborn. George Lewis specialized in bankruptcies and was an "expert in 'arranging' the insolvencies of gentlemen of the leisured and professional classes";[101] James became the "principal attorney" of the Old Bailey.[102] Said to have resembled a genial sea captain rather than a lawyer, and reputed to have inspired the character of Jaggers in *Great Expectations*, James Lewis was respected as much for his humanity and compassion as for his considerable legal abilities and became known as "the Poor Man's Lawyer."[103] His son George, who took over the business, was to dominate defense practice in London until his retirement in 1909.[104]

On the prosecution side two equally respectable attorneys commanded the lion's share of business: Humphreys and Wontner.[105] Thomas Wontner was the anonymous author of a scathing condemnation of the administration of criminal justice in London, published in 1833;[106] Humphreys attracted much praise from Charles Phillips during his lifetime. "He is one of the most respectable men I met in the profession," Phillips wrote, a year after leaving criminal practice,[107] "not only an honest man, but a very discreet & cautious one" who always made sure of his facts,[108] "a man in every respect fully to be relied upon . . . more competent than any man in London, and so rigidly honourable . . . that he may be trusted to any extent." Humphreys,

Phillips told Brougham, was the "only attorney" he had ever asked within his doors, in either England or Ireland.[109]

These reputable attorneys notwithstanding, London's criminal courts were also plagued by less savory—and often unqualified—characters.[110] In 1844 the counsel practicing at the Old Bailey were reported to have held a meeting to resolve upon measures "for putting a stop to the business of the vagabonds who lurk about the prisons and courts, and conduct, as attorneys, the defences of the unsuspecting prisoners, upon whom they practise the most grievous impositions."[111] The problem had a long history. During a trial for assault heard in 1788 Garrow accused the prosecutor of earning his living as an attorney (in particular, of attending regularly at the Clerkenwell sessions) without having been admitted to the rolls.[112] William Ballantine complained in the early 1830s of agents "clean neither in character nor person," while the *Westminster Review* lamented two years later that "a considerable portion of the gaol business" lay "in the hands of some of the most disreputable individuals in the metropolis. Attornies who have been struck off the rolls, discharged penny-a-line men who have obtained a prison connexion while themselves under confinement, in short the worst description of agents that can be found call themselves solicitors."[113] Such men rendered little honest service and frequently no service at all to their clients, disappearing after pocketing the fee.[114]

Reports of other irregular practices were made in the nineteenth century. In the 1830s convicts in Newgate prison seem to have been allowed to prepare "briefs" for fellow inmates and to retain a five shilling fee per brief;[115] in the 1840s the governor of Newgate appears to have taken on the role of solicitor himself.[116] What, asked the *Law Times*, was the meaning of "leaving money at the gate," and why should a prisoner not hand it directly to an attorney? It suspected the practice was "a means taken to secure a monopoly of prisoners' defences." A letter to the editor of this paper suggested that in "the case of the poor prisoner who is able to raise his guinea fee for a defence and no more," his poverty should be openly stated in court and the prisoner then allowed "*there* to name a counsel, to whom he may hand over his fee."[117]

The practice by which counsel communicated directly with prisoners at the bar also occasioned complaint on the part of solicitors. An anonymous member of the criminal bar wrote to the *Legal Observer* in 1843 to point out that such work was usually performed gratuitously.[118] But that paper believed it would be best "if some understanding were to be come to on this head: if the bar, in criminal or any other business, is to dispense with the attorney, let it be at once known, and so settled . . . the theory, we apprehend, at present is, that the attorney shall be employed, as the medium between the bar and the public, and that the barrister shall not receive business except through the attorney. If another rule is to be laid down and followed, all that we ask is, that it shall be so understood, in order that it may be fairly discussed." In the paper's view, the rule ought not to be changed, and "[p]ublicity and open comment" remained the only remedies to be used against barristers who departed from the established rule.[119] A month earlier, however, the *Law Times* had accepted that it was permissible for a barrister to receive a brief directly from a criminal client, provided the brief was handed from the prisoner to counsel over the bar.[120]

In 1844 a recently called member of the bar, Newton Crouch, unwittingly found himself at the center of a professional scandal for having taken instruction not from a prisoner but from a prosecutor without the intervention of an attorney. The case itself—*R. v. Pond*—was a minor one, tried in the evening sessions at the Central Criminal Court[121] before the common serjeant. In the course of his cross-examination, counsel for the defense, Charles Wilkins, had asked the prosecutor, a Mr. Stewart, whether he had employed an attorney. When Stewart replied that he had not, the common serjeant (Mirehouse) interrupted to ask him to explain, as such a course of action was both irregular and unusual. Stewart replied that he knew the barrister personally and had approached him. The common serjeant continued to insist that the procedure was highly unusual, but Crouch asserted that it was not, that it occurred at the Old Bailey "every day." When he "appealed to the gentlemen at the bar to bear him out," however, he found no support.[122] The *Morning Chronicle*, which reported the case at some length, commented two days later on practice at the Old Bailey. There had once, it reported, been a famous body snatcher named Crouch; the present Crouch was no less famous as a "snatcher of briefs."[123] The silence of senior counsel on the issue it also considered suspicious.[124] If they did come forward, "then we shall believe that the stories of jobbing, and monopoly, and exclusion, and the system of cadding by clerks, and hooking and plucking by low retainers in the precincts of the Old Bailey courts, is a mere 'coinage of the brain' of some briefless would-be brief-snatcher, less successful in action." But "as at present advised," the paper wrote, "we consider these practices by no means of uncommon occurrence, though we are willing to admit that they have been only recently publicly noticed and denounced." Is there "a man in or out of the profession," it continued, "who does not know that the Old Bailey was, to all intents and purposes, and is yet, to the generality of practitioners, as close a borough as were Gatton and Old Sarum to the Parliamentary candidates before the passing of the Reform

Bill? Is there a man who does not know that business was and is jobbed there in the grossest and unfairest way, and that an embryo ERSKINE would be 'mute and inglorious' for evermore, if he had to begin at the Old Bailey without the proper freemasonry of the craft of the trade, for it would be a prostitution of the name to call it profession. . . . There is a taint in the very atmosphere of the Old Bailey."[125] The next day the paper reported a case of nuisance tried at the Middlesex sessions in which the prosecutor, a Mr. Pyke, had "acted in the capacity of prosecutor and solicitor, and in the latter character had drawn and delivered the briefs to counsel, and when the solicitor on the other side declined to hold any communication except with another professional gentleman, he received an anonymous letter, proved to be in the handwriting of Mr. Pyke, intimating that Mr. Kirk, of Symonds-Inn, was retained as solicitor for the prosecution." Pyke's conduct had been condemned by the judge as "derogatory to the character of a gentleman of the bar."[126]

Crouch wrote to both the *Legal Observer* and the *Law Times* offering a defense for his conduct, conceding "that *in all cases whatever*, either *criminal or civil*, the *agency* of an *attorney* is most advantageous to the client, and ought never, if possible, be dispensed with by counsel." He then went on to examine practice at the London sessions. Crouch claimed that in his experience the "first and best" business of the Central Criminal Court was conducted by a "few respectable attorneys" who employed the leading counsel and from which there was but little chance of juniors getting a brief, thus in effect confirming the *Morning Chronicle*'s characterization of the Old Bailey as a "close borough." He outlined the circumstances of the particular case as follows: the prosecutor had been known to him and had told Crouch that the case was a simple one for which he did not intend to hire an attorney. He had then given Crouch the depositions and sent further information in writing a few days later. Crouch had taken no notes and conducted no examination. The next time he saw the prosecutor was at the Central Criminal Court on the first day of the session, at which time he was paid two guineas before the bill was found, four days before the trial itself. Crouch had seen none of the witnesses until they got into the box to give their evidence. He insisted that he had acted neither unprofessionally nor unusually, and that if the practice of accepting briefs from clients in person were condemned, he ought not to be singled out for particular condemnation as he had merely followed "the long-established usage of the court he practised in."[127] In his letter to the *Law Times* he claimed that London's criminal bar had met at the Middlesex sessions to discuss the issue and had collectively agreed "[t]hat the practice of the Bar attending [the Old Bailey] had *always allowed* the *barrister* to *act* as *counsel* either for the PROSECUTOR or the *prisoner, although* no *attorney* was *employed* by the *parties*."[128]

Self-interest obviously fueled the discontent expressed by qualified members of the lower branch of the legal profession, who jealously guarded their role as intermediaries between lay client and barrister.[129] But the practices complained of in the 1840s speak to other issues as well. First, they reveal the vulnerability of persons accused of criminal offenses. To prisoners awaiting trial, the niceties of proper professional relations between barrister and solicitor were irrelevant. They simply wanted help, and their economic circumstances, and in some cases their inexperience, put them at risk of being offered second-rate service, or no service at all, from unqualified persons. Second, newly called barristers and others struggling for a share of business may not have been overscrupulous in inquiring as to whether the name inscribed on a brief was that of a solicitor on the rolls. They may also have been willing to receive instructions directly from prosecutors as well as defendants. As a later critic was to put it: "Competition is fierce. The briefless are many."[130]

Income at the Criminal Bar

Criminal work was by no means as lucrative as civil practice in the superior courts. The fees typically charged for defense work, if beyond the means of many prisoners, were low: a guinea in the eighteenth century, possibly two or three guineas in the early nineteenth century, by which time "there was an understanding that men in good practice should not take guinea briefs."[131] Attorney Thomas Wontner reported sending fees of "one, two, or three guineas" with the twenty or so prosecution briefs he wrote for the first day of an early nineteenth-century sessions at the Old Bailey.[132] The City of London appears to have paid three guineas to leading counsel and two to juniors during the same period, although the fees earned in some cases were slightly higher.[133] In *R. v. Baker* William Bolland was paid five guineas by the City for leading the prosecution; he had already received two guineas for "perusing and settling" the indictment.[134] Barristers' fees for the prosecution of James Smith et al., charged in 1812 with conspiracy to commit fraud, totaled £23, shared among three counsel. John Gurney's fees for an embezzlement case tried in the same year totaled ten guineas: two for a consultation, six for the trial, and two in the form of refreshers.[135] The fee earned also varied according to the court in which the case was tried. Briefs drawn up for the most minor cases heard in the King's Bench or the Court of Chancery were routinely marked upwards of seven guineas for leading counsel and one or two guineas less for the counsel who assisted him; assize briefs among the

City solicitor's papers were marked in the three to five guinea range; those drawn for quarter sessions cases were marked at between two and four guineas.[136]

Charles Phillips, employed primarily by the defense, estimated that his criminal practice earned him just over £2,000 a year, and when his will was proved in 1859 he left a personalty of £30,000.[137] In 1828 he claimed to have defended "no less than 800 Prisoners at the Old Bailey and on the Oxford Circuit," which would suggest that his fees for individual cases fell within the two to three guinea range.[138] Where criminal practice was concerned the lower branch of the legal profession appears to have been more lucrative: Harmer was said to have earned £4,000 a year in 1833, and he left legacies totaling £70,000 on his death in 1853.[139] Phillips's annual income, moreover, was well below that of leaders in civil practice in the eighteenth, let alone the nineteenth, century.[140] Judging by the estates they left, Alley and Adolphus earned more modest incomes still. Where John Gurney, who proceeded from the Old Bailey to Westminster Hall and was eventually made a baron of the Exchequer, left legacies in the thousands of pounds, Alley left £500 to a niece and £100 each to his two nephews (he had no children), and a further £100 to his clerk.[141] When Adolphus died the inventory of his goods and chattels was valued at £6,000, £2,000 of which he had inherited four years earlier from Tom Richards, for many years clerk of the peace on the Home circuit.[142] The only truly spectacular financial success among the metropolitan barristers was Francis Const. Const was reported to have been worth £150,000 at his death and to have left legacies of £1,000 each to many of his friends. This wealth was attributed to "great parsimony and extensive speculation in early life."[143]

Success and Failure

As described in the previous chapter, the length of time counsel attended at the Old Bailey varied considerably. For some barristers, Old Bailey practice was simply a stage in the early years of their career. Thus in 1835 the *Westminster Review* reported, "[A] young man who had provided himself with a wife, was recently heard to declare, that he would go to the Old Bailey because he must make money somewhere."[144] The low fees probably account for the defections of the successful. Barristers such as Garrow, Gurney, and Brodrick prospered in the superior courts and abandoned a regular attendance in London's criminal courts. In other cases discontinuing criminal practice indicated failure rather than success, for prisoners, it seemed, had "a propensity to enquire into the qualifications of those persons with whom they trust[ed] their necks and liberties."[145] Henry Crabb Robinson, who like many young barristers was frequently employed in Crown cases on circuit, was advised early in his career to attend at the Old Bailey sessions as well, but he never managed to secure any business there.[146] The short attachment of a considerable number of barristers to the metropolitan sessions, together with a marked opacity in their later careers, testifies to a general lack of success at the bar. For men such as Knapp and Curwood, Adolphus and Alley, however, the Old Bailey provided lifelong employment.[147]

CHAPTER FOUR

The Criminal Trial
before the Prisoners' Counsel Act

The criminal trial in the eighteenth and early nineteenth centuries is best described as being in a state of flux. In London, despite the emergence of an Old Bailey bar, the majority of felony trials continued to take place without counsel being engaged on either side. And even in the rare instances in which barristers were employed by both the prosecution and the defense, the ensuing professional contest was an uneven one. A key element of the old-style trial continued: defendants were required to make their own defense, and defense counsel were forbidden to speak on their behalf. In acknowledgment of the restrictions on the participation of counsel for the defense, prosecuting counsel exercised a degree of restraint. The unwritten, self-imposed rules governing their conduct appear to have varied throughout the country, and in the nineteenth century, on at least one circuit, opening speeches were by and large eschewed. In London this was not the case, but counsel for the prosecution constrained their efforts within certain recognizable boundaries. Professional, adversarial contests were thus by no means the norm. The irregular employment of counsel at the Old Bailey nonetheless introduced change and altered the dynamic of the felony trial, and where employed, counsel certainly influenced the outcome of trials. In the eighteenth century, in fact, the influence of the nascent Old Bailey bar on the administration of justice is discernible at the level of pretrial as well as trial proceedings.

Pretrial Proceedings

When the sessions opened at the Old Bailey a dozen or so barristers would be found sitting beneath the bench, some briefed, others hoping to be. But their involvement in criminal proceedings often began at an earlier stage: the pretrial hearing before a magistrate. These preliminary proceedings, like trial for felony, were subject to profound alteration during the eighteenth century, acquiring a more public and a more formal character. From the mid-sixteenth century the duty of the magistrate had essentially consisted of assembling the case for the prosecution: he examined and took depositions from the victim/prosecutor and his or her witnesses and committed the accused to prison to await trial. Magistrates were advised to commit all suspected felons rather than exercise their own judgment as to whether there was a strong enough case to proceed.[1] Over the course of the eighteenth century, however, the pretrial examination in London gradually evolved into a judicialized inquiry into whether there was a charge to be answered. In the City a rotation system was developed after 1737 whereby the aldermen took it in turns to sit daily as magistrate at a Justice Room in the Guildhall. This room soon took on the appearance of a courtroom, with the magistrate sitting behind a bar, an attorney to keep the record, and a clerk. The lord mayor, the City's chief magistrate, likewise had a Justice Room at Mansion House from the 1750s.[2] A form of public office emerged in Westminster at roughly the same time, when magistrate Thomas de Veil moved to Bow Street in 1739. His successors, Henry and John Fielding, would make the Bow Street office famous, and a model for other rotation offices.[3] While the impulse to conduct a genuine inquiry into the charge, rather than simply to ensure that an accused would be sent to trial, predates the physical transformation of the magistrate's office, that transformation facilitated the change in direction.

The increasing importance attached to pretrial inquiry into the evidence against the accused can be seen in a notable development of the 1780s: the categoric rejection of committal on suspicion. Traditionally the law had provided that a suspect could be committed without a full hearing, on the basis of oaths sworn against him by respectable members of society. This practice was challenged in 1785 by one of its victims, a publican named Burgess. A seaman had applied to Burgess for a loan to take out administration of a will; the will in question turned out to have been forged, and Burgess was wrongly assumed to have been involved in or aware of the forgery. He was committed by Bow Street magistrate Addington on suspicion of forgery on the basis of two oaths sworn against him. Burgess was not allowed to call for a witness who could exonerate him, and it was five days before a hearing was convened. When the hearing finally took place, the outraged publican was immediately released. He then instituted a civil action against Justice Addington in the Court of Common Pleas and won £300 in damages plus the full cost of his suit. Bow Street had pleaded the press of business, but Lord Loughborough, the presiding judge, strongly condemned the practice of committal without an examination. Those "who had not time to do justice," he said, "should not act as magistrates." *The Times* was subsequently careful to distinguish between those "committed" by Bow Street magistrates and those "fully committed" (i.e., examined) by the City's aldermen.[4] The accused still labored under disadvantages, however. Over thirty years later Frederick Carrington, who practiced at the Old Bailey from the mid-1820s into the 1840s, wrote: "[I]t is provided that it shall not be compulsory on any justice or justices to hear evidence on the part of the accused, unless it shall appear to be conducive to the ends of justice to hear it." To this comment he appended the mild footnote: "It seems difficult to suppose any case, where, if a prisoner said that he had evidence, it would not appear to be conducive to the ends of justice for the magistrate to hear it."[5]

The transformation of the magistrate's office into a courtroom, which enabled greater public access, and a growing conviction that pretrial hearings ought fully to examine the charges brought before them no doubt contributed to the entry of lawyers into these proceedings. The accused had no more right to representation by counsel at the pretrial hearing than he did at the trial: "A person under examination before a justice on a charge of felony, has no *right* to have his legal adviser present, still less to have him examine or cross-examine the witnesses; this, when allowed, being quite in the discretion of the justice: and the justice is justified in excluding such legal adviser from being present at the examination."[6] This prohibition continued past 1836 into the second half of the nineteenth century.[7] But it is clear from newspaper coverage of the rotation offices that counsel for both the prosecution and the defense were sometimes engaged. By 1820 multiple hearings before a magistrate preceded the trial. Newspaper evidence suggests that in the nineteenth century pretrial representation increasingly fell within the purview of the lower branch of the legal profession,[8] and in Charles Dickens's *Great Expectations* it is an attorney, the famous Mr. Jaggers, who strikes terror into the hearts of magistrates and thief-takers as well as thieves.[9] In the eighteenth century, however, barristers undertook this work themselves. Thus in 1778 the *Morning Chronicle* reported that counselor [William] Fielding persuaded Sir John Fielding to release his client, charged with putting his name to a forged power of attorney, arguing that there was no felonious intent as required by statute.[10] *The Times*'s report of the examination before the justices at the rotation office in Whitechapel of a linen draper and his wife accused of arson similarly reveals the intervention of Old Bailey counsel. Newman Knowlys appeared for the prosecutor, Leonard MacNally for the defendants, and MacNally succeeded in having the charges against his clients dropped:

The fact of burning was fully and substantially proved by an overseer who examined the premises; after which a maid servant to the prisoner being examined for Mr. Knowles, counsel for the prosecution, she gave a long and circumstantial account of her having being employed by her master and mistress to set fire to the shop; but on her cross-examination by Mr. MacNally, who was counsel for the prisoners, she acknowledged that she had not accused her master and mistress, till after she was informed of her own danger, and that to save herself she became evidence. Mr. MacNally being informed by the Bench that there were no other witnesses to be produced against the prisoners, advised them not to call any witnesses or make any defence, as no evidence had been given that could affect them upon a trial. The servant, he said, was not only incredible, but an incompetent witness.[11]

The prisoners were discharged. When (or indeed whether) barristers were entirely supplanted by attorneys in pretrial proceedings I cannot say, but the involvement of Old Bailey counsel continued in the opening decades of the new century at least: Peter Alley and Thomas Andrews were found arguing for both the prosecution and the defense at Bow Street in 1815.[12]

As at the Old Bailey, pretrial hearings did not necessarily involve counsel. Moreover, at this stage in the process, the prosecution could request that defense counsel be excluded.[13] But where counsel were employed the proceedings appear to have been formal; there was a genuine inquiry into the evidence presented against the accused; and the participation of defense counsel could result in the charges being dropped. Where they failed to achieve this result, counsel could still provide assistance: Peter Alley, representing two men charged with the murder of an excise officer, could not prevent their committal for further examination, but he did secure permission for the prisoners' solicitor and friends to have ready access to them while in prison, "as they had only a fortnight to prepare their defence."[14]

Preparing for Trial

Whether the barristers who appeared before metropolitan London's magistrates were instructed through attorneys or directly by lay clients is unknown. Once a cause reached the Old Bailey, however, barristers cannot have preferred to do without the services of an attorney. It seems obvious from the way in which some cases were presented, and from the thoroughness and effectiveness of certain defenses, that considerable preparation had preceded the trial—and that in cases where counsel had not been fully briefed the result could be disastrous. For example, in prosecuting William Stevenson, a watchman of Clerkenwell Prison charged with murdering one of the prisoners in a disturbance, barrister Richard Peatt called as a witness a man named Hopkins, another of the prison's inmates. When it came time for cross-examination Silvester, who appeared for the defense, had a field day exploring Hopkins's previous appearances at the Old Bailey. After listening to a history of repeat offenses the judge interrupted to inform Peatt that he would "do well not to bring witnesses such as that." Peatt responded with the extraordinary remark, "My Lord, I know nothing of the case nor of the witnesses."[15] While prosecuting counsel could in theory construct a case directly from the depositions taken against the accused and a verbal briefing from the victim (Peatt's entire ignorance in the Stevenson case must have been unusual), the defense barrister who lacked the assistance of an attorney was placed at a considerable disadvantage. Like the accused himself, counsel for the defense had no right to a copy of either the formal charge or the depositions taken against his client; moreover, professional etiquette prohibited him from entering a gaol and thus from interviewing the client. Basil Montagu mentioned in passing being employed as a go-between while he was a student, sent to Newgate to question a prisoner.[16] The extent to which this practice was common, however, is again unknown. Questions of "proper" relations between the upper and lower branches of the legal profession aside, there can be no doubt that attorneys made a valuable contribution to the construction of a case to be presented in court.

As discussed in the previous chapter, early-nineteenth-century attorneys are much more visible than their eighteenth-century counterparts. Details of their legal practice, however, have largely vanished. This was perhaps deliberate: the famous Victorian criminal attorney George Lewis burned his records upon retirement.[17] The records which do survive tend to be those of the solicitors for institutional prosecutors—the solicitors for the Mint, the Bank of England, and the Post Office, and the Treasury solicitor—and even within these records briefs prepared for counsel are rare. As John Langbein remarks, once a trial had concluded there was little reason to keep a brief to counsel.[18] The City solicitor's briefs, however, have fortunately been preserved from the 1780s into the mid-nineteenth century.[19] These are overwhelmingly briefs for the prosecution, but the City would apparently, in "cases of interest," procure funds for a prisoner's defense,[20] and in one case an alderman presumably went so far as to request that the City solicitor himself prepare the brief: in 1809 Jerome William Knapp was engaged by the City to defend a young man (William Webb) committed to Newgate for the theft of a silk handkerchief belonging to his employers.[21] Also preserved among the City solicitor's papers, for less obvious reasons, is Charles Isaacs's brief to Charles Ewan Law for the defense of Thomas Dean et al.

(1826).[22] The City records thus afford some evidence—albeit slight—of the form of defense briefs as well as those prepared for the prosecution.[23]

When employed, the attorney collected and examined witnesses, who were listed within the brief in the order in which they were to be called, with notes of the purpose of their testimony. The attorney might also research applicable law and provide the barrister with references. The City solicitor gathered, for instance, legal authorities in the brief for the prosecution in *R. v. Harris* (1817) to establish that, when an officer or an assistant to an officer was slain in the course of duty, the offense was always murder, even where no malice was established or where the exercise of duty was erroneous, citing extensively from Viner's *Abridgment*, Leach's *Crown Law*, Hale, *History of the Pleas of the Crown*, Strange, Foster's *Crown Law*, Comyns's *Digest*, Hawkins's *Pleas of the Crown*, and the *State Trials*.[24] The attorney, or his clerk, conducted interviews with incarcerated clients, and it was the attorney who prepared the brief for counsel. A brief for the prosecution consisted of the indictment, set out in full, the defendant's plea, and the case to be made for the prosecution; it closed with a list of proofs and witnesses to support the case.[25] For example, the brief in *R. v. Skinner* (1786), in which the defendant was indicted for perjury in a previous trial, listed three witnesses who could be called to prove the burglary in the original trial, two to prove the accusations made by the defendant against the individuals who stood trial for the crime, a witness to produce all three examinations of the defendant, one to "falsify" the examinations, and six others to prove that Skinner had later contradicted himself.[26] The solicitor thus not only engaged in significant investigative work, identifying and selecting witnesses, but offered a strategy for making the case in court.

Attorneys for the defense labored under severe restrictions. Like the prisoner, the defense attorney was not entitled to a copy of the indictment—a prohibition which remained in effect throughout the nineteenth century—and he thus had to prepare a case uncertain of the exact charges laid against the client.[27] The City solicitor's brief for the defense of William Webb demonstrates the potential problems faced by defense counsel. Webb had been committed to Newgate for the theft of a silk handkerchief from his employers, a pair of linen drapers in Oxford Street. His sister, however, informed the City solicitor that a second charge might be laid against her brother: five yards of cambric had been found in Webb's bed after he had been committed, and one of the partners had carried the cloth to the magistrate's office. The accused himself knew nothing of the second charge, and as the brief prepared for Knapp indicated, it was unclear whether it would form part of the indictment.[28]

Defense attorneys also suffered from the disadvantage of being refused copies of the depositions sworn against their clients. Even a sight of these, Harmer lamented, would be useful, if only to inform the attorney of the witnesses to be called against his client. The attorney would then be able to "enquire into their credibility": "The facts sworn may be false; but how are they to be investigated and disproved, unless they be known?"[29] No remedy was provided for this situation until 1836. Informations were publicly read during the final examination of the accused before the magistrate, but attorneys were not usually employed until after the commitment, and the prisoner was frequently unable to give a clear account of what had been sworn against him.[30]

The brief delivered to the barrister for the defense also consisted of three parts. The first stated that the accused had been committed to gaol by a particular magistrate for a specified offense and identified the prosecutor. The second described the defendant's background and character, outlined the events leading to his or her arrest, and provided any facts tending to disprove the client's guilt. Defense briefs concluded with the evidence on behalf of the defendant, again listing witnesses and what they could be called upon to prove. The City solicitor's brief to Knapp in *R. v. Webb* established the good reputation Webb had enjoyed in Gloucester, where his family lived, and traced his history from the time of his arrival in London. Webb had been in continuous employment until his committal: prior to his service with the prosecutors, Evans and Savage, he had worked for two other drapers' firms, the names and addresses of which were provided, along with the periods of his employment. "It may," wrote the City solicitor, "be material for the Prisoner's benefit to shew that he is not a common thief on the town or an idler." He then moved on to provide a detailed account of Webb's version of the events leading to his arrest. Webb pointed to malice on the part of another employee, Bevan, who he said had laid "traps" to incriminate Webb with their employers on previous occasions. Bevan, according to Webb, had harbored a grudge against the accused since he had been forced to share his Christmas tips with him. Knapp was requested to cross-examine the drapers and Bevan if they appeared as witnesses for the prosecution, and to call them if they did not, to establish Bevan's malice. Two further witnesses were to be called to prove that Bevan had boasted of receiving £5 in Christmas tips but admitted only thirty-five shillings to his employers when he was forced to share. Three of Webb's former employers would testify both to the fact of his good service and his general good character; four family members would also speak to his character.

While the case for the defendant had been strong enough for the City to bear the costs of Webb's defense, he was nevertheless convicted, sentenced to six months' imprisonment in the House of Correction, and fined a shilling. Knapp's presence in court, confirmed by his signature on the front of the brief and notes taken of one of the drapers' testimony on the back, is undetectable from the report of the trial in the OBSP. The prisoner's defense was recorded as "Henry Bevan owed me a spite ever since Christmas; he would not share the Christmas box with me; I told Master, he made him." Four unspecified witnesses gave him a good character.[31]

Charles Isaacs's brief to Law in the case of *R. v. Dean et al.* (1826)[32] similarly contains a wealth of information that is not available in the Sessions Papers. The OBSP recorded that Thomas, Elizabeth, John, and William Dean and Ann Cox were indicted for breaking and entering the dwelling house of Robert Poynton and stealing "1 coat 3s; 1 waistcoat 5s; 1 pair of boots 21; 2 pair of gaiters, 10s; 1 pair of shoes 5s; 3 watches, 31; 1 hat, 2s; 1 umbrella, 10s; 1 bed, value 11; 2 blankets, 15s; 1 coverlid, 1; 6 chairs, 30s; 1 table, 11; the goods of Ann Allen."[33] Isaacs's brief reveals that the defendants were a family of publicans. Mr. Allen, the husband of the prosecutor, had lodged with them for thirteen weeks, having agreed to pay fourteen shillings a week. When he moved to private premises he owed the Deans a total of £50 9s., this sum consisting of back rent plus a loan. Allen became ill and went into hospital, at which time he requested Thomas Dean, in the presence of two witnesses, to see him decently buried in the event of his death, and to take possession of his furniture and effects at his lodging in payment of his rent and funeral expenses. He left the key with the landlord, who delivered it to Dean but subsequently refused him entry. Dean, with the assistance of the other defendants, forced the lock and conveyed the items specified in the indictment to his own residence, believing that he had a "just right" to do so. "The manner in which Dean his family wife & child were taken up," wrote Isaacs indignantly, "reflects little credit upon the score of humanity upon the prosecutor or her agent Mr. Burnell who we verily believe has been the sole means of instigating the prosecutrix to prefer this bill of indictment." Burnell, he said, had acted with "spite and malice." The brief continued: "Having put counsel in possession of the facts which gave rise to the preferring the Bill of Indictment we will proceed & put him in possession of the evidence which we shall produce at the trial of this Indictment and also call witnesses to the character of the Defendants Dean which when done we say the Court and jury will concur with us in the opinion that the Defendants are neither of them guilty to the charges laid to them & acquit them of this most foul and scandalous charge." Isaacs then listed the names of witnesses who would confirm both Allen's debt and that Allen had instructed

Dean to take possession of his personal effects. In this particular instance the attorney's efforts proved unnecessary. When the case came to trial the prosecutor did not appear, and the prisoners were acquitted.

Where they were employed, attorneys were obviously largely responsible for providing the strategy of the case. Given that the majority of defendants were poor, however, and found it difficult to scrape together the sum required to retain counsel ("the bed being often sold from under their wives and children for that purpose"),[34] briefs were frequently prepared and supplied to the barrister at the last moment. James Harmer recounted that he had been employed for the defense of John Holloway, charged with Owen Haggerty with murder, only a few days before the sessions began (there were ten days between Holloway's committal and his trial), because Holloway's father could not find the fee until then.[35] Harmer delivered his brief to Thomas Andrews the following morning. In his pamphlet account of the trial—Harmer believed Holloway and Haggerty to have been wrongly convicted—he wrote, "[I]n my humble opinion, the public have much reason to regret, that these unfortunate men were unprovided with the means of defence. . . . The prosecution was carried on under the direction of the government, and with public money; the minute investigation respecting the prisoners must have shewn . . . that they were in the greatest indigence, and even without a shilling."[36] In another murder case, *R. v. Patmore* (1789), Richard Peatt received his brief halfway through the trial. The accused cross-examined the first two prosecution witnesses, and Peatt took over in the middle of Patmore's cross-examination of the third. His client later lamented in court, "Every thing [was] not put into the brief that should have been, because [there was] not time."[37] Similarly, William Priddle, charged with rape (1775), had found that some evidence had emerged in the course of the trial about which his counsel had "no instructions," and he requested the judge's permission to ask a few questions of his own.[38]

No provision for legal aid was made until the early twentieth century, and indigence clearly prevented most defendants from employing counsel: "[T]here was nothing in the process that matched counsel to cases that most need or deserved representation . . . in allocating counsel, money talked, for both the prosecution and for the defense."[39] What defendants could expect to pay the attorney, on top of the minimum of a guinea to the barrister he employed, is again unclear. Among the City solicitor's papers, however, is an itemized bill of costs for undertaking a Mrs. Hicks's prosecution of William Sparry for assault (1760) totaling £16 10s. 6d. This sum included a fee of a guinea to counsel, Mr. Stow, a pound paid to witnesses, and fees paid to various officials at different stages of the proceedings as well as moneys paid to the solicitor himself for taking the prosecutor's instructions, drawing an affidavit for habeas corpus, preferring the bill of indictment, drafting instructions for counsel to move to put off trial, drawing a draft brief, preparing a "Fair Copy" for counsel, attending counsel "several times," attending court when the trial was heard, and a number of other tasks, closing with an "Ending fee &c" of 6s. 8d. Many of the charges incurred in conducting a prosecution would not apply to defense work, but attorneys must have charged for discovering and interviewing witnesses, preparing drafts and fair copies of the brief(s) to counsel, consultations with both the accused and his or her counsel, correspondence, and so forth. The City solicitor charged 3s. 4d. per consultation, 6s. 8d. for preparing the brief, and a further 3s. 4d. for the copy provided to the barrister.[40]

At the Old Bailey

When a particular sessions opened at the Old Bailey at least some of the barristers seated at the green baize table beneath the bench would already have been briefed, and for multiple causes. Adolphus began to suffer from cataracts in 1834, and his clerk read his briefs to him the night before he was due in court; on one occasion they numbered thirteen.[41] Other counsel arrived hoping to be employed at the eleventh hour; thus James Lewis's movements "were watched with anxiety and hope as he quietly walked about and slipped a brief into the hands of a pleased recipient."[42] At the Clerkenwell Sessions House Peter Alley was said to be "punctilious" about everyone keeping to their proper place in court, and his usual address to the usher was "Keep this space clear; I shall be poisoned. Gin and cheese second-hand will be the death of me." When, however, he saw the usher resisting the entrance of "a young man in the costume of a Clerkenwell solicitor, — coat buttoned to the chin, linen not visible, — with a brief in his hand," he had a different criticism: "Usher, why do you stand staring about you there? You let in all the blackguards, and keep out gentlemen who are coming on business. Let this gentleman in." Unfortunately, on admittance the attorney asked Alley if he were Charles Phillips.[43]

Once the sessions began, the pace at which criminal trials proceeded would astonish a modern observer. Even where counsel were employed, most were probably concluded in less than an hour, many of them perhaps in a matter of minutes. In the 1780s twenty or so trials per twelve-hour day seems to have been the norm at the Old Bailey sessions. As both London's population and the crime rate increased in the opening decades of the nineteenth century, the time allotted to individual trials may have decreased.

Metropolitan London continued to grow at a phenomenal rate, its population reaching 2,685,000 by 1851, while criminal statistics, collected nationally and published on an annual basis from 1810, reveal an almost sevenfold increase in committals between 1805 and 1842. The pressure of numbers in London is immediately obvious from a comparison of the annual volumes of the eighteenth-century OBSP with those of the nineteenth century: in the 1780s and 1790s the number of cases tried annually at the Old Bailey ranged between 500 and 1,000; by 1820 this number had increased to just over 1,500, and in 1830 slightly more than 2,100 cases were tried in that court.[44] Murder trials not uncommonly took up a day or more,[45] but Wontner calculated that the average time occupied by trials at the Old Bailey in the early 1830s "never . . . exceeded eight and a half minutes."[46] The *Westminster Review* took issue with this calculation, arguing that the average time per trial was just over twenty-two minutes. The writer of the article admitted, however, that excessive speed was a problem in other of London's criminal courts. The chairman of the Clerkenwell sessions had tried sixteen prisoners within an hour, thirteen of whom were transported, while on another occasion eight prisoners were tried in twenty minutes, five of whom were transported. "In these instances," it was conceded, "a little more time might have been taken, without being guilty of useless delay."[47] Charles Phillips wrote indignantly that "the hurry-scurry with which men are bundled out of the dock on their way to Botany Bay is often not merely reprehensible, but most revolting!" At the Middlesex sessions he had witnessed "13 fellow creatures arraigned, tried, convicted & transported, on several indictments, too—all within an hour!"[48]

The Role of Counsel

Evidence of the role played by counsel in trials at the Old Bailey in the eighteenth century is derived principally from the OBSP. The reliability and usefulness of these reports varied over time, but between 1770 and 1800, and particularly in the 1780s and 1790s, they were comparatively rich in detail with respect to the participation of lawyers. From 1783 counsel were identified by name, and their opening speeches and arguments with judges—and each other—over points of law were occasionally reproduced. The dynamics of the eighteenth-century courtroom come vividly to life in these reports. In the early nineteenth century, however, the reports become much more circumspect about the activities of the bar. This variation owes in part to changes in proprietorship:[49] the reports produced during the tenure of Edward Hodgson (1782–92) are particularly detailed; those produced during that of Robert Butler (1805–16) are particularly poor. But the varying needs and concerns of the City of London also influenced the content of the reports. The City increasingly involved itself with publication of the Sessions Papers from the mid-1770s, in part because it wanted a record that could be referred to and relied upon when the authorities were considering which of London's capital convicts to pardon and which to hang, but also, according to Simon Devereaux, because it wanted to convey a "particular vision" of the criminal trial to the public, one which stressed the justice of the system.[50] The shorthand writers were thus exhorted to provide "faithful and accurate" accounts, and those who failed to do so were called to account. The City was decidedly unhappy with Butler's performance: he was reprimanded for reproducing indecent material and asked to "pay more attention and fulfill his contract better than he ha[d] hitherto done." The recorder, John Silvester, complained that "the printing was frequently very inaccurate and the whole badly executed." When Butler still failed to produce the kinds of reports desired, his contract was terminated.[51]

Butler cannot be blamed, however, for the nineteenth-century Sessions Papers' lack of detail with respect to the participation of lawyers, for in 1805 the City voted to expunge the direct or indirect arguments of counsel from the record.[52] Barristers continued to be named, albeit sporadically (the final years of Butler's proprietorship, 1811–16, are especially bad),[53] and Butler routinely flattered the barristers he occasionally mentioned: "MR. GURNEY, with his usual perspicuity, stated the case to the jury"; "MR. WALFORD comment[ed] to the Jury [in a trial of misdemeanor] with a considerable degree of vivacity and warmth of expression on the part of the prisoner"; "MR. ARABIN, as counsel for the prisoner [again in a trial of misdemeanor] entered into an ingenious address to the jury, in his defense; and commented a good deal upon the prisoner's conduct, as neither being extraordinary or remarkable."[54] These tributes, however, deliberately conveyed little information about what counsel actually said. Butler and his successor, Henry Buckler, occasionally broke the rules, so that the gist of a speech in a trial of misdemeanor or a glimpse of a counsel's style of address were captured.[55] Generally, however, under the new rules for reporting, the opening addresses of prosecution counsel, which were occasionally reproduced in the earlier period, no longer appear, and even the conduct of cross-examinations can be difficult to reconstruct. Sometimes a series of questions appears to have been accurately transcribed, but in other instances only an indication of who cross-examined appears, followed by the substance of the answer, with the question itself left unrecorded. By the 1820s cross-examinations were frequently telescoped, with counsel's initial question reported, followed by the answer not only to it but to subsequent, unspecified questioning.[56] In other words, the evidence was reproduced but not the manner in which it was elicited. This was deliberate. The City did not want counsel's "ingenious addresses" to form part of the public record; it was interested in the evidence alone and did not want to educate criminals in how to escape from justice.[57] In the nineteenth century, therefore, newspaper reports of Old Bailey trials tend to be more useful, although only the more spectacular trials are reported in detail, and again a synopsis of the evidence adduced from an examination or cross-examination is more likely to be reproduced than a verbatim account of questions and answers.[58] The newspapers had from the late 1780s regarded with a degree of suspicion "those various *legal modes*, the ingenuity of Council has adopted to save a culprit from conviction."[59]

Counsel for the Prosecution

Imperfect as they are, the eighteenth-century OBSP allow considerable insight into the form of the criminal trial and the role played by counsel in the pre–Prisoners' Counsel Act era. Prior to 1836 that role differed markedly between trials of felony and trials of misdemeanor, and where the felony trial was concerned practice throughout England was by no means uniform. On the Midland circuit in the early nineteenth century, for instance, there was "no case without a prosecuting counsel," but it was "unusual for the Counsel for the prosecution to make to the Jury even a single statement of facts."[60] Similarly, in the county of Stafford on the Oxford circuit in the same period it was "a Custom adopted by the Bar never to open the Case for the Prosecution, never to state the Case against the Prisoner, unless it be a Case of Murder, and in Circumstances where it is necessary for the understanding of the Case and for the Benefit of the Prisoner."[61] At the Old Bailey, prosecuting counsel did make a speech after the indictment had been read. It was observed by contemporaries that in doing so they observed "a great decency of language," refraining from appeals to the jury's feelings and stating the case to be made against the accused in a cool and restrained manner. William Bolland, in particular, was remembered as leaning "rather largely to the side of mercy" in opening the case for the prosecution.[62] The evidence of the OBSP tends on the whole to confirm this assessment. Opening addresses in trials of felony are markedly different from those in trials of misdemeanor and follow a readily identifiable formula. Counsel repeatedly emphasized their "painful duty," and the duty which lay equally heavily on the jury, of weighing the prisoner's interest against the public good. They were careful always to indicate the consequences of conviction but reminded the jury of the competing interests of the prosecutors and the public as a whole. Thus in *R. v. Vandercom* (1796) Jonathan Raine stated: "Gentlemen, you cannot but be well aware that this is a capital offence; and I state this to you at the outset by way of requesting your most serious attention to a charge of such magnitude [burglary]; involving, as you very well know, the lives of the two men at the bar; the interests of the persons for whom I have the honour to be concerned; and, what is still more, the interest of the public."[63] Newman Knowlys's opening speech in *R. v. Ward* (1789) is also quite typical: "Gentlemen of the jury, you have heard the indictment opened by my learned friend, which contains the charge of murder, and when I am addressing myself to a jury who has discharged their duty so well this sessions, I need say nothing to you to call your attention to so important a charge; you well know what is due to publick justice upon a satisfactory conviction of such a crime; you likewise well know how immense a stake a prisoner has who stands under such accusation: gentlemen, I will state the case to you, as shortly as I can."[64] He then briefly outlined the case against Ward, charged with killing Edwin Swain in a fight. Knowlys concluded his account by explaining the legal difference between murder and manslaughter and informed the jury that it was up to them to decide which was the most applicable in the circumstances.

In lieu of directing an outright attack on the accused, prosecuting counsel asked the jury to weigh the pros and cons of a conviction. Thus Garrow concluded his opening address in the prosecution of James Templeman and George Platt for highway robbery (1790):

> Gentlemen, I shall lay before you the evidence. On the one hand, the growing experience of the times shews us that these accusations, which are very easily made, which are extremely difficult to be refuted, which may be made by the worst of men against the best members of society, have grown to an amazing heigth, and it is a duty you owe to the publick to make the prisoners the sacrifices of their own delinquency, if you believe them guilty; but on the other hand, however much you may abhor and detest the crime you ought not to involve innocent persons in the consequences of guilt. Gentlemen, I have no doubt but you will attend to the evidence with the care and impartiallity which must always, and which, thank God, always does, characterize an English jury. I shall call the witnesses with no anxiety about the result of the case, having no doubt but public justice will be satisfied.[65]

Garrow, of course, when opening a prosecution, could play up the fact that he had frequently appeared for the defense and was therefore not insensitive to the plight of the accused: "Gentlemen, I am of counsel in this case for the prosecutor against the two men at the bar; and it has very often been my fortune to stand in this place, in the situation which my learned friend [Knowlys] stands to-night, called upon to do the best in the compass of my power, to defend real or supposed innocence: Gentlemen, I have not taken leave of the feeling which must necessarily operate on the minds of advocates placed in so painful a situation, in a place too in which by the wisdom of the law it is denied to the advocate, on the part of his client, to make any address in his defense."[66]

There was clearly an established etiquette to be observed in opening a felony prosecution. Counsel might dwell on the seriousness of the crime and perhaps, in asking the jury to weigh the competing interests of the prisoner's and the public good, lean slightly in the direction of the latter, but they were not to declare any personal belief in the guilt of the accused. Instead, they were to refer to their instructions. Thus Knowlys, opening *R. v. Martin* (1786), informed the jury that the prosecutor would be produced, and it would "hear from her whether she is as certain as I am instructed she is, that the prisoner is the man" guilty of the assault charged.[67] Opening speeches almost invariably closed with phrases to the effect that, if the case counsel had made out against the accused was proved by the evidence presented, the jury must convict, but if they entertained any doubt to the prisoner's advantage, it became their duty to acquit him. John Silvester frequently told the jury that if the case could not be proved to its satisfaction, he would "rejoice" with it in the accused's acquittal.[68] The "duty of restraint" eventually made its way into a nineteenth-century textbook. Dickenson and Talfourd's *Practical Guide to the Quarter Sessions and Other Sessions of the Peace* (1829) instructed that prosecuting counsel addressing the jury in a case of felony

> ought to confine himself to a simple detail of the facts he expects to prove, because the prisoner has no opportunity of laying his case before the jury by his counsel; and even the privilege of stating circumstances, however dryly, in such order and direction as may tend most directly to a particular conclusion is, of itself, no small advantage accorded to the prosecutor, and certainly should be exercised with great forbearance and caution. . . . In cases of misdemeanour, the prosecuting counsel is not thus restricted, because here the defendant is allowed to make a real defence by his counsel, and, therefore, here the counsel for the prosecutor may not only state his facts, but reason upon them, and anticipate any line of defence which his opponent may probably adopt.[69]

Convention, however, allowed for considerable leeway, and in many prosecution speeches the obligatory reference to the accused's right became a token gesture. In *R. v. Ash* (1784) Silvester informed the jury that there could be no doubt in the mind of any man who heard him that the accused had indeed committed the crime with which he was charged but added, "[A]t the same time, I do not mean to influence your minds by anything that I can say, but I only wish you to try this case as every other case ought to be tried, upon facts produced by the evidence; if those facts are true, it becomes your duty, though a melancholy one it is indeed, to pronounce that verdict; if the facts are not proved, you will acquit him."[70] William Fielding also trod a little near the line in his opening speech in *R. v. Dingler* (1791). The accused was charged with murdering his wife. After outlining the evidence against Dingler, Fielding, anticipating Garrow's defense, reminded the jury that with a charge of murder, malice aforethought must be established or the charge would be reduced to manslaughter. But, he said, it appeared to him that "the present case will preclude the prisoner at the bar from all such considerations . . . if there should appear any cause, which I at present cannot think can appear; if there should appear any possibility for his accounting for this horrid transaction, by any thing that can furnish the least degree of excuse, you will hear that excuse with wonderful satisfaction." He reminded the jury that in cases between man and man, the distinction frequently did occur, "but, as between man and wife, nay as between man and woman without that connection, it appears to me that the distinction of manslaughter can rarely ever arise when the crime has been attended with circumstances like those I have described to you." He concluded, "[O]n occasion like the present, I should think myself extremely to blame, if I was to comment more on a case like the present," but by this point he had already indulged in considerable comment.[71]

Examples can also be found among the OBSP of occasional appeals to the jury's feelings. Peatt, opening the prosecution of Stevenson, the watchman of Clerkenwell Prison charged with murdering one of the prisoners in the course of a disturbance, told the jury, "[T]he deceased, as I understand, has two children, and was gone seven months with child; but this I mention as a circumstance to be lamented, than as a matter for your consideration."[72] On the evidence of the OBSP, such lapses appear to have been rare. How far counsel were willing to strain against etiquette depended to a great extent on the circumstances of the crime and the evidence available. Silvester, for instance, displayed considerable lenience in opening an infanticide case, while Garrow, likewise employed for the prosecution, interrupted the testimony of the first witness to cross-examine for the defense: "The poor woman has no Council, I will ask you what character she had?"[73] Garrow's conduct in the prosecution of Richard Patch, however, was very different.[74] Although he refrained from appeals to emotion, his opening speech in *R. v. Patch* (1806), a case tried not at the Old Bailey but at the sessions house in

Newington, Surrey, would be repeatedly cited in the debate which arose over the Prisoners' Counsel Act as a "hanging speech."[75]

The conventions involved in prosecuting a felony become clear when a comparison is made of the same barristers' conduct in opening the prosecution in a trial of misdemeanor. The latter could in theory take the form of a fully fledged adversarial contest, with counsel engaged on both sides. The OBSP and anecdotal evidence suggest that such contests were not uncommon, although the proportion of misdemeanor trials which took the form of a professional contest remains unknown.[76] Defense counsel were permitted to address the jury in such trials, and consequently the restraint exercised in opening a felony case was abandoned. Prosecuting counsel, although expected again to refrain from "indulging in invective" and from appeals "to the prejudices or passions of the jury,"[77] argued the case against the accused much more forcefully and, rather than referring to their instructions as to the prosecutor's belief, declared vehemently the certain guilt of the accused. These addresses concluded with strong words to the effect that the miscreant must be punished. Thus in *R. v. Oliver* (1791) Garrow told the jury that he hoped the accused would "be made an example to others," while in *R. v. Jacques et al.* (1790) Silvester had concluded, "I sit down perfectly satisfied, that I shall prove [the] facts, [the] connections between the parties, as not to leave the least doubt in the mind of any man, but that they are all guilty of the charge; and it is high time that justice should overtake these delinquents."[78] In opening *R. v. Priddle et al.* (1787) Silvester was able to warn the jury against allowing Thomas Erskine, who appeared for the defendants, to lead them astray. "You will admire his talent, you will say, pity so much ingenuity should be exerted on behalf of men so undeserving," but "Gentlemen, if the evidence comes up to but half of what I have opened, you will not let the able harangue of my learned and eloquent friend, Mr. Erskine, outweigh the testimony of so many witnesses . . . and I trust that you will, after a serious investigation of the facts . . . give these men over to that punishment, which they so wholly deserve."[79] Barristers' aggressive advocacy of just punishment for misdemeanants owed, no doubt, to the fact that such punishments were noncapital: vehement arguments that accused felons "wholly deserved" to be hanged were unlikely to have been made even if counsel for the defense had been permitted to reply.

Reminders of the accused's rights, of the necessity of proving the case to the jury's satisfaction, and of the dreadful consequences of a conviction could not disguise the fact that it was the prosecuting counsel's task in felony trials, as in trials for misdemeanor, to secure a conviction. During this period a defendant was entitled to an acquittal if the slightest error was contained in the indictment drawn against him, and barristers were consequently often hired to "peruse" a particular indictment before it was presented in court. Silvester took the drafting of indictments very seriously indeed, compiling a selection of precedents from the records of the Old Bailey which, by 1790, comprised four stout volumes of more than seven hundred pages apiece.[80] The collection was carefully arranged by subject matter under headings provided by John Reeves's *Chart of Penal Law*. On the verso of the title page of the first volume he inscribed a verse from the Old Testament:

> Arthxerxes Longimanus, King of Persia, in the 7th year of his Reign, and 457 years B.C. appointed Ezra to the Government of Judea.
>
> And thou, Ezra, after the wisdom of thy God, that is in thine hands, set Magistrates and Judges, which may judge all the people that are beyond the River, all such as know the Law of thy God, and teach ye them that know them not. And whoever will not do the law of the God, and the Law of the King, let Judgment be executed speedily upon him, whether it be unto Death, or to Banishment, or to confiscation of Goods, or to Imprisonment.
>
> Vide Ezra 7 ch : 25 verse

Silvester also took pains to acquaint himself with London's criminal underworld, and with its slang. In its report of the trial at quarter sessions of James Banner for an assault on Elizabeth Lear (1790), *The Times* stated: "Mr. *Silvester* opened this case on the part of the prosecution. He said, the prisoner was of two professions: he was a *Peterman* and a *Nuckler*. Taking it for granted, these terms were not understood by the younger part of the profession, he condescended to explain them. By a *Peterman* was meant, any blackguard who earned his living by cutting portmanteaus from behind post-chaises; and by a *nuckler* was understood a pickpocket."[81] Two notebooks also survive of Silvester's recordership, in which he noted not only the haunts of known thieves but a dictionary of their slang.[82]

After opening the indictment and stating the prosecution's case to the jury, counsel for the prosecution examined the prosecutor and his or her witnesses. Apart from material witnesses, counsel might call witnesses to speak to the prosecutor's character, thus establishing that the prosecution was brought in good faith. Counsel for the prosecution naturally undertook the cross-examination of any material witnesses produced by the defense. Such witnesses were questioned incessantly with respect to how they could recollect the time or events in question with certainty. In *R. v. Wood & Brown* (1784) Mary Wilson testified that Wood had never been out of her sight on the night he had supposedly committed a robbery. How, Silvester asked, could she remember every detail of a conversation Wood, a publican, had had with a customer? Had she written it down? Why were the events of that particular day so clear in her mind? Had she been told of the importance of that date? Who told her that the robbery had been committed on that night? He pressed the customer, Jane Saunders, equally hard when it was her turn to testify.[83] Prosecuting counsel also had the right to cross-examine the accused's witnesses to character, but it was customary that, if he intended to do so, notice of his intention would be given to the prisoner's counsel, who could then exercise his discretion as to whether to call them.[84] This courtesy may have been the reason Garrow declined to examine any more witnesses and attempted to dissuade his client from doing so in *R. v. Martin* (1786).[85]

As prosecuting counsel Garrow was wont to treat these encounters as sport. Opening his cross-examination of one of the prisoner's witnesses in *R. v. Plata et al.* (1791) he asked, "What do you shake so for?" and then set to work:

> You were never in this court before?—Not as a witness.
>
> No! a witness! No; how long was it since you was here?—Six years, eight years, I was tried here.
>
> God bless me! What for pray?—Tried, I was arraigned, there was no witness against me.
>
> What was you tried for?—A charge of house-breaking.
>
> God bless me! House-breaking![86]

Continued attendance at the Old Bailey meant familiarity with prosecutors and witnesses as well as those who regularly appeared in the dock. The OBSP contain a number of trials in which counsel for the prosecution were able to demolish the credibility of a witness for the defense on the basis of previous knowledge of that witness. In *R. v. Jacques* (1790) more than one defense witness was known to Silvester. When Benjamin Griffen Jackson was sworn the barrister greeted him with, "Well, Mr. Jackson, this is not the first time we have met here?" In the course of his cross-examination it emerged that Jackson had once been convicted of an assault:

> *Mr. Silvester.* You had counsel, I take it then?—I had you for a counsel; I think so.
>
> And all I could do for you, you was sent to Newgate?—Yes.

Another of Jacques's witnesses was greeted in similar terms: "I know you very well, Mr. Johnson?" Johnson reacted defensively, defying Silvester or anyone else to say anything against his character.[87]

Counsel for the Defense

In trials of felony the role of defense counsel was restricted before 1836. As the court informed Benjamin Russen, charged in 1777 with rape: "Your counsel are not at liberty to state any matter of fact, they are permitted to examine your witnesses, and they are here to speak to any matters of law that may arise; but if your defence arises out of matter of fact, you must yourself state it to me and the jury."[88] Some prisoners chose to hire an attorney to prepare a written defense, which they would read out in court when called upon to state their case. Precisely when this development emerged is difficult to determine. There are occasional references to written defenses in the eighteenth century,[89] but the bulk of the evidence is found in the early decades of the nineteenth century.[90] For example, James Ripley, charged with murder in 1815, was represented at trial by the attorney general, Mr. Serjeant Best, Knapp, and Garrow. Called upon to offer his defense, Ripley submitted a lengthy written statement that had clearly been drafted by a lawyer.[91] Harmer testified before the commissioners on the criminal law in 1836 that, because defense counsel were prohibited from addressing the jury, "the only thing [he] could do as a remedy was, to prepare a written defence for the accused." After acquainting himself with the facts of the case he would prepare a defense he thought best calculated to explain them to his client's advantage. But of course, he acknowledged, "circumstances may arise in the course of a trial which would render the defence mischievous instead of beneficial."[92] Defense counsel were equally aware of the potential damage that could result from a written defense. In *R. v. Parr* (1787) Knowlys demanded of the prisoner, just as he was about to read his defense to the court, "Hand it here first that we may see if it is proper to be read."[93]

In a few very rare instances counsel for the defense appears to have made some sort of opening statement.[94] Generally, however, the work of defense counsel began when the indictment was read out in court at the beginning of the trial. Even if briefed, this was the first time he was made aware of the formal charge against his client, and that client was entitled to an acquittal if the indictment contained the slightest flaw. Knowlys pointed out the difficulties experienced by counsel in the *Parr* case: "I have to lament an old rule, that counsel for prisoners in cases in which indictments are of a very long and intricate nature, are obliged to pick out from the short reading which they hear of that indictment from the officer of the Court, such objections, as perhaps might be much multiplied if they had the perusal of them."[95] In spite of this handicap defense counsel were often able to detect from that single hearing of the indictment whether the charge fit within the relevant statute. Garrow was able to win an acquittal for George Pitt when he demonstrated that, in Pitt's case, it did not.[96]

Sometimes counsel relied heavily on technical objections. In *R. v. Lee* (1784) the defendant began by successfully challenging a jury member, who was replaced. Silvester then argued at some length with the presiding judges, Ashurst and Heath, about the form of the indictment. Lee was charged with forging a bill of exchange "directed to the Pay Office in the Ordnance Office, Whitehall, requiring the proper person, in such Pay Office, at the Ordnance Office, Whitehall, to pay Mr. John Lee or order, on demand, the sum of 15l. sterling." The bill was signed "Townsend, M.G. Pay Office, Ordnance Office, Whitehall." Silvester argued that since every count in the indictment had stated that Townsend was Master General of the Ordnance, it was necessary for the prosecution to prove that fact and that there was such an office as the Pay Office, and he drew the judges' attention to a case tried before Lord Mansfield in support of his position. This line of attack was unsuccessful, but Silvester did not give up. "My Lord," he said, "it is my duty standing here as a council for a prisoner to take every objection that lays in my power, for a man standing in his unfortunate situation, therefore I shall make no apology for troubling your lordship with a further objection." Quoting an act of Parliament which required every bill of exchange to be stamped, he referred the judges to *R. v. Hawkins*, in which William Baldwin had objected that a forged bill was not stamped and Mr. Justice Buller had reserved the case for the twelve judges. Again he was unsuccessful: Heath told Silvester that the meaning of the act did not extend to criminal suits. Silvester's final ploy was to suggest that the bill read "Jownsend" and not "Townsend": "[I]f my Lord Townsend's name had not been mentioned, I believe nobody would have thought of it."[97]

Defense counsel frequently attempted to cast doubt on the prosecutor's identification of the prisoner, calling into question his or her eyesight or sobriety, or seeking to establish that poor lighting at the scene of the crime made certain identification impossible.[98] In the trial of Joseph Phillips and William Andrews (1788), Knowlys was able to establish that the prosecutor, Richard Dale, had been so drunk at the time he was robbed that he was incapable of identifying the men who had robbed him. In court he demonstrated that Dale was in fact unable to tell the two prisoners apart. Mr. Justice Wilson concluded the trial by saying, "[S]omebody has seen him drunk and robbed him, but there seems to be no more reason for charging these two men, than any others." Both the accused were acquitted.[99]

Counsel for the defense also exposed less than creditable episodes in the lives of prosecutors. In *R. v. Backow & Backow* (1796) Knowlys opened his examination of prosecutor Benjamin Davis with the command, "Keep up your voice, and speak as loud as when you cry bad shillings," and proceeded to force Davis to reveal that he had with his brothers been taken up on suspicion of being a "smasher," a "putter off of bad money."[100] Peter Alley used the same tactic in *R. v. Hartshorn* (1811), asking the prosecutor if he had not himself been tried at the Old Bailey, convicted of a libel, and put in the pillory. Alley further accused him of offering to drop the prosecution if the defendant's father "made him a compromise." Hartshorn was acquitted.[101] Charles Phillips opened his cross-examination of one of the prosecutors in *R. v. McCabe* (1830) by demanding to know how many gaols he had been in in the course of his life and extracted the fact that he had spent two years in Newgate. Again, the accused was acquitted.[102]

The OBSP contain many examples of defense counsel effectively putting the prosecutor on trial, and not always where they suspected a false or malicious prosecution. Jerome William Knapp managed to reverse the proceedings in *R. v. Tilly* (1792). Tilly was prosecuted by a Bank of England clerk who claimed she had picked him up in the Piazza one night on his way to the theater. He went with her to her lodgings and was there some time; then, he said, Tilly had run away with his watch. Knapp first questioned whether Pilleau, the prosecutor, could be sure he had identified the correct person, but he quickly changed tack. With a series of questions, during the course of which Pilleau was advised not to "shuffle," Knapp established that the bank clerk, a married man with six children, had been with the same woman on several occasions. When Pilleau pleaded that "most men do foolish things sometimes," Knapp replied that it was a "disgrace to come with such a prosecution into court." Neither the identity of the accused nor the theft itself were mentioned again. Knapp raised further instances of "indecent conduct" on the part of the prosecutor, and Tilly was acquitted.[103] Alley similarly did his best to expose the prosecutor in *R. v. Weston* (1812) as an immoral, irreligious man who had been unfaithful to his dying wife.[104] While defense counsel were quick to take advantage of the prosecutor's past, however, the same men, when employed for the prosecution, attempted to prevent their opponents from using this strategy: "I must once more ask whether the private history of a man's life is to be brought into question?"[105]

Some efforts were made by defense counsel to build a positive case for the accused via the evidence of material witnesses. Unrepresented defendants, incarcerated in Newgate, were seldom able to track down eyewitnesses or alibis, but counsel, probably aided by attorneys, occasionally produced such persons.[106] They also, of course, called character witnesses, sometimes amassing extraordinary numbers. In *Parr* Knowlys informed the court that he had eighty-four character witnesses and was prepared to call them all; in the trial of Joseph Slack he called thirteen character witnesses and again was prepared to call "many more," but the court ruled that character could be taken no further. The testimony of twenty-nine character witnesses was permitted in the trial of St. John Long (1830), a physician charged with murdering one of his patients.[107]

Defense counsel, however, devoted the bulk of their efforts to testing, and demolishing where possible, the prosecution's case. They frequently attacked the competency of the prosecution's witnesses, attempting to prevent their evidence from being heard.[108] Once a witness had been permitted to testify, defense counsel engaged in damage control, attempting to limit the evidence he or she was allowed to present. As Langbein argues, "[T]he rules of evidence crystallized out of the judge's discretion over the conduct of trials in his courtroom," but they also acted to empower counsel.[109] In *R. v. Smith* (1783) Silvester objected twice to the admission of evidence and once to its relevance.[110] Similarly, Fielding objected to irrelevant evidence in *R. v. Clary & Gombert* (1788).[111] Alley raised the issue of "best evidence," albeit unsuccessfully, in *R. v. Hindes* (1797).[112] Defense counsel also, although not consistently, attempted to prevent the prosecutor and his or her witnesses from indulging in speculation. Silvester, who appeared for the defense in *R. v. Wilson et al.* (1784), reminded one witness: "You know when you are upon your oath you are to tell us the facts, and not the mind of any man, because it is impossible for you to know the mind of any man, or to know that the intent of one was this, and another was this."[113] Garrow, in *R. v. Matthews & Matthews* (1786), interrupted the prosecutor by ordering, "Do not tell us what you suppose."[114] A brief discussion of legal evidence published in *The Times* in 1789 stated firmly: "Nothing is evidence but what a man knows of his own knowledge, nothing but what he saw or heard." In continuing, however, the paper overstated practice with respect to hearsay evidence: "No hearsay evidence is admitted, except the person affected by such testimony was present, and who consequently had an opportunity of contradicting it, if it was not true."[115] Counsel did sometimes object to hearsay evidence, once thought to have been excluded by the early eighteenth century, but they did not do so consistently, and it continued to be advanced and accepted by the court into the nineteenth century.[116]

Habitual attendance at the Old Bailey resulted in a familiarity with legal precedents and accepted practice. Counsel frequently cited from trials reported in Leach or Foster which, unlike the OBSP, were aimed specifically at the legal profession and dealt solely with points of law.[117] In *R. v. Clinch* (1791) Knowlys, in objecting to the form of the indictment against his client, cited "the case of Mary Mitchell, in Foster's Reports, and a subsequent case of the King and Williams, in Term Law," which ruled that in order to fall within the statute in question, "the thing purporting to be forged" must be an order from some person(s) having the authority to dispose of the goods. The court reserved judgment on this point for the twelve judges. Knowlys then made further technical objections; Garrow, who opposed him, countered with "Lockitt's case," disputed Knowlys's reading of Mitchell, and drew the court's attention to "a case of Jones, which was in October sessions, 1764, before the late Lord Chief Baron Smythe; Lord Mansfield and Mr. Justice Bathurst were present." That case, he informed the court, was "in print in a collection of crown cases."[118]

Garrow and Silvester in particular referred extensively not only to published cases but to trials in which they personally had been previously employed. Thus Garrow commented, with false humility, in *R. v. Baert* (1790), "Mine is not a long experience, yet it has been a busy experience, and I have seen much of the practice of others much abler than myself; and I have practised a little law here also; and I have had the good fortune, I thank God, to do it with some success: and I remember a case . . ."[119] Discussing the admissibility of a confession in *R. v. Hoy* (1788), he was able to remind the court of words spoken by Mr. Justice Grose "on our last circuit": the accused "must neither be influenced by hopes nor awed by fears" in making a confession.[120] Similarly, Silvester, opposing an objection made by Garrow in the *Wooldridge* case, was able to complain that he had made the same objection himself in a previous trial and had been overruled.[121]

In some instances the discussion that ensued over points of law enabled the accused's counsel to make a de facto speech. In 1785 James Adair, the recorder of London, commented, "You have had ground enough in this case, Mr. Garrow, to entitle you, in point of law, to observe the evidence by a side wind, which you have done very efficiently."[122] One of the best examples in the OBSP may be found in *R. v. Davis* (1786). Davis was charged with the murder of William Watson and was represented at trial by Silvester and Garrow. When it came time for Davis to make his defense, Silvester drew the court's attention to a case reported by Keeling in which a fatal shooting had been deemed accidental, the accused having been unaware that his gun was loaded. He quoted from the case at considerable length, and when he concluded Garrow rose to speak "a few words in addition." These few words were only very loosely tied to Silvester's citation. Garrow in fact argued the case to be made in Davis's favor, at some length and in a style reminiscent of that of John Mortimer's fictional twentieth-century barrister, Horace Rumpole, with his flattering of the jury and requests that judgment be tempered with mercy. Garrow concluded, "[T]hank God, we are prepared with that sort of proof, that will amply convince the jury of the innocence of the prisoner at the bar." The court, unmoved, responded curtly: "Then I desire you will enter into that proof, for I am sure there is no proof of it yet."[123]

The chief service provided by defense counsel during the period in which they remained barred from speaking directly to the jury was cross-examination of the prosecutor and his or her witnesses.[124] "Even Bentham," "the most caustic contemporary critic of the early-nineteenth-century English law of evidence," Langbein notes, accepted the utility of cross-examination: "Against erroneous or mendacious testimony, the grand security is cross-examination."[125] Bentham was not alone in this belief: by the early nineteenth century writers of legal treatises generally demonstrated a similar faith in cross-examination.[126] Through cross-examination the prisoner's counsel could expose not only factual weaknesses in the prosecution's case but also any unworthy motivation for the prosecution itself.

In some cases the defense barrister's line of questioning reflected investigative work undertaken by an attorney. Comments to the effect that more was known of the history of a prosecutor than he or she supposed, together with the doggedness with which counsel pursued lines of questioning, suggest a considerable degree of pretrial legwork. But barristers' personal memories again often proved useful. In *R. v. Homedon* (1794) the accused was charged with stealing goods from the shop of John Disney. Knowlys began his cross-examination of the prosecutor with a series of questions to establish the value of the articles stolen but soon turned to Disney himself.

> Q. I did my duty for you before; I think I recollect seeing your face?
> —Very possibly you might.
> Q. Where do you think I recollect seeing your face?—I cannot tell; you may have seen me in my shop perhaps.
> Q. I never dealt with you, and I assure you I never will. Cannot you guess some other place?—It may be a great many places, perhaps; you might have seen me in Covent-Garden Theatre.
> Q. I may to be sure. Now I will guess where I see you, the last place an honest man should stand, at the bar of the Old Bailey?

Disney continued with evasive answers, but Knowlys eventually forced from him the fact that he had been prosecuted and acquitted of forgery at the Old Bailey and subsequently convicted of fraud at Clerkenwell and imprisoned for a year.[127]

As argued in Chapters 1 and 2, false and malicious prosecution posed continuing problems to justice in the late eighteenth and early nineteenth centuries. The attorney Thomas Wontner complained in *Old Bailey Experience* that some people prosecuted with "the diabolical desire of destroying an innocent person through the prejudice and hastiness of Old Bailey proceedings,"[128] and there is considerable evidence to support this view.[129] Malice appears to have underlain the prosecution of William Webb, and although in this case counsel failed to prove it at trial, the OBSP contain numerous examples of counsel exposing private malice. In *R. v. Pudding* (1789), for instance, Garrow succeeded in establishing that the motives of the prosecutor, Mary Osliffe, were less than creditable. The accused in this case was Osliffe's servant, charged with theft from her mistress. When the prosecutor objected to Garrow's attempts to establish a history of "bickering" between the two women as "impertinent," Garrow informed the judge that he intended to prove that the prosecution owed to the prisoner's knowledge of certain "epistolary productions" of the prosecutor. Garrow was allowed to continue, and Pudding was acquitted.[130] In another case, however, the strategy backfired. Defending Rachel Turner, a servant charged with stealing from her employers, Garrow argued that she had confessed only because her master had promised that if she did she would come to no harm. He further insinuated that there had been some sort of relationship between Turner and her master and that certain gossip had resulted in her mistress becoming "a little matter jealous." This tactic brought down the wrath of Mr. Justice Heath on Turner's head: "This is a very improper return you have made to the mercy of the prosecutor; you have thought it proper to instruct your counsel to throw out such insinuations, the object of which was to destroy the domestic peace of your master and mistress and therefore it will be considered in your punishment."[131] Turner was sentenced to seven years' transportation.

Through cross-examination counsel could attempt, often with success, to destroy the credibility of witnesses as well as prosecutors, and hence that of their testimony. Accomplices testifying to avoid prosecution themselves were frequent targets. The testimony of an accomplice "alone and unsupported" was not, from the middle of the eighteenth century, sufficient to secure a conviction,[132] and defense counsel frequently objected to allowing accomplices to testify at all. In 1787 Garrow made an impassioned plea that Francis Fleming be prevented from testifying against Durham and Crowther: "He has the indemnity of the magistrate, having admitted him as a witness, and he cannot now be prosecuted. My Lord, you have no testimony to confirm this man. . . . [T]here is not one single circumstance in the evidence that confirms this man. . . . [H]e comes here as an accomplice. . . .

My Lord, he is sent here, he does not come here. . . . I therefore humbly hope, that Mr. Fleming . . . will be sent away and his testimony rejected. I humbly hope your lordship will say, we run no risk in this case, in trusting to the baseness, the infamy, the falsity, or malicious testimony of a man who confesses himself unworthy to live in society."[133] A few years earlier, however, when Silvester had similarly objected to an accomplice testifying, Garrow had countered, "If that is to be objected to witnesses, every third person may deprive the King of his witnesses."[134]

Unable to exclude Crown witnesses, defense counsel did their best to discredit them. Thus Garrow, employed for the defense in *R. v. Langford* (1788), addressed Robert Kimber, a witness for the prosecution, as follows:

> This is an unexpected pleasure to you to get into this part of the Court [the witness box rather than the dock]?—It is.
> How long have you been in Newgate?—About a week.
> They talked of sending you to Botany Bay for seven years; did not they—I was afraid so.
> So you are swearing now to get yourself out of a scrape?—Yes.[135]

"Swearing to get out of a scrape" was one incentive to perjured testimony; another was the government's rewards system. Defense counsel were keen to sniff out, expose, and discredit those who prosecuted or gave evidence in the hope of financial gain. "When you came into court, did you not expect, and believe, that you should share the reward?" is a question found over and over again in the eighteenth-century OBSP.[136] Justice personnel were not immune from temptation: in 1786, for example, a runner attached to one of the rotation offices "offended the Court" by straining the evidence against the prisoner, who stood accused of a robbery.[137] In the 1780s *The Times* appears to have been convinced that such behavior was the rule rather than the exception where Bow Street was concerned. The £40 reward for a successful conviction, "though unquestionably well intended by the Legislature, to encourage prosecutors to bring offenders to justice, makes some men look rather too sharp in criminal prosecutions."[138]

Counsel were much better able to detect and reveal perjured evidence than were defendants, and the most severe of their cross-examinations were reserved for persons who came into court determined to lie under oath. In one complicated case (1786) a notorious offender, Robert Jacques, added a twist to this scenario by bringing a false prosecution (at Hicks' Hall) for perjury against John Lacy, with respect to an affidavit made in a Chancery suit. Before the jury was sworn, John Silvester, acting for Lacy, brought charges against Jacques for altering the indictment after the grand jury had found a true bill. Garrow, Jacques's counsel, said he could not proceed with the case if what Silvester alleged were true. When it was proved the record had been altered, "Mr. Silvester rose and said, he thought it a duty he owed the public to bring such men to justice, and therefore he would, in order to prosecute Jacques and Crosley, come forward without a fee; and that he would take the conduct of the prosecution upon himself." MacNally and several other counsel instantly made the same offer.[139]

Defense counsel were frequently instrumental in ensuring that those who attempted to pervert the course of justice were themselves prosecuted. In *R. v. Joseph Percival* (1787) and *R. v. Robert Percival* (1792),[140] for example, Garrow moved that witnesses be committed for perjury, while at the conclusion of the trial of John Burrows (1790) he asked for a copy of the indictment so that his acquitted client could proceed against the prosecutor, William Moore. Burrows's trial was reported only in the "squib" format, so details of the case itself are lost,[141] but Garrow, incensed on behalf of his client, waxed so eloquent that the shorthand writer devoted an entire page to reproducing his application to the judge, thus affording a rare instance of his rhetorical style:

> *Mr. Garrow.* May it please your Lordship; my Lord, I stand at this moment in a situation, in which I hardly know how to address myself with proper decorum to the Court, because I have to night experienced one of the most uncomfortable scenes that can belong to human nature, in the course of having been called upon as a feeble and very unworthy member of a very honourable profession, to endeavour to preserve the life of a fellow subject; and I have had the good fortune to assist an enlightened jury; I have had the good fortune to be (without any of the affectation of those who talk of the divinity of their nature) able to defeat as nefarious, as abandoned, and as profligate a prosecution as the annals of human depravity can afford; but, my lord, my duty will not permit me to stop here, and your lordship, I will be bold to say, would not do your duty if you caused me to stop here, if you denied me the requisition I ask: my lord, without meaning to give any offence (for it cannot be my interest, and it is not my inclination) I DEMAND of your lordship, that this innocent, this injured, this oppressed man, whose life has been attacked by perjury . . . may be furnished with the means of further vindicating his injured innocence; your lordship knows, you have the means of damming up the fountain of justice; and though he would not have had much to lament, I agree, after the reparation which he has already had; after twelve of his fellow citizens; careful, intelligent, enlightened men, hearing this prosecutor's story; after such a

jury have, without any directions from your lordship, without any witnesses to his character; with hearing half his case; when they have said, that they cannot see it necessary to continue the trial any longer; God knows, the prisoner is a happy man, and may retire with comfort and satisfaction. . . . My lord, I ask no commitment of this prosecutor for perjury, I repeat it, for *murderous perjury*; let him go to his bed with that peace he can enjoy; I do not ask you to set him in the pillory; I do not ask you to confine him within those walls, though he is the only man in court who does not feel that he deserves such punishment, for the wickedness of that perjury, which must have been fatal to the life of that innocent man, if indeed the ways of providence were not above the ways of those weak, miserable mortals, who fancy they can elude its all-searching eye; my lord, all I ask is, that you do not deprive the man at the bar of the means of applying to the future justice of the country; your lordship knows, that without a copy of the indictment Mr. Burrows cannot maintain an action against this prosecutor, which, by your lordship's granting that copy, and the assistance of some generous public spirits . . . he may be enabled to maintain, and to prove, that a malicious prosecutor he was; that aimed a shaft at the life of an innocent man; and to call for a satisfaction before twelve other men, in the character of a civil jury; my lord, will any body say this is not a demand of justice? Let this man put his defense on the record; let him justify his conduct and join issue with us on the fact; I desire to meet an English jury; I desire to come to an investigation, that is all I ask; I ask only the means of bringing an action, which I pledge myself the poverty of Mr. Burrows shall not prevent his prosecuting with effect.[142]

Garrow was indeed, as James Scarlett described him, "an eloquent scolder." Scarlett also accused the star of the Old Bailey of being overly theatrical and prone to "affected arrangement,"[143] but there can be little doubt that Garrow, like Silvester and other members of the Old Bailey's bar, was genuinely outraged by perjury, which struck at the heart of justice. It was in all likelihood the subject and occasion of Garrow's speech, as well as its style, moreover, that attracted the attention of the shorthand writer.

Conclusion

As described in Chapter 1, the entry of the lawyers into felony proceedings was the result of a set of circumstances peculiar to the eighteenth century. In those circumstances defense counsel, in particular, made a substantial contribution to both truth and justice. As long as the death penalty

attached to felonies, and the reward system continued, the lives of innocent men and women were in danger. Through the exposure of perjured
testimony and false or malicious prosecution, barristers did much to reveal the absolute truth, to uncover facts that prosecutors and witnesses
had endeavored to subvert or conceal. In other cases the efforts of counsel promoted justice, for in the era of the "Bloody Code" the "truth" of
the crime was only one issue at trial: the jury had also to decide whether
what the defendant had done merited the death penalty. "Too much truth,"
in this period, "meant too much death."[144] "Pious perjury" in the form
of partial verdicts, in which juries acquitted the accused of the indicted
offense but convicted him on a lesser, noncapital charge contained within
it, uncommon in the Elizabethan-Jacobean period, was frequently found
in the eighteenth-century courtroom.[145] The establishment of a secondary punishment—transportation—and an increased aversion to the death
penalty allowed for this development, and counsel undoubtedly encouraged
the practice. The OBSP contain numerous examples of appeals to humanity
or exposure of its absence. Garrow, for instance, dealt severely with a witness
testifying against Elizabeth Holmes:

> *Mr. Garrow.* I will only ask you, after the last observation you made
> with a smile, whether you know that this case affects the life of the pris-
> oner?—That is not material; I have told nothing but the truth.
>
> You mean to state, at the time you made a not very decent nor a very
> pertinent observation, you knew that this case affects the life of the
> prisoner?—I do not know; I am not sure that I do.
>
> Do you not know that this is an indictment calculated to affect her
> life?—It may be.
>
> Do you not know that it is?—I do not understand that it is so.
>
> Do you expect a jury more likely to credit you, when you declare
> that it is immaterial to you, whether the woman is to be executed in
> consequence of your evidence, or not?

Holmes, charged with stealing from a dwelling house goods to the value of
£5, was convicted only to the value of thirty-nine shillings (forty shillings
or more would have demanded the death penalty), sentenced to be imprisoned twelve months, and fined a shilling.[146] In *R. v. Collings* (1795) Newman
Knowlys asked the prosecutor directly to reconsider the value he had placed
on goods stolen from him: "Perhaps you would change the selling price on
them, you have put them at three pounds in the indictment, but perhaps,
you would not put them at above thirty-nine shillings, where a man's life is
at stake?" The prosecutor objected that the items in question would sell for

much more, but Knowlys pressed the point home: "It is very hard to pay your profit with our lives." The jury found Collings guilty of theft to the value of thirty-nine shillings, and he was thus sentenced to be transported rather than hanged.[147]

While the activities of defense counsel may in some instances have resulted in the acquittal of the guilty, they also corrected problems introduced by the reward system and ameliorated the effects of a severe criminal code. Despite these contributions to the administration of justice, however, criminal counsel were not celebrated. And as we will see in the following chapters, neither the bench, the bar, nor the public anticipated or desired any further expansion of their duties.

CHAPTER FIVE

Public Reaction
and Professional Concerns

The Old Bailey Bar and the Press

The gradual emergence of Old Bailey counsel coincided with a marked expansion of the periodical press, which, in the turbulent opening years of the reign of George III, acquired a new power and influence.[1] Forerunners of the newspaper had first appeared in London in the 1620s,[2] while the first daily paper, the *Daily Courant*, was published in 1702. Both the number of papers and their circulation grew over the course of the eighteenth century. In 1770 London had five daily papers plus a number of others published on a weekly and triweekly basis; by the 1780s there were nine dailies, eight triweeklies, and about nine weekly papers; by the 1790s the number of dailies had risen to fourteen, with a further seven papers published triweekly and two weekly. Jeremy Black estimates that in 1782 25,000 papers were produced each day, and that each paper was read by twenty or more people for a total readership of 500,000.[3] Hannah Barker argues more cautiously for a readership half that size. Her figure of 250,000 readers remains a sizable proportion of London's total population (750,000 in 1780), and although that readership corresponds roughly to estimates of the size of London's "middling classes," Barker argues against conflating the two: newspaper readers were socially diverse.[4] Perhaps the best portrait of eighteenth-century newspaper readers is that provided by Bob Harris, who describes them as occupying "a series of concentric circles, with the smallest circle signifying the parliamentary classes, a larger circle their allies among the gentry, clergy, and urban elites, and even yet larger circles signifying the middling sort and those on their lower boundaries, the skilled working classes."[5]

Although the space allocated to advertisements roughly equaled that apportioned to news, newspaper revenues derived primarily from circulation: owners were thus motivated to address issues that would attract readers in high numbers. Britain was almost constantly at war in the late eighteenth century, and foreign affairs were afforded considerable coverage. Domestic politics also featured prominently, and Parliament's ceding of control over reports of its proceedings in 1771 allowed the newspaper press access to a regular source of copy while Parliament was in session.[6] Andrew and McGowen argue that the press had by the 1770s instigated a transformation of the political world. This transformation was achieved in part, however, by appealing to the public's appetite for "the sensational and salacious": discussion of serious issues of policy was combined with virulent personal abuse of ministers.[7] Crime and criminal justice could, like politics, be counted on to boost circulation, and coverage of those topics displayed a similar dichotomy. Lurid accounts of crime and criminals are guaranteed to attract readership in any age, and by the mid-eighteenth century pamphlet accounts of trials and biographies of notorious criminals had long been popular with the public.[8] Newspaper coverage of crime and punishment continued a well-established tradition in that sensational trials—such as those of the Perreau brothers and Mrs. Rudd in 1775—were reported and discussed in minute detail.[9] Columns entitled "Bow Street Intelligence" and "Old Bailey Intelligence" were likewise a feature in most papers. Reporting of the more routine proceedings tended to be cursory, frequently consisting of a single paragraph citing the number of persons who had been tried and sentenced,[10] and in some instances little more than a statement to the effect that nothing worthy of attention had occurred.[11] Gruesome details that emerged in a trial for murder occasionally swelled these columns. In 1762, for example, the *Gazeteer and London Daily Advertiser* reported some of the "acts of inhumanity" perpetrated by Sarah Metyard and Sarah Morgan Metyard, convicted for the murder of their apprentice, as well as details of their execution.[12] But anxiety about rising crime rates and the apparent failure of the criminal justice system to detect, apprehend, convict, and adequately punish criminals also fueled interest in more serious discussion of criminal administration.

While the newspaper press was clearly willing to cater to the public's desire for gory detail, it offered as well a forum in which the operation of criminal justice could be examined, for the papers did not merely report the news, they allowed the public to participate in debates about current affairs. It is now commonly acknowledged that the newspaper press was instrumental in creating a "public sphere," although opinion is divided as to the timing of this development. Jürgen Habermas identified 1694–95 as the critical period, but the emergence of popular political opinion and debate has subsequently been pushed back as far as the 1640s, or even earlier.[13] Some of this public debate took place in coffee houses and other public spaces in which individuals could discuss what they had read. But debate also occurred within the newspapers themselves, for apart from the papers' own reports and editorial comment significant space was allotted to correspondence. As Jeremy Black indicates, limited financial resources and small numbers of staff meant that the newspapers happily accepted contributions from their readers and printed them with a minimum of editorial intervention.[14] The papers thus disseminated the opinions of members of the public as well as informing that opinion. Where criminal justice was concerned, discussion ranged over a broad array of issues, among which policing and capital punishment were prominent.

In the 1780s England's criminal justice system was in a state of crisis. At the close of the war with America in 1782 prosecution rates soared, while the same conflict had effectively terminated the transportation of convicted criminals.[15] During this crisis the City of London continued to pin its faith in the deterrent effect of public execution. In his address to the capital convicts at the close of the Old Bailey's January sessions in 1785 the recorder warned that "crimes were become so numerous and notorious, that exemplary punishments were essentially necessary to preserve the public safety and tranquillity." The laws of England, he said, "were not laws of vengeance, designed to torture the expiring offender, but intended to deter the survivors from the commission of similar malefactions."[16] The "Bloody Code," however, was consistently attacked in the press. The *St. James Chronicle* reported the "shocking Spectacle" that ensued at the close of that particular sessions, in which "twenty miserable Wretches were, in one Moment, plunged into eternity. . . . So great a number had not been executed at one time since the Year 1740."[17] *The Times* similarly lamented the existence of a criminal code that was both barbarous and ineffective: "If any man still entertains a doubt of the insufficiency of our police for the prevention of crimes, let him only read the long and dreadful list of persons ordered for execution on Wednesday next. Every country in Europe will hear of it with astonishment; they will naturally suppose, that in England there is no more government, than in a horde of wandering Tartars, or among the Arabian banditti."[18] *The Times* recommended a fundamental revision of the nation's sanguinary laws.[19] England executed more criminals in the space of a year than all the cities in Europe put together,[20] and every sessions at the Old Bailey held forth the "melancholy prospect of carnage."[21] The frequency of public hangings and the number of persons hanged served to demonstrate that England's laws were "calculated solely to punish, and not to prevent the commission of crimes."[22] The paper urged instead the establishment of penitentiary houses—existing prisons were merely "seminaries of

guilt"—in which solitary confinement and "proper instruction" would produce genuine repentance,[23] and it cautiously applauded the opening of a new
penal colony in Botany Bay.[24]

The concern expressed was not solely humanitarian, for while *The Times*
deplored the carnage of the mass executions which followed the close of each
Old Bailey sessions, it was equally unhappy with the "prevailing evil" of frequent pardons, which loosed upon the public "swarms of felons" who were
sure to offend again.[25] The *St. James Chronicle* similarly noted with horror
that more than six hundred persons were scheduled to be tried for felonies
at the Lent assizes in 1785.[26] Magistrates were repeatedly encouraged to pay
greater attention to lesser offenders: "[T]o nip the bud of vice in its earliest stage is sounder policy, than to let the fruit ripen to maturity."[27] The
press also constantly drew attention to the dangers posed by public houses
and public drunkenness ("ebriety," to use the contemporary term) and asked
that licensing laws be more rigorously enforced.

Crime and the administration of criminal justice had become central pre-
occupations of the London press by the 1780s, and the newspapers commented extensively on the causes of criminal behavior, the activities of
metropolitan magistrates, London's overcrowded gaols, public execution,
and England's capital code in general. Both reform of the criminal law and
protection of the liberties of the English subject were very much in the public eye. The right of a defendant in a felony trial to employ legal counsel,
however, was not. The introduction of counsel to the criminal trial in the
eighteenth century seems to have attracted little contemporary reaction,
and the emergence of a criminal bar in London went largely unremarked by
a press that demonstrated enormous concern for virtually every other as-
pect of the criminal justice system. The papers rarely commented on the
activities of counsel in the criminal courts. Their presence was occasionally noted, and sometimes the gist of a cross-examination or an objection
raised was reported, but little judgment was passed by the press on the innovation of counsel. William Garrow's ascendancy at the Old Bailey certainly
attracted notice,[28] but his success served primarily as a subject for jests—
witness the following extracts from *The Times*:

> *A set down.*—I say to you once again, *Feller*, (says *Garrow*,)—at the Old
> Bailey—my honest friend,—are not you a *Thief Taker*?—"Vell, vat if I
> am," said honest *Nob*,—nattily enough—"an't you a Thief's Counsel—
> so there's *tit* for *tat*."[29]

> Judge —— asked a brother Judge after dinner, what he thought of Mr.
> Garrow's speech—think, says the other—"I think it is like a race horse,
> it runs fast because it *carries a feather*."[30]

Or, in a column entitled "Extraordinary Wants" (for Fox, the office of prime minister, for example): "WANTED by Mr. *Garrow*, more wisdom and less loquacity."[31]

While both the papers and the public clearly found Garrow amusing, there is no evidence to suggest that the eighteenth-century English public wanted or expected to see the criminal trial transformed into a professional contest, or that the bar itself was pushing in this direction. Individual defendants requested in court to be allowed to make their full defense by counsel, and reference was occasionally made in various public forums to the imbalance which had resulted from the entry of counsel for the prosecution and the unfairness of a system that allowed prosecuting counsel to make speeches but prohibited defense counsel from doing so. In Henry Fielding's novel *Tom Jones* (1749), for instance, the schoolmaster Partridge remarks, "It is indeed charming sport to hear trials upon life and death. One thing I own I thought a little hard, that the prisoner's counsel was not suffered to speak for him, though he desired only to be heard one very short word; but my lord would not hearken to him, though he suffered a counsellor to talk against him above half an hour."[32] Whether Fielding himself thought that defense counsel ought to be allowed to address the jury is another matter entirely. High-profile criminal trials, such as those of the Perreau brothers and Mrs. Rudd for forgery, might have attracted some attention to the issue.[33] A lengthy defense of Robert Perreau published in the *Public Advertiser* on 21 August 1775, which subjected England's criminal law to a wide-ranging critique, opened with a complaint that persons accused of capital offenses were denied the right to counsel.[34] But such complaints were few and far between. While, in 1781, Coachmakers' Hall advertised in the *Morning Chronicle* a debate on the question "Is that part of our criminal law just, which prevents a prisoner from making a *full defence*, as well as to matters of *fact*, as to matters of law by Council?,"[35] the issue was not taken up by the press itself.

It might be argued that the relative silence on the subject of prisoners' counsel owes in part to class prejudice: the bourgeois newspaper-reading public may simply have been uninterested in the rights of the poor, the illiterate, and the disreputable persons who made up a large portion of those who appeared in the dock at the Old Bailey and in other courts. Yet they were interested in reducing the severity of the punishment meted out to many of these individuals, and for humanitarian as well as utilitarian reasons; bourgeois callousness is therefore unlikely to explain the lack of public interest in prisoners' counsel. The public was also clearly interested in the rights of those placed under arrest and the treatment of prisoners by magistrates.[36]

Middlesex and Westminster justices of the peace were suspected of routinely ignoring constitutional principles, resulting in "extraordinary, peculiar, and novel oppressions."[37] Mainwaring's police bill of 1785, which would have empowered constables to search on suspicion and increased summary jurisdiction, was denounced as a threat to "that great bulwark of liberty, trial by jury,"[38] and when the bill failed *The Times* advocated that its rejection should be followed by an act to regulate the offices of the justices of the peace.[39] Where the criminal trial was concerned, however, the overriding public concern as evidenced by the newspaper press was, as described in Chapter 2, not the rights of prisoners but the grave problems posed to justice by perjury.

The Reputation of Lawyers

On the rare occasions when the issue of defense counsel was raised among the general public the concern was principally one of fairness: powerful prosecutors like the Bank of England routinely engaged counsel for the prosecution, and where counsel on one side were a fact it seemed unjust to prohibit counsel—or to allow only limited participation—to the other. Working against this sense of fair play, however, was the reputation of lawyers. To the men and women he defended, an Old Bailey barrister, whether gentleman or "bar-bully," must have appeared as a potential savior, standing as he often did between the prisoner and the gallows or the convict ship. One felon, considering his options while being held pre-trial, was overheard deliberating as to the counsel he would choose if charged with the crime. Peter Alley was his initial choice: "If I get committed for the job, I will have a counsel; I will have Alley." But he later reconsidered: "Knapp is a d——d good one, he will bother some of them."[40] Similarly, when John Disney, accused of forging and uttering a promissory note, was advised by his attorney to go before Bow Street magistrate Sir Sampson Wright, his unnamed companion said, "[N]o, we will not go into the lion's mouth, we will go first and consult Mr. Garrow."[41] Counsel knew the criminal law, and they knew the legal system; they could expose, through vigorous cross-examination, any weaknesses in the evidence or discreditable motives of witnesses and prosecutors. They could also be kind. A pickpocket once cursed William Bodkin in court for prosecuting him, but he was instantly commanded by a codefendant to hold his tongue: "[T]hat toff in the klobber wig often defended my old mother and arter the case was over, he'd slip the fee back into 'er 'and and say, ' 'Ere you want it more nor I do.' "[42] Garrow, during his roughly ten-year reign at the Old Bailey, must have assumed the stature of a folk hero, as John Adolphus did some twenty years later. Adolphus's daughter Emily told a story of her father being recognized while making his way home from his chambers one night: "[As he was] walking through St. Giles's [a notoriously dangerous neighborhood] by way of a short cut . . . an Irish woman came up to him. 'Why, Misther Adolphus! and who'd a'thought of seeing you in the Holy Ground?' 'And how are you to know who I am?' said my father. 'Lord bless and save ye, Sir! not know ye? Why I'd know ye if ye was boiled up in soup!' "[43] When Emily married a few months after her father's death, she found a crowd waiting for her outside the church: "I was astonished at the number of very common-looking people who crowded round the church door and looked at me with such unusual interest, some making remarks such as 'I would not have missed seeing his daughter for the world.' "[44] Outside of the circle of their clients, however, the Old Bailey bar enjoyed a much more checkered reputation. As David Lemmings has commented, "Even the humblest Englishman seems to have been certain of his superior 'birthright' to liberty and justice under the common law, normally identified with freedom from arbitrary arrest and trial by a jury of his peers in the event of prosecution at the suit of the Crown."[45] But if the English exalted the rule of law they looked with a jaundiced eye on legal practitioners, and the mixed reputation of the legal profession must have disinclined the public to look to their increased participation in the criminal trial as a means of advancing truth and justice.

Public mistrust of lawyers has a long history, and in England the stereotype of the greedy, grasping, deceitful, and dishonest lawyer had been firmly in place since the Middle Ages.[46] Hostility is said to have escalated from the late sixteenth century, when the legal profession had experienced considerable growth in size, influence, and social status.[47] The established elite—clergy and gentry—may have both envied and resented the sudden rise of competitors. But lawyers were also seen as disruptive of society, promoting conflicts so that they became legal actions and prolonging those actions to their own financial advantage. In the late seventeenth century the public image of the legal profession suffered also from the "political pliancy" of many of its leading members. Royal manipulation of the judiciary threatened the integrity of the bar; the "coarseness and gross partiallity" of chief justices George Jeffreys and William Scroggs and the tendency of at least some counsel to fawn on them inevitably cast a shadow over the entire profession.[48] It is possible that standards of practice improved by the early eighteenth century: changes in the constitutional position of judges created an image of judicial impartiality and dignity that filtered down to the bar. It has also been suggested that the distinction in both institutional base and function of the barrister and the attorney or solicitor that occurred after

1660 enabled the bar to assume both intellectual and social superiority over the lower branch of the profession, the "pettyfoggers and vipers" of the law, who continued to attract opprobrium.[49] The Inns of Court, from which attorneys were excluded by the mid-sixteenth century, became associated with the academic training of an elite, and snobbish distinctions arose between the theoretical learning and liberal education of barristers and the purely "mechanical" learning or apprenticeship undertaken by attorneys, which did not allow them to participate in the association of law and gentility. Certainly attorneys enjoyed little public reputation. Hence Samuel Johnson's curt dismissal of someone whose name had come up in conversation: Johnson "did not care to speak ill of any man behind his back, but he believed the gentleman was an *attorney*."[50] "An Attorney at Law was indicted," *The Times* reported in a similar spirit, "on the Oxford Circuit, for stealing a silver punch ladle.—The Counsel for the Crown making some sarcastic remarks on the prisoner, the Judge said to the Counsel, in a whisper, 'Don't make the matter worse than it is; for if the fellow had been an Attorney, you may depend upon it, he would have taken the bowl too."[51]

Where criminal practitioners were concerned, the strongest attack at mid-century was indeed aimed not against the upper branch of the legal profession but at solicitors or attorneys, specifically, at the sinister figure of the "Newgate solicitor." A pamphlet published in 1728 warned that prosecuting solicitors at the Old Bailey were involved in a variety of nefarious practices. They would, "for a Fee from the Prisoner, advise the Prosecutor to compound the Felony before Sessions, or not to appear" (nonappearance of a prosecutor itself constituted a felony).[52] Newgate solicitors were further accused of bribing or attempting to bribe juries, of bringing false prosecutions, and of coaching witnesses.[53] Henry Fielding refers in *Tom Jones* to "those sages of the law, called Newgate solicitors" who treat with disdain the qualms of conscience of a young witness.[54] He subsequently comments in passing on pretrial preparation: "There is nothing so dangerous as a question which comes by surprize on a man, whose business it is to conceal truth, or to defend falsehood. For which reason those worldly personages, whose noble office it is to save the lives of their fellow creatures at the Old-Bailey, take the utmost care, by frequent previous examination, to divine every question, which may be asked their clients on the day of trial, that they may be supply'd with proper and ready answers, which the most fertile invention cannot supply in an instant."[55] The Newgate solicitor subverted rather than revealed the truth, and encouraged rather than prevented perjury.

Barristers too, although their reputation may have marginally improved during the Augustan period, continued to attract abuse, remaining targets of criticism on grounds established centuries earlier. In fact, by the late eighteenth century the bar suffered "a crisis of unpopularity."[56] *The Times* from its inception contained various barbs directed at lawyers, of which the following is typical: "A foreign Gentleman supposed the *Temple*—from its name to be a place of worship, particularly as a Divine was supposed to be the master of it; but, on being informed that nobody lived there at present but Lawyers, though it was originally a holy place, he archly replied, 'well, we may wish to say with the scriptures, this *was* my House, but *now* you have made it a den of thieves.'"[57] Eighteenth-century satirical prints reveal two recurring themes where the lawyer is concerned: greed and a close association with the devil. Two prints dating from around 1760 contrast the prosperous lawyer with his penurious client, while others portray the devil handing out briefs on the first day of term, acting as the lawyer's agent, and supervising the winding up of accounts.[58] Greed, as even Bentham would admit, was generally not a charge that could be levied at the fledgling criminal bar. Unlike property law, the criminal law afforded few opportunities for barristers to fleece their clients, who tended for the most part to be very poor. But when William Davy was called to task by his brothers for disgracing the profession by "taking silver from a client"—that is, for accepting a brief for a fee of less than a guinea—his response was: "I took silver because I could not get gold, but I took every farthing the fellow had in the world, and I hope you don't call *that* disgracing the profession."[59]

The most common criticism levied at those members of the bar who practiced at the Old Bailey, however, involved not greediness for fees but lack of manners. The way in which they conducted cross-examinations, in particular, often attracted public censure. Davy's defense of Mrs. Rudd provides an example of the type of criticism that would increasingly be expressed. His cross-examination of prosecution witness Mrs. Perreau was denounced in the press: Davy had been so "extremely abrupt," his manner and language so cruel, as to reduce the witness at least to tears, some said to fainting.[60] Jury members or spectators in the public gallery might occasionally thrill to the eloquence of a particular advocate or admire a well-executed cross-examination. Often, however, the public condemned the aggression typical of counsel at the Old Bailey. In 1786 *The Times* reported an exchange heard at that court: "An evidence . . . swore positively to the identity of a culprit merely from the recollection of his voice. It is somewhat singular, said Mr. Sylvester, that you should speak so decidedly from such a circumstance: Pray did his voice bear any resemblance to mine? Oh Lord! no Sir replied the man with the utmost *naievete*, for *he* addressed me very *politely*."[61] The following year the paper reported: "An Old Bailey Barrister has received a

"Being nervous and cross-examined by Mr. Garrow"
(Copyright The British Museum)

letter from a Gentleman, who lately fell to his lot in a cross examination, couched in terms to provoke resentment, while it cautiously avoids any expression which may be food for litigation. Whether the lawyer will *gorge* the pill, or not, has not yet transpired."[62] In all likelihood the barrister in question was William Garrow; if so, the letter in question was not the last he would receive on the subject of his behavior in court. Ten years later Matthew Concannen would publish a letter addressed to Garrow "On the Subject of his Illiberal Behaviour to the Author" during a civil trial, in which he referred to "the arts by which professional dignity is brought into contempt, engendered in *low debating societies*, and brought forth in the schools of *scrutinizing virulence*."[63] Yet another *Letter to William Garrow, Esquire* was published in 1808, *in which*, the title continued, *the Conduct of Counsel in the Cross-examination of Witnesses and Commenting on their Testimony is fully discussed, and the Licentiousness of the Bar Exposed*.[64] Hague's examples were drawn primarily from civil cases tried in the Court of King's Bench, but the practices he condemned were bred, he claimed, in "spouting clubs" and at the Old Bailey, the "cradle" of Garrow's oratory. Hague described Garrow as pert, vulgar, and garrulous and argued that the "brutal insolence" and "wanton scurrility" he employed in cross-examining witnesses wounded private feelings, insulted the dignity of the court, and violated public decorum; more important, it tended to disrupt the ends of justice.[65]

Garrow's successors at the Old Bailey would be subject to the same kinds of attack. Michael Prendergast once so incensed the foreman of a jury by his cross-examination of a witness that the foreman stood up and shouted that "he would rather be robbed of any amount than act as a witness and be browbeaten by counsel."[66] The behavior of prosecuting counsel was less frequently the subject of censure, but in 1790 *The Times* devoted roughly a quarter of a column to the "Impudence of Counsel in a Prosecution": "The liberties taken by Gentlemen of the long robe in charging a defendant with more than he has committed—with blackening his character to a Jury, and endeavour to do all in their power to aggravate his crime by the introduction of matter not in the record, have long been complained of as a most intolerable grievance. . . . [T]he Gentlemen of the tailed wig and black gown are licensed to abuse and vilify any man in open Court."[67]

Similar criticisms may be found in the early nineteenth century: the lay press delighted in reporting the occasional "legal fracas" and "curious scenes" at the Old Bailey.[68] Some members of the public, however, were willing to acknowledge that aggressive cross-examinations might contribute to a determination of the truth. Sydney Smith dismissed criticisms of ungentlemanly behavior in no uncertain terms:

> Of what importance is a little disgust at professional tricks, if the solid advantage gained is a nearer approximation to truth? Can anything be more prepostrous than this preference of taste to justice, and of solemnity to truth? What a eulogium of a trial to say, "I am by no means satisfied that the jury were right in finding the prisoner guilty; but everything was carried on with the utmost decorum. The verdict was wrong; but there was the most perfect propriety and order in the proceedings. The man will be unfairly hanged; but all was genteel!" If solemnity is what is principally wanted in a court of justice, we had better study the manners of the old Spanish Inquisition; but if battles with the Judge, and battles among the counsel are the best method, as they certainly are, of getting at the truth, better tolerate the philosophical Billingsgate than persevere, *because* the life of a man is at stake, in solemn and polished unjustice.[69]

But not everyone was convinced that "battles among counsel" were the best way of arriving at the truth.

The absence of a public campaign for the right of defense counsel to make speeches is not surprising, given the public's suspicion of paid advocacy. In *Gulliver's Travels* (1726) Jonathan Swift described the bar as "a society of men . . . bred up from their youth in the art of proving by words multiplied for the purpose, that white is black, and black is white, according as they are paid."[70] The criticism was a persistent one. The same sentiment was expressed by Robert Southey, among others, in a poem published more than a hundred years later: the lawyer "proves by reason in reason's despite / That right is wrong, and wrong is right, / And white is black and black is white."[71] Barristers would happily argue any position provided that they received their fee, and loyalty to the client, that tenet of modern professionalism, was believed to preclude loyalty to the truth. "Lawyers like soldiers of fortune," wrote *The Times*, "never trouble themselves about the justice of the cause they are engaged in; and they gain superior advantages from endeavouring to make a bad cause appear like a good one."[72] There was no humor in that paper's report that Garrow was preparing for a political career: "Some of the papers have been recommending Mr. *Garrow* as a proper person to sit in the House of Commons;—God forbid, says the writer of this, that any such an event should ever take place.—There are too many lawyers there already,—too many speakers whose bread depends upon letting out their voice to any purchaser, and . . . to either and so both sides of the question, arguing, that *black was white* one day, and that the very same white was black the next day. We want men of independence, of honour, and not of oratory and loquaciousness in the House of Commons."[73]

   Accusations of lawyerly indifference to or deliberate misrepresentation of the truth in the criminal trial were relatively infrequent in the pre–Prisoners' Counsel Act era, when the scope of advocacy remained limited. Nevertheless, the talents of Old Bailey counsel were thought by some to be as often employed in "perplexing and confounding witnesses," in suppressing the truth and suggesting the false, as they were in revealing the true facts of a case. A satirical print tentatively dated 1789 depicted "The Old Bailey Advocate Bringing Off a Thief," in which the barrister's brief is labeled "Insinuations versus Truth," and Truth is being vigorously trampled under the counsel's foot. The poem below the cartoon reads:

> Did not the Felon firmly fix his hope
> On flaw or jaw, and so escape the rope,
> Justly he'd meet that Fate without reprieve,
> (Which comes when Advocate fails to deceive,)
> Or, doom made sure for want of quibling aid
> He'd quit bad ways to seek an honest trade.[74]

"The Old Bailey Advocate Bringing Off a Thief," eighteenth-century evidence of public mistrust of paid advocacy—and advocates—in the criminal courts (Copyright The British Museum)

Reflections published in Knapp and Baldwin's *Newgate Calendar* on "the comparative functions of the JUDGES and COUNSELLORS" were likewise less than complimentary to the bar:

> The *Judge* labours to discover the truth.
> The *Pleader* takes pains to conceal or disguise it.
> The *Judge* seeks that medium which is the seat of equity.
> The *Pleader* contends for extremes.
> The *Judge* must act up to the strict letter of the law, severe, rigid, and inflexible, in some cases—merciful in others.
> The *Pleader* is supple, pliant, fawning, flattering his client, and espousing his interest.
> The *Judge*, constant, uniform, invariable.
> The *Pleader*, ever changing sides.
> The *Judge* divests himself of passions.
> The *Pleader* assumes them, and endeavours to raise them in others.
> The *Judge* holds an even balance in the scales of Justice; but
> The *Pleader* ever endeavours to make one or the other preponderate.[75]

The theme of lawyers' deceptive practices was taken up by the essayist William Hazlitt, who wrote in 1816 that "the lawyer's business" was to "confound truth and falsehood in the minds of his hearers" and that, as a "natural" consequence, he confounded them in his own: the "confirmed habit of looking at any side of a question with a view to make the worse appear the better reason . . . must make truth and falsehood sit loose upon him, and lead him to 'look on both indifferently,' at his convenience." Hazlitt then offered a highly jaundiced view of Garrow's performance in the House of Commons in support of his position:

> We have heard him stringing contradictions there with the fluency of water, every third sentence giving the lie to the two former; gabbling folly as if it were the last opportunity he might ever have, and as regularly put down as he rose up—not for false statements, not for false reasoning, nor for common-place absurdities or vulgar prejudices, (there is enough of these to be found there without going to the bar), but for such things as nobody but a lawyer could utter, and as nobody (not even a lawyer) could believe. . . . [N]o one there but a lawyer fancies himself holding a brief in his hand as a *carte blanche* for vanity and impertinence—no one else thinks he has got an *ad libitum* right to express any absurd or nonsensical opinions he pleases, because he is not supposed to hold the opinions he expresses.[76]

A decade later (at roughly the same time, that is, that the Reverend Sydney Smith was defending defense counsel) John Stuart Mill likewise weighed in against the lawyers in a speech prepared for a debate on whether their influence was not "pernicious to Morals Jurisprudence & Government":

> We hear lawyers continually talking of themselves as the guardians of justice, the defenders of innocence, and so forth, and they are right to put the best face upon the thing as people usually do when they are giving an account of themselves. It would not quite do to stand forward and say "I live by roguery." But amid all this fine language one thing is always forgotten, that to every cause there are two sides, and that of these one only can be the right. At least one half therefore of a lawyer's business is deception, and avowedly so. . . . Even when a cause is good a lawyer has not done his duty by it unless he has given it all the gloss and varnish of which it is susceptible, disguised all its weak parts and heightened its strong ones by artificial colouring. Not one half only but three-fourths at least of his business is deception. Sir, it is not easy for a man who gets his bread by insincerity to remain entirely free from it in his other concerns; it is not easy for him one half of whose life is spent in making the worse appear the better cause, and the other half in making the good cause appear better than it is, to retain that simplicity and singleness of purpose, that passionate love of truth and abhorrence of artifice and deceit without which, in my estimation at least, there can be no perfect character. Supposing even the purity of his intentions to remain unimpaired, yet the habit of making falsehood plausible begets a coolness with regard to the interests of truth. . . . [When] no part of their daily occupation tends to strengthen those faculties of their minds which would enable them to distinguish falsehood from truth, they soon begin to fancy that they cannot be distinguished . . . and that truth is placed beyond the reach of the human faculties. This state of the intellectual part of their minds co-operating with the diminished sensibility of the moral part, they soon learn to be utterly indifferent what opinions they take up and advocate; and where their interest is not concerned they are determined by mere vanity and choose that side of a question which affords the greatest scope for their ingenuity, that is most commonly the wrong side.[77]

Spanning a hundred years, these various assertions that the activities of lawyers tend to deception, and to the suppression rather than the revelation of the truth, testify to a longstanding public mistrust of paid advocacy. In all likelihood, the lack of any concerted public agitation for prisoners' counsel owed to this mistrust.[78]

Professional Concerns

If the public was occasionally exasperated or offended by the antics of criminal counsel in the late eighteenth and early nineteenth centuries, the legal profession had its own objections to the conduct of London's emerging criminal bar. In his memoir of Garrow, Adolphus wrote that the Old Bailey barrister needed to possess "great intellectual vigour," "a learned insight into the criminal law; a discerning tact in the practice of evidence; the acquisition of a scholar and the manners of a gentleman."[79] Few of his contemporaries in the legal profession would have agreed with him. While acknowledging the need for barristers to represent both the protection of society and the rights of the accused, the bar had mixed feelings about the men who actually performed these duties. As a blanket description, "Old Bailey barrister" quickly acquired negative associations, and the posthumous reputation of most practitioners is ambiguous. One historian has written that the Old Bailey in the early nineteenth century was "regarded as a forum for dishonest hacks" and that the bar had "strong suspicions that beneath the level of a few outstanding advocates such as Phillips work was distributed to those with influence rather than ability."[80] Even the Old Bailey's outstanding advocates, however, were regarded with a degree of suspicion.

Criminal practice was considered sordid, and aspiring barristers were advised to avoid Old Bailey practice. "How ignominious the name and character of a mere Old Bailey counsel may justly appear," wrote Joseph Simpson in *Reflections on the Natural and Acquired Endowments Requisite for the Study of the Law* (1764).[81] This sentiment was expanded on some thirty years later:

> [F]ew Gentlemen of the profession chuse to make their *debut* at Hick's-hall, or the Old Bailey; it is possible they may fancy there is something *ominous* in commencing their career in those Courts; however necessary for the safety of society it may be, that there should be found Counsel to lead the prosecution; or for the defence of the prisoner's life, liberty, and reputation, that Gentlemen of the profession astute in all the law, and chicanery of the Criminal Courts, should be willing to accept a fee, and undertake his defence; yet it is not to be supposed, that a Barrister, just emerged from a Pleader's office, should be chosen for this purpose; and if chosen, it would better become him to decline the brief, unless he determines to confine his future business to what is called Old Bailey practice; by which, although it must be confessed, that many Gentlemen have acquired large incomes, with more credit to themselves, than the general reputation of the practice there would urge us to suppose; yet, on the whole, the Crown Courts are not the

cleanest to sit down in; as it is morally impossible, but that somewhat of
the dirt and pollution which so closely adhere to those wretches, who
are the objects of prosecution at the Old Bailey, must infect those also,
who by their counsel, and assistance at the Bar of that Tribunal, are the
means of these marauders mixing again in society, with all their imper-
fections on their head.[82]

The Crown side of circuit business would provide the barrister with sufficient knowledge to enable him to appear competent if engaged in criminal
business in the higher courts; not only was knowledge of Old Bailey practice
inessential to the "rising barrister," but ignorance of it "might be thought
conducive to his future fame."[83] Such opinions persisted into the nineteenth
century. Indeed, the bar's opinion of Old Bailey counsel worsened, so that
when William Ballantine began his long career at the Old Bailey in 1834,
"the mode in which business was conducted in that tribunal made it a term
of opprobrium to be called an Old Bailey barrister."[84] The *Westminster Review* commented similarly in 1835 that "the title of Old Bailey Barrister is
claimed by no one, and is generally esteemed a term of reproach."[85]

The image of the Old Bailey barrister was not an issue which the legal
profession regarded lightly, for the honor and integrity of the bar as a whole
were at stake. The problem was there were no fixed, written rules of conduct or standards guiding professional behavior in the eighteenth and early
nineteenth centuries. Daniel Duman divided an unwritten code of legal etiquette into four categories: "1. rules defining the parameters of professional
practice and the relationship between barrister and lay client; 2. restrictive
practices relating to the employment of barristers; 3. regulations concerning
the conduct of barristers on circuit; 4. rules of circuit membership."[86] The
majority of these rules were thus intended to control competition among
barristers and maintain "honourable relations" between barristers and solicitors or attorneys; they did not speak to conduct in the courtroom. Discipline of the bar, moreover, was shared among a variety of institutions. Each
of the four Inns of Court had authority over its members, exercised by the
benchers who had the (rarely used) power to "disbar" or expel a barrister
from the profession. Judges of the superior courts supervised the conduct of
barristers who appeared before them, while circuit messes, rather like clubs
for barristers attending the assize circuits, monitored the behavior of their
members while they were on circuit.[87] Each circuit had its own mess which
established its own rules and conducted "trials" for those who breached
them. The most severe sanction was expulsion from the mess, but token fines
(frequently in bottles of wine) were more usual. Expulsion, while a social

sanction, invariably affected a barrister's business: attorneys were unlikely to give briefs to a man whose character and professional integrity had been condemned by his peers.[88] The circuit messes, together with "the general sentiment of the profession,"[89] thus played an important role in the day-to-day discipline of the bar, and some attributed the problems at the Old Bailey in part to the absence of anything corresponding to the circuit mess. This criticism was acknowledged by members of the bar at that court: "[E]very man did what seemed good or profitable in his own eyes. Nothing short of being disbarred prevented his being heard, and there was no punishment for obtaining business irregularly, except professional disapprobation."[90] Bar etiquette was at its weakest at the Old Bailey as far as the legal profession was concerned, and practice at that court became a source of both anxiety and exasperation.

In the nineteenth century the subject of Old Bailey practice was frequently taken up in a new forum: the legal periodical press. When Garrow began to practice at the Old Bailey in the 1780s this press was virtually non-existent. There had been a few short-lived journals—the *Lawyer's Magazine* (1761), *The Templar* (1789), *Lawyer's and Magistrate's Magazine* (1790-94), and the *Law Journal (Morgan and Williams)* (1803-4)—the contents of which consisted largely of reports or digests of recent case law.[91] *The Templar*'s two volumes were slightly different in that they included short articles on the study of law, legal biography, proposed legislation, the trial of Hastings, debating societies, the English constitution, and so forth. *The Templar* initially contained reports of trials at the Old Bailey as well, although the activities of counsel were not recorded. A note near the end of volume 1, however, stated: "It is intended, by the editor of the Templar, to discontinue the publication of the trials at the Old Bailey, unless when anything uncommonly interesting shall occur; and to insert, in their place, something more worthy of attention.—This has been done at the express solicitation of a great number of our readers."[92]

In the first quarter of the nineteenth century what has been described as a period of experimentation ensued in legal publishing. Most of the legal journals published were again short-lived,[93] and the more influential periodicals did not appear until the late 1820s and early 1830s. These included a number of weekly papers: the *Jurist, or Quarterly Journal of Jurisprudence and Legislation* (1827-33), the *Legal Observer* (1830-56), the *Legal Examiner* (1831-33), and the *Legal Examiner and Law Chronicle* (1833-35). Apart from commenting on current case and statute law they published correspondence on various issues affecting both branches of the legal profession, biographical sketches of prominent members of the bar, book reviews, obituaries, notices of professional promotion, and so forth.[94] The *Law Magazine or Quarterly Review* (1828–56), whose roots, as Hines points out, lay in the eighteenth-century tradition of journalism for the intelligent layperson, published lengthy articles on more general subjects. The early-nineteenth-century journals varied in political orientation as well as content: the *Jurist* was Benthamite; the short-lived *Legal Reformer* (1819–20), as its title implied, was intended to draw public attention to the need for reform of the law; the *Law Magazine* was founded "as a defensive measure for rallying the bar against the impending storm" of reform.[95]

Sustained consideration of the duties and obligations of counsel in criminal cases is rarely found within the early-nineteenth-century legal journals. The *Legal Review* did take up the subject in 1813, prompted by what it saw as a wrongful acquittal. Public suspicion of the hired advocate was echoed in its discussion of "Kendall's Trial": "It is certainly questionable, how far a man, paid for the habitual perversion of truth, and the disguise of the most atrocious falsehoods in the semblances of truth, should be allowed to stand up in a court of justice, and in defiance of every principle of honour and integrity, exercise a trade, by which the guilty are made to change place with the innocent, and the innocent with the guilty: a trade by which ignominy is often attempted to be transferred, and too often with success, from a great offender against the laws, to those whom a sense of public duty had urged to drag that offender to a criminal bar."[96] The review acknowledged and accepted the argument that the criminal advocate's business was to detect and expose perjury, and that if counsel were prohibited from pursuing this end the innocent "might frequently become victims" to it.[97] Malice must not be allowed to triumph over innocence, nor perjury over truth. But this task was not allotted to counsel alone: it was the duty of judge and jury as well. The review's ultimate concern was that "trick, chicanery, and imposition"[98] were being allowed to obstruct the operation of the law.

After 1836, and particularly in the 1840s, professional questioning of the rights and duties of criminal advocates would become widespread.[99] In the opening decades of the nineteenth century, however, the bar's complaints where Old Bailey counsel were concerned more often centered on manners rather than morality. Unseemly bickering between counsel in criminal trials was prominent among repeated criticisms. A letter to the editor of the *Legal Examiner* in 1831 reported an exchange overheard in a magistrate's office between two Old Bailey counsel given the pseudonyms of "Mr. Pert" and "Mr. Malbred":

> *Mr. Malbred.*—. . . The conduct of my client throughout the entire affair is unimpeachable. What! can it be entertained for one moment

as a serious charge, that he has had the courage to expose his life in support of his honour. I ask, what is honour without courage? what is honour without courage!—why, it is like a barrister without a brief, or a contingent remainder without a particular estate to support it. I submit, Sir, that my client should be discharged, and that Mahoney [the prosecutor] should be held to bail, to answer the charge at the next sessions.

Mr. Pert.—My more learned than temperate friend, has been pleased to indulge in flippant ribaldry respecting my client; I tell my rude and learned friend, that his abusive epithets are more applicable to himself than to Mr. Mahoney.

Mr. Malbred.—You lie, Sir, you are as great a blackguard as he is, and you are a coward into the bargain.

Magistrate.—Gentlemen, (if it be not a profanation to call you so,) I can no longer listen to such language in this place. It is a subject of melancholy regret, that all who are gentlemen by profession, are not so in reality, whereby the law is at variance with the fact. It grieves me to perceive a respectable profession disgraced by such conduct as I have witnessed here today; from the language which you have used, and temper which you have manifested, I feel it my duty, before I proceed further, to call upon you both for sureties to keep the peace towards each other.

Mr. Malbred.—Bless your soul, Sir, you completely mistake us; if you were in the habit of attending at the Old Bailey Sessions, you would not say that we have transgressed the usual bounds of decorum.

Mr. Pert.—Such is our usual way of doing business, Sir. Our feelings are proof against the shafts of the tongue; to convince you of our mutual cordiality—(Here they both shook hands.)

Mahoney informed the magistrate that "these Old Bailey lawyers are gentlemen only by fiction of law."[100]

While the real names in this instance were suppressed, the scene described is reminiscent of a dispute reported in the OBSP in 1796. In the prosecution of Charles Scoldwell for the theft of two live tame ducks, Newman Knowlys, counsel for the defendant, objected to the way in which Peter Alley opened the case, and relations between the two barristers deteriorated from then on.[101] At one point the shorthand writer recorded that "a skirmish ensued between the Counsel of rather a serious nature" over a piece of paper in the hands of a witness, and there were numerous heated exchanges that required the intervention of the judge. When Alley objected to a question asked by Knowlys, the latter retorted, "I care not for your observations, I know you too well to care for them." Knowlys repeated the question, and Alley the objection; Knowlys then replied that he would attend only to his lordship. Alley later accused Knowlys of "indecent, unbecoming, and ungentlemanlike behaviour"; Knowlys asked the judge to "silence" his opponent.[102]

Such behavior was undoubtedly entertaining, but it did little to advance a client's cause, nor did it enhance the reputation of the bar. It is small wonder that judges found Old Bailey counsel exhausting, even when they restricted themselves to a "becoming zeal" for their clients. Counsel were rude not only to each other but to the presiding judge. Beattie cites one exchange between Garrow and Heath,[103] and the following was reported in an anonymous barrister's unlicensed trial notes. "The Court" in this instance was Serjeant Arabin.[104]

> After a conference between the Court, Phillips and Clarkson, the prisoner pleaded Guilty.
> The Court. Mr. Phillips, you must distinctly understand that I know nothing of the arrangement.
> Phillips. Yes my Lord it is thoroughly understood that your Lordship knows nothing.[105]

Midleton J., asked in 1803 if he intended to preside at the adjournment of the Guildford Sessions, answered that he found himself "wholly unequal to contend with a dozen Old Bailey counsel" and that he "could not think of it."[106]

The hot-tempered Peter Alley was involved in another dispute, one which became very public, in 1816. It began during a trial held at the Old Bailey in October, in which Alley appeared for the prosecution and John Adolphus for the defense. The OBSP made no mention of an argument, but the *Observer* reported it the following Sunday, describing a "warmth of feeling" on the part of the advocates that degenerated into personal insult. The *Observer*'s coverage was picked up by the *Courier* and *The Times* on 14 October, and the papers followed the development of events over the following month. Adolphus felt compelled to contribute his own version of events, which appeared, under the headline "Quarrel at the Bar," in *The Times* on 18 October. This unprofessional squabble was subsequently translated into a duel after further correspondence in the papers. Bound over by a Bow Street magistrate to keep the peace, Alley—accompanied by colleagues James Agar and Robert Beville—and Adolphus departed for Calais, where they fought with pistols. Alley's shot went over his opponent's head while Adolphus's bullet wounded his opponent in the arm. The combatants then reconciled and remained on friendly terms until Alley's death.[107]

"A Barristerial Duel," featuring Old Bailey counsel Peter Alley (left) and John Adolphus (right), who fought a duel in Calais in 1816 (Copyright The British Museum)

Apart from quarreling among themselves and insulting the bench, Old Bailey barristers were further accused of playing to the jury. Adolphus's son reported that in his father's generation there was a practice "of plying the jury with a sort of by-play, stares, shrugs, laughs (I have even heard of winks), while the adverse counsel was addressing them. Chaste practitioners condemned, though few altogether refrained from it."[108] Contempt for the skills of the criminal practitioner is evident in the *Dictionary of National Biography* entry for George Bond (1750–1796), famous in his day as a criminal pleader at the Surrey sessions: "He belonged to a class of lawyers now happily approaching extinction, whose chief strength consists in playing upon the susceptibilities of ignorant juries. Enthralled by his coarse and vulgar humor, the jurors of his native county, Surrey, were almost at his mercy, and tradition says that a not uncommon form of verdict at the Surrey Sessions was: 'We find for Serjeant Bond and costs.'"

The criticisms leveled at the Old Bailey bar are particularly interesting for the light they shed on the way in which the bar as a whole constructed its professional identity in the early nineteenth century. Two persistent complaints recur: first, Old Bailey barristers did not behave like gentlemen; second, they were ignorant of the law. The first concern reflects what historians of the professions have labeled an "aristocratic ideology": early nineteenth-century barristers, it has been argued, defined themselves by reference "to criteria that seem startlingly irrelevant to modern observers,"[109] that is, a classical education, gentlemanly or refined feelings, good character, and aristocratic disinterestedness. David Lemmings has argued that "social elitism" rather than "educational utility" lay behind a shift in legal education away from clerical apprenticeship and toward university and pupilage in the late eighteenth century;[110] he notes similarly that the "Vinerian/Blackstonian lecturing and publishing project" "was ultimately intended to transform the culture of Westminster Hall by appropriating a distinctive version of the gentlemanly ideal."[111] The eighteenth-century bar, in his view, "nourished a culture which was deliberately exclusive."[112] In the process, increasing social restrictions were placed on those admitted to the Inns: membership was denied to attorneys, clerks in Chancery and Exchequer, and proctors or articled clerks of attorneys unless they had ceased to practice their former business for at least two years, and in 1790 an order was made forbidding the appointment or election to any place or society in the Inner Temple of any person who kept a public house.[113] Class bias was inherent in a prescriptive text of the 1790s, *The Barrister; or strictures on education proper to the bar* (1792). The law was to be kept clean of "persons emerging from inferior situations, whatever their abilities may be": "not all the fees in

WESTMINSTER HALL can convert the low bred man into the Scholar or the Gentleman."[114] Class prejudice is equally apparent in an article on the profession of the bar published in 1867: "Here and there in the crowd we mark, with pity for his too certain fate, the careworn face of some self-educated peasant. The ambition which has aspired his toil in the unwonted field of legal labour is doomed to inevitable blight. He may have assiduously sown, but to him the harvest-time comes not, and at length, with broken heart, and perhaps, alas! in the bitterness of poverty, he learns how fallacious have been his hopes—how fatal his mistake."[115] All but gentlemen were to be prevented from entering the Inns, and once called to the bar, they were expected to behave in accordance with their gentlemanly social status. Hence the exasperation expressed by the magistrate forced to listen to "Pert" and "Malbred," who found it a "subject of melancholy regret, that all who are gentlemen by profession, are not so in reality." This view of the legal profession, as Wesley Pue has demonstrated, can be heard repeatedly in the testimony of those who gave evidence before the 1846 Committee on Legal Education.[116]

Pue also argues, however, that early-nineteenth-century barristers did not think of themselves as "'well-trained professionals' or [attempt] to justify their position in society by reference to objectively demonstrable practical experience."[117] It is true that barristers in the late eighteenth and early nineteenth centuries received little in the way of formal training, nor were they examined by the Inns of Court. Any acquisition of legal knowledge "very much depended upon the individual intelligence and exertion of the pupil."[118] But this does not mean that barristers were not expected to exert themselves and learn the law. James Scarlett's appraisal of Garrow—"without education, without taste, without law"—reveals the characteristics thought desirable in a barrister: a classical education, gentlemanly feelings, *and* specialized knowledge. Ruggles employed the same criteria in describing the barrister: "the Scholar, the Lawyer, the Man of honourable Character, the polite and accomplished Gentleman."[119] A lack of technical expertise meant that John Campbell could dismiss Randle Jackson as "a declamatory speaker . . . who despised all technicalities, and tried to storm the court by the force of eloquence."[120] Adolphus's defense of the criminal bar is based on the same assumptions and contains the same elements: specialized knowledge (criminal law, the law of evidence), a classical education ("the acquisitions of a scholar"), and the behavior of a gentleman. And it was the combination of these qualities that drew praise for William Brodrick: "[H]is knowledge of the law was, for his standing, both extensive and deep, his industry was indefatigable, his mode of speaking, though perhaps never rising into eloquence, was always plain, clear, and persuasive. In the conduct of a cause he was firm, zealous, and undaunted. . . . The happy medium seemed to have been obtained by him, that while he pressed his client's cause with all necessary boldness, he never infringed on the proper rules of respect towards the court."[121] Another testimonial to Brodrick said simply: "Few men knew more; scarcely any applied their knowledge better."[122] The early-nineteenth-century bar clearly valued legal knowledge as much as it did the manners of a gentleman, and mistrust of criminal practitioners was to a great extent founded on a mistrust of success based on "chicanery" or tricks. As the laws of evidence were developed they provided the criminal bar with its own brand of specialized (if limited) knowledge, allowing the Old Bailey bar to defend itself in accordance with the accepted criteria of the bar as a whole.

It is also clear that the bar's criticism was leveled at a particular group of practitioners: those barristers who regularly practiced criminal law *in London*. The *Legal Observer* wrote indignantly in 1834: "We have the most sufficient proof that criminal business can be conducted with perfect order and becoming dispatch, in every assize town. Why is the metropolis to bear the disgrace of being worse off than the provinces?"[123] The *Westminster Review* expressed similar views the following year, remarking that the "prosecuting or defending a felon cannot *per se* be less reputable [at the Old Bailey] than at Norwich or York," but it certainly had the reputation among both the bar and general public for being so.[124] The difference may partially be explained by the lack of controls over behavior previously discussed. When on circuit Old Bailey counsel were subject to the standards of behavior imposed by the mess—thus Adolphus and Andrews were immediately hauled onto the carpet for an ungentlemanly altercation. An "intemperate quarrel" attracted the wrath of their colleagues on the Home circuit, who requested that the leader of the circuit, Serjeant Onslow, investigate the conduct of the two barristers: it was anticipated that they would be banned from the circuit mess.[125] This incident is captured in a contemporary cartoon in which Adolphus is shown hitting Andrews over the head with an umbrella.[126] But it seems equally likely that contemporaries exaggerated when discussing Old Bailey practice. Serjeant Robinson, who made his acquaintance with the Old Bailey in the late 1830s, when Phillips, Clarkson, and Bodkin dominated business there, commented mildly that with a few "trifling exceptions," "the business was conducted as fairly and respectably as in any of the courts of Westminster Hall. I may say further that I have heard much more slang talked of the Old Bailey than ever I heard uttered within its walls."[127]

Full often we're Told and true it may be
That two of a Trade can never agree.

The Learned A——S or a legal Construction of Rogues and Vagrants

June 6 1817

"The Learned A——S or a Legal Construction of Rogues and Vagrants,"
showing John Adolphus hitting Thomas Andrews over the head with an umbrella
(Copyright The British Museum)

Unquestionably, a certain amount of professional snobbishness can be detected in the bar's criticism of Old Bailey practice. In the eyes of their profession, Old Bailey barristers simply belonged to an inferior grade of practitioner. Outside of London, criminal practice was the preserve of junior members of the bar. Barristers were expected eventually to relinquish such work once their civil practice expanded, for reasons of taste as well as income. As we have seen, few Old Bailey barristers acquired substantial practice in the superior courts; they tended rather to be confined to the metropolitan sessions and customary courts. And while their work in those tribunals may have been useful, it conferred no professional prestige. When not "bullying" witnesses and "confounding" juries in the criminal courts, where was the Old Bailey barrister habitually to be found? "Passing paupers" and opposing tavern licenses at the quarter sessions. Enjoying a monopoly of practice in the City courts which owed to money rather than talent. Setting potentially fraudulent bankrupts free at the Insolvent Debtors' Court.

In the eyes of their colleagues at the bar, such practice was less than distinguished.

Conclusion

By the nineteenth century the conduct of the bar found at the Old Bailey had become a source of concern to a profession increasingly preoccupied with its reputation. The legal profession seems to have accepted that cross-examination was crucial to establishing the truth. The bar, however, desired that it be conducted without undue aggression or rudeness. Thus Erskine, as Lemmings indicates, had been singled out for his "unfailing courtesy in the courtroom" and "gentlemanlike" examinations of witnesses"[128] at the Old Bailey as elsewhere in the country. More generally, the bar wanted its members to behave like gentlemen. This preference for taste and gentlemanly behavior would become more marked as the nineteenth century progressed. The bar wanted its members to conduct themselves as legal versions of Dickens's ultrarespectable Podsnap, a character found in *Our Mutual Friend*.[129] To its despair, the Old Bailey barrister would instead be caricatured by Trollope as Chaffanbrass.[130]

The public's reaction to the emergence of a criminal bar in London was more complex. Among defendants, and the lower classes from whom defendants were generally drawn, prominent Old Bailey counsel acquired a cult status that allowed them to walk with safety through some of the most dangerous areas of London. Those less likely to meet the criminal law as sanction viewed the advent of defense counsel in particular with tempered enthusiasm. But the public did not call for defense counsel to be excluded from the trial. It was the behavior of counsel in court, not the fact of their presence, that attracted negative comment: "[T]he personalities, the wranglings, the explosions of brutal intemperance, [were] a disgrace to the bar"; the Old Bailey had become a "by word expressive of everything coarse and indecent in the business of advocacy."[131] There are a few instances of public grumbling about the participation of defense counsel resulting in the acquittal of the guilty, and public indignation about the rough handling of witnesses is evident from the 1760s. In the eighteenth and early nineteenth centuries, however, the activities and behavior of Old Bailey counsel were more likely to provoke sarcasm and exasperation than moral outrage.

This must owe in large part to two circumstances: the limited role permitted to defense counsel before 1836 and the problems posed to the administration of the criminal law by a system which relied on private prosecution. Anxiety about the extent and effect of perjured testimony may have inclined not merely the bench and the bar but the public to tolerate, if not to welcome, the presence of counsel in trials of felony. The limited activity of defense counsel did much to reveal the truth, rather than subvert or conceal it. The means by which they did so may have from time to time attracted disapprobation, and distaste was occasionally expressed for a choice of practice that involved regular contact with the underworld, but the barristers who practiced in the criminal courts were seldom attacked as amoral. While the accused retained responsibility for mounting his own defense, counsel were to an extent able to distance themselves from their clients. Before 1836 the moral responsibility for a plea of not guilty rested primarily, although not entirely, with the accused himself. It was paid advocacy that worried the public, and advocacy was limited in the criminal courts prior to the enactment of the Prisoners' Counsel Act. During the period in which defense counsel were forbidden to address the jury, public criticism of their participation in felony trials was comparatively muted. This situation would change dramatically once the Prisoners' Counsel Act was in place.

CHAPTER SIX

The Bar, the Bench,
and the Central Criminal Court

As discussed in Chapter 4, metropolitan London continued to expand in the nineteenth century, its population increasing from 1,117,000 in 1801 to 2,685,000 in 1851. Criminal prosecutions at the Old Bailey also rose dramatically, the number of trials heard annually almost tripling between the turn of the nineteenth century and 1830. The pressure of these rising numbers necessitated administrative changes at the Old Bailey.

The first efforts to address the increase in business were made by the City of London in the early 1820s, when it authorized both the construction of a second Old Bailey courtroom and the creation of a new legal officer, a "third civic judge," to serve as a deputy to the recorder and common serjeant.[1] The City Lands Committee met in 1822 to consider plans for holding two courts at the Old Bailey, and by the following year a decision had been made to convert a building on the south side of the Sessions House, at the time used as a record office for the clerk of the arraigns, into an additional court. The "New Court" was ready by 1824,[2] and to coincide with its opening, the Court of Aldermen appointed William St. Julien Arabin, formerly an Old Bailey counsel and City common pleader and recently elected a judge of the Sheriffs' Court (1822),[3] "to perform the Judicial Duties at the Sessions at the Old Bailey, in the absence of the Judges, and to discharge the respective duties of Mr. Recorder and Mr. Common Serjeant at the Said Sessions in their unavoidable absence by illness or otherwise." A letter from Arabin, who took "the degree of Serjeant at Law, with a view to add to the dignity of the office," outlined his judicial duties. He was to sit daily during the attendance of the judges between 9 and 10 A.M. and 5 and 9 P.M., or as long as necessary; he was to be available to sit at other times; and he was to attend at the sessions at the Guildhall and in the Borough Court of Southwark when the recorder and common serjeant were unable to do so.[4]

By the early nineteenth century, the City of London was but a small enclave within the metropolis as a whole. Nonetheless, it not only retained but extended the ancient right of its elected legal officers to sit as criminal judges at the Old Bailey. In 1790 it had formally extended that right to an existing officer (the common serjeant); in 1824 it created a new judicial appointment. It was the City judges, rather than those from the superior courts, who would preside over the bulk of trials heard at the Old Bailey, and the incumbents of the offices in question were to a man former members of the bar found at that court. The bench and bar of England's premier criminal court had become intimately connected.

The Central Criminal Court Act

The City was not alone in recognizing London's changing geographic and demographic realities: in 1834 the boundaries of criminal jurisdiction were officially redrawn by the Central Criminal Court Act to include metropolitan Essex, Kent, and Surrey.[5] The Central Criminal Court, as the Old Bailey was now officially to be known, opened on Saturday, 1 November 1834 (the occasion was marked by a fifteen-minute ceremony). The court was also granted jurisdiction of the Admiralty Sessions, and its sessions of oyer and terminer and gaol delivery were to be held twelve rather than eight times per year. As predicted, the recent innovation of a winter circuit in the Home counties affected by the act was dispensed with.[6] This reorganization did not in itself attract controversy—the need to adjust jurisdictional boundaries was patently obvious—and much of the contemporary discussion of the statute postdated its implementation. A minor squabble did arise in *The Times* over who, precisely, was responsible for the act. Charles Phillips was keen to attribute it to his friend the lord chancellor—"To Lord Brougham, and Lord Brougham alone, are the public indebted for this vast improvement."[7] But plans for the legislation appear to have dated back at least thirty years. Peter Alley drew attention to a draft drawn up by the Old Bailey's former clerk of arraigns, Thomas Shelton, and revised by John Silvester in the early years of his recordership.[8] *The Times* thought a more accurate attribution of the 1834 act would acknowledge not only Shelton's original sketch and Silvester's revisions but the intervention of the Court of Aldermen and the current clerk of arraigns, John Clarke (Shelton's nephew), who insured the early draft was passed on to the Home Office via Lord Melbourne. There, according to *The Times*, it underwent further revision by Undersecretary Phillips, Sir Frederick Roe, and Clarke himself before being forwarded to Brougham.[9] *The Times*, no friend to Brougham, was as keen to play down his contribution as Charles Phillips was to promote it.[10]

Ultimately, this debate was of little consequence. Whatever its origins, the Central Criminal Court Act, as the *Westminster Review* commented, was not passed before its time: the steady growth of metropolitan London had rendered the older jurisdictional boundaries obsolete (London's bridges had, for instance, "virtually repealed the distinction between Middlesex and Surrey"),[11] and Middlesex gaols were so routinely overcrowded that the county's magistrates had instituted an intermediate sessions. The addition would not have been a bad plan in itself, conceded the journal, had the county bench been adequate.[12] Middlesex magistrates, however, had long been under attack as incompetent, and commonly cited as among the benefits of the Central Criminal Court Act was the fact that it contracted their jurisdiction. Charles Phillips dealt at length with this issue in a letter to Brougham: "The comparative solemnity of a court where the King's judges shall preside contrasted with that held by county justices is unquestionable—the importance of that solemnity in the administration of criminal justice where life & liberty are constantly at stake is equally indisputable—it alone goes a great way in establishing that confidence in the administration of the laws inseparable from their respect by the people." More important still was the "legal education & practical experience" requisite for a judge. In trials of any offense for which a conviction would result in transportation—the conditions of which, Phillips noted, had become more severe as the scope of capital punishment was restricted—the public had "a right to expect that the King's judges" would try them. He pointed to the errors likely to arise where judges had no legal training. Middlesex magistrate Sir William Curtis, while "no doubt, a respectable banker & an honourable Man," was nonetheless ignorant of the most common rules of evidence. Yet he was constantly deputed to try felonies. The chairman of the sessions, Rotch, was even worse, having sentenced to fourteen years' transportation a man named Palmer despite the fact that the principal in the case had been acquitted by three of the royal judges on the grounds that the offense charged was no offense in law. After six months in prison Palmer obtained a free pardon. The "monstrous anomoly" of a principal acquitted and an accessory convicted was no oversight, Phillips wrote; the mistake had been made after repeated warnings from counsel and "persevered in with contumelious obstinacy."[13] Phillips returned to the subject of the Middlesex bench in more than one letter, advising Brougham against any scruples of conscience with respect to restricting the jurisdiction of Middlesex magistrates and not those of other counties: "[T]hey have brought it on themselves by grasping . . . at a jurisdiction which did not belong to them & by their glaring & repeated blunders of late which have worked so much private misery & grievously disgraced the administration of justice." It would, he thought, be in the inter-

ests of justice eventually to restrict the jurisdiction of magistrates throughout the country as a whole, but the Middlesex bench was "beyond all doubt,
the very worst in England."[14]

In reducing the jurisdiction of Clerkenwell the Central Criminal Court
Act resolved the problems identified with entrusting trials of felony to magistrates with no legal training. But the statute did nothing to lessen the ancient rights and privileges of the Corporation of the City of London, which
were confirmed and upheld in section 23: "[N]othing in this Act contained
shall extend or be construed to extend to prejudice or affect the rights, interests, privileges, franchises, or authorities of the lord mayor, aldermen, and
recorder of the city of London, or their successors, the sheriffs of the city of
London and county of Middlesex . . . or to prohibit, defeat, alter, or diminish
any power, authority, or jurisdiction which at the time of making this Act the
said lord mayor, aldermen, and recorder for the time being, of the said city,
did or might lawfully use or exercise." The continuation of these privileges
caused considerable disappointment. The *Westminster Review*, hesitating to
anticipate any evil from what it considered to be a generally positive piece
of legislation, concluded that nothing short of a repeal of section 23 and "an
entire sweeping away of the Lord Mayor and Aldermen" would allow the
Central Criminal Court to achieve a level of efficiency and respectability
appropriate to "the principal court of criminal jurisdiction in the empire."[15]
The necessity of an alderman's presence on the bench, which often caused
delay, was resented,[16] and Phillips later claimed that the aldermen interfered
with the sentences passed by the City's judges: "[M]en are constantly transported by their interference or imprisoned."[17] But the City judgeships attracted the greatest criticism. In a review of Wontner's *Old Bailey Experience*, published in 1833, the *Law Magazine* had condemned the constitution
of London's chief criminal court as "vicious, inasmuch as the judges are too
much within the influence of local and subordinate interests."[18] Similarly,
the *Westminster Review* commented, "That which is managed by a corporation almost inevitably becomes corrupt."[19] The appointment of the Old
Bailey's judges, it was argued, ought to be removed from the City and vested
in the Crown: "no part" of England's law gave "such general satisfaction"
or "less require[d] revision" than the trials of prisoners by the Westminster judges at the assizes.[20] Phillips similarly wrote to Brougham that the
administration of criminal justice was "too sacred a trust to be left at the
mercy of any corporation in England. Their members are not the persons
who ought to appoint judges,"[21] while William Ballantine condemned the
process by which a "canvass amongst a parcel of by no means the highest
class of tradesmen, who were quite incompetent to form a judgment, ob-

tained for candidates the places of Common Serjeant and Commissioner,"[22] as London's third civic judge was now known.

The dissatisfaction expressed owed in large part to the behavior of the men who held the City offices in the early nineteenth century: John Silvester (recorder, 1803–22), Newman Knowlys (common serjeant, 1803–22; recorder, 1822–33), John Mirehouse (common serjeant, 1833–50), and William St. Julien Arabin (third civic judge/commissioner, 1824–41). Their experience at the bar of the Old Bailey might logically be assumed to have proved an asset on promotion to the bench; indeed, as we saw in Chapter 4, it did provide them with a degree of familiarity with the records and reputation of those who appeared in the witness stand as well as in the dock. As judges, however, Silvester and Knowlys were deemed uncouth and overly severe, while Arabin and Mirehouse were found ridiculous.

The City's Judges

As discussed in Chapter 1, the common serjeant and recorder were elected by the City of London's governing bodies, the Court of Common Council and the Court of Aldermen. Prior to the nineteenth century these elections had been relatively open: some successful candidates had connections with the City, others did not. There were precedents for a common serjeant proceeding to the office of recorder,[23] and in other instances the recorder had formerly held a different City office, a pleadership or judgeship of the Sheriffs' Court of London.[24] But John Silvester provides the first example of the City regularly promoting its officers. When, in 1803, Silvester was chosen recorder by a unanimous Court of Aldermen, he was the first since George Jeffreys (an inauspicious predecessor) to have previously held the serjeantcy, and the first to have occupied successively the offices of City common pleader, common serjeant, and recorder. Newman Knowlys followed in Silvester's footsteps, and in the year prior to the creation of the Central Criminal Court, Charles Ewan Law had "rotated" in his turn to the recordership. By that date the elections had become a source of public outrage, and disgust with the process must be tied directly to its results. Whatever their talents as advocates, in their tenure as recorders Silvester and Knowlys did much to bring the office, and more broadly the administration of criminal justice in London, into disrepute.

Although, in an obituary published in the *Gentleman's Magazine*, Silvester was praised for discharging his judicial duties "in a faithful, zealous, and conscientious manner,"[25] other contemporaries were less flattering. Silvester was said to have "rendered himself exceedingly obnoxious by his

"A Levee Day," portraying John Silvester, recorder of London, on the right,
waiting to present his report of capital convicts to the Prince Regent
(Copyright The British Museum)

coarseness, the violence of his temper, and his utter disregard for the rules
of courtesy."[26] In caricatures he consistently appears as bloated and corpu-
lent—perhaps the consequence of too much of the City's rich turtle soup.
"The Recorder of London," wrote Farington in his famous diary, "indulges
much at the table."[27] Cruickshank drew a fat-faced recorder clutching
"Black Jack's Black Bag" (the report on capital convicts) in a cartoon entitled
"A Levee Day"; in "The Night Mayor" he added a dark, five-o'clock shadow.
Williams, for his part, gave the recorder a grotesquely bloated face in "City
Scavengers Cleansing the London Streets of Impurities" (Silvester is reading the Riot Act).[28] There were rumors of sexual impropriety and abuse of
power: Silvester was accused by William Jerdan of demanding sexual favors
from a woman who approached him to appeal for his assistance in obtaining a pardon for her husband.[29] He was also widely (although not consistently) condemned for a severe summing up in the trial of Eliza Fenning, a
servant girl hanged for the attempted murder of her master and his family
and popularly believed to be innocent. Some 10,000 people were reputed
to have followed Fenning to her execution.[30] Silvester's conduct in the Fenning trial was probably less blameworthy than many contemporaries believed, but as the *Morning Chronicle* commented, his "public character" had
not been "peculiarly calculated to inspire respect for the judicial office."[31]
If popular with the City government, Silvester failed to win the public's approval.

When John Silvester died in office in 1822 the newspapers tended to dwell

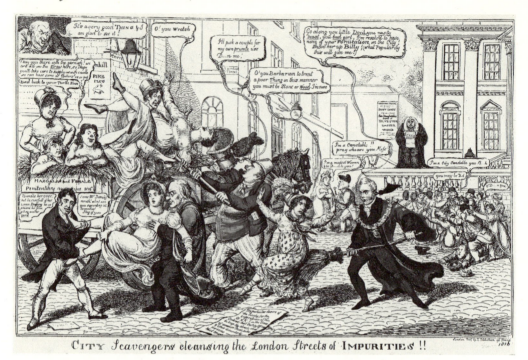

"City Scavengers Cleansing the London Streets of Impurities," showing city
officials at work ridding the streets of prostitutes. John Silvester, recorder of
London, appears in the upper righthand corner, reading the Riot Act.
(Copyright The British Museum)

on the desired requirements of the new recorder rather than to enumerate
the failings of the late incumbent. Offering advice to the Court of Aldermen, *The Times* emphasized the recorder's role as a "Criminal Judge." The
ideal recorder should have "an intellect at once enlarged and discriminating,
with a patient temper, and a considerate, humane, and merciful disposition,"
given that the "life or death of his fellow-creatures rests more frequently
upon his personal responsibility than on that . . . of any other minister of
the laws of England."[32] When it became apparent that Newman Knowlys
would succeed Silvester the press was quick to challenge what it saw as an
unwelcome development. Knowlys was elected unanimously as the only candidate for the office left vacant by Silvester's death, but on 6 April *The Times*
had reported that James Mackintosh would accept the position if it were
offered. Alderman Robert Waithman, convinced that Knowlys possessed
neither "that personal dignity" nor "those eminent legal abilities" requisite

for a position that had in former times served as a stepping stone to the highest offices in the land—previous recorders of London had subsequently been appointed chief baron of the Exchequer, chief justice of the Courts of King's Bench and Common Pleas, and a few even lord chancellor[33]—nominated Mackintosh for the office, but the nomination came too late. A canvass had been held, and the majority of aldermen backed Knowlys. Opinion had been set, Waithman lamented, before all the candidates were known. Mackintosh's nomination was withdrawn.[34]

The aldermen were extremely unlikely to have elected Mackintosh in any case, as his politics would not have won the votes of more than a few of them. Prior to the reign of Queen Victoria politics played a role in both the election and subsequent behavior of the aldermen, and while the majority of the Common Council became "very violently Whig" soon after the beginning of the Revolutionary War with France in 1793, the aldermen did not follow suit.[35] The few radicals who transferred from the council to the Court of Alderman in the early nineteenth century—including Waithman and Matthew Wood[36]—were in the minority. In 1822 the Court of Alderman consisted of fifteen Tories (plus the Tory lord mayor) and ten Whigs, three of whom subsequently joined the Tory Party.[37] James Mackintosh would not have appealed to the Tory majority, as by 1822 he was well known for his liberal opinions. An "able and faithful defender of liberal principles," Mackintosh had, on Samuel Romilly's death in 1818, assumed the lead in the parliamentary campaign to reduce the severity of England's criminal code. In the following year he had carried a motion against the Tory government to strike a committee to consider capital punishment, and in 1820 he introduced six bills based on the recommendations of that committee, three of which became law.[38] Knowlys, in contrast, was, like Silvester, known to oppose any further repeal of capital statutes.[39]

If the Court of Aldermen found Knowlys's conservatism attractive, it drew censure from other quarters, and during his tenure as common serjeant Knowlys was the subject of attack in the newspaper press on more than one occasion. The *Morning Chronicle* in particular despised him for his reactionary opinions and for his behavior on the bench. Only a month previous to his appointment as recorder the *Chronicle* had printed letters condemning his conduct in a trial of libel, in which the accused was a seventeen-year-old shop-boy of Richard Carlile.[40] Knowlys was accused of descending to personal attack on the defense counsel and of positively misdirecting the jury. One angry correspondent wrote that he had never witnessed "so barefaced a system of *frightening* a jury into a verdict of conviction."[41] In the days that followed the *Morning Chronicle* made further digs at Knowlys, comparing him to George Jeffreys, who had been notorious for insulting the bar and perverting the course of justice. Knowlys, the paper reported indignantly, was known to dispatch sixty criminals a day.[42] But the paper had been under no illusion that Mackintosh might succeed. Prior to Knowlys's election it reported: "[T]he recent conduct of the Common Serjeant at the Old Bailey, so severely animadverted in the House of Commons the other evening, when not one voice was raised in his favour, will, no doubt, point him out . . . as peculiarly qualified" for the office of recorder. "Possessing . . . as Mr. Knowlys unquestionably does, qualities so congenial with those of the Court of Aldermen, his election may be presumed a matter of certainty, and all observations on the subject would only be thrown away," the *Chronicle* despaired, as the Court of Aldermen was "known to be ultra-illiberal."[43] Instead, the paper urged the Court of Common Council in electing a new common serjeant to choose "some Gentleman alike distinguished by the possession of professional character and true constitutional principles."[44]

The 1822 election of a new common serjeant, unlike that of the recorder, proved to be hotly contested, for the unanimity displayed by the Court of Aldermen was conspicuously absent in the City's lower chamber. Once Knowlys had been installed as recorder, a requisition was made to convene the Court of Common Council to consider the vacancy left by his promotion. It was immediately apparent that the council was divided over the issue of rotation of City offices. A number of councilmen were uneasy with the precedent set by Knowlys's election and unhappy with the prospect of a competition for election to the office of common serjeant closed to any but the City common pleaders. Twice the Court of Aldermen had promoted the common serjeant to recorder. If this practice were to become routine, critics argued, it was imperative that the Common Council be free to elect their serjeant from among the most distinguished members of the bar. Those responsible for the requisition claimed to have been influenced "by no party feelings" but were "anxious that the office should be thrown open to the bar in general, in order that it might be filled by an individual of talent and high legal character." While it "had been customary to select" one of the City's common pleaders, "who all purchased their places, to fill the office," Councilman Slade was convinced that "this was a sort of trammel which the Court ought to get rid of."[45] A standing order to the effect that no City office could be held by anyone who had not received the freedom of the City two years earlier ought also to be removed. Other councilmen, however, were convinced that the office should be reserved for the city's pleaders. In a council meeting held on 3 April it was "objected, but not very forcibly" that an outside candidate would not be as well versed in London's municipal law.[46] In the event, the standing order requiring candidates to have possessed the freedom of the City for at least two years was rescinded and an election called for 25 April. The election lay between an outside candidate, Thomas Denman,[47] and William Bolland, Old Bailey counsel and senior City common pleader.

In 1822 Denman was riding a wave of enormous popularity as the result of his defense of Queen Caroline.[48] The case had won him the long-standing enmity of the king and cost him a well-deserved promotion to the rank of King's Counsel, but both Denman and Henry Brougham had been presented with a vote of thanks and the freedom of the City in 1821. Denman's application to stand for the vacancy in the common serjeantship had been solicited by a member of council, and he was known to be willing to accept the office. Councilman Slade drew attention to Denman's "talents and integrity" and argued that he "was not at all likely to mix up political prepossessions and antipathies with his judgment upon the rights and privileges of his Majesty's subjects."[49]

Both *The Times* and the *Morning Chronicle* supported Denman's candidacy, although *The Times* commented that "under present circumstances" the common serjeantcy was beneath Denman's seeking or acceptance. It had "long ceased to be an office of dignity." *The Times* further expressed the hope that the Court of Common Council would refuse to recognize any claim to the office by virtue of the (purchased) possession of a pleadership: "[T]he yielding to such a claim would prevent their selecting from amongst the most distinguished and meritorious members of the bar."[50] The "criminal tribunal of the city of London," it had argued two days earlier, "ought not to be open to *purchase*; nor to be arrived at through mere routine by men who have bought, not by parts or character, but by money, a previous monopoly of city practice."[51] In a subsequent issue the paper drew attention to the system of rotation that had become established with respect to City offices. The public, it said, was unaware that pleaderships were "mere matters of bargain and sale." Silvester, after purchasing a pleadership, had stepped from the office to that of common serjeant and from thence to the office of recorder, Knowlys had followed in his wake, and now William Bolland, to whom Knowlys had sold his pleadership in 1803, by putting himself forward for the office of common serjeant, seemed to be following in Knowlys's footsteps. The "city lottery of the law" was "without blanks, and the capital prizes in it [were] two of the highest judicial offices in the kingdom." In encouraging this serial promotion the Corporation sacrificed "both their own priviliges and their duty to the public."[52]

In its criticism of the rotation of City offices *The Times* was careful to cast no aspersions on Bolland personally. As described in Chapter 2 above, Bolland was "one of the most popular men of his time," pleasant, kind, and benevolent, "an amiable and honourable man," if not remarkable for his legal talent.[53] An advertisement placed in *The Times* by Bolland's supporters the day before the election commented plaintively that "surely it would be to act [on] absurd and unfair grounds in deciding that a candidate is positively disqualified, whatever may be his other merits, merely because he happens to have been a Common Pleader."[54] Denman himself described Bolland as "one of the most blameless and honourable men living, possessed of very competent talents and much curious learning (especially in early English literature)," albeit "rather deficient in nerve and promptitude of business."[55]

On the election day 24 of the 26 aldermen and 226 of the 236 commoners turned out to vote, and despite Denman's popularity the contest was close. He won by a majority of 12 (131 to 119). The *Morning Chronicle* was delighted by his success and reported that the election result was "a subject for public congratulations." Denman was unconnected with the City, and his public character was "unreproachable."[56] But the controversy did not end with his election: a petition citing a sixteenth-century by-law that ordered that the recorder, under-sheriffs, and common serjeant be chosen from among the ranks of the City's lower offices was quickly presented to the Court of Aldermen. Councilmen Dixon, Crocker, Brook, Smith, Gibbs, and Stuart protested against swearing Denman into office, claiming that he was ineligible to be elected, and requested that Bolland be admitted in his place.[57] The aldermen varied in their response. Like the election, the petition occasioned great public interest, and some felt that the opinion of the recorder ought to be consulted. But Alderman Brown, although he had supported Bolland, spoke out strongly against it. The petition attempted to revive an "obsolete" by-law passed nearly three hundred years earlier (1554) and perhaps never acted upon, and its effect would be "to render all the great and important offices of the city purchasable by money" and deprive the court "of even the shadow of an election."[58] Waithman made the same objections, and Denman was duly sworn into office. His performance of the duties of common serjeant during the eight years he remained in office "was deservedly the subject of high and general approbation. [Denman] displayed on the Old Bailey bench . . . firmness tempered with lenity, the strictest impartiality, and a determination to have every case tried on its merits; towards the Bar, a dignified courtesy of demeanour, and a total abstinence from those interruptions and interlocutory comments from the Bench which tend to irritate the temper of counsel, and seriously to retard the despatch of business."[59] During the same period Knowlys, as recorder, contrived to turn the Old Bailey into a "bear garden."[60]

"March of Intellect or an Opera without Music," portraying
Newman Knowlys, recorder of London, on the bench at the Guildhall,
"a worthy successor of Dingy Old Jack"
(Copyright The British Museum)

When Denman surrendered the serjeantcy on being appointed attorney general in 1830 the controversy over the rotation of City offices emerged once more. In December of that year an election was held to fill the vacancy left in the office of common serjeant, and as in 1822 the contest lay once again between a Tory City official of little or no professional reputation and an outside candidate known to hold liberal opinions. The City candidate in this instance was Charles Ewan Law. In politics Law's "distinctive characteristic was a jealous and unflinching adherence to the opinions and practice generally called 'Tory.'"[61] Called to the bar in 1817, Law had been a City common pleader, like Silvester, Knowlys, and Bolland, although he was elected to this position (in 1823) rather than purchasing it.[62] In 1827 he had been appointed a judge of the Sheriffs' Court.[63] Although he was made a King's Counsel in 1829, Law "signally failed" to establish himself in the superior courts,[64] and his legal practice was chiefly of the metropolitan variety described in Chapter 3; he had appeared regularly in London's customary courts as well as at the Old Bailey, where for a few years (1821–26) he appears to have rivaled Andrews and Adolphus.[65] His competitor presented a marked contrast. Matthew Davenport Hill, friend of both Bentham and Thomas Macaulay, was a radical, and he was retained for the defense in many political trials. On his first circuit he had defended Major John Cartwright et al. for conspiracy (1819); he subsequently defended Richard Carlile's wife (1820) and shop-boy (1822), against charges of selling a seditious libel and disseminating blasphemy, respectively. Throughout his career Hill was a fervent advocate of both political reform and reform of the criminal law.[66]

As in 1822 the Common Council was divided over the issue of whether to promote a City official or elect an outsider. Again the election was won by a fairly narrow margin, and this time the City's candidate triumphed, 118 to 100.[67] Hill, however, was soon to have another chance to win the office, when Knowlys's judicial career came to an inglorious end in 1833. As recorder Knowlys appears to have fully justified the *Morning Chronicle*'s opinion of him. In 1831 a petition was presented to the House of Commons from Richard Carlile requesting that it inquire into the circumstances under which his conviction for libel had been obtained, praying for a pardon, and asking that some alteration be made "in the existing Jury laws, so as to prevent Juries from being starved and exhausted into a verdict." The petition stated that Carlile's trial had lasted from nine in the morning until two o'clock the next morning. The recorder and counsel left the court to dine, but Carlile had been kept at the bar and allowed no refreshment for the whole of this time, which he quite reasonably argued had affected his ability to mount a defense. The jury had retired at nine that evening and returned at eleven, stating that they could not agree on a verdict. The recorder sent them back twice and finally threatened "in uncourteous language" to lock them up fasting for the remainder of the night, leave the court, and not to receive their verdict until the next day. After retiring twice more, an exhausted jury rendered a guilty verdict. In passing sentence the recorder added insult to injury by claiming that the jury's "great deliberation" "required the exercise of additional severity on his part." John Wood, who presented Carlile's petition, told the House of Commons that if this were a true account of the proceedings, "the case would require some further investigation by [the] House, and some further proceedings would be necessary against that Judge"; if the information contained in the petition were true, the jury had indeed been starved and bullied into their verdict.[68] Two weeks later Wood indicated his intention to have the petition printed. Although it came from a private individual, "the subject of it was of public character, and involved a great charge against a public officer." Daniel O'Connell agreed, as the petition "stated what appeared to be a gross case of the maladministration of justice."[69]

As recorder Knowlys thus continued to engage in the same kind of behavior that had so infuriated the *Morning Chronicle* during his common serjeantcy. But the end to his tenure in office must surely have exceeded even the *Chronicle*'s expectations: Knowlys was forced to resign when it was discovered that he had sent a warrant to Newgate for the execution of Job Cox, a convict who had been granted a royal pardon. But for a chance conversation between the chief justice of the Court of King's Bench and one of the undersheriffs, it was claimed, Cox would have been hanged. Councilman Stevens, who called these circumstances to the attention of the Court of Common Council, condemned Knowlys as "an old man, imbecile, and utterly unfit to perform the duties of the office he held."[70] Councilman Haines referred the court to a motion he had attempted to bring forward "about two years ago" relative to the recorder's behavior, which he characterized as "a natural forerunner of the late mistake" and deeply reprobated.[71] Knowlys resigned in disgrace and died two years later.

In 1833 the *Morning Chronicle* emphasized the political dimensions by now evident in the aldermen's choice of their legal officer: "[T]he most popularly elected Magistrates of the first city in the world, are at this moment said to be deliberating whether or not the appointment of their highest judicial officer—of the man whose professional, intellectual, and moral qualifications, and the lives and liberties of thousands of their fellow creatures, must from time to time be dependent—shall or shall not, be determined by reference to party politics."[72] But *The Times* expected that Law would be nominated to the vacancy created by Knowlys's resignation,[73] and any hopes the *Chronicle* had were soon dashed. Undeterred by the performance and reputations of Silvester and Knowlys, and in the face of considerable public criticism, the aldermen stubbornly continued to adhere to the principle of rotation, unanimously electing Law in Knowlys's place on 2 July 1833.[74] The principle of rotation thus continued as Law, like Silvester and Knowlys, rose from City common pleader to occupy first the office of common serjeant and ultimately that of recorder.

Rotation continued as well in the election of yet another pleader, John Mirehouse, to the serjeantcy left vacant on Law's promotion. Mirehouse's career followed a now familiar pattern: City common pleader (1823), then judge of the Sheriffs' Court (1831).[75] His attachment to the Old Bailey appears to have been of brief duration (he was named in the *Law List* as attending the London, Middlesex, and Westminster sessions from 1830 to 1833), and he was far less successful than Law or other of his predecessors, but this lack of success may owe in large part to the stranglehold Phillips exercised on Old Bailey practice during the years in question.[76] In the election of 1833 Mirehouse's competitor was Law's opponent in 1830: the radical Matthew Davenport Hill. *The Times* once again took the opportunity to comment on the qualities desired in the City's common serjeant: while the office "ought not to be a political one," "the officer ought to be a man whose politics do not run counter to the general spirit of the age, for there is always a feeling of contempt for the understanding of any man (not an old one) who is not alive to the moving world about him, and who would stagnate in the dull ditch of obsolete custom rather than flow on with the running stream of wholesome improvement."[77] Both the *Morning Chronicle* and *The Times* supported Hill in the contest and derided Mirehouse's candidacy. *The Times* wrote that the merits of Hill were well known to the public: "[W]e may say, without fear of contradiction, that Mr. Hill, as well in as out of Parliament, has been constant and steady, both in principle and in practice, to protect, to strengthen, and to extend the rights and liberties of the people." Of Mirehouse nothing more was known "than if he has ever been in a situation of proving himself a friend to the people, his talent has been hidden in a napkin, or he has done the people wrong, and, being insignificant, the thing is not now remembered." The paper had "no doubt" that Hill would succeed: "[H]owever irrecoverably a few of the citizens of London may be given over to the canker of Toryism, and however the good and generous spirit of a still smaller number of them may for a time be fly-blown with the dirt of ultra-radicalism or *destructiveness*, there is a vast deal too much of sterling merit and of solid good sense in that body to suffer the majority of them ever to go wrong for many times together or for any considerable period."[78] Contrasting the professional reputations of the two candidates *The Times* asked, "Who in Westminster-hall "*has heard* MR. MIREHOUSE or *heard of* him?"[79] The *Morning Chronicle* concurred in *The Times*'s estimation of the merits of poor Mirehouse—his qualities were "those of a dormouse . . . unseen and unknown"—but was less sanguine about the chances of a radical candidate's winning the election.[80] It had earlier reported, somewhat hysterically, rumors of a "City cabal" among the Court of Aldermen to defeat the election of Hill as common serjeant by passing over Law and electing William St. Julien Arabin, "a gentleman cast in the antique mold of a Knowlys," as recorder.[81] Arabin too had been a City common pleader

(1807), Old Bailey barrister (1804–22), and subsequently a judge of the Sheriffs' Court (1822). He had, as described above, served as a deputy judge at the Old Bailey since the creation of the New Court in 1824. A "thin, old, wizen-faced old man," both short-sighted and deaf,[82] Arabin quickly gained a reputation for "enunciating absurdities."[83]

In the serjeantcy election of 1833 the Court of Common Council remained divided in its opinion of rotation. Councilman Wood, who claimed to be indifferent to the outcome of the election, argued that "the principle of rotation should not be entirely thrown away" and that the council "should follow something like candour and justice in advancing those gentlemen who had already served the corporation, when they came forward as candidates for the office of judge."[84] Charles Pearson,[85] however, pointed out that "that mode of supplying the office had not provided the public with judges whose legal attainments afforded any recommendation for its continuance." John Silvester's name would "descend to posterity in connexion with that of Eliza Fenning," while the "awful mistake" that had occasioned Knowlys's resignation was unlikely "soon to be forgotten." Such precedents "were hardly likely, even in the eyes of the dearest lovers of rotation, to furnish an argument for their imitation."[86] Pearson then moved that a committee be appointed to inquire into the extent of the practice of both candidates, having already intimated that Mirehouse's would bear no close examination. Although the qualifications of the candidates for the City's judicial offices had never been subject to official scrutiny in the past, and not everyone agreed that the extent and nature of a candidate's practice as an advocate was the best criterion for assessing his fitness for office, the motion was affirmed. Both Mirehouse and Hill agreed to furnish the court with statements in writing that would summarize their standing at the bar as well as indicate whether they were freemen of the City, and if so, how long they had held that status.[87]

Mirehouse's statement, submitted to the council on 16 July, informed the court that he had been educated at Harrow and held an M.A. from Cambridge. Called to the bar in 1817, he had since published two (minor) law treatises, one on tithes and the other on advowsons.[88] He claimed to have acquired a "more than average proportion" of cases both civil and criminal on the Home circuit, and in 1832 he had won a general retainer from the Bank of England to act as its counsel on that circuit. At the Hertfordshire and Essex quarter sessions he was engaged in three-quarters of the appeals, and at the assizes he was employed in about a third of the cases heard. As a judge of the Sheriffs' Court Mirehouse occasionally presided at the Old Bailey when one of the other City officials was ill. Clearly upset by the adverse publicity that attended his candidacy, Mirehouse appended to his statement a list of the hundred or so solicitors who had engaged him as well as two letters requesting opinions of his professional character from senior judges in Westminster Hall, together with the responses received. "I should not at my time of life have thought it necessary to appeal to them for my character," he wrote, "had I not been attacked as incompetent to discharge the duties of the situation."[89] These testimonials had been circulated among the councilmen before Mirehouse formally submitted his statement. Judge Bayley, before whom Mirehouse had appeared on the Home circuit and at the Old Bailey, responded that Mirehouse had "the feelings of a gentleman, and inflexible integrity" as well as the requisite legal ability for the office of common serjeant, but he was careful to add that he had no wish to interfere with the appointment or to weigh Mirehouse's merits against those of another candidate. Judge Parke returned a brief note which indicated his belief that Mirehouse was "fully competent" for any judicial City office.

The statement submitted by Matthew Davenport Hill reflected a greater professional standing and emphasized the civil side of his practice. Hill had been called to the bar in 1819. He traveled the Midland circuit, and although in the early years of his practice his business had been largely confined to the criminal side, particularly at the Nottingham and Warwick sessions, he had more recently been "too much engaged" in nisi prius trials to attend much to criminal business. His sessions work in the previous seven years had consisted chiefly of appeal cases, "which are considered the highest branch of the sessions practice," and he had been engaged in 140 of the 150 appeals tried at the sessions he attended. Hill appeared regularly in Westminster Hall, chiefly in the common law courts, although he occasionally practiced in equity. He also practiced in bankruptcy and was employed as counsel at elections. Convinced by his friends that the circulation amongst the council of the letters Mirehouse had solicited from the Westminster judges "imposed" upon him the duty of seeking written testimonials of his own, Hill attached letters from Judges Bayley, Parke, and Bolland; the current and former chairs of the Warwick quarter sessions; the recorder of Coventry; the town clerks of Coventry, Lincoln, and Nottingham; various leading counsel on the Midland circuit; and prominent members of the bar at Westminster Hall, including Serjeant Wilde and Frederick Pollock, KC. Among his references was a letter from University of London law professor Andrew Amos, while John Campbell, then solicitor general, testified to Hill's King's Bench practice.[90]

Mirehouse *was* unknown at Westminster Hall while Hill was not, and if the candidates were to be judged solely by their respective practices at the

us by any flashes of wit or humour, nor exhibited any peculiar eccentricities that might furnish us with food for ridicule. He was a solemn, steady, sententious person, too respectable to wish to be made the subject of remark, whether with reference to praise or blame."[102] But even Law's critics admitted that, in marked contrast to his predecessors, as recorder he was both considerate and merciful. Four years into his recordership one contemporary reported:

> I have never seen one who seemed to me to be more deeply or more permanently impressed with a sense of the serious responsibility of his situation. . . . He unites in a rare degree the gravity of the judge with the mildness and manners of a gentleman. He is ever anxious to anticipate the wishes of the unfortunate parties at the bar; and to afford them every opportunity of doing everything which the law allows, to procure their acquittal. He listens most patiently to everything they have to say, at whatever sacrifice of his own time, and however great the amount of personal labour to himself. He does this even when his most decided impression is, that there is not the slightest chance of an acquittal. A more humane judge never sat in a court of justice: you see kindness in his looks; humanity shows itself in every word he utters. His leanings, wherever the case can admit of leaning, are always on mercy's side.[103]

John Mirehouse attracted more criticism. A Welshman commonly referred to as "Taffy," Mirehouse was said to have turned the Old Bailey into "a low-comedy theatre."[104] While the barristers who appeared before him described the common serjeant as "good-humoured and kindly enough,"[105] the press proved more censorious. "If the judge allow himself to degenerate into the jester," wrote *The Times* in disgust, "if the court of criminal justice is to be transformed into a theatre of mirth — the judge on the bench the chief actor in the farce — in the name of consistency, let him throw off the costume under which a decent solemnity has been wont to be exhibited, and let the cap and bells be substituted for the coif, and the particoloured coat for the judicial robe!" Better still, "let him vacate the bench, for which his mirthful propensities render him unfit."[106] The speed at which Mirehouse conducted trials was also censured. Robinson cited the following as typical of the sort of trial over which Mirehouse presided in the New Court:

> The Common Serjeant to the prosecutrix, after getting her name and address:
> "Were you in such a street on such a day?"
> "Yes, my lord."

"Had you a purse in your hand?"

"Yes, my lord."

"Policeman, produce the purse. Is that your purse?"

"Yes, my lord."

"Did you see the prisoner?"

"Yes, my lord."

"What did he do?"

"He snatched the purse from me, and ran away."

Mirehouse to the prisoner: "Prisoner, do you wish to ask the witness anything?"

"No, my lord."

"Policeman, did you apprehend the prisoner?"

"Yes, my lord, and found this purse upon him."

"Did he say anything?"

"He said he picked it up in the street."

"Prisoner, do you wish to say anything to the jury?"

"No, my lord, except that what I told the policeman is true."

Mirehouse. "Well, gentlemen of the jury, if you believe the evidence, you will say that the prisoner is guilty. He says he picked up the purse in the street. I have walked the streets of London for many years now, and I have never been lucky enough to pick up a purse; perhaps some of you have. Consider your verdict."[107]

Serjeant Robinson described Mirehouse as "a blunt, honest, straight-forward dispenser of justice, who never wasted time." He acknowledged the "celerity" with which Mirehouse dispensed justice—"I have known him more than once sentence a man to seven years' transportation at the end of as many minutes from the commencement of the trial"[108]—but Robinson did not believe that the speed produced injustice. *The Times*, however, was not of the same opinion. Reporting a trial conducted with similar speed, it wrote: "Five or six witnesses examined—as many clever jokes perpetrated—a prisoner bantered—a jury charged—the verdict returned—the criminal sentenced to transportation—and all *in six minutes!*"[109] Mirehouse seems to have taken the criticism to heart, for about a week later the paper re-ported a "marvellous change for the better." The common serjeant managed to preserve "a degree of gravity and decorum which was truly edifying," re-fraining from making even a single joke at a prisoner's expense and taking "nearly two minutes" to sum up cases for the jury. Unlike his predecessors, *The Times* concluded, Mirehouse appeared to be sensitive to public opinion, and hopes were held out for continued improvement.[110]

The way in which the City judges administered justice was a matter of no small import, for they in fact presided over most of the cases tried at the Central Criminal Court. The official division of labor was spelled out in the *Westminster Review*. In the Old Court, two judges of the superior courts tried capital cases from ten until five o'clock; after five the recorder sat with a London jury until nine. In the New Court, the common serjeant and commissioner tried noncapital cases, judge and jury again being changed at five o'clock. In practice, this division was sometimes blurred, the high court judges trying larcenies in the absence of capital cases, and the City judges given capital cases if larcenies ran out.[111] The House of Lords Papers for 1835 provide hard evidence of the actual apportioning of business. A return drawn up by John Clarke, who had been officially reinstalled as clerk of arraigns when the Old Bailey became the Central Criminal Court, shows the number of cases heard before the City officers and the Westminster judges, respectively, breaking the totals down by offense for the six months ending 5 April 1835 (the six months, that is, following the opening of the Central Criminal Court) and the equivalent periods for 1830 to 1834. Between November and April 1835 the City judges had heard a total of 860 cases, the superior court judges 132. The Westminster judges had tried the majority of burglary and housebreaking cases, as well as those of murder and rape, but the most common charge was some form of larceny, and these cases were tried before the recorder, common serjeant, and commissioner (674 of their total of 860).[112] Three years later the *Monthly Law Magazine* likewise turned its attention to the division of labor between the Westminster judges and City officers. The judges of the King's Bench, Common Pleas, and Exchequer, it claimed, attended in rotation "during one-third of the sittings only." The "real, permanent, and influential judges are the Lord Mayor for the time being of the city of London; the aldermen of the city of London; the Recorder, the Common-Serjeant, and the judges of the Sheriff's Court of the city of London." Of roughly 136 hours of business in a typical sessions it estimated the queen's judges were present for a mere 28; "notwithstanding the parade of high-sounding names in the first section" of the Central Criminal Court Act, the City authorities, it concluded in horror, transacted four-fifths of the business.[113] The remainder of the article was devoted to an explication of the "glaring impolicy" of such a system.

The Bar and the Central Criminal Court

If the City's wings had not been clipped in the legislation of 1834, many still hoped that the opening of the Central Criminal Court would prove something of a watershed in the administration of criminal justice in London. Apart from the benefits arising from more frequent sessions and jurisdictional boundaries that provided an accurate reflection of contemporary urban geography, professionals and laypersons alike anticipated an improvement in the professional tone of the court. Writing on 8 November 1834, the *Legal Observer* commented at length on the perceived benefits of the act. At the Old Bailey, the paper wrote, "we have here seen counsel forget not only all respect for the Bench, but all respect for themselves; we have here seen attorneys resort to means and take up expedients disgraceful in the extreme; we have here seen the faults of a few practitioners throw a shade over the whole Court; we have here also seen Judges give way to petulance and ill-breeding." The creation of the Central Criminal Court presented an opportunity for change:

> [W]e must express a hope, that with the new Court may arise a new school of practitioners—that we shall cease to consider persons exclusively practising in this Court as belonging to an inferior grade in the profession—that we shall not see the administration of justice impeded and defaced by indecent exhibitions of temper, or open defiance of professional superiors. We have the most sufficient proof that criminal business can be conducted with perfect order and becoming dispatch, in every assize town. Why is the metropolis to bear the disgrace of being worse off than the provinces? Why is her great Criminal Court to be the place in which all the intestine broil of lawyers are to be settled? Jealous of the honour and good name of our profession, we, who in common with all its members, have witnessed the injury which is done to it, with the public, by such scenes, that we fain trust that they are never again to be enacted—that lawyers will not here forget to be gentlemen, and that the manners and practices—we hardly make use of language too strong—of the criminals at the bar, may be confined to *them*.[114]

The Times similarly expressed the hope that the reorganization of London's premier criminal court would lead to improvements in professional behavior: "It is true that to put a pig in a drawing-room will not make a gentleman out of him, but it denies him the opportunity of wallowing."[115] Where the bar was concerned the Central Criminal Court Act did have one immediate effect in that the number of barristers attached to the criminal court almost doubled. *The Times* reported that on the opening of the new court, counsel "mustered unusually strong" and "the place appropriated for them could only with difficulty contain them."[116] Those counsel, roughly twenty-five in number, previously recorded in the *Law List* as attending the London, Middlesex, and Westminster sessions were now listed as well under a new heading, "Counsel, Central Criminal Court," but under that heading were also to be found a further nineteen men, presumably anticipating that the court's expanded jurisdiction would create opportunities for employment.[117] *The Times* looked with some hope to the benefits anticipated of expansion alone, believing it would contribute to an elevated professional atmosphere. "Too close neighbourhood" fostered petty envy and jealousy, the paper claimed, and opening the competition would eliminate such problems.[118] By the early 1840s, however, the number of counsel attached to the Central Criminal Court had dropped again by roughly half, returning to a figure of twenty or so.[119] Business, moreover, continued to be concentrated in the hands of a very few barristers after the Central Criminal Court Act as before. Charles Phillips retained an effective monopoly until his retirement from practice in 1842, after which time William Ballantine, who began to practice in London's criminal courts in 1834, assumed the lead. Any attempt to unseat Phillips when the Central Criminal Court opened would have been futile. The man Ballantine "feared most," "the man most in [his] line," was the "loud-voiced and swaggering" Clarkson. "[I]t soon became apparent," Ballantine said, "that either he or I must go to the wall. I infinitely preferred that it should be he, and so I devoted my whole life to worrying him. I drove him first to sedative pills, and finally to carbuncles—and he died."[120]

Ballantine's own reputation, like that of the barristers who preceded him, was mixed. He was remembered by colleagues as an "advocate of quite extraordinary skill," "a man of remarkable power," a barrister with a facility for thinking on his feet, picking up a case as it went along and relying on a quick consultation with his junior rather than a thorough reading of his brief. His curious, somewhat hesitant drawl, whether due to infirmity or affectation, proved highly effective, and Ballantine was soon recognized as a "great verdict-getter."[121] He had charm and the ability to dominate a courtroom, leading or coercing witnesses, judge, and jury alike. Like that of his predecessors at the Old Bailey, Ballantine's knowledge of the law was not deep, but he was a highly skilled advocate with a marked talent for cross-examination. He shared with Peter Alley a reputation for a violent temper and bitter sarcasm, but while his "combative tendency" ensured success at the bar, Ballantine, his colleagues argued, was "certainly . . . not amenable to the censure frequently cast on the Bar generally, of needlessly harassing witnesses with questions injurious to their character, and only calculated to outrage their feelings." "I have," Robinson wrote, "known many instances in which a witness has been produced against him, whose reputation he might have torn to shreds, if it had served the purpose of his client to have the lash administered; but, when the testimony was of no great importance, he has allowed the witness to go down with scarcely a question put to him."[122] Robinson also claimed, however, that in his personal life Ballantine had no fixity of opinion: "In truth, every sentiment he uttered was the result of mere temporary impulse. . . . He got a reputation for being utterly destitute of all creed, because he represented so many, at various times. . . . He was very like a chameleon."[123]

As argued in the preceding chapter, reports of professional misconduct at the Old Bailey may have been exaggerated. But even if the majority of business contracted at the Old Bailey was conducted in a seemly fashion, that court had nonetheless acquired a bad reputation in both the lay and professional press.[124] In attributing blame for the unruly conduct of some members of London's criminal bar, many pointed accusing fingers at the bench, in particular at the City judges. The *Monthly Law Magazine* commented at some length on "the interdependence of character between the bench and the bar": "[A] vicious and ignorant judge will produce a corrupt and contemptible bar."[125] The City judges, it was commonly believed, whose own behavior was so frequently the source of controversy, were less likely than the judges of the superior courts to check those excesses of behavior thought typical of the Old Bailey's bar. Turning to the specific occupants of the City offices when the Central Criminal Court came into being—Law, Mirehouse, and Arabin—the *Monthly Law Magazine* wrote that "the first is the only one who requires any consideration there, as we believe he is the only one possessing any elsewhere."[126] Mirehouse and Arabin might be gentlemen of "excellent pedigree" and highly respectable in their private lives, but a worse choice of judges to preside at the Old Bailey could not have been made: "If there be anything about them that is entitled to distinction, it is a distinguished want of all the endowments necessary to the situations which they hold. They are bad in manners, bad in temper, bad in law, and bad in English."[127] The journal granted that the City had been more fortunate in the appointment of its recorder (which good fortune it attributed entirely to luck), and praised Law at some length, but lamented the fact that he did not apply himself to correcting the abuses found within his court. His bearing toward the bar was "not only utterly deficient in steadiness, but . . . calculated to encourage all those vices which appear to be engendered by the very atmosphere of the Old Bailey." Old Bailey barristers, the journal argued, were distinguished by a desire to overbear the judge. But instead of endeavoring to improve the conduct of the counsel who routinely appeared before him, or to invite the presence of other and better counsel, Law merely made obvious his "*contempt*" for them, and his desire that "there should be no counsel at all." That contempt, and a continual interference with the proceedings of counsel, rather than proving them to be unnecessary, merely demonstrated that Law considered counsel "very much in the way."[128]

Evening Sittings and Civic Hospitality

Evening sittings at the Old Bailey had been a cause of complaint since the late eighteenth century[129] and attracted sustained criticism in the first half of the nineteenth century. Low professional standards were thought to fall even lower after five o'clock, for although judges were changed then, counsel were not. Moreover, both counsel and judges had dined well at the City's expense. The long-standing tradition of civic hospitality during the sessions became itself the subject of widespread criticism. "Judicial guzzling" at the Old Bailey, it was complained in Parliament, "materially interfered with the ends of justice."[130] Two dinners were served, hosted by the sheriffs, one at three o'clock for the judges and aldermen sitting in the evening, and one at five for those coming off duty. Counsel were often invited to partake, and the Ordinary (the chaplain of Newgate) reputedly dined at both; Montagu Williams reported later in the century that he "seemed as though he were literally saturated with City feasts."[131] Marrow puddings and beefsteaks figured prominently on the menu, and the wine flowed liberally. "[O]ne cannot but look back with a feeling of disgust to the mode in which eating and drinking, transporting and hanging, were shuffled together," wrote Serjeant Ballantine.[132] The City's judges "rush[ed] from the table to take their seats upon the bench, the jokes of the table scarcely out of their lips, and the amount of wine drunk, not rendered less apparent from having been drunk quickly."[133] Another contemporary recalled:

> The dinners were good, the wines abundant, and the results visible at the evening sittings. A barrister who had been cross-examining, and speaking for eight hours, was not unlikely to take more than a little wine for his stomach's sake, and was sometimes called down to defend a prisoner without any very clear notion that he was not to prosecute. The juries who came to sit at five, of course had dined, and living men have seen a judge (not one of the fifteen) descend the stairs, holding fast by the bannister, not in wantonness of care, and afterwards trying prisoners, when unable to read the depositions accurately, or to understand the witnesses' answers, yet getting through the work from memory and

habit. The witnesses, who had been waiting all the day in the Old Bailey public houses, were often very drunk. One alderman must always be in the court; no one knows why, but such is the law, and his worship was frequently in a state of modified sobriety. Quarrels of the most discreditable order might be expected from a court so composed. It is better not to attempt a description of the *rows*. Those who have been present at them will remember; those who have not would disbelieve.[134]

The novelist Theodore Hook—an acquaintance if not close friend of John Adolphus, and a friend of Ballantine[135]—mocked the dinners served at the Central Criminal Court in *Gilbert Gurney* (1836), tying the recorder's sentencing decisions directly to the quality of the wine served:

> "Walter Cutts, stealing two loaves—seven years for him, I think. Did you ever taste such stuff as that wine, Mr. Ordinary?" . . .
>
> ". . . [I]t is an absolute insult.—Well—Stephen Robinson, for stealing two pewter pots—upon my honour it is enough to bring on a cholera morbus—Robinson, seven years' transportation. Vinegar would be just as palatable. Rachel Marsh, fourteen years—abominable woman. Simon Warner, pair of boots, umph—oh, I recollect that case—transportation for life . . ."
>
> "Will your lordship please to try this," said Mr. Butler, proffering a new bottle. His lordship, still muttering indignation, filled his glass, and after smelling its *bouquet*, and looking at its brightness, swallowed the contents. "Ah," said his lordship, "this is something like wine—why did not you give us this at first, Mr. Butler? Fill my glass again—hand it round. . . . [E]xcellent, excellent wine indeed. Well, let us finish our business. Robert Holland, stealing fourteen gold watches, thirty-four gold chains, six timekeepers, and sundry loose diamonds, oh—in a dwelling-house—well, let's say three months for him—capital wine, isn't it, Mr. Clerk—capital. Roger Perkins, three mares and a foal—six weeks' imprisonment. Anne Griffiths, administering poison to her mother, aunt, and two sisters—poor girl—case of mistake, eh—pass that bottle, Mr. Ordinary—what shall we say—childish carelessness—one month. Simmons, cow—oh—fine one shilling and discharge—that's the last—the last."[136]

In 1832 the editor of the *Legal Examiner* had beseeched the magistrates of the City of London to "lift up their eyes even to the bench, and amongst themselves." Some "of the after-dinner trials we have witnessed, induce us to propose for the adoption of their worships, the following club-like regulation: — 'When prisoners are to be tried after dinner, no alderman or other officer to be allowed more than four glasses of wine; — at other times he may drink any quantity.' "[137] The *Monthly Law Magazine*, for its part, called the evening sittings "very abominations" and urged their abolition.[138] Writing in the late 1880s, Serjeant Robinson insisted that neither Ballantine nor other contemporaries had "at all exaggerated the unseemly condition which the subordinate occupants of the Bench presented on very many occasions." He denied that "any serious injustice" was likely to result from a drunken bench and bar: "[T]he clerks of the court were steady, responsible men," and prevented proceedings from going seriously awry. Still, he admitted, "it was a grievous scandal, that the courts presented the appearance they so frequently did."[139]

In the 1830s many members of the public clearly agreed. The issue of evening sittings was taken up in the newspaper press, and in 1838 the *Morning Herald* reported that a grand jury's presentment requesting that the court sit from nine to six had been met with a threat to resign by several aldermen, who estimated that the alteration would extend the sessions by three or four extra days.[140] While the sheriffs' dinners continued until 1877, the evening sessions were finally abolished in 1844,[141] and from that date the City judges began to do "soberly and demurely by day what they had been in the habit of doing so questionably by night."[142]

Conclusion

The reconstitution of the Old Bailey as the Central Criminal Court ultimately served to extend the authority of the City of London where criminal justice was concerned. The City retained its ancient privileges with respect to the composition of the bench, and it was the City judges — the recorder, common serjeant, and commissioner — who absorbed the steady increase in business. But those judges, and the process by which they reached the bench, had by the 1830s become the focus of considerable controversy. The practice of rotation of City offices, first evident in the career of John Silvester, had taken firm root, largely for political reasons. The promotion of junior City officials provided the Court of Aldermen with a means by which to exclude those candidates for election to higher office whose reform-minded politics were deemed objectionable, and the overlap among the incumbents of the lowest offices — the common pleaderships — and Old Bailey practitioners resulted in the promotion of a number of Old Bailey counsel to the bench. But in the first half of the nineteenth century this development had adverse consequences for justice. The barristers promoted on the basis of their political

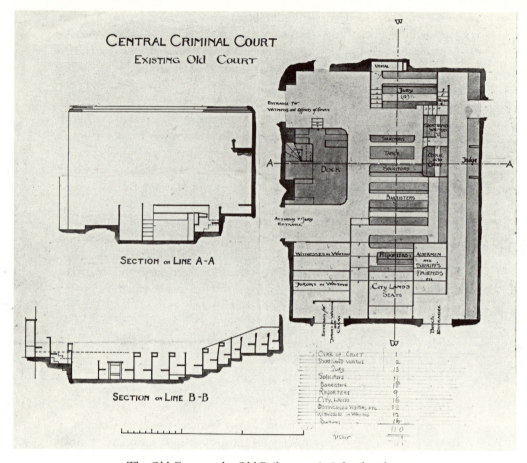

The Old Court at the Old Bailey, ca. 1848; by that date
two courtrooms were no longer sufficient, and a third was added
(Corporation of London Records Office)

conservatism possessed little professional reputation, and with the exception of Law, once on the bench they consistently attracted negative comment. Silvester and Knowlys lacked compassion, Mirehouse and Arabin the gravitas becoming to a judge.

The reputation of the City judges would improve somewhat in the second half of the nineteenth century. R. M. Kerr, who served as commissioner from 1859 until 1901, was admittedly something of an anachronism. Kerr was described as "a law unto himself, an able but cantankerous lawyer, who lacked both polish and reasonableness."[143] But his superiors enjoyed a more positive reputation. When Charles Ewan Law died in 1850 he was succeeded as recorder by a comparatively distinguished outsider, Sir J. A. Stuart Wortley, who went on to become solicitor general. Wortley, Ballantine reported, "was as good a criminal judge as ever sat upon the Bench. I never saw him out of temper. He was a sound lawyer, and managed the court admirably."[144] In Wortley's successor, Russell Gurney, QC, MP, the principle of rotation was revived, but with a positive result.[145] Gurney was elected common serjeant in April 1856 and recorder in December of the same year.[146] The grandson of eighteenth-century shorthand reporter Joseph Gurney and son of former Old Bailey barrister turned baron of the Exchequer John Gurney, Russell had, like his early-nineteenth-century predecessors, combined practice at the Central Criminal Court with a City pleadership, and he had been elected a judge of the Sheriffs' Court in 1850. But his lengthy recordership (1856–78) attracted praise rather than censure or ridicule. "Mr. Gurney," the *Law Journal* reported on his death in 1878, "was of that type of lawyer and gentleman of which the profession and the country are justly proud, and the recollection of his sterling qualities will not soon fade away."[147] Gurney was also a man of liberal principles, championing not only reform of the criminal law but the rights of women.[148] While the days in which a recorder of London went on to become chief justice of the Court of King's Bench or lord chancellor were over, so too were those in which London's senior legal officer was despised as an ill-mannered reactionary.

CHAPTER SEVEN

Changing the Rules:
The Prisoners' Counsel Act

When the Old Bailey reopened as the Central Criminal Court in 1834, the rules under which its counsel operated remained essentially the same. Defense counsel were prohibited from addressing the jury, and, in recognition of this handicap, counsel for the prosecution continued to restrain their opening addresses. The evidence of the OBSP suggests that the proportion of cases in which counsel appeared on both sides had changed little from the beginning of the century. The majority of cases were tried without any counsel at all. But even in the small percentage of trials (between 6 and 12 percent in the first three decades of the nineteenth century)[1] in which counsel were engaged for both the prosecution and the defense, no full-fledged adversarial contest could take place. Two years later, however, an act was passed that would radically alter both the dynamic of the felony trial and the duties of defense counsel.

The Prisoners' Counsel Act, which recognized the right of a defendant to legal counsel and allowed defense counsel to address the jury on their clients' behalf, forms part of the larger process of the legislative dismantling of the ancien régime. It can be grouped with the repeal of the Test and Corporation Acts, Catholic emancipation, the Reform Act of 1832, the new poor law, municipal reform, and, in particular, the reduction of the scope of the death penalty. Together these various measures signaled the end of an era. Unlike the removal of religious restrictions on political participation or the expansion of the franchise, however, this particular reform never became a truly "public" issue. The English public did not take to heart the plight of those accused of felony as they did, for instance, the suffering of slaves. While defendants had from the eighteenth century repeatedly requested in court that they be allowed to make their case via counsel, rather than being forced to speak for themselves, there is no evidence of sustained popular agitation for

such a right. The people did not take to the streets to demonstrate on behalf of prisoners, nor did they systematically petition Parliament. When, in
1824, a group of Old Bailey jurors presented a petition in favor of the prisoners' counsel bill then under consideration, Lord North snorted, "A single
petition! Were the people of England in the habit of expressing their opinions or wishes upon a great public question by a single petition?"[2] Even the
bills' supporters were forced to acknowledge that "the people" might not
have formed any opinion at all on the issue. Sydney Smith's scathing indictment of the unreformed system in the *Edinburgh Review* in 1827[3] was unique:
the bourgeois public—the "rate-paying, opinion-forming middle class"[4]—
remained largely silent on the subject of the rights of prisoners. Debate over
the issue of prisoners' counsel thus took place for the most part in Parliament and, to a lesser extent, in the legal professional press.

The Campaign for Reform

Prisoners' counsel first became a political issue in 1821, when an independent
MP named Richard Martin[5] introduced the first bill proposing to allow per-
sons charged with capital felonies to make their defense by counsel.[6] Martin
would introduce the majority of the bills presented to the House in the
1820s (four of six); he was supported in his efforts by reform-minded Whigs:
Sir James Mackintosh, Stephen Lushington,[7] Thomas Denman, Thomas
Spring Rice, and George Lamb, among others. Lamb, the brother of Lord
Melbourne, introduced a prisoners' counsel bill of his own in 1824.

As the parliamentary campaign for the act progressed, the scope of the
proposals broadened. Where Martin's one-clause bills proposed that defendants charged with capital offenses be granted the right to make their defense by counsel, Lamb's bill of 1824 would have entitled any defendant to
the same right, regardless of the penalty attached to the crime as charged.
At the time such a proposal was so unacceptable to the government that
even its introduction was overwhelmingly opposed. Prisoners' counsel received little support from the Tory-dominated, anti-reform government of
the 1820s (both the attorney general and the solicitor general were against
the measure), and only the bill of 1825 passed the second reading stage.

By the 1830s, however, political circumstances were radically altered—the
Tory government fell in 1830 over the issue of parliamentary reform—and
the campaign for prisoners' counsel entered a second phase: the bills introduced by William Ewart[8] in 1833, 1834, 1835, and 1836 had the broad approval
of a reform-minded government. A lawyer himself, Ewart also supported
radical parliamentary reform and the total abolition of the death penalty,

and his prisoners' counsel bills went further in terms of content than their predecessors. He proposed not only to grant the right to a full legal defense to any defendant, regardless of the charge, but to reserve for defense counsel the right to make the final speech to the jury. Ewart also included provision for the establishment of a form of legal aid: where a defendant could not afford to employ counsel the judge would be required to assign a barrister in attendance to his or her case, whose services would be provided without a fee. Finally, he proposed that defendants be granted the right to be represented before justices in summary proceedings and to be provided with copies of the depositions to be sworn against them. Neither the provision for legal aid nor the right of defense counsel to have the final word survived in the act of 1836.

As the arguments made in Parliament for and against the Prisoners' Counsel Act have been thoroughly addressed by both John Beattie and David Cairns, I will only summarize them here. Proponents of the legislation stressed the unfairness of a system in which a dazed and frightened defendant, ignorant of the law and of criminal procedure, was forced to make his or her own defense, while the prosecution may have been undertaken by a professional advocate, whose opening remarks frequently created a prejudice among the jury against the accused. Those against the alteration argued that the defendant had no need of independent counsel, as the judge could be relied upon to protect his or her interest. Moreover, prosecuting counsel, aware of the advantage they possessed, could be depended upon to exercise restraint in their opening remarks—a restraint, based on the evidence of the OBSP, that generally appears to have been observed. The existing system, the opposition claimed, worked to the advantage of the accused; allowing a full-fledged adversarial contest between professional advocates to occur would be detrimental to his or her interests. Passion and bias would be introduced, and the criminal trial would be "turned into an arena for ingenious display."[9] The reformers repeatedly drew attention to the theoretical inconsistency of a system which allowed persons accused of misdemeanors the right to a full legal defense but denied that right to accused felons. Opponents of the legislation, however, suggested that a closer look might be taken at the effects of adversarial procedure in trials of misdemeanor.

At issue during the debates was not merely the unfairness of a system that denied to prisoners the right to a full legal defense but, more important, the best method for determining the truth of a charge against a prisoner. John Copley (later Lord Lyndhurst), who had entered Parliament in 1818, based his arguments first against a Prisoners' Counsel Act and then in favor of one on the assumption that a trial was an investigation of "truth."[10] The object of a court of justice was to elicit "the truth," and the principal point at issue when contemplating altering the form of the criminal trial was "the best mode of investigating the truth."[11] Copley presumably spoke from his experience of criminal trials on the Midland circuit and elsewhere.[12] Thomas Denman, politically of a very different stripe, had used the same wording in the 1824 debates: "[T]he discovery of the truth should be allowed to take its chances in a contest of equal talents. . . . All minor considerations should be sacrificed to the larger and more important question of the best mode of coming at the truth."[13] James Scarlett, one of the most famous advocates of the day,[14] likewise argued that the object in the criminal trial, as in its civil counterpart, was "the investigation of truth"; the object of the prisoners' counsel bill was "that the truth should be investigated," and in his opinion it would be better investigated if a free discussion of the charges was allowed to both sides.[15] The Commission on the Criminal Law, established in 1833 by the lord chancellor, Henry Brougham, to codify the criminal law, similarly introduced the subject of prisoners' counsel by stating that its inquiry seemed to involve "two principal questions": "Whether the allowing a defence by the speech of Counsel on charges of Felony tend to the discovery of truth; and if so, Whether that advantage be counterbalanced by any inconveniences inseparable from the practice."[16] The relationship between truth and advocacy was thus the key issue in the debates leading up to the Prisoners' Counsel Act.[17]

The "truth" in question was the truth of the facts of individual crimes, and this emphasis was made possible by the increasingly restricted application of the death penalty. As we saw in Chapter 4, while capital punishment attached to felonies the question at trial was frequently more than the literal or moral guilt of the accused. Whether the defendant had committed the offense charged in the indictment was certainly an issue, but there were further considerations at play in the decision-making process, for the jury had also to decide whether what he had done merited the death penalty. Albany Fonblanque, writing for the radical weekly, the *Examiner*, pointed to this stumbling block to an investigation of the truth in 1827: "A common effect of the severity of the Law is, to turn the humanity of society to the account of criminals, and to habituate men in the discharge of a most solemn duty to the violation of truth. In trying a prisoner, regard is generally had to the nature of the punishment awaiting him, before the inquiry is directed to the truth of the charge, and belief or disbelief of the evidence is proportioned to the probable character of the sentence."[18] A jury convinced that the punishment awaiting a convicted felon would be proportionate to the offense committed would be more likely to render a "true" verdict. The timing of the Prisoners' Counsel Act is thus "intimately linked," as Beattie points out, to a broader reform of the criminal law, and the campaigns for repeal of the death penalty and for the prisoner's right to counsel involved many of the same MPS.[19]

When Silvester and Garrow, Knowlys and Knapp embarked upon their legal careers in the late eighteenth century, the death penalty was prescribed for the majority of serious offenses. By the time of Garrow's call to the bar, however, the traditional penal code was under attack. Both the use of terror and the exercise of mercy were condemned by reformers who argued that certain punishment, proportionate to the offense, would be both more humane and more effective. These principles had been articulated by Cesare Beccaria in a work translated into English in 1767 as *Of Crimes and Punishments*.[20] Beccaria argued that a system of punishment that centered on the death penalty was not only barbaric but did not work: that is, it failed to reduce the incidence of crime. Arbitrary and discretionary punishments must therefore be replaced by those which were explicable and rational. The parliamentary campaign for the reduction of capital punishment began in the early nineteenth century, under the leadership first of Samuel Romilly and then, after Romilly's death in 1819, of James Mackintosh. Robert Peel, during his tenure at the Home Office in the 1820s, removed capital punishment from a variety of minor offenses and between 1827 and 1830 consolidated the criminal law into four major statutes. Benefit of clergy was abolished, and the entire law relating to theft was consolidated; the distinction between grand and petty larceny was eliminated, and the amount beyond which stealing from a dwelling house became a capital offense was raised to £5. Dramatic decline in the application of the death penalty, however, occurred in the 1830s: by 1839 only fifteen capital statutes remained in force.[21] This reform was not purely humanitarian in intent. The unreformed system of punishment, as Beattie argues, allowed "too much scope for discretionary and essentially personal and irregular decisions," and discretion and uncertainty in the administration of the criminal law were anathema to the nineteenth-century reformers.[22] The granting of the right to counsel, while rooted in a general rejection of paternalism and representing an affirmation of individual rights, owed equally to a rejection of discretionary justice and a desire for greater certainty in the criminal trial.[23] A reduction in the scope of capital punishment and the introduction of punishment that was both less severe and proportionate to the offense freed juries from considerations external to the question of whether a prisoner was guilty as charged, allowing them to focus on the truth of the charges laid: "justice" and "truth" now converged. Debate over the Prisoners' Counsel Act thus turned on whether permitting defense counsel to address the jury would promote or impede discovery of the truth.

The Prisoners' Counsel Act and the Legal Periodical Press

In the 1830s support for the various prisoners' counsel bills was voiced in much of the newly emerged legal professional press—a press that had been virtually nonexistent when the first bills were introduced a decade earlier.[24] Many of the new journals were progressive in their views. *The Jurist*, for instance, established with the help of Henry Brougham and edited by Henry Roscoe, a reforming Whig, offered Whig criticism of the law. Given the character of the professional press, it is not surprising to find it supporting a prisoner's right to make his or her full defense by counsel. "H. W. G.," writing in the *Legal Observer* in 1834, hoped the proposed bill would be carried: "[I]t has always appeared to us a piece of cruelty and absurdity, that when a prisoner is tried for any capital felony his counsel is not allowed to speak for him." What was wanted was "fair-play speech" for both the prosecution and the defense or "speech for none."[25] When the bill passed the House of Commons in July 1835 the *Legal Observer* commented, somewhat regally, "[W]e are inclined to give it our concurrence," arguing that there were cases in the experience of almost every barrister "where a speech may unquestionably save an innocent man, and where it is his only chance": "[A]s a general rule, discussion will confirm the escape of the innocent, but must clinch the punishment of the guilty."[26] It subsequently argued that an accused should be entitled to pretrial professional assistance, in order that witnesses might be cross-examined and "observations" made to the magistrate "as may be deemed necessary."[27] When the act finally passed in 1836, the journal commented with some satisfaction that its benefits would soon become obvious once the novelty had worn off: "It seems to have created some surprise that although prisoners employ counsel, who address the jury in their behalf under the act, they are nevertheless convicted; but a different result, as a general rule, was never expected or wished by the supporters of the measure. At least nine out of ten prisoners tried for criminal offenses are guilty, and it was always urged that the effect of the act would be to make their guilt more evident, by causing a fuller investigation into it. No one ever desired that the rogues should escape, but simply that honest men should come by their own."[28] The *Legal Examiner* likewise expressed its approval of the measure. An article published in that paper in 1832 pointed to the fact that England was unique in prohibiting legal counsel to speak for the accused in felony trials and, like the parliamentary reformers, emphasized the disadvantages experienced by the defendant—"natural incapacity . . . want of education, or even . . . an overwhelming sense of disgrace or danger"—forced to make his or her own defense. The journal rejected the view that the judge acted as a safeguard of the accused's interest and equally dismissed the notion that allowing defense counsel to speak to the jury would reduce the contest to one of "passions and feelings." The article concluded, however, not with further consideration of the benefits to the accused, but with the potential benefit to the bar. If the bill were adopted, it might create "a wider field for the display of eloquence in our Courts," causing "that noble and valuable talent to be more assiduously and effectively cultivated amongst us than at present."[29]

Only the *Law Magazine* seemed lukewarm about the reform. In 1835 it drew attention to the fact that the bill then before the House of Commons passed "by a majority of one; a sufficient proof that it was opposed to the conviction of the House." For their part, the editors believed the importance of the measure to have been "greatly overrated": "[I]t is capable neither of so much good nor of so much evil as its advocates and adversaries contend; but we anticipate much more evil than good from it if it is passed." "Will any good result," they wrote, "from . . . exposing juries to have their own plain impressions disordered by the glosses counsel may put upon the facts? or will even the prisoner be a gainer by the privilege, with a judge released from the direct responsibility of protecting him, and a prosecuting counsel set free from the restraints imposed upon this peculiar department of advocacy?"[30] An article published in the following year specifically denied both the efficacy of allowing defense counsel in felony trials the right to make a speech and the utility of professional adversarial process in the criminal trial: "It is our firm conviction that truth is, after all, most imperfectly elicited by the contention of the bar; the side that wins may be the right side, but it often, too often, wins by tact, by trickery, by manoeuvring, by chance. Talk over their field-days with the leaders of the bar, and you will be told repeatedly that the verdict hung trembling in the balance from circumstances wholly independent of the merits, and was won or lost eventually, not by soundness of argument or weight of proof, but by exciting or soothing some prejudice of the jury or the judge, by suppressing or injudiciously producing a document, by calling evidence and giving, or keeping back evidence with the view of preventing, the reply."[31] In civil cases counsel's speeches, "with all their tendency to mislead," constituted a lesser evil. In determining complicated questions of damages or liability—unlike the simple question of guilt or innocence—both judge and jury often required the assistance of counsel. Moreover, both parties to a civil action were likely to have relatively equal means of retaining counsel. The resulting contest would therefore be reasonably balanced. The "real remedy" for the disadvantages suffered by prisoners had, the journal pointed out, been identified by one of the bill's opponents: "[A]gents should be employed at the public expense to inquire into criminal charges on behalf of the prisoner."[32] Permitting counsel to make speeches would only aggravate the existing inequality between prosecution and defense. The article concluded by pointing to the additional time and, consequently, expense required if the bill were to become law.

The Bench and the Bar

The support expressed in the legal periodical press for the proposals made by the various prisoners' counsel bills by and large did not reflect the sentiments of either the judiciary or the practicing bar, including that found at the Old Bailey. Few members of the legal profession welcomed the changes the measure would introduce. The *Law Magazine* reported that "a large proportion of the profession (including three-fourths of the judges)" were not in favor of the prisoners' counsel bill,[33] and professional hostility was equally admitted by the reformers themselves. George Lamb commented when he introduced his bill of 1824 that "the profession of the law were in general hostile to the change which he wished to make"; James Mackintosh allowed that "it might, perhaps, be said, with truth, that the majority of that learned profession were opposed to the measure" under consideration.[34] These opinions remained unchanged in the 1830s. Defense attorney James Harmer testified to the criminal law commissioners in May 1835 that he found "the generality of the profession are of opinion that counsel ought not to be allowed to speak for a prisoner, and that the practice would be injurious to the accused"; during debate in the House in 1836 Sir Eardley Wilmot similarly commented that "nine-tenths of the profession and the Judges were decidedly hostile to the alteration."[35] John Campbell, who supported the proposed legislation, testified to judicial antagonism in particular, recording in his diary, "I am sorry to say that twelve out of the fifteen [Westminster] judges strongly condemned the Prisoners' counsel bill." Mr. Justice James Allan Park had gone so far as to threaten to resign if Campbell allowed it to pass.[36]

The hostility of the bench, as Campbell noted with regret, perhaps owed in large part to self-interest. Some of the judges who opposed the Prisoners' Counsel Act, he feared, were "actuated unconsciously by the apprehension of the boring speeches they must listen to, and the additional labour which would be cast upon them."[37] The reluctance of other members of the

bench to listen to the speeches of defense counsel in felony trials undoubtedly stemmed from their experience of hearing such counsel hold forth in
trials of misdemeanor. The aggression typical of defense counsel in such
cases may also have contributed to judicial antagonism. The *Legal Observer*
commented in 1835 that "one or two Chairmen of Quarter Sessions, probably fatigued by the brawling of some hard-fighting junior, cannot endure
the thought of giving him unlimited time and scope for his tongue."[38] Professional conservatism, as Mackintosh recognized, was also at play. During debates in the House of Commons he identified "a feeling which he
feared might have powerfully influenced . . . members of the profession—
the strong effect of habit—the repugnance to change long-established rules
—the partiality they naturally felt for those forms of practice which they followed from the earliest days of their professional lives, and for that system
under which they had so long acted, and under which they had earned both
fortune and character."[39] Bentham had commented to the same effect, albeit
not in connection with the criminal law, "[I]n the eyes of the lawyers . . . the
is and the *ought to be*" are "one and indivisible"; Francis Horner, for his part,
wrote, "Of all persons, those that give you the least aid, when any thing is
to be done by legislation, are your ancient barristers; the two opinions of
mind, knowing what the laws are, and seeing what they had better be, seem
almost incompatible."[40]

Neither conservatism nor self-interest, however, can account entirely for
the bar's reaction to the Prisoners' Counsel Act. In a pamphlet published
in 1836, barrister Frederic Calvert agreed with the reformers that the "sole
object" of the criminal trial was to ascertain "the truth." He also accepted
that the prosecution and the defense ought to be accorded "perfectly equal
terms." But allowing a full, professional adversarial contest to develop, he
said, would serve only to aggravate the inequality between the prosecutor
and the accused: the prosecutor was usually wealthier than the defendant
and would be able to hire the better counsel. Why not instead, he suggested,
employ government agents at public expense to inquire into the charges,
on the prisoner's behalf? Admitting the discrepancy in procedure between
trials of felony and those of misdemeanor, Calvert argued that the proper
solution was to remove speech-making from trials of misdemeanor rather
than extend it to felony trials. Contrasting criminal trials with civil ones, he
pointed, as did many critics of the various prisoners' counsel bills, to the fact
that commercial transactions and those involving landed property would
be unintelligible to jurors without some explanation, whereas the "subject-
matter of criminal trials is almost always familiar to their minds" and required no explication by counsel. Moreover, the question to be determined

in criminal cases was a simple one: "[T]he prisoner either did, or did not do the act."[41]

Other members of the bar voiced similar opinions before the criminal law commissioners in 1835. Consultation with representatives of the legal profession had naturally been undertaken during the parliamentary campaign for a Prisoners' Counsel Act, and the partisan commissioners' leading questions did not always extract the answers they sought. Ewart, the MP responsible for introducing the prisoners' counsel bills of the 1830s, naturally pressed the case for reform; Sir Frederick Pollock and Stephen Lushington likewise expressed full support for prisoners' counsel. Serjeant D'Oyley, however, dissented. D'Oyley, whose knowledge of criminal practice was rooted in his attendance at the Sussex sessions, acknowledged that the procedural distinctions affecting trials of felony and misdemeanor were "almost a disgrace to the criminal judicature," but like Calvert he did not believe that the solution was to extend speech-making to felony trials: "I should rather have given my opinion the other way. . . . [A] criminal trial is better conducted without speeches."[42] Although the commissioners pressed the serjeant very hard, he did not waver in his position.[43] Serjeant Spankie concurred with D'Oyley's opinion.[44] He was not sure, he told the commissioners, that the "parade and array of counsel" in trials of misdemeanor had contributed to just verdicts or the protection of innocence. "The inquiry on the trial of a crime turns upon the truth of positive facts," he said. What was desired in the criminal trial was "a dispassionate inquiry" into that truth, an inquiry "relieved from the obstreperous contention of counsel." Spankie believed that the existing system presented a model of such inquiry. He also displayed very little confidence—in fact, none at all—in the response of the legal profession to the changes proposed. Advocates, he said, would not restrain themselves to commenting on evidence: juries would routinely be "flattered, or threatened, or deceived," resulting in verdicts against the evidence. "It appears to me . . . the effect of allowing counsel in felonies would totally destroy the temper, moderation, and sobriety of the administration of criminal justice. The counsel for the prosecution would follow the bad example of the counsel for the prisoner. In a public contest the strict discharge of duty would yield to the fame of eloquence and the ardour of victory; the authority of the judge would be despised; the jury would be exposed to the corruptions of the worst arts of the forum." Moreover, "the bar would be corrupted by the temptation to address speeches, not only to the juries, but to the audience; not only to the audience, but to political parties, or religious sects, all over the country, through the press." Spankie concluded that he could see "no good in the proposed experiment."[45]

What of those lawyers who practiced at the Old Bailey? Leading members of the lower branch of the legal profession came out strongly in favor of the bill, on the basis of their long-term experience of justice in metropolitan London's criminal courts. Both James Harmer, who dominated defense practice in the metropolis for the first three decades of the nineteenth century, and Thomas Wontner, usually employed by the prosecution, were firmly convinced that denying defense counsel the opportunity to comment on the evidence frequently resulted in the conviction of innocent persons.

Wontner's views on the subject appear in his *Old Bailey Experience*, one section of which was devoted to a report and commentary on the debate in the House of Commons on 28 March 1833 over the first of Ewart's bills. "Not to permit a prisoner to make a *full defence*," he wrote, "or, in other words, to oblige him to make an imperfect defence, while the accusation is pressed against him with all the aid of eloquent statement and ingenuity, is such gross and flagrant injustice, that it can only be accounted for on the principle that there is nothing, however monstrous or absurd in the institution of society, to which long habit cannot reconcile the human mind."[46] Answering the argument that an advocate could only worsen the accused's position, Wontner replied that the objection was ridiculous: advocacy could not harm innocent prisoners, for they had nothing to hide. And if an advocate would "provoke opposition and elicit more truths, and thereby occasion more convictions," was this outcome too not "very desirable"?[47] The object of the law was to acquit the innocent and punish the guilty. Contrasting practice in the criminal courts with that found in their civil counterparts, he pointed not to the complexity of issues in civil cases but to the issue of class: the legislators would not, in a property case, wish "to answer a declaration in ejectment without a counsel, so much more value is there set, in this 'Christian country,' on the property of the rich than the lives of the poor."[48] Wontner's concluding remarks were devoted to the inexperience of members of parliament with criminal procedure. They argued, he said, only from theory, without being possessed of the true facts: "[S]uch reasoners will ever fall into error."[49] Moreover, lacking the requisite knowledge themselves, they relied too heavily on the opinions of the ever-conservative bar. "[T]hose engaged in legislation," he warned, should beware of pinning their faith "on the evidence of those employed in carrying on the system as it now works."[50]

Harmer's views on the subject of prisoners' counsel are found in both his own published works and his testimony before the law commissioners.[51] By the 1830s James Harmer had long been a critic of the unreformed system. Like others who supported the prisoners' counsel bills, he deplored the discrepancy between the rules governing felony trials and those which applied to trials of high treason or misdemeanor and highlighted the factors preventing defendants from making an adequate defense on their own. Agitated, ignorant of the law, inarticulate, and unqualified for public debate, "[i]s a man, thus circumstanced, enabled to address the jury with effect?"[52] Not only was Harmer in favor of removing the restrictions on the activities of defense counsel, but like Ewart he recognized the need for some form of legal aid. Merely assigning counsel at the time of the trial, however, did not adequately address the problem. Preparation for trial had to be made well in advance, allowing for investigation into the circumstances of the crime. Even those accused who employed counsel suffered under a disadvantage; being poor, they were usually unable to raise the requisite fees until the last moment, so their defense was hastily assembled. Harmer also lamented the fact that defense counsel and attorneys were denied a copy of the indictment and thus forced to prepare for trial uncertain of the exact charges facing their client. Their exclusion from pretrial hearings at the whim of a magistrate was further cause for complaint. This exclusion particularly affected the innocent: a habitual thief "would tell [his attorney] every point of evidence against him, and what every man had said before a magistrate; but not so with a man that is innocent; he would be hardly able to tell . . . what had passed."[53]

The restrictions against which Harmer chafed all had their origins in the older form of trial, in which the accused's unrehearsed reaction to the charge in court was deemed essential to a determination of his guilt or innocence. His objections to being denied a copy of the indictment, to the authority of a magistrate to bar him from a pretrial hearing, and to the rule forbidding counsel to address the jury together constitute an unequivocal rejection of the traditional felony trial. Harmer wanted to be able to construct a complete case for the defendant, one which in court would be conducted and controlled by the barrister.

Harmer's professional clients—Old Bailey barristers—did not share his opinions. Experienced Old Bailey counsel as well as attorneys had been approached by the reformers as sources of potential support, and their opinions were solicited by the government in 1835. Among those who testified were Charles Ewan Law and Charles Phillips. As discussed in the previous chapter, Law, in 1835 recorder of London, had had an active Old Bailey practice before his elevation to the bench. His experience of London's criminal courts stretched back to 1820; he had also traveled the Home circuit and been employed at the Kent sessions. Charles Phillips, for his part, had dominated practice at the Old Bailey from the mid-1820s. Both men were emphatically opposed to allowing defense counsel to make speeches.

Law claimed that it was not in the prisoner's interest that his counsel should be allowed to address the jury, as he might have had the misfortune of employing an unsuccessful barrister.[54] In evidence given before the House of Lords Select Committee he pointed out that prosecutors were more likely to be in a position to hire the better counsel, while prisoners would rely on the young and inexperienced barristers who haunted the criminal sessions in search of work. Moreover, allowing prisoners' counsel to make speeches would introduce professional rivalries to the courtroom, and this would not be in the prisoners' best interest. He further stated: "My Opinion is, that to give the Prisoner a fairer and fuller Opportunity of Defence you would not resort so much to the Speeches of Counsel as affording him Facilities before the Trial of distinctly understanding the Sort of Charge made against him. I think the Depositions taken before the Magistrates should be delivered to him (they are in the Hands of the Prosecution), and a Copy of the Indictment. I think that every Means of thoroughly understanding and meeting the Charge should be given to the Prisoner, and that on the Trial he should be put on a Perfect Equality with the Prosecutor."[55] Law was not therefore advocating that the old form of criminal trial be retained: he did not believe that a prisoner should first hear of the exact charges against him in the courtroom. He did, however, like Spankie and D'Oyley, express a lack of faith in the potential of professional advocacy to contribute to a determination of the truth.

> I am not of opinion that the Speech of Counsel on one Side or the other is at all calculated to advance the Cause of Truth. I think there may be particular Cases in which the Talents of an Advocate, brought to bear upon the Facts, may be of Assistance to a Judge in the Train of Thought he may pursue, and enabling him perhaps in certain Instances more effectively to do his Duty; but I think that is rather the Exception than the Rule. I think that the Speeches of Counsel in Civil as well as in Criminal Cases do not lead to a satisfactory Issue in a Variety of Instances; and my Opinion is, that if the Speeches of Counsel were excluded, both for and against the Prisoner, (without any Remark on the Manner in which they are allowed in Civil Cases,) the Effect would be to produce greater Certainty in the Result of the Trial, and that the Result would in a greater Degree depend upon the Facts of the Case.[56]

When questioned as to whether the same argument would not apply to trials of misdemeanor, Law agreed, and he stated later in his testimony, "I think in Cases of Misdemeanour there have been a great many Acquittals contrary to the Effect of the Evidence."[57] Asked again if the proposed innovation, "[w]ithout regard to whether it is to the Benefit of the Prisoner or not," would introduce "the best Mode of investigating truth" he replied, "My Opinion rests upon that, that it does not advance the Cause of Truth and Justice."[58]

The common serjeant of London, John Mirehouse, similarly appears to have opposed the enactment of a Prisoners' Counsel Act that allowed defense counsel to make speeches, calling Ewart a "sugar hog's-head" when he succeeded in carrying it.[59] And while the views of the barristers then practicing at the Central Criminal Court are more difficult to determine, there is no evidence of any agitation among them for an expansion of their duties. In a case tried in Essex in 1800 Garrow had argued, "I had a right, if I could, indirectly to convey observations to the fact; and whatever other people may say, I shall certainly take the liberty of doing it; for what the law of England will not permit me to do directly, I will do indirectly, where I can."[60] Yet neither Garrow nor his successors at the Old Bailey appear to have actively promoted a Prisoners' Counsel Act. Indeed, few seem to have spoken publicly on the issue at all. Although it is always dangerous to argue from silence, their silence is at least suggestive of acceptance of the unreformed system. If they pressed hard against the rules that constrained their activities in court, Old Bailey counsel do not appear to have wanted those rules removed.

Charles Phillips, leader of London's criminal bar in the 1830s, was convinced that the Prisoners' Counsel Act was a mistake, and he argued vehemently against the proposal both in correspondence with his friend Henry Brougham and in testimony before the Lords' committee in 1835. His opposition was based on an intimate experience of the administration of criminal justice in London and on the Oxford circuit. "There can be no doubt," he wrote to Brougham, "that the prisoners counsel bill must materially change the whole system of our present administration of criminal law." He pointed first to practical concerns, to the increased time required per trial if defense counsel were allowed to address the jury, using the example not of the Old Bailey but of a recent Gloucester assizes. Eighty-eight prisoners had been tried, exclusive of those out on bail, and every case employed prosecution counsel. If every defendant had also had counsel, and those counsel were allowed to make speeches, Phillips estimated that an additional forty-four hours, or four and a half working days, would have been added. "I know very well," he wrote, "that on this question of time, men who never held a criminal brief in their lives say—'Oh, but, the cross-examinations will be shortened'—Do you find this to be the case at Nisi-prius? The thing is perfectly ridiculous. If a man means to speak at all, he must lay the foundation for the speech by the cross examination. Besides, these people never consider that the business will not be confined merely to persons of experience. Young

men, to whom a display is every thing will hold, as now, their briefs of fa-
vouritism and then what becomes of my average?" Like other critics Phillips
also pointed to existing practice in trials of misdemeanor: "We have Bacon's
test of *experiment* to guide us. The system has been long & long at work in
cases of misdemeanour—and what has been the consequence? Did you ever
know a man decline to make a speech? Do we find cross-examinations shortened? I never did. But I do find, putting aside all complicated cases, such as
perjury, conspiracy &c that the everyday questions, even those of common
assault, take double the time they would if there were no speeches."[61] Time
and expense were of course of no consideration if they would result in an
improvement in justice, but to Phillips's mind they would not: the proposal
was unlikely to result in any benefit to the prisoner or to promote determination of the truth. Like Law, Phillips conceded that granting defendants
the right to copies of the depositions sworn against them would indeed be
a "real boon." Allowing counsel to speak for their clients, however, would
"make life & liberty subjects of a trial of skill. Verdicts will often depend,
not on innocence but on eloquence. Those who are employed as advocates
must act as advocates—& the most awful of considerations may become the
victim of sophistry. Look at your Courts of Common law—one fourth of
their time consumed in motions for new trials, on the ground that the verdicts were given *against evidence*. How obtained? *The speech of Wilde did it!!*
And to this human life is to be subject!"[62] "You must remember," he told
Brougham, "that I have literally been toiling night & day, for sixteen long
years, in the proposed scene of this experiment. I have had ample means of
anticipating its operation. I confess at once that many of my objections may
be obviated, & I admit also that a very considerable expenditure in thus ob-
viating them, ought not to stand in the way. . . . But even when all those
objections of detail are surrendered, my principal ones remain untouched.
This bill will place prisoners in a much worse situation than they were before—it will make the judges objects rather of commiseration than envy—
as above all, it will *not* forward the interests of justice."[63]

Before the Lords' committee Phillips again spoke first of the practical
problems posed by the introduction of speech making. The Central Criminal Court in 1835 tried between 250 and 300 prisoners at each of its twelve
sessions, over the course of about six days. Speeches by defense counsel
would in themselves lengthen the time of trials; moreover, the judge would
in some instances feel compelled to "counteract the Effect of a sophisti-
cal Speech for the Defence."[64] Both the time of trials and expense of witnesses would be doubled. He also argued that the proposal would do prisoners "Mischief." When questioned as to whether it would promote "the

Investigation of Truth," Phillips responded, "I confess I think not." While there was "no Doubt neither Time nor Expense should be spared to promote the Ends of Justice," what would result from transforming the felony trial into a professional altercation was a contest that would depend "almost altogether" on the talents of the advocates involved. As prosecutors generally had "the longest Purse," prisoners would "labour under the Grievance of having the best Talents arrayed against them." Like Spankie, D'Oyley, and Law, Phillips displayed little confidence in how the bar would behave under the new rules. There was, he said, a "great Variety of Talent at the Bar," and some men would mislead juries to obtain verdicts against the merits of the case. The prisoners' counsel bill would compel prosecuting counsel to "colour" cases.[65] Barristers must "struggle for Success or lose Character"; since lack of success meant lack of employment, pride and self-interest would guide their actions. "The Bar will not be allowed to consult their own good Feelings; how can they, with the Consciousness that their all in Life depends on their succeeding? If any momentary Scruple should induce them to falter, they will feel their Children pulling at their Gowns, and calling to them for Bread." These tendencies, Phillips argued, were already evident in the civil courts and should not be introduced to criminal administration, where "Passion should never enter." The prisoners' counsel bill would turn the "Courts into a mere Arena, turn the Counsel into Gladiators, and compel the Judge himself to descend from the Bench and mingle with the Combatants."[66] "Counsel, whether for the Prisoner or with the Prosecution, if they are put in competition, would be apt to do it with Heat and Zeal; and in place of the Investigation of Truth being forwarded by a Speech of Counsel, I should rather say Facts would be distorted and Circumstances discoloured, for the Purpose of favouring the side on which Counsel is employed."[67] Phillips again referred to his vast experience—most of the evidence he gave before the Lords' committee was drawn not from the Old Bailey but from the Stafford assizes—and to the general opposition of the bar to the measure. Four-fifths of the "practical men" were against it.[68] He argued that under the existing system prosecuting counsel, when they made a speech at all, exercised discretion and refrained from any unbecoming zeal; the case of *Patch*, so commonly referred to by the reformers, was the exception rather than the rule.[69] Like Spankie, Phillips praised the judiciary for protecting the interests of prisoners: "Of course there are Exceptions, but as far as my Experience has gone, both in England and in Ireland, the Judge has done Justice according to the Talents he is possessed of, and has spared neither Time nor Trouble nor Anxiety to elucidate the Truth, never deviating to the Right Hand nor the Left, unless he has felt the Duty of doing so for the

Advantage of the Prisoner."[70] He was able in 1835 to include the recorder of London, Law, within the compass of these remarks but was careful to establish that he alluded to the current judges at the Central Criminal Court rather than their predecessors.

As it became increasingly clear that the 1836 bill would pass into law, Phillips did not waver in his opinion. In a letter to Brougham written a few months before the bill passed, he praised both Calvert's "excellent pamphlet" and the "sensible article" recently published in the *Law Magazine*.[71] He also appears to have believed at the time that the "experiment" of the Prisoners' Counsel Act would be confined to the assizes,[72] presumably based on the mistaken impression of Brougham, who had written to Phillips on 14 April 1836, "I certainly agree so far with you that I do not think the Central Court *would* be a fair trial," adding that he had "not yet heard" that the experiment was to be made in that court.[73] Phillips was also exceedingly angry with Lyndhurst: "I suppose you may have observed," he wrote to Brougham,

> that [Lyndhurst] volunteered to *nurse* the prisoners' counsel bill in the Lords—he has smothered the child. He struck out deliberately the only two clauses which were of any use to prisoners—the giving them the depositions & giving them the last word—in his first speech he said he founded himself on the law of France—now the Code Napoleon says under all circumstances the accused shall have the last word and then— *he* struck it out. . . . [I]n my conscience I believe he intended from the beginning to *burke* the bill. . . . He has made it an atrocious bill as it stands against prisoners & I should not be at all surprised at the Commons refusing it. Ignatius Loyola himself could not exceed this. His Marshal asked me how I like his speech—"You may tell him from me (Ld L) that his speech in *36 for* the bill was the best on the subject always excepting his speech in *26* against it." When a man speaks pro and con, he is sure to be right one time or the other.[74]

Admittedly, there is an element of self-interest in Phillips's criticisms of the proposed legislation. During the second reading of the prisoners' counsel bill in 1836 Phillips was accused by Daniel O'Connell—somewhat churlishly, given Phillips's efforts to promote O'Connell's political career—of basing his opposition "on the inconvenience & loss of income which the bill would occasion" to defense counsel.[75] Phillips naturally took offense at this accusation and argued that the bill would have the "very opposite effect,"[76] but there is no doubt that passage of the legislation greatly increased the exertions required of defense counsel, and given the relative poverty of the majority of their clients, any substantial increase in fees would only result in fewer briefs. Phillips himself anticipated that his strength would "not long resist the operation of the Bill"[77] and after it passed commented on the burden the act placed on him: "[E]very session makes its demand of forty to fifty speeches, in each of which a fellow creature, standing before you, not only seems to have, but very often has, all that is dear to man depending."[78] In his testimony before the Lords' committee he had also argued vigorously against a clause, which did not survive in the act, that would have empowered judges to "call upon Counsel to defend Prisoners gratuitously, on their mere Representation that they have not the Means of retaining them." This he referred to as the "greatest Spoliation of the Profession ever attempted," the clause "not merely depriving Counsel of the Fruits of their Profession, but compelling them to expend their Lives in thankless and most anxious Labour." Barristers, he said, had never been found unwilling when so called upon, but must they "be placed at the Beck of every Prisoner who chooses to say he is without funds?"[79] Self-interest aside, however, he was clearly convinced that the existing form of the criminal trial was better able to promote a determination of the truth and that full-fledged advocacy would serve only to obscure it.

Phillips also argued that the worst effects of the Prisoners' Counsel Act would be felt in London, at the Central Criminal Court. The reformers typically assumed the fact of prosecution counsel, but in Phillips's experience the majority of cases tried at the Old Bailey were tried without such counsel, for the simple reason that Middlesex magistrates refused to grant the costs of employing them: "In every other court in England the county in which it is held provides counsel to prosecute. The County of Middlesex refuses to do so and therefore in nineteen cases out of twenty there are no counsel employed for the prosecution." The admittance of counsel to cross-examine on behalf of defendants had consequently skewed the trial process: it became the "odious, but bounden duty of the judge to unwind the web of the defence and expose the guilt of the prisoner."[80] The anecdote related of Serjeant Arabin, in which the serjeant, about to try a particular case in the New Court, asked who appeared for the prosecution and, receiving the reply that no one did, responded, "Then, I do. Here goes," assumes a certain logic in these circumstances.[81] Judges were handed the depositions in court, interrogated the prisoners from them, and wrote down their answers. "Now," wrote Phillips to Brougham, "to metamorphise the judge into an advocate, is surely not the way to make him respected."[82] But in the absence of a public prosecutor, the prisoners' counsel bill allowed no alternative. This was not only a slow and expensive way of proceeding, Phillips argued, it also greatly damaged the reputation of the judiciary and brought the administration of justice into disrepute. How could judges appear to be impartial when the role of prosecutor was thrust upon them?

The issue of prosecuting counsel was an important one, as an adversarial contest requires counsel on both sides. As described in Chapter 4, the presence and activities of prosecuting counsel varied among the circuits and between the circuits and the Old Bailey. Those not actively involved in or familiar with criminal practice at the Central Criminal Court were presumably unaware of the imbalance between prosecuting and defense counsel and perhaps argued on the basis that counsel for the prosecution were a fixture.[83] A few, however, were willing to query the wisdom of leaving the responsibility for hiring counsel for the prosecution with the victim of the crime, and to entertain the possibility of establishing some form of state prosecution.

Public Prosecution

The issue of public prosecution had been raised a number of times before the 1830s, although the term "meant different things to different people."[84] The introduction of some form of public prosecution was recommended by a select committee in 1798; Jeremy Bentham, who had compared the systems of prosecution in England and France in 1790,[85] turned his attention to the issue twice in the early nineteenth century; Patrick Colquhoun likewise developed a plan to address the problems posed by private prosecution; and among the Old Bailey's bar William Fielding had argued in 1816 (by which time he had become a Westminster magistrate) for the institution of a "public accuser."[86] Romilly appears to have supported the concept of public prosecution,[87] as did Denman[88] and Sir Robert Peel. In 1826 Peel had argued: "If we were legislating *de novo*, without reference to previous customs and formed habits, I for one should not hesitate to relieve private individuals from the charge of prosecution in the case of criminal offences justly called by writers upon law—public wrongs. I would have a public prosecutor acting in each case on principal, and not on the heated and vindictive feelings of the individual sufferer, on which we mainly rely at present for the due execution of justice . . . and I would by the appointment of a public prosecutor guard against malicious or frivolous prosecutions on the one hand, and on the other, I would ensure prosecution in cases in which justice might require it."[89] Previous customs and formed habits, however, mitigated against the innovation, for the English were wont to equate public prosecution with political tyranny.

In the 1830s public prosecution was not in the forefront of the reform-

require "almost the exclusive devotion of a professional life."[96] Apart from desiring the office for himself, however, Phillips believed the introduction of public prosecution was essential once the Prisoners' Counsel Act came into effect. "To render the measure not effective, but *practicable*," he wrote to Brougham, "you must have counsel to prosecute."[97]

Phillips continued to hope into the late summer of 1834, and with some justification, for he had Brougham's support on the issue. The lord chancellor forwarded extracts from Phillips's proposal to Lord John Russell, arguing that the evidence provided with respect to existing criminal practice underlined the necessity of instituting a system of public prosecution.[98] On 22 September Brougham wrote that the chief justice intended to open the Central Criminal Court "in style & state," and that he hoped "the arrangement of public prosecutor will then be completed," allowing Phillips to appear in his "due rank."[99] The *Law Magazine* (no friend of Brougham), for its part, commented on newspaper rumors to the effect that Phillips was to be appointed "to the office of public prosecutor in the new Metropolitan Criminal Court," citing a salary of "about 2000*l.* a year," but expressed skepticism as to the likelihood of the appointment. There was nothing in the Central Criminal Court Act to support it.[100] The following year the journal noted that "the notion of a public prosecutor, in the sense in which Lord Brougham and Mr. Charles Phillips understood it, has . . . declined with its originator."[101] Private prosecution remained the general rule, although it was increasingly questioned. It would be some years before the government undertook any substantive reform of the system.[102]

Practice under the Prisoners' Counsel Act

The Prisoners' Counsel Act passed in 1836 granted defendants the right to make "their full Answer and Defence" by "Counsel learned in the Law"; the second clause extended to them the same right in cases tried summarily by magistrates (although they were not entitled to counsel in pretrial hearings). The act further entitled defendants to copies of examinations of witnesses and depositions made against them. Commenting on the immediate effects of the legislation, Brougham noted that according to Denman it had not lengthened the sessions to the extent anticipated, adding no more than twenty-four days in the year, and, further, that time was not the issue: "[I]f necessary for justice, the country is bound to find the time." Brougham did, however, record "a general belief," to his mind well-grounded, that the measure had led to "no small number" of acquittals "against the truth of the case." This, he said, was not the fault of the bill but owed rather to the ab-

sence of prosecuting counsel. "Though the Bill had never passed, I should
have said a prosecution without counsel ought not to be, but the Bill makes
it quite clear something must be done to remedy this glaring defect."[103]
Given the imbalance between prosecuting and defense counsel at the Central Criminal Court, and the failure to implement any form of state prosecution, professional adversarialism was not immediately to become the norm
in that court: any speeches heard at the Old Bailey after 1836 were most
likely to be those of prisoners' counsel.

The brief act was silent on a number of issues, and details of practice
under it were discussed by magistrates, judges, and lawyers alike. Shortly
before the statute came into effect, the chairman of the Middlesex sessions,
Mr. Serjeant Adams, "threw out" to the counsel at Clerkenwell "such suggestions, as a perusal of the enactments of the measure had presented to his

mind." Those suggestions were published in the *Legal Observer*.[104] Adams
first proposed that counsel for the prisoner be given the option of addressing the jury either before or after he had examined his witnesses. Second, he
suggested that, where the prisoner had counsel, counsel for the prosecution
not be restrained from cross-examining the prisoner's character witnesses.
He also wondered whether counsel for the prosecution should be allowed to
exercise the right of reply to character witnesses. Some brief discussion ensued, and Charles Heaton, who had been practicing at the Old Bailey since
1829,[105] cautioned against laying down any strict rules of practice without
"much consideration, the more particularly as the country sessions would
look anxiously to the regulations of [the Central Criminal] Court as a guide
for themselves."[106] "A Barrister" replied with some exasperation in a subsequent issue of the journal that the answers to these questions would "readily
occur to those who are conversant with the practice of our Criminal Courts.
The only inexplicable problem is, how they could have been seriously entertained for a moment by the Clerkenwell chairman." The Prisoners' Counsel
Act, the writer continued, clearly specified that defense counsel were to address the jury "after the close of the case for the prosecution." Witnesses
solely to character had not been addressed in the act itself, but prosecuting
counsel already had the right to cross-examine such witnesses: the practice
at the bar was to give notice to the prisoner's counsel if he intended to do
so, to allow the defense the choice of not calling such witnesses. Where witnesses were called solely to speak to character, prosecuting counsel (other
than the attorney or solicitor general) was not entitled to a general reply.
The barrister himself raised a further question, however: was a prisoner
tried for felony to be permitted to address the jury himself, even when he
had counsel? Two cases "universally acted on in trials for misdemeanour"

had ruled against it, as did further rules at nisi prius. He presumed—correctly, as it turned out—that the same prohibition would be extended to cases of felony.[107]

Practice under the act was also considered by England's judiciary: in 1837 twelve of the fifteen high court judges discussed its implications before setting off on the spring circuit. Their decisions were published in the *Law Magazine*, and given judicial resistance to the Prisoners' Counsel Act, it is not surprising that they acted to constrain the advantages it granted. Prisoners had won the right to copies of the depositions sworn against them, but prisoners' counsel, the judges instructed, could not refer to a deposition, or to any statement made by a witness before a magistrate, until that deposition had been read as part of the evidence of the defense. They also ruled that prosecuting counsel were entitled to a reply to any evidence called, and thus to the ever-important last word.[108] This ruling, as Cairns has noted, must have made defense counsel reluctant to use depositions.[109] The judges also spoke to the issue of character witnesses, contradicting the rule outlined by "A Barrister" and specifying that even if the only evidence called by the prisoner was evidence to character, counsel for the prosecution *was* entitled to reply, although he could exercise his discretion whether to do so or not: "Cases may occur in which it may be fit and proper so to do." Finally, they instructed that in felony prosecutions instituted by the Crown, "the law officers of the Crown, and those who represent them, are, in strictness, entitled to the reply, although no evidence is produced on the part of the prisoner."[110] These various stipulations thus all ceded the last word to the prosecution.

The first counsel to appear for the defense after the passage of the Prisoners' Counsel Act was that veteran of the Old Bailey, John Adolphus. His client was indicted for stealing from a shop, and the trial was held not at the Central Criminal Court but at the Westminster quarter sessions on 13 October 1836, before chairman Francis Const—a former member of the Old Bailey bar—and a full bench of magistrates. Before making a speech on behalf of his client Adolphus addressed a few remarks to the court which the *Legal Observer* thought fit to record. He began by noting that a "most important alteration in the practice of the criminal law" had been effected, which he hoped "would prove as great a blessing to the community as the benevolent persons who framed and supported it could expect. Much of the benefit to be derived from it would depend on the conduct of those to whom the administration of justice was confided, and more especially the bar."[111] Adolphus's support for the act seems somewhat lukewarm; the majority of his comments related to the consideration owed to the prosecutor, and he

took pains to differentiate the respective positions of a prosecutor for felony
and someone who brought an action for damages or for a misdemeanor. In
the case of felony, unlike in the latter instances, the prosecutor and his witnesses were bound over with heavy recognizances and effectively compelled
to prosecute, in the interests of public justice. Const, however, in giving
judgment, congratulated the jury and the court "on the time having at length
arrived when counsel were permitted to reply for prisoners charged with
felony." Alluding to Adolphus's speech, he agreed that the newly won right
of defense counsel to address the jury would be a great blessing indeed, "if
properly used."[112]

Conclusion

In the absence of both public prosecution and legal aid for defendants,
felony trials in the mid-Victorian period would not consistently take the
form of a professional, adversarial contest. Many cases continued to be tried
without counsel, or with counsel engaged on only one side. This was true
throughout England: in 1856 the *Law Times* reproduced a notice published
in the *Bath Herald* reporting that at the last quarter sessions, "of nearly
twelve barristers present at the court . . . only three or four found briefs,
and those for the prosecution. Not a single prisoner engaged counsel to defend him."[113]

As David Bentley indicates, the Prisoners' Counsel Act was "cruelly irrelevant" to the majority of prisoners.[114] Most prisoners could not afford
counsel,[115] and even defendants in murder trials thus appeared in court
without legal representation.[116] Judges were increasingly inclined to assign
counsel where someone accused of murder, to which the death penalty still
attached, would otherwise go undefended. The assistance provided by assigned counsel was limited, however, as the (unpaid) advocate worked under
the same conditions as his eighteenth-century predecessors, being brought
in at the eleventh hour without having been briefed. Moreover, counsel were
rarely assigned in trials for crimes other than murder.

While theory and practice diverged throughout the nineteenth century, a
fundamental transformation of the felony trial had nonetheless been made
possible by the Prisoners' Counsel Act. This transformation owed neither
to public pressure nor to pressure from the bar but was instead the result
of determined effort by a small group of Whig politicians. England's bench
and bar clearly did not regard the Prisoners' Counsel Act as an inevitable
conclusion to the entry of lawyers into the criminal trial, or even a desirable one. The majority of the legal profession opposed the implementation
of the statute.

Just as the "coming of the lawyers" cannot be accounted for by politics, it would be wrong to posit support for and opposition to the Prisoners' Counsel Act among the legal profession, if not among the politicians, solely along Whig and Tory lines. The argument that the proposed change would "work utterly against the accused" was not simply a Tory argument. Charles Phillips was not a reactionary where the criminal law was concerned. Like Ewart he was in favor of the total abolition of the death penalty;[117] he was also in favor of granting defendants full access to the evidence sworn against them. What was at issue was thus not paternalism versus individual rights. Rather, concerns were expressed about balance in the criminal trial. Without a system of public prosecution there was no guarantee that the Prisoners' Counsel Act would not, in metropolitan London at least, simply skew the advantage in the trial toward the defendant. Reformers believed that the unreformed system placed the accused at a disadvantage: an unrepresented defendant might meet with a lawyer-driven prosecution. But as Phillips pointed out, under the existing system, in London it was actually the prosecutor who suffered the disadvantage, a disadvantage that would only be aggravated by the Prisoners' Counsel Act.

Even the instigation of public prosecution, however, would not have solved the problems anticipated. Phillips and other members of the practicing bar simply did not believe that professional adversarialism advanced the truth. They did not trust advocacy. For reasons that will become clear in the next chapter, Old Bailey counsel may also have preferred the restrictions that largely confined their duties to testing the legal strength of the prosecution's case through cross-examination and left responsibility for mounting an active defense with the accused.

CHAPTER EIGHT

Justifying Advocacy

If Charles Phillips had been able to see into the future, one can only imagine that his resistance to the Prisoners' Counsel Act would have increased tenfold, for four years after the passage of the act his speech in defense of a criminal client was to embroil him in a scandal that left his professional reputation permanently tarnished. The subject of the five-clause statute that revolutionized the English felony trial was the prisoner's right to a full legal defense. The act did not address the relationship between the prisoner and his or her counsel, and it provided no guidelines for the conduct of a prisoner's defense.[1] As William Forsyth noted in his "historical essay" on the subject, nowhere had the state interfered so little with the conduct of advocacy as in England. In imperial Rome the rights, privileges, and duties of advocates were regulated with "minute care"; in early-nineteenth-century France the conduct of advocates was similarly subject to restraints. In England, however, "in a legislative sense," the state may be said to have "almost ignored" the existence of advocates.[2] When Phillips stood up to address the jury in 1840, what precisely constituted the duties of defense counsel and what, if any, restrictions ought to be placed upon their activities remained unspecified. Much of what the bar eventually determined to be appropriate conduct, and the rules which govern English advocates today,[3] can be traced back to what would prove to be Phillips's ordeal by fire.

During parliamentary debate over the issue of prisoners' counsel in the 1820s and 1830s the reformers had argued that allowing defense counsel to comment on the evidence would protect the innocent from wrongful conviction and secure the conviction of the guilty, as jurors, no longer troubled by a system that seemed unduly weighted in favor of the prosecution, would be more inclined to reach their verdicts on the facts. The nature of the duty owed by counsel to a guilty client did not form part of the politicians' discus-

Charles Phillips, leader in practice at the Old Bailey, ca. 1825–42 (Harvard Law Art Collection)

sion. The issue was raised only incidentally. In 1826 both Thomas Denman and James Scarlett had argued that in many instances counsel would allow a conviction "when they saw they could make no defence."[4] Scarlett made the same point ten years later: where the prisoner's guilt had been "clearly proved" in court, "no counsel of the least discretion would think of addressing the jury to assert his innocence."[5] Long famous as a "verdict-getter," Scarlett himself had never relied on eloquence and was known instead for clear and lucid statements of the facts.[6] No doubt his argument here was personal, rooted in his own standards of professional conduct.

The limited parliamentary discussion of the guilty client addressed only what counsel ought to do once the evidence presented in court had proved his client guilty. It did not touch on the problems posed by either a private confession or a barrister's strong suspicion prior to the commencement of the trial that his client was indeed guilty as charged. Defense counsel, however, were well aware that many of their clients were guilty,[7] and from 1836 they were obliged to become the "mouthpiece" for these clients—if they accepted them. Here too was an issue left unresolved by the Prisoners' Counsel Act. After 1836 counsel *could* mount a full defense for a criminal client, but was he obliged to? Could clients be rejected outright or abandoned in midtrial? If not, how was the barrister to conduct the defense of a client he knew or suspected to be guilty? No formal rules or regulations were forthcoming from the legal profession itself; there were indeed as yet no written standards of professional conduct for the bar as a whole. Acceptable practice was monitored on an informal basis by the circuit messes,[8] and, as Phillips would discover, there was considerable disagreement among the bar about the proper limits to advocacy in the criminal courts.

Defending Advocacy

Advocacy in general, and the boundaries within which the advocate was permitted to operate, had been subject to limited and frequently defensive discussion prior to the enactment of the Prisoners' Counsel Act. In 1820 Brougham characterized the advocate's duty toward his client in a passionate speech made during the proceedings in the House of Lords against Queen Caroline:

> [A]n advocate, by the sacred duty which he owes his client, knows, in the discharge of that office, but one person in the world, THAT CLIENT AND NONE OTHER. To save that client by all expedient means, — to protect that client at all hazards and costs to all others, and among others to himself, — is the highest and most unquestioned of his duties; and he must not regard the alarm — the suffering — the torment — the destruction — which he may bring upon any other. Nay, separating even the duties of a patriot from those of an advocate, and casting them, if need be, to the wind, he must go on reckless of the consequences, if his fate it should unhappily be, to involve his country in confusion for his client's protection![9]

As Brougham himself acknowledged, his statement was made in the course of a particular, extraordinary trial and was "anything rather than a deliberate and well-considered opinion."[10] His intent was to threaten the king and his ministers rather than to elaborate a theory of advocacy. But Brougham's words, in particular the doctrine of all expedient means, were immediately controversial and would subsequently attract sustained criticism. Disraeli commented that he had from Brougham's speech "imbibed an opinion that it is the duty a counsel owes his client to *adjust* him by all possible means, just or unjust, and even to commit a crime for his assistance or extrication."[11] According to Brougham, Disraeli noted, counsel's duty might extend so far as to allow him "even to commit treason."[12]

The duty of an advocate to his noncriminal client was subsequently spelled out in less provocative language—indeed somewhat primly—by Basil Montagu in *The Jurist* in 1832.[13] Except where a man's life was at stake, he wrote (at the time anonymously), it was deemed expedient that a judge should hear the opposite statements of men better able than individual suitors to do justice to their respective causes. The advocate might in the course of his duties be required to profess that which he did not feel and to support causes in which he did not believe or which he knew to be wrong. This, however, was nothing but "a species of acting without an avowal that it is acting."[14] The advocate did not mix himself with either his client or that client's cause; he lent his exertions but not himself. He exercised no discretion as to whom he would plead for; to do so would prejudice the suitor. Here Montagu relied on the famous justification for advocacy offered by Thomas Erskine in his defense of Tom Paine, charged in 1792 with seditious libel: "[I]f the advocate refuses to defend from what he may think of the charge or of the defence, he assumes the character of the judge—nay, he assumes it before the hour of judgment—and, in proportion to his rank and his reputation, puts the heavy influence of perhaps a mistaken opinion into the scale against the accused, in whose favour the benevolent principle of the English law makes all presumptions."[15]

Samuel Johnson had made the same argument some twenty years earlier. When asked by Boswell (in 1768) what he thought of supporting a cause which he knew to be bad, Johnson retorted, "Sir, you do not know it to be good or bad till the Judge determines it. . . . [Y]ou are not to be confident in your own opinion that a cause is bad, but to say all you can for your client, and then hear the Judge's opinion."[16] He repeated this argument at greater length in 1773:

> Sir, . . . a lawyer has no business with the justice or injustice of the cause which he undertakes. . . . The justice, or injustice, of the cause is to be decided by the judge. Consider, Sir; what is the purpose of courts of justice? It is, that every man may have his cause fairly tried, by men appointed to try causes. A lawyer is not to tell what he knows to be a lie: he is not to produce what he knows to be a false deed; but he is not to usurp the province of the jury and of the judge, and determine what shall be the effect of evidence,—what shall be the result of legal argument. As it rarely happens that a man is fit to plead his own cause, lawyers are a class of the community, who, by study and experience, have acquired the art and power of arranging evidence, and of applying to the points at issue what the law has settled. A lawyer is to do for his client all that his client might fairly do for himself, if he could. . . . If lawyers were to

undertake no causes till they were sure they were just, a man might be precluded altogether from a trial of his claim, though, were it judicially examined, it might be found a very just claim.[17]

Johnson's dictum ran directly counter to advice provided to the bar in the previous century, when it was frequently argued that advocates should not accept bad cases. Sir John Davies, Irish attorney general in the reign of James I, wrote in the preface to his *Reports* (1615): "[G]ood lawyers have not with us that liberty which good Physicians have: for a good Physician may lawfully undertake the cure of a foul and desperate disease, but a good lawyer cannot honestly undertake the defence of a foul and desperate Cause." If the good advocate found himself engaged in a cause which had seemed honest but subsequently proved unjust, he was to follow "the good counsel of the schoolman Thomas Acquinas," that is, he should endeavor to persuade his client to yield or compromise on the issue and, failing that, to give up the cause without disclosing its secrets to the contending party.[18] In *The Holy State* (1642) Thomas Fuller wrote that the good advocate "is one that will not plead that cause, wherein his tongue must be confuted by his conscience. It is the praise of the Spanish souldier, that (whilst all other Nations are mercenary, and for money will serve on any side) he will never fight against his own King: nor will our Advocate against the Sovereigne Truth, plainly appearing to his conscience."[19] John Cook, solicitor general to the Regicides at the trial of Charles I, argued in 1646 that "to speak well in a bad cause is but to goe to Hell with a little better grace but without repentence."[20] As David Mellinkoff warns, the clergy's repeated reminders that an advocate should not set his tongue and his conscience at odds presumably indicate that in practice the seventeenth-century advocate frequently did just that.[21] In theory, however, advocates were advised to discriminate. As late as 1756 this older advice continued to be reiterated: the "Good lawyer" "exerts all the generous Powers and Faculties of his Soul in the ever honoured Cause of Truth; but when he discovers the least Fraud, Falsehood, or Chicanery, detests the Notion; that it is his duty to employ his Skill and his Eloquence in Defence of Wickedness, and to serve his Client, be he right or wrong."[22]

By the late eighteenth century a shift in the theory of advocacy forbade the advocate to prejudge a client or his cause. But even those who upheld the new principles which allowed a barrister to take on any cause, or insisted that it was his duty to do so, retained doubts about the effects of such a course on the advocate's private character. Johnson had argued that "a man will no more carry the artifice of the bar into the common intercourse of society, than a man who is paid for tumbling upon his hands will continue to tumble upon his hands when he should walk on his feet,"[23] but others were persuaded that the advocate's indiscriminate defense of right and wrong, while necessary to the administration of justice, was potentially dangerous for society as a whole. Fears for the advocate's character, and its potentially adverse effects on public life, were voiced within the legal profession in the nineteenth century, although most were expressed from without. An article published in *The Jurist* in 1828, for example, warned that indiscriminate advocacy "has a tendency, unless counteracted by strength of mind and vigilance" to generate in the barrister "indifference to truth on other occasions; and, when the distant prospect appears desirable, to induce him not to be very scrupulous as to the foulness of the road over which he has to pass to attain it."[24] Samuel Taylor Coleridge agreed. While acknowledging that it was the advocate's duty as well as his right "to do every thing which his Client might honestly do—and to do it with all the effect which any exercise of skill, talent or knowledge of his own may produce," he also believed that "upon the whole the Advocate is placed in an unfavourable position for his moral being." Coleridge recommended that the advocate devote some of his leisure time to the "study of the metaphysics of the Mind or metaphysics of Theology—something . . . which shall call forth all his powers and center his wishes in the investigation of Truth alone, without reference to a side to be supported."[25]

Advocacy specifically in the criminal courts received less sustained attention prior to the enactment of the Prisoners' Counsel Act. Denman, however, did touch directly on an issue which would come to preoccupy Phillips, the bar, and the public: the consequences of a full confession to counsel on a prisoner's defense. In a review of *Traité des Preuves Judiciares* (1823), a French edition of Bentham's *Rationale of Judicial Evidence*,[26] Denman took issue with Bentham's position on criminal advocacy. Bentham, whose views of the legal profession are well known, compared the relation of advocate and client "to a compact of guilt between two confederated malefactors" and argued that any confidences made by the client to his lawyer should be made public.[27] Denman, in contrast, maintained that even "in the very few instances where the accused has intrusted his defender with a full confession of his crime," the prisoner could still be lawfully defended: "The guilt of which he may be conscious, and which he may have so disclosed, he has still a right to see distinctly proved upon him by legal evidence. . . . [T]here is no reason why any party should not, by fair and animated arguments, demonstrate the insufficiency of that testimony, on which alone a righteous judgment can be pronounced to his destruction. Human beings are never to be run down, like beasts of prey, without respect to the laws of the chase.

If society must make a sacrifice of any one of its members, let it proceed according to general rules, upon known principles, and with clear proof of necessity."[28]

These views do not seem to have been shared by the public at large. In 1829 Jonathan Dymond repudiated both advocates and advocacy in an essay on morality.[29] The "original fault," he claimed, lay with the law itself.[30] Where fixed rules were established, it was an inevitable consequence that equity must at times be sacrificed to those rules, and it was the lawyer's duty to enforce their literal application. The law, moreover, was over-complicated and encumbered with technicalities allowing counsel to achieve less-than-moral successes. But lawyers too were to blame, in accepting that whatever was legally right was right, and they proceeded from evil to evil: "If a material informality in an instrument is to them a sufficient justification of a sacrifice of [the dictates of equity], they will soon sacrifice them because a word is misspelt by an attorney's clerk. When they have gone thus far, they will go further. The practice of disregarding rectitude in courts of justice will become habitual. They will go onward, from insisting upon legal technicalities to an endeavour to *pervert* the law, then to the giving a false colouring to facts, and then onward and still onward until witnesses are abashed and confounded, until juries are misled by impassioned appeals to their feelings, until deliberate untruths are solemnly averred."[31] William Paley had commented in the eighteenth century, "There are falsehoods which are not criminal; as where no one is deceived, which is the case with an advocate in asserting the justice, or his belief of the justice, of his client's cause,"[32] while Thomas Gisborne had justified lawyers' conduct on the basis that the standard to be applied was neither the law of reason nor that of God but the law of the land and argued that the lawyer's task was prove the side of a question which was legally rather than morally right.[33] Dymond rejected both views. If no one ever believed what an advocate said, why did they continue to speak? And the lawyer's task ideally extended beyond merely applying the law. Adhering to the seventeenth-century belief that the good advocate did not undertake bad causes — except to prevent a client from "suffering too far"[34] — he castigated those willing to take on any cause for their deliberate intention and endeavors to mislead. An advocate's indifference to the causes he undertook to defend amounted to nothing less than "intellectual and moral prostitution."[35] Turning specifically to criminal lawyers, Dymond went so far as to argue, quite unfairly, that it was "their regular and constant endeavour to prevent justice from being administered to offenders"; he concluded that "he who wards off punishment from swindlers and robbers, and sends them among the public upon the work of fraud and plunder again, surely deserves worse of his country than many a hungry man who filches a loaf or a trinket from a stall."[36]

Fictional representations of advocacy in the criminal courts advanced the same view. The campaign for the Prisoners' Counsel Act coincided with the emergence of what came to be known disparagingly as "Newgate novels"; Bulwer's *Paul Clifford* (1830) and *Eugene Aram* (1832) and Ainsworth's *Rookwood* (1834) and *Jack Sheppard* (1839–40) belong to this category of fiction, as does Dickens's *Oliver Twist* (1837–39).[37] These novels represent a refashioning of the older tradition of criminal biography: *Rookwood* retells the story of the eighteenth-century highwayman, Dick Turpin; Eugene Aram and Jack Sheppard were likewise famous eighteenth-century criminals, while the nineteenth-century forger/poisoner Thomas Wainewright inspired the character Gabriel Varney in Bulwer's *Lucretia* (1846).[38] The Newgate novels were also intended in part to promote reform of England's sanguinary criminal law—this was the primary aim of *Paul Clifford*. In no way, however, can they be said to promote the cause of prisoners' counsel. At issue once again was the relationship between advocacy and truth, and the portrayal of barristers in these novels can be summed up with the same word employed by Mellinkoff to describe criticism of the bar generally: "Liars!"[39] Look, for example, at the description of Bulwer's Dyebright, one of the counsel engaged in the trial of highwayman Paul Clifford:

> Mr. Dyebright was a lawyer of great eminence: he had been a Whig all his life, but had latterly become remarkable for his insincerity, and subservience to the wishes of the higher powers. His talents were peculiar and effective . . . [for he] possessed the secret of addressing a jury. Winningly familiar, seemingly candid to a degree that scarcely did justice to his cause, as if he were in an agony lest he should persuade you to lean a hair-breadth more on his side of the case than justice would allow; apparently all made up of good, homely, virtuous feeling: a disinterested regard for truth; a blunt yet tender honesty, seasoned with a few amiable fireside prejudices . . . versed in all the niceties of language, and the magic of names; if he were defending crime, carefully calling it misfortune; if attacking misfortune, constantly calling it crime; *Mr. Dyebright was exactly the man born to pervert justice, to tickle jurors, to cozen truth with a friendly smile, and to obtain a vast reputation as an excellent advocate.*[40]

At the same time the Whig politicians were arguing that advocacy in the criminal courts would serve to promote the truth, the English reading public was presented with fictional representations of advocates achieving precisely the opposite effect, representations that cannot but have served to reinforce centuries-old prejudice.[41]

Only too aware of the public's deep-seated suspicion of advocacy, Brougham published a defense of its principles (to coincide with the enactment of the Prisoners' Counsel Act) in which he addressed several of the issues which would plague Phillips, including personal belief and the consequences of a private confession. The article, ostensibly a review of Samuel Warren's *Popular and Practical Introduction to Law Studies* (1835), opened with a discussion of the negative reputation of advocates. "The multitude," Brougham wrote, "regard the learned objects of their invective as persons wholly devoid of common honesty, because they are ready to attack or defend any person, or any position, for hire; to ruin the innocent and screen the guilty, if paid for it; utterly confounding all distinctions of right and wrong, to support any proposition for money."[42] He divided the critics into three groups. The ignorant appeared to believe that advocates commonly auctioned themselves off to the highest bidder in any given dispute. "Better informed and more reflecting persons" believed the profession of an advocate to be "of doubtful honesty, and of pernicious tendency." This group acknowledged that advocates might further injustice without being aware of doing so but also condemned them for persisting in "patronising wrong" even when they became aware of the fact. A third group accused advocates of being accessories to the perversion or suppression of the truth. Brougham placed Jonathan Swift in the first category, Jeremy Bentham in the second, and William Paley in the third.[43] He himself found all of these accusations groundless and believed that it was impossible to administer justice—in its broadest sense, not merely criminal justice—without professional advocates.

In the course of his justification Brougham argued, as Samuel Johnson had done roughly a hundred years earlier, that the advocate merely did and said what his client would do and say himself, given the requisite capacity. The advocate did not appear in his own person, and whatever he stated to the judge must be considered to have been offered by his client. "All the zeal with which he can support [a] statement—all the ingenuity by which he can reconcile it to the evidence—all the pathos by which he can appeal to the feelings in its behalf—must be taken as the effusions of the client."[44] Paley had claimed that the advocate's falsehoods deceived no one and were therefore innocent; Brougham countered that the advocate did pretend to state the facts truthfully and desired to be believed, but the promise he made was to speak the truth of what his client represented to him, not the truth of his own beliefs. Brougham, like others before him, continually stressed the distance between the advocate and his client's cause. If put in the position of having to state in court things which he suspected were not true, the advocate had no right to act upon his suspicions. His individual belief was not the ground of any statements made in court. Nor was it the advocate's business to prejudge a client or anticipate the office of the judge. Briefly addressing advocacy in the criminal courts, Brougham's stance was unequivocal and rooted in the presumption of innocence. The accused was presumed innocent until proven guilty on the evidence presented in court: "[E]ven when the party confided to his advocate the utter groundlessness of his defence," an advocate was bound to undertake that person's defense and to do his best to succeed if the party in question was charged with a crime or confronted with a civil suit that attempted to prove against him criminal conduct.[45]

Brougham's emphasis on the distance between the advocate and the cause for which he pleaded notwithstanding, in practice this distance seems frequently to have been eroded well into the nineteenth century. In 1837 the *Legal Observer* spoke to the issue, lamenting that younger barristers in particular were prone to the "very grave error" of avowals of personal belief in the justice of their client's cause. Such protestations, which often carried great weight with juries, involved the advocate in a lie, dulled his sense of right and wrong, and brought the profession into public disrepute.[46] Brougham himself had personally vouched for his client and the cause he represented when defending Queen Caroline: "I am borne up in my task with that conviction of its justice, and of the innocence of my illustrious client."[47] Denman likewise made what "can only be classed as an expression of personal belief"[48] when he indicated in closing that the evidence presented in court had satisfied his own mind that the queen must be acquitted.[49] In committing themselves both personally and professionally to the vindication of their client Denman and Brougham followed in the footsteps of their renowned predecessor, Erskine, who had argued from personal conviction in both his defense of Paine in 1792 and his prosecution of the publisher of the *Age of Reason* five years later.[50] While Erskine made a distinction between ordinary cases and cases affecting public right, Mellinkoff claims this was merely a private, personal rationalization. Erskine's injection of personal opinion was "the passing style of the day"; it belonged to an older tradition of advocacy.[51] From the evidence of Henry Crabb Robinson's recollections alone Mellinkoff would appear to be correct. At the age of sixteen Robinson had witnessed Erskine's efforts on behalf of the plaintiff in a trial that turned on the validity of a will: "[T]he sentence that weighed on my spirits," he wrote, "was a pathetic exclamation, 'If, gentlemen, you should by your verdict annihilate an instrument so solemnly framed, *I should retire a troubled man from this court.*' And as he uttered the word *court*, he beat his breast and I had a difficulty in not crying out."[52] From the late 1830s, this tradition and style of advocacy came increasingly under attack.

The Trial of François Benjamin Courvoisier

The principles of advocacy outlined by Montagu, Denman, and Brougham were to be put to the test in the aftermath of an infamous nineteenth-century trial: that of François Benjamin Courvoisier, a Swiss valet accused of the murder of his master, Lord William Russell.[53] On Tuesday, 5 May 1840, the seventy-three-year-old Russell, a widower who lived alone but for three servants, had retired to bed at half past twelve. When his housemaid rose the next morning she discovered the house had been ransacked and her master murdered. The coroner's jury returned a verdict of murder by persons unknown. Two days later, however, the valet was taken into custody.

The circumstances of this particular murder ensured intense public attention. Russell, aged and infirm, a member of one of England's leading families (the Bedfords), had been murdered at home in his sleep, his throat slashed so violently as to nearly sever his head from his body. In this crime the worst fears not only of the aristocracy but of everyone who employed a servant appeared to have been realized. The trial of Courvoisier, which spanned three days in June, consequently occasioned enormous public interest.[54] Six pre-trial examinations were reported at length in *The Times* and the *Morning Chronicle*, as well as many other papers, and a biographical sketch of the accused was published for readers eager for detail. When the trial opened on the 18th of June extra seating had to be provided as spectators thronged to the Central Criminal Court (*The Times* commented that the public anxiety to witness these particular proceedings was unprecedented), while on the bench Lord Chief Justice Sir Nicholas Tindal and Mr. Baron James Parke were hemmed in by the "extensive draperies" of surrounding aristocratic ladies.[55] His Royal Highness the Duke of Sussex was also in attendance, occupying the seat at the center of the bench normally reserved for the mayor of London and shouting "hear! hear!" during the course of the proceedings.[56]

John Adolphus led the prosecution and was assisted by William Bodkin and Montagu Chambers. Adolphus was convinced Courvoisier was guilty: "I saw the bed on which [Russell] was murdered, just as it was, the pillow saturated with blood, and the furniture in disorder. I viewed the pantry, and all the places where property had been found. I have not the slightest doubt of the wretch's guilt."[57] He was concerned, however, that the jury might be reluctant to convict, given that all of the evidence against the valet was circumstantial, and he devoted the day before Courvoisier's trial to arranging and digesting the facts of the murder from the depositions made before the coroner and the Bow Street magistrates. At trial Adolphus would face a formidable opponent, for Sir George Beaumont had advanced £50 to allow Courvoisier to engage counsel (Courvoisier's uncle, "a person of great respectability," had been in Beaumont's employ for eighteen years). A subscription was also raised on Courvoisier's behalf among foreign servants in London.[58] The Swiss valet was thus able to hire a solicitor named Flowers,[59] who in turn briefed Charles Phillips.

Adolphus's opening speech and the examination and cross-examination of Russell's two female servants took up the first day of the trial. Adolphus admitted that the evidence against the valet was purely circumstantial and that there was no apparent motive for the murder. But he reminded the court that Courvoisier was after all a foreigner. Englishmen "were not in the habit of considering murder as a prelude to plunder," but with foreigners it was different. He then proceeded to anticipate the defense. The character of one of the female servants, Sarah Mancer, might be found unworthy of credit, and a similar attack might be made on the police. Their efforts at discovering the identity of the murderer might, he argued, be thought to be motivated by reward money totaling £450 (the government had offered £200 and the Bedford family a further £200, plus £50 for the recovery of missing items from his lordship's plate).[60] At the end of the day the case against Courvoisier did not appear to be too black. That night, however, important new evidence was brought to the attention of the police. A woman had come forward to claim that prior to the murder the valet had left a brown paper parcel with her for safekeeping. When opened, that parcel was found to contain various articles belonging to William Russell. The new witness for the prosecution, Madame Piolaire, and various police officers were examined on the second day of the trial. On the third day the court reconvened and, despite Phillips's best efforts, Courvoisier was convicted and sentenced to death. The publicity attendant on his trial, however, continued: a fresh source of outrage emerged when it was revealed that Courvoisier had confessed his guilt to his counsel halfway through the trial. Learning of the new evidence against him on the second day, he had summoned Phillips and Clarkson, the junior counsel, to the dock and said, "I have sent for you, gentlemen, to tell you I have committed the murder." Upon being asked whether he intended to change his plea to guilty, he replied that he did not, and that he expected Phillips to defend him "to the utmost." Courvoisier pressed his point home at the end of the day, sending a message via his attorney: "Tell Mr. Phillips, my counsel, that I consider he has my life in his hands."[61]

The Trial of Charles Phillips

That Charles Phillips should have played the central role in the ensuing de-
bacle was ironic, given his strenuous opposition to the Prisoners' Counsel
Act. Obliged from 1836 to participate in a form of trial of which he did
not in his heart approve, Phillips found himself in 1840 in what must have
seemed a nightmare. While barristers faced with a confession of guilt in the
early twenty-first century can turn to the professional *Code of Conduct*[62] for
guidance, no such help was available to him. Phillips's first instinct was to
withdraw from the case, and he was only prevented from doing so by the
solicitations of his junior. Clarkson persuaded him to seek the opinion of
Baron Parke, who sat on the bench to assist Tindal but did not try the case.
The judge advised that if the prisoner insisted that he wanted Phillips to
continue in his defense Phillips was bound to do so, "and to use all fair arguments arising on the evidence." Phillips himself had come to the conclusion
that he could not relinquish his brief: "I had no right to throw up my brief,
and turn traitor to the wretch, wretch though he was, who had confided in
me. The counsel for a prisoner has no option. The moment he accepts his
brief, every faculty he has becomes his client's property. It is an implied
contract between him and the man who trusts him."[63]

When news of Courvoisier's confession spread, however—*The Times* reported it immediately following its coverage of the final day of the trial[64]—
the public and various members of the bar disagreed. Phillips's conduct was
attacked from various quarters. Some of the criticisms pertained to circumstances particular to the case, while others addressed the broader issues involved. Was Phillips right to continue at all? What exactly were his obligations to his client in the circumstances? Many members of the public, and
some barristers, were clearly uncomfortable with the idea that counsel made
fully aware of his client's guilt must continue in that client's defense. Charles
Phillips's conduct of the defense in the *Courvoisier* trial provoked what was
to become a ten-year debate on the ethics of criminal advocacy and standards of professional conduct for defense counsel, a debate conducted in
both the lay and the professional press.

The newspapers had reported Courvoisier's trial in detail, and it was in
the papers that the debate opened. Charles Dickens, signing himself "Manlius," was among the first to attack Phillips's defense of his client, accusing
him of seeking to cast the blame on another servant, of unjust allegations
of police misconduct, of casting aspersions on the character of one of the
witnesses for the prosecution, and of appealing to God "on behalf of a man
whose hands he knew were reeking with venerable blood, most savagely, bar-

barously, and inhumanly shed." As a "plain man," Dickens concluded, he was "perhaps unable to balance the advantages of continuing that license which is extended to counsel, against the disadvantage of restricting and confining it within more limited bounds." But proceedings in the *Courvoisier* trial had convinced the novelist that no practical man would "stretch out [his] hand to arrest a murderer, with these pains and penalties before [him]" and that "no earthly consideration" would induce him to allow his wife or daughter to give evidence at the Old Bailey.[65]

Some of Dickens's criticisms thus echoed long-standing concerns about the rough cross-examinations typical of criminal trials. But he also effectively accused Phillips of lying in court in an attempt to secure the acquittal of his client: Phillips had attacked "with violent language the witnesses for the prosecution, *whose evidence he [knew to be] true.*"[66] "A Well-Meaning Person" wrote to the *Morning Chronicle* in a similar vein. The duties of counsel must be consistent with the duties of man, including adherence to the truth: "[E]vasions, subterfuges, and efforts to conceal and stifle truth which would disgrace a gentleman" could not, by the mere acceptance of a fee, become honorable or laudable in legal counsel.[67] The bishop of London had equal difficulty reconciling "the propriety of any man taking a reward to prove that to be otherwise which the accused himself had distinctly confessed"[68] with passages of Scripture. On the 10th of August he presented a petition in the House of Lords "from the inhabitants of London" requesting that the principle of allowing prisoners' counsel the right to address the jury be reconsidered, as that principle was now revealed to be of "exceedingly questionable propriety." Brougham, who was present in the Lords, responded that the privilege in question belonged not to counsel but to the prisoner, and that on it depended "the elucidation of truth" and the prevention of injustice. Conceding that counsel were not at liberty to decline a brief, the bishop nevertheless lamented the hardship imposed on counsel by the Prisoners' Counsel Act, which "might compel a man to that which is against his own conscience, namely to defend by a speech a man whom he knows to be guilty."[69]

The concerns of the public were shared by some members of the bar. An anonymous barrister belonging to Gray's Inn wrote to *The Times* that after reading Phillips's address in defense of Courvoisier a doubt had entered his mind "whether a profession in which a man employs his talent to 'screen the guilty, and to varnish crime' can be considered honourable." Had Phillips's eloquence succeeded, "the result would have been, that through his instrumentality a confessed murderer would have been turned loose upon society, perhaps again to imbrue his hands in the blood of the sleeping, and to be

again rescued by the ingenuity and astuteness of counsel from the justly
offended laws of his country." Unlike "Manlius," he cast no aspersions on
Phillips's character but viewed the question "abstractedly" to conclude: "I
am simple enough to consider that he who defends the guilty, knowing him
to be so, forgets alike honour and honesty, and is false to God and man!"[70]
Other members of the bar, however, supported both Phillips's conduct of the
defense and the right of the accused to a defense, regardless of any private
confession. "Vindex" wrote from the Temple that it was "perfectly honourable for an advocate, although he is confidant his client is guilty, to lend his
assistance as far as to prevent a prisoner being convicted by any other than
legal means, for if this were not so, the amount of evil would far outweigh
the good."[71] "A Middle Templar"—perhaps Phillips himself—expanded on
these views in a response to Dickens's criticisms. He "entirely dissent[ed]"
from the notion that counsel ought not to defend a person of whom he
entertained suspicions of guilt or was positively convinced had committed
the offense charged. In a criminal trial, the jury's task was not to determine
whether the accused was guilty but whether the evidence presented in court
established his guilt beyond reasonable doubt. The duty of defense counsel
was to procure his client's acquittal "by every means in his power," or, failing that, at least to see that he was legally convicted.[72] Phillips was therefore
fully justified, in principle, in pursuing the course of action that he chose.
He had a perfect right to point out any discrepancies in the evidence: in fact,
it was his duty to do so. In making this argument the barrister in question
referred to Erskine's defense of Paine.

Was Phillips actually guilty of concealing or stifling the truth? This question naturally turned on a close examination of his address to the jury.[73]
Phillips began by drawing the jury's attention to the fact that there was no
apparent motive for his client to have murdered William Russell, and that all
of the evidence against him was circumstantial. He pointed out inconsistencies in the testimony of Courvoisier's fellow servant, Sarah Mancer, in the
course of which he cast mild aspersions on her character, noting an unlady-
like use of language. But his most severe attack was reserved for the conduct
of the policemen involved in the investigation of the crime. It was obvious
that his client had been the victim "of an unjust and depraved conspiracy."
Motivated by the prospect of a reward, when the police could find no evidence they planted it. On initial examination the servant's box of personal
possessions had contained no incriminating evidence; a subsequent search
revealed bloody gloves, a stained handkerchief, and a stained shirt frill. (The
police evidence was so patently manufactured that, in the absence of Courvoisier's confession, Phillips could have had plausible doubt with respect
to his client's guilt.) Phillips also severely condemned the police interviews

with his client, comparing them to the Inquisition. He complained bitterly about the way in which new evidence had been sprung against the defense, "like a mine under their feet," and suggested that the timing of its appearance was linked to that of the offer of a reward. Madame Piolaire's evidence was not to be trusted. In the various accounts of his speech Phillips invoked the deity, but the words attributed to him varied.

The Times considered Phillips to have acted with restraint: both that paper and the *Chronicle* had anticipated a much more severe attack on the fellow servants and the police.[74] Phillips, *The Times* concluded, had "made the best of a very bad case"; surrounded by difficulties, he had with "honourable zeal" made an energetic and impressive speech on behalf of his client. There were no allegations of misconduct here.[75] The *Herald* likewise took a lenient view, arguing that Phillips had done his best for his unfortunate client while "abstaining from indulging in insinuations respecting the prisoner's fellow-servants or the police."[76] The *Examiner*, however, launched a full-scale and prolonged attack. Its original accusations were published on 28 June and 12 July 1840; the attack on the legal profession—"the Profession of the Lie"[77]—in general continued throughout the 1840s, with the specific allegations against Phillips renewed nine years later on 24 November and 8 December 1849.

By 1840 the *Examiner*, a weekly magazine founded by John and Leigh Hunt[78] in 1808 and now owned by Albany Fonblanque, had become a "household word" in metropolitan London and was acknowledged as "the chief organ of high-class intellectual radicalism."[79] Although it championed the radical cause in Parliament, supporting Brougham and Sir Francis Burdett and advocating the political ideas of Bentham and Robert Owen, among others, the paper had also won the respect of the Tories. While disagreeing with its principles they recognized its integrity. Fonblanque, friend of Bentham and the Mills and a leading contributor to the *Westminster Review* from 1823, had been the *Examiner*'s principal leader writer since 1826.[80] He had a reputation for being an "uncompromising advocate of the most Liberal principles," "incessant in his attacks on a Tory oligarchy, and a most strenuous asserter of the rights of the people," and he was equally well known for quiet sarcasm.[81] The son of a lawyer—his father was John Samuel Martin Fonblanque, author of *A Treatise on Equity* (1793)—Fonblanque had himself briefly studied law, but he evidently shared Bentham's distaste for the English legal system. In 1827 he wrote:

If falsehood were supposed to be an exhaustible body, nothing could be conceived more politic than the system of English law, which would in this case expend so many lies in its own forms and proceedings as to leave none for the use of rogues in evidence: but unfortunately such is not the moral philosophy; and the witness who goes into one of our courts, the vital atmosphere of which is charged with fiction, is too likely to have his inward and latent mendacity provoked by the example. He sees, in the reputed sacred forms of justice, that the falsehood which is accounted convenient is not esteemed shameful. . . . The end sanctions the means. We cannot touch pitch without defilement, and it is impossible that a people can be familiarised with falsehood, and reconciled to it on the pretence of its utility, without detriment to their morals.[82]

Fonblanque's attacks on Charles Phillips and his denunciation of the morality of the bar did much to stimulate professional debate on the ethics of advocacy.

What Phillips's colleagues at the Old Bailey thought of his conduct of Courvoisier's defense is difficult to determine. Certainly none of them appears publicly to have leapt to his defense. Many years after the fact William Ballantine discussed the *Courvoisier* case in his memoirs. Ballantine's feelings toward Phillips were mixed. He had resented the Irish barrister's hold on criminal business and what he regarded as uncharitable behavior toward his juniors, and his view of Phillips's conduct may as a result be less than charitable. Ultimately Ballantine condemned his brother at the bar, arguing that the course of action Phillips had pursued following his client's confession "showed the inherent weakness of his character."[83] His communication of the confession had violated confidentiality with his client and placed Parke in a painful position.

Ballantine was unique in condemning Phillips for approaching the bench for advice. The charges laid against Courvoisier's counsel were generally threefold: he was condemned for retaining his client's brief after a full confession, accused of asserting his personal belief in Courvoisier's innocence and of appealing to Heaven for his sincerity, and further accused of attempting to lay the blame for the murder on innocent others. The incriminating words upon which the second charge was based were "The omniscient God alone knows who did this crime," and whether or not Phillips had uttered them became itself the subject of fierce debate. He vehemently denied having done so: "What! Appeal to Heaven for its testimony to a lie, and not expect to be hit by lightning!"[84] A report from a third person published in *The Times* the day after the trial had ended said that far from making any appeal to God, Phillips had "cautiously abstained" from adopting such a course and had done his best for his client against his "own feelings and conviction."[85]

Much of the debate owed its existence to the fact that no official text of that speech existed. By this date the OBSP accounts of trials strictly limited their coverage of the activities of counsel and published neither opening nor closing addresses. The versions published in the newspapers varied. The *Courier* reported Phillips as declaring "From my soul, I believe Courvoisier innocent of the crime" and "The omniscient God alone knows who's guilty and I cannot throw a shred of light upon the terrible deed of darkness."[86] When challenged, the paper stoutly defended the accuracy of its report.[87] Ballantine refreshed his memory by consulting Irving's *Annals of Our Time*, which reported Phillips as having said "Supposing him to be guilty of the murder, which is known to Almighty God alone" and "I hope for the sake of his eternal soul that he is innocent." In making such remarks, Ballantine commented, Phillips "scarcely escaped conveying a positive falsehood." "It is of the essence of advocacy," he wrote, "that counsel should under no circumstance convey his own belief, or use expressions calculated to do so."[88] The statement reported in *The Times* was "The omniscient God alone knew who did this crime."[89] Samuel Warren pointed out in the *Law Review* that this report was given in the third person, where "the slightest turn of expression, unconsciously, would make all the difference."[90] In 1849 a barrister who had attended the trial was willing to state on oath that Phillips's exact words had been "But you will say to me, if the prisoner did it not, who did? I answer, *ask the Omniscient Being above us, who did it*: ask not me . . . ask the prosecutor who did it; — it is for *him* to tell you who did it; it is not for *me* to tell you who did it; and until he shall have proved, by the clearest evidence, that it was the prisoner at the bar, beware of how you imbrue your hands in the blood of that young man."[91]

The legal periodical press seems, with one exception, to have been united in its belief that Phillips had had no choice but to retain his brief, a point conceded even by the *Examiner*,[92] but it divided over the question of whether his subsequent conduct of the defense was appropriate, given Courvoisier's admission of guilt. The *Law Magazine*, the "premier periodical" of its kind,[93] declared that Phillips had overstepped the bounds of legitimate advocacy: "[T]here was no occasion for insinuations against the maid-servants; nor was it in good taste, to say the least of it, to attempt to work upon the timid consciences of the jurymen, by holding out the apprehension of a never-dying omnipresent feeling of remorse." Phillips had only to take one step further before the "melodramatic absurdities" of the French courts would be introduced and advocates would be seen to embrace their clients to convey belief in their innocence.[94]

The Bar and the Lay Press

The controversy over Phillips's defense of Courvoisier was not easily laid to rest. The public had been made aware of the implications of the Prisoners' Counsel Act, and advocacy became a sensitive issue. The *Examiner* in particular refused to drop the issue, and Fonblanque continued his attack on the legal profession throughout the 1840s. In 1842 he contrasted the Duke of Wellington's assertion that "the foundation, the means, the end of justice is truth" with Mr. Justice Cresswell's recent advice to a prisoner who had pleaded guilty to consider the punishment attached to the crime of which he was charged (the gentleman in question had fired randomly during an attack on his house, accidentally killing a servant) and change his plea to not guilty. What, Fonblanque asked, was a plea of guilty, but the confession of the truth? Was it decent for "the very ministers of truth" to recommend the substitution of a lie?[95] In the following year he claimed that crime was to the lawyer "precisely what the fox is to the sportsman": the lawyer's object was not to capture the beast at once but to enjoy a good run and the opportunity to "exhibit skill and address in the chase." He compared confession to the surrender of the fox to the hounds, detested by lawyers because it spoiled the thrill of the chase.[96] In yet another article he wrote:

> Country people pronounce the word lawyer as liar, a corruption which a thousand years hence may be taken for the restoration of the proper word. In a dictionary in the year 3000 may appear, under the head of Lawyers corruptly so called, but properly Liars, a class of men who indiscriminately advocated right or wrong for hire. "They were called Liars because their greatest triumph was to give falsehood the victory over truth, to bring off the guilty or procure an unjust judgment against the innocent. In some old works mention is made of the Profession of the Law, but this is obviously a corruption, the true reading being the Profession of the Lie, the followers of which were accordingly named the Liars."

The morality of the bar was "vicious and mischievous," and barristers "the advocates of falsehood for a guinea."[97]

Punch, a recently launched satirical magazine, joined in the condemnation of "the Bar Humbug":

> When we talk of roguish lawyers, as talk we do—lawyers are supposed to mean attorneys—the Bar somehow escapes scot-free; there's no stain upon *them*, they get such large fees, they become barons and earls so often; above all they prate so magnificently and constantly about their

own honour and dignity, that the public believes them; they reap the dignity, and the poor attorney comes in for all the odium.

And yet these men are but the creatures of the Attorneys: they go where the latter bid them, they state what the Attorneys tell them. . . . If an honest man is to be bullied in a witness-box, the barrister is instructed to bully him. If a murderer is to be rescued from the gallows, the barrister blubbers over him . . . or accuses the wrong person, as in COURVOISIER's case. If a naughty woman is to be screened, a barrister will bring Heaven itself into court, and call Providence to witness that she is pure and spotless, as a certain great advocate . . . did for a certain lamented QUEEN CAROLINE.

They are sold to the highest bidder, these folks of the long robe.

Punch's sarcasm was in this instance inspired by the recent decision taken by the members of the Western and Oxford circuits that it was not consistent with the dignity and the independence of the bar for a barrister to report to the newspapers. Such employment had long been resorted to by penurious young barristers with little legal practice. Oh yes, said *Punch*, a man could be expelled from the bar mess for a connection with the press, but he was not expelled—in fact he would eventually be promoted—for "disgusting hypocrisy," for bearing false witness, and for "artful dodges" to disguise fraud and falsehood.[98] "A Barrister may be a very honourable man; *but* many things which professional *etiquette* allows him to do, would be thought disgraceful and dishonest among ordinary people."[99] In the same issue the magazine published a poem entitled "The Jolly Young Barrister":

> And did you not hear of a jolly young Barrister,
>   At the Old Bailey who used for to ply?
> He made out his case with such skill and
>   dexterity,
> Twisting each fact, while he glozed o'er each lie.
> He stuck at nothing; and that so steadily,
> The felons all sought his aid so readily,
> And he saved from conviction so many a thief,
> That this Barrister ne'er was in want of a brief.
>
> What sights of fine rogues he got off by his
>   blarney;
> His tongue was so glib, and so specious withal;
> He was always retained by the great City forgers
>   To Newgate from Mansion House sent, or Guildhall.
> And often the Press would be gibing and jeering,

But 'twas all one to him, its carping and sneering;
He'd swear black was white in behalf of a thief,
So this Barrister ne'er was in want of a brief.

And yet, only think what strange morals have lawyers,
    The Bar of such conduct think nothing at all;
Whilst should any poor Counsel report for a paper,
    "To Coventry with him!" that instant they call;
From their mess they'll expel him, he'll find, to his sorrow;
But they'll dine with the housebreaker's hireling to-morrow;
Then hurrah !—though his client be swindler or thief,—
For the Barrister never in want of a brief.[100]

In the face of these repeated attacks the bar could not remain silent, and in 1846 Thomas Noon Talfourd attempted a response to the accusations levied against advocates and advocacy.[101] Advocacy, Talfourd wrote, consisted "in the substitution of persons professing skill and learning in litigated matters for the actual litigants, to do on their behalf and in their stead, all which they might, if gifted with sufficient knowledge and ability, do for themselves, with fairness to their opponents."[102] Should no defendant who had been condemned in public opinion be entitled to legal representation? Must he find counsel willing to prejudge him and declare him innocent before accepting the case? If this were true, those defendants most in need of a legal defense would be denied it. The accused's right to counsel had only recently been won. Must it now be taken away from some defendants? The law as it stood allowed technical defenses to the accused, and while it did so, such defenses remained the accused's right. In answer to the specific question of whether counsel were justified in defending the guilty Talfourd replied, "[Y]es, often."[103] Otherwise, the accused's guilt must be determined by the press or by the bar. And even where the person's guilt seemed certain, "the intervention of an acute mind, expressly and avowedly engaged to make every inquiry and suggestion which can render it doubtful, conduces to the satisfaction with which it is desirable the administration of criminal justice should be regarded."[104] Thus, according to Talfourd, in defending the potentially guilty client the barrister promoted both justice itself, contributing to a determination of the truth, and public confidence that justice had been done.

Talfourd had acknowledged in previous work that men of mediocre talents and possessed of something less than intellectual honesty could and did succeed at the bar, and that a barrister's "taste, feeling, and judgment" in certain instances—such as cross-examination—could prove a positive hindrance to success. The "pliable temperament" which enabled the advocate to argue any cause also meant that he was not in fact likely to be known for an exalted sense of principle.[105] In 1846 however, while stressing, like Brougham, the necessity of advocates for justice, Talfourd conceded that their practice must be consistent with "personal truth and honour."[106] In other words, he repudiated the doctrine of all expedient means. And he offered human nature as the explanation for the professional conduct that attracted public censure.[107] Man was by nature partisan, and a barrister's forensic zeal was a manifestation of this fact. Counsel's sympathy for his client might lead him to errors of judgment that he would later regret: "[H]is client's case becomes part of his own being. . . . [H]is belief in its justice insensibly but inseparably blends with his natural desire to succeed. . . . [H]e hears all the arguments and regards all the testimony against it with the surprise, dislike, and incredulity of inveterate opinion sharpened by zeal. The irregularities which counsel sometimes commit, when betrayed into conversational attacks on each other, and the petulance with which they occasionally treat opposing witnesses, — faults often to be severely censured, and always to be deplored, — generally arise from the excess of this conviction, and the irritation consequent on an attempt to defeat it."[108] Specifically addressing the alleged abuses of defense counsel in criminal trials, Talfourd reiterated that counsel could not refuse or abandon clients, but his duty following a confession was confined to detecting defects in the evidence offered in court and suggesting any legal difficulties to which even the "most guilty" was entitled.[109] Returning to the issue of Phillips's defense of Courvoisier, Talfourd stated in no uncertain terms that Phillips had been entirely correct to continue after his client's confession. He wavered, however, on the other charges, in one sentence trusting that Phillips had not attempted to implicate the innocent but in the next asserting that if he had, the public had no reason to assume that such conduct was sanctioned by the bar.[110]

Talfourd's article offered only qualified reassurance, and in the following year (1847) the conduct of defense counsel — in this instance not Old Bailey barristers — in another murder trial again occasioned public controversy, resulting in a fresh examination by the bar of the limits of advocacy in the criminal courts. Patrick Reid and Michael M'Cabe, two itinerant peddlers, were charged with the murders of James Wraith, his wife Ann, and their servant Caroline Ellis (commonly known as the Mirfield murders).[111] M'Cabe, who consistently maintained his innocence, turned state's evidence at Reid's trial for the murder of James Wraith, receiving a £100 reward as well as a pardon. Reid, who was defended by Serjeant Wilkins and William Seymour, was acquitted. Both men were subsequently brought to trial for the murder of Ellis, and new evidence placed them at the scene of the crime. Seymour, who again appeared for Reid, argued that M'Cabe was the murderer. Despite the judge's summing up strongly in favor of M'Cabe's innocence, the jury convicted both men. Once back in his cell, however, Reid confessed that he alone was responsible for all three murders, and it was widely rumored that he had confessed both his guilt and M'Cabe's innocence to Seymour prior to the commencement of the trial. Seymour denied the confession, claiming he had had strong reason to presume that his client was guilty but no evidence "irreconcilable with the supposition of M'Cabe's guilt." In a letter to *The Times* he continued with a defense of advocacy guaranteed to offend the lay public:

> When a counsel accepts a brief for a prisoner he becomes, in my opinion, bound by a twofold obligation. I esteem it in the first place to be his strict and solemn duty to keep faithful to his client during the trial, and to hold his secrets as a religious trust. . . . [I]t is equally his bounden duty to frame the best defence in his power from the evidence at the trial. If a prisoner confesses his guilt, or makes admissions which tend to criminate him while they acquit his fellow prisoner, is his counsel to hurry into the witness-box to ruin and betray him? If not, then his confession is not in evidence; and does a counsel overstep his duty who adopts a line of defence wholly irrespective of that confession, but which is founded on the evidence before the jury, borne out, and justified by it? When a veto is put upon this exercise of a counsel's discretion—when, instead of his argument being weighed and measured by the nature of the evidence, his motives and private opinions are publicly submitted to a rigid moral test—the relation of client and counsel will be deranged, and their mutual confidence interupted; the independence of the bar will be violated, and the principle of advocacy will be abolished altogether.[112]

An editorial published the same day responded shortly that if Seymour's principles were true the abolition of the office of the advocate would be "very desirable." An advocate fully conscious of his client's guilt could never be justified in saving that client at the expense of an innocent man. The paper which had supported Phillips in 1840 now turned against him, reminding its readers that "the last remarkable incidence . . . of unscrupulous advocacy" had been defense counsel's attempt to lay the blame of William Russell's murder on one of Courvoisier's innocent fellow servants.[113] The *Examiner* responded similarly to Seymour's articulation of the principles of advocacy, arguing that if this were indeed the morality of the law, then either "a better morality" should be invented or the profession of law be abolished entirely. If M'Cabe had been hanged, "Mr Seymour would have richly deserved to swing from the same gallows."[114] Nor were the lay papers the sole critics: the *Law Magazine* remarked acidly that it believed Brougham, Phillips, and Seymour must share "the enviable distinction" of giving sanction to the idea that it would be justifiable in both a prisoner and his counsel "to get an innocent man hanged in order to save his own neck from a halter."[115]

Two years later the issue of the advocate's duty to his client again resurfaced, this time as the result of the conduct of the defense of the Mannings, a husband and wife charged with the murder of Mrs. Manning's lover, Patrick O'Connor.[116] Mr. Manning was represented at trial by Serjeant Wilkins, while his wife's counsel was William Ballantine, by this time the leader in practice at the Old Bailey. Wilkins defended Manning by means of a violent attack on his wife, allowing Ballantine to assume the moral high ground. Ballantine declared that he would not follow the example of his colleague at the bar: "I will do that which is my duty as an advocate; but if my duty as an advocate requires that I should cast upon the male prisoner the sort of observations and accusations which have been made against the woman, I would feel that my profession was a disgrace, and that the sooner I abandoned it for one somewhat more creditable, the sooner I would be a respected, an honest, an honourable, and an upright man, and placed in a position better to respect myself."[117] These were creditable sentiments but also shrewd ones, possessing an undoubted public appeal. Where Wilkins's conduct was denounced in the press, that of Ballantine was consistently praised.[118]

The trial of the Mannings led to a reexamination of Phillips's defense of Courvoisier, and again the *Examiner* took the lead in the attack. Far worse than Wilkins's attempt to lay the blame for O'Connor's murder on Mrs. Manning, it said, had been Charles Phillips's attempt to cast suspicion on innocent female servants in the murder of Lord William Russell. One of those servants was now in a pauper lunatic asylum, "driven mad by the terrors that had successively beset her," whereas Phillips had been so little prejudiced by his "horrible endeavour" that he had been advanced to the bench.[119]

The *Examiner* had by the mid-1840s moved away from its radical past. Now best described as "a liberal paper with Whiggish leanings,"[120] it was largely under the direction of John Forster.[121] Like Fonblanque, Forster abandoned the law for a career in journalism,[122] and among the more famous of his literary reviews is a savage attack on one of the Newgate novels, Ainsworth's *Jack Sheppard*, the novel Courvoisier claimed had led him into error.[123] Forster railed against both the publicity *Jack Sheppard* had received and the "moral capabilities, nice emotions, and sensitive affections" it attributed to "thieves and murderers." The real-life Jack Sheppard, he wrote, had been "of the very refuse of the rope."[124] Many years later Dickens would caricature Forster as Podsnap in *Our Mutual Friend*.[125] But there was more to Forster than Dickens's portrait allows. His obsession with dignity and respectability derived from a Unitarian upbringing; his sense of morality was outraged by romanticized portraits of criminals, and he was equally outraged by the conduct of the criminal bar. Forster's attacks on Phillips's handling of the *Courvoisier* case were both more hostile and more personal than those made by Fonblanque a few years earlier, and Phillips must have found them extremely wounding.[126]

When the charges against his conduct in Courvoisier's defense case were reopened Phillips was no longer practicing criminal law. He had retired in 1842, having solicited, through Brougham, a less arduous post from Lyndhurst, the lord chancellor. "The truth seriously is," he wrote, "my strength is by no means what it used to be and is becoming sensibly & daily inadequate to the physical labour & mental anxiety which the prisoners' counsel bill entails on me. . . . [E]very session makes its demand of from forty to fifty speeches, on each of which, a fellow creature, standing before you, not only seems to have, but very often has, all that is dear to man depending. Under such circumstances, to spare one's-self would be an actual crime."[127] Public and professional response to the *Courvoisier* trial must also have dampened considerably his enthusiasm for criminal practice. Originally unable to acquire a post that would allow him to remain based in London—he had wanted to be appointed a County Court judge or to obtain a lunacy commission—Phillips accepted a position as a bankruptcy commissioner in Liverpool. He was later transferred back to the metropolis and spent the remainder of his career in relative obscurity, sharing the bench of the Insolvent Debtor's Court with another former Old Bailey barrister, Henry Revell Reynolds. The *Examiner* begrudged him even this lowly position. Both that paper and *Punch* believed Phillips to have prospered professionally despite dishonorable conduct as a barrister.[128]

Stung by the assertion that he was unfit for any judicial office, Phillips could remain silent no longer, and on 20 November 1849 he undertook to refute the charges made against him, publishing his correspondence with the legal writer Samuel Warren on the subject in *The Times*. In explaining his predicament, Phillips wrote of the "wretched night" he passed before the final day of the *Courvoisier* trial: "If I slumbered for a moment, the murderer's form arose before me, scaring sleep away, now muttering his awful

which argued that even if Phillips had not uttered the words attributed to him he had acted a lie, persisted in its attack on a gentleman who had "maintained a character of undoubted integrity" throughout a long professional career.[147] The charges against Phillips were revisited in two further notices, in each of which the barrister was stoutly defended while the conduct of which he was accused was condemned.

The response from other legal periodicals was less favorable. The *Law Magazine*, which in the 1830s had been ambivalent about the benefits of enacting a Prisoners' Counsel Act, continued to believe that Phillips had gone too far.[148] The paper admitted that he had been perfectly justified in retaining his brief after Courvoisier's confession, as it was no part of the contract that lay between an advocate and his client that the client be innocent. Guilty men had a right to be defended, and that right furthered public justice; no one should be convicted except on legal and sufficient evidence. The paper, moreover, sympathized with the extremely awkward position in which Phillips had been placed: prior to his client's confession he had pursued a line of cross-examination rooted in the plausibility of Courvoisier's innocence. Acting on Baron Parke's advice doomed him to failure. While blaming Phillips for his course of action, the *Law Magazine* believed he was entitled to "lenient consideration," but it condemned emphatically his "use of the name of the Almighty." Conceding, after a comparison of the wording found in the various newspaper accounts, that he had made no direct appeal to Heaven to bear testimony to Courvoisier's innocence, the journal argued that he had nonetheless coupled the name of God "with a misstatement calculated to convey that impression."[149] The *Law Magazine* regretfully concluded that the *Examiner*'s condemnation of Phillips's conduct was just.

The *Jurist*, after chasing in circles and reversing its opinion twice, eventually condemned Phillips on the strength of the wording in *The Times*.[150] It believed him to be guilty of conscious misrepresentations of the evidence and of the character and motives of the witnesses. The discussion found in this periodical is particularly interesting, as it reveals the lack of professional consensus in 1840 on the proper limitations to advocacy in the criminal courts. Without referring explicitly to the case, roughly a month after the *Courvoisier* trial the paper outlined what it believed to be the existing practice of the profession and the principles on which that practice was defended. It was clear, The *Jurist* argued, that counsel were "not at liberty to refuse to defend a prisoner by reason of any preconceived notions of their own as to his guilt or innocence," and that once having undertaken a defense an advocate was bound to say for his client "all that he might be reasonably supposed to say for himself."[151] In *The Jurist*'s opinion, the question that remained to be answered was how far such a rule could be carried "consistently with the dictates of morality and sound policy?"[152] Existing practice was grounded in the presumption of innocence, in the right of a prisoner to make his or her defense by counsel, in the belief that counsel must on no account usurp the place of the court and prejudge the prisoner, and in the distinction made between the counsel speaking merely as the mouthpiece of his client rather than in his own character, according to which he assumed no moral responsibility for what he said on his client's behalf.

The Jurist, in contrast, argued in 1840 that the presumption of innocence applied between the accused and his judges, rather than his chosen advocate. Under existing practice, the paper claimed, defense counsel was frequently put in the position "of having to say that which is directly contrary to his own mental impressions": "We believe we are not stating the practice too strongly in saying, that it is considered his professional duty to conceal, or at least withhold, all the facts that tell against his client; to colour those that he cannot conceal; to give, by astute arguments, a meaning and construction to fact, which, in sound reasoning, they may not in his opinion bear; in fact, to guide the jury and court, if possible, to the conclusion that his client is innocent, without reference to whether he is or not. . . . This, we apprehend, is a system which is not to be reconciled with sound policy or high morality."[153] In sum, it was considered the duty of defense counsel "to practise a voluntary conceit"; the customary rule of the bar, at odds with morality, amounted to "neither more nor less than that a man is bound to deceive, if it be for the interest of his client."[154] *The Jurist* rejected the argument that counsel was merely the mouthpiece of the accused; if this were true then there would be no difference between the defense made by the best advocate in the land and the same address delivered by anyone who could read. In speaking for the accused the barrister retained his own individuality; his talent, status, and reputation inevitably affected the outcome of the trial. The paper further rejected the argument that by refusing to defend, the barrister usurped the place of the court and deprived the accused of his or her right to a defense. In refusing to defend, the barrister merely expressed an opinion which, unlike the disposition of the court, had no binding effect. But *The Jurist*'s central argument against allowing counsel to defend a client he knew to be guilty was that such a person had no right to a defense. It was that journal's opinion in 1840 that if the accused were "really guilty" any attempt on his part to evade punishment by attempting, via counsel or otherwise, to persuade his judges that he was innocent itself constituted a crime:

The doctrine, as we conceive, on principles of a high morality, would be this: that the accused is entitled to defence only so long as it is uncertain whether he is guilty or not, and from such persons only as are ignorant whether he is so. But he is not entitled, in point of morality, to defence from any person who knows his guilt. And the extent to which such person knows or believes his guilt should be, it seems to us, the measure of the duty of that counsel in defending him.

In our view, unless the public is to be considered interested in the escape of criminals, it would be a rule more consistent with public policy as well as with morality, that the duty of the advocate should be, to go in defence of his client only so far as his own mental conviction extends.[155]

In 1848 *The Jurist*, responding to the public hostility aroused by the trial of Reid and M'Cabe, regretted that the bar had not laid down and publicly stated the rules governing professional conduct. The paper had itself "no manner of doubt" about the "true rule": "[W]e believe it to be this, that counsel is at liberty to reason as much as he will upon the law and facts, and to influence, as far as he can, the . . . tribunal that he addresses; but he is not at liberty to mislead it, whether it be judge or jury, upon facts," regardless of the manner in which the facts had come to his knowledge.[156] There is some evidence in this article of a slight withdrawal from the high moral ground assumed in 1840: "If he is aware of facts prejudicial to his client, [counsel] is not, indeed, bound to communicate them to the tribunal; for it is the proper business of his opponent to find out and communicate all such facts as are necessary to make out his own case. Counsel is not, therefore, bound to call witnesses, whose evidence would be against his client; nor to ask of witnesses already before the Court, questions which would bring out facts prejudicial to his client's case. . . . Nor is he bound, so far to play the part of assistant to justice, as to take the case out of the evidence that is before the tribunal, and to bring forward matter which he knows only from the communications confidentially made to him by his client."[157] In the *Courvoisier* case in particular, "the proper practice would be, for the prisoner's counsel to watch rather than to act. To take care that no evidence was admitted against his client but under strictest scrutiny; to use every technical defence in his power; to take care, in fact, that his client should not be convicted, except strictly according to law."[158]

No mention was made in this 1848 article of the possibility of rejecting or abandoning cases for reasons of conscience, and in 1849, although it ultimately condemned Phillip's defense of Courvoisier, *The Jurist* was willing to concede that "for a client, if he be a person charged with crime, to avow his criminality, or for a party to a civil proceeding to avow that he has no moral claim, is no ground for his counsel, who has accepted his brief, to throw it up."[159] "A criminal is to be convicted only upon legal evidence, and his moral guilt may be consistent with a legal defence, to the benefit of which the law gives him a title. This, we fear, is a necessary though undoubtedly a large concession to guilt."[160]

Accepting the accused's right to counsel regardless of confession, *The Jurist* turned to the distinctions to be made between moral and legal guilt and with the restrictions a confession imposed on the client's advocate. Counsel, the paper stated, are not priests: "It is not their duty to rebuke men for their moral iniquities, or to see that they are dealt with according to their moral merits or demerits. In judicial proceedings, the rights of suitors are dealt with according to the law of the country, and by their compliance with or departure from the rules of that law, are they to be judged."[161] Civil rights were the creation of municipal law; the advocate's duty was to ensure that his client received the rights to which he was by law entitled. "If, by the rules of the law, a man actually guilty in a moral point of view, is not legally guilty, it would be as gross an act of injustice in his counsel to abandon him, as it would be in his judges to condemn him."[162] *The Jurist* then proceeded to reconcile moral wrong with legal right. It was not advocating the encouragement of moral wrong through the means of legal technicality; it merely argued for the enforcement of laws which, after all, represented "the average morality of the community."[163] Every man's notions of right and wrong were different—if it were otherwise, there would be no need for the law at all. Laws were made to regulate the conduct of men in the absence of any universal standard of high morality. It thereby followed that the "general cause of morality is better served by maintaining a general adherence to the fixed standard of morality"[164] as established by law, than by each individual attempting to set up his own standard, which would invariably be questioned by his neighbors. An advocate, by restricting himself to enforcing his client's legal rights without reference to his own particular view of morality, actually did more to "uphold the general morality of the community" than he would if he allowed himself to be influenced by his own opinion. This would introduce uncertainty, whereas certainty was the object of all legislation. That an advocate ensured that his client was convicted "*according to law*" was not only a defensible course of action but one which benefited the community.[165] A confession of guilt, however, did impose restrictions on the conduct of the defense. Defense counsel must, in such circumstances, confine himself to pointing out the defects in the evidence and preventing his client from being convicted on insufficient evidence or against the forms of law. To ensure that defense counsel did not trespass beyond the bounds of justifiable practice, *The Jurist* recommended the abolition of trial by jury in nonpolitical trials: the "gesticulations" of counsel and their "expressions of emotion"—the lie acted if not spoken—would then be of no effect.[166]

Truth versus Justice

David Mellinkoff notes that the modern Anglo-American "system of *justice* is just that . . . it searches not for truth but justice."[167] "The great function of the lawyer in our society is not to establish or disprove guilt, but to see to it that an orderly process of justice is indeed continuous."[168] Lawyers play a vital role in furthering justice, and the lawyer's conscience is not like that of other men. It is "a learned thing, not intuitive, untutored, abstract; it is not everyman's conscience. Applied to a specific case, the lawyer's conscience is a reflection of an educated sense of justice under law."[169] The lawyer's truths are law and evidence rather than " 'truth' in an absolute sense."[170] This is essentially what Denman and Brougham had argued in the periodical press in the 1820s and 1830s and what Talfourd had argued in 1846, and it was the position eventually accepted by *The Jurist*. It was not, however, what had been argued during debates over the Prisoners' Counsel Act. As described in the previous chapter, in the parliamentary debates over the issue of prisoners' counsel the argument had been couched in terms of an inquiry into the truth. Defending advocacy in the House of Lords against the bishop of London, Brougham highlighted its necessity not merely to justice but to "the elucidation of truth," just as his criminal law commissioners—Thomas Starkie, William Wightman, Henry Bellenden Ker, Andrew Amos, and John Austin[171]—had emphasized in their *Second Report* that the participation of counsel in the criminal trial was essential to investigation of "the truth." The "truth" in question was the truth of the facts of individual crimes, given that one of the aims of these same politicians in removing the death penalty from the majority of felonies was to enable juries to come to verdicts based on the facts. In the 1840s "justice" gradually superseded "truth" in the professional debates, and a new standard of justice was articulated, one rooted in the presumption of innocence, the right to counsel, an onus on the prosecution rather than the defense, a high standard of evidentiary proof, and a belief in adversarial procedure.

While the bar accepted the distinction between truth and justice in the nineteenth-century criminal trial relatively quickly, that distinction continued to distress the English public. The public remained very much interested in the truth in individual cases: "Did he do it?" rather than "Was he proven to have done it beyond reasonable doubt based on the evidence presented in court?" was frequently the foremost question in the public mind. This division between the bar and the public's concerns was nicely captured by Anthony Trollope in *Phineas Redux*, in an exchange between his fictional Old Bailey barrister, Chaffanbrass, and the attorney who employs him to defend Phineas Finn on a murder charge. The attorney is urging a reluctant Chaffanbrass to see his client before the trial:

> "I hate seeing a client. — What comes of it?"
>
> "Of course he wants to tell his own story."
>
> "But I don't want to hear his own story. What good will his own story do me? He'll tell me either one of two things. He'll swear he didn't murder the man — "
>
> "That's what he'll say."
>
> "Which can have no effect on me one way or the other; or else he'll say that he did, — which would cripple me altogether."
>
> "He won't say that, Mr. Chaffanbrass."
>
> "There's no knowing what they'll say. A man will go on swearing by his God that he is innocent, till at last, in a moment of emotion, he breaks down, and out comes the truth. In a case such as this I do not in the least want to know the truth about the murder."

"That is what the public wants to know," reminds the attorney. Chaffanbrass responds: "Because the public is ignorant. The public should not wish to know anything of the kind. What we should all wish to get at is the truth of the evidence about the murder. The man is to be hung not because he committed the murder, — as to which no positive knowledge is attainable; but because he has been proved to have committed the murder."[172] The *Examiner* and its readers refused to accept this position and never forgave Phillips for his defense of Courvoisier. "Liar!" remained its angry response.

Conclusion

Fourteen years after the passage of the Prisoners' Counsel Act the English bar had executed a complete about-face. Initially unconvinced of the suitability of advocacy in the criminal courts, it had by 1849 reversed its position and derived a sophisticated justification for the necessity of advocates to criminal justice. From the middle of the nineteenth century efforts to improve the reputation of the criminal bar would be directed primarily toward establishing behavioral restraints on counsel. Phillips's florid oratory and the theatrical behavior typical of the early criminal bar would not be ac-

ceptable in the late-Victorian courtroom.[173] But while the bar was willing
to modify the style of its advocacy, it had accepted advocacy in principle.
The professional response of the Victorian bar to continued public doubts
is summed up in Chaffanbrass's response to the attorney in *Phineas Redux*:
"[T]he public is ignorant."

In establishing what is essentially its modern position on the rights and
duties of advocates the bar rejected the notion that the "good advocate"
should accept only "good causes." In point of fact, the mere appearance of
counsel in the criminal courts was at odds with Sir John Davies's seventeenth-century prescription,[174] for when he wrote his preface any criminal
cause was automatically excluded from the realm of good causes. Davies had
argued that one of the many reasons the law denied counsel to those indicted
for treason and other capital offenses was to prevent "any professor of the
law of England" from dishonoring himself "as the advocates and orators in
other countries do . . . by defending such offenders."[175] By the nineteenth
century this reasoning had become offensive. "As if," William Forsyth wrote
indignantly, "the guilt or innocence of the accused could depend on the
enormity of the charge! And as if the maxim of our law were to be reversed,
and every man upon his trial were presumed guilty until he could prove
himself to be innocent!"[176] But the "maxim of the law" in question—the
presumption of innocence—was an eighteenth-century development. It did
not exist in 1615. At the time Davies was writing, prisoners were indeed faced
with the task of proving themselves innocent.[177]

The development of the concept of the presumption of innocence in the
eighteenth century made the theory of "good causes" untenable. Its aban-
donment, however, led to new moral dilemmas. The new principle of advocacy prohibiting a barrister from prejudging his client, which found its
most famous expression in Erskine's speech in defense of Paine, was almost
certainly the cause of mounting professional disapprobation of expressions
of personal belief. But personal belief aside, the question of how far a barrister ought to go in defense of his client remained. Ultimately, the bar repudiated the doctrine of all expedient means: while the guilty client was
entitled to a full legal defense, there were moral limits to his counsel's advocacy of his cause; there was "an honourable way of defending the worst
of cases."[178] As Forsyth and others noted, "the utmost circumspection" was
required to prevent a barrister from crossing an invisible line, and observ-
ing "the proper medium" had become one of the chief trials of the legal
profession.[179] Charles Phillips was widely held to have failed to observe this
medium, and his reputation was a casualty of the nineteenth-century bar's
justification of advocacy. For nine years after the *Courvoisier* trial Phillips's

name had been blackened, and even after 1849 a stain remained. *Punch* proclaimed, "Public Opinion—assuming for a brief space the Bench of justice, and addressing the COMMISSIONER in his own daily phrase, says—'CHARLES PHILLIPS, after a careful reading of your petition, it does not appear that you have any standing in court. CHARLES PHILLIPS, your petition is dismissed.'" [180]

Conclusion

In explaining the rise of professional adversarialism at the Old Bailey and in England's criminal courts more generally we must look well beyond the concerns of the practicing bar. As discussed in Chapter 1, the entry of counsel into felony trials in the early eighteenth century was client-driven; it was rooted in changes in prosecutorial behavior, changes which in turn inclined the English bench to permit a limited role to defense counsel. These early developments were not inspired by any politics of reform; they were instead ad hoc developments, the product of practical concerns relating specifically to the administration of criminal justice. Government initiatives designed to encourage private prosecution had placed defendants at a new disadvantage and created a new imbalance in the courtroom. The judiciary's informal decision to allow defense counsel to examine and cross-examine private prosecutors and witnesses constituted an attempt to redress this imbalance, to re-create a level playing field.

Although their participation in late-eighteenth- and early-nineteenth-century criminal trials did much to impel the trial in the direction of a professional contest, the advocates had mixed feelings about this result. They had never intended to effect a fundamental transformation of trial process, and given the choice, counsel themselves would not have taken the final step toward adversarial procedure in trials of felony. A small core of Whig politicians effected that change, in the face of professional hostility. The opposition of the bar to the changes made by the Prisoners' Counsel Act undeniably owed much to self-interest: the act increased the workload of defense counsel, and given the poverty of most of their clients, no corresponding increase in pay was likely. But Charles Phillips and other barristers genuinely believed that the adversarial process which typified civil cases and trials of misdemeanor often resulted in verdicts against the evidence rather than increasing the frequency of true ones.

[237]

While professional doubts about the utility of adversarialism in the criminal courts were overridden, the enactment of the Prisoners' Counsel Act
was not sufficient in itself to transform felony trials into professional contests. The clause which would have assigned counsel, without a fee, to prisoners who could not afford to hire them did not survive in the final act, and
although the plight of the "poor prisoner" — "the spectacle of poverty baited
by wealth" in England's criminal courts — was raised again in the 1840s,[1] no
formal provision of legal aid would be forthcoming until 1903.[2] In its absence, many defendants at the Old Bailey continued to appear without legal
representation.

The presence of counsel for the prosecution, too, was by no means a certainty in the mid-nineteenth century. The lack of systematic public prosecution was increasingly felt in the 1840s, and a full-blown parliamentary
campaign for its institution emerged in the following decade, but changes
in practice evolved slowly.[3] Provision was made for increased state participation in serious cases via an expansion in the role played by the Treasury
solicitor: in 1841 duties once performed by the solicitor to the Home Office
were absorbed by the Treasury and, as J. Ll. Edwards points out in his history of the *Law Officers of the Crown*, from this amalgamation emerged the
practice of nominating Treasury counsel in serious cases arising within the
Metropolitan Police District of Greater London and tried at the Central
Criminal Court or the Middlesex or Surrey sessions. In 1849 the Treasury
solicitor's responsibilities were expanded again, when the office of solicitor
to the Mint was abolished; the Treasury from this date assumed the duty of
prosecuting counterfeit and coinage cases.[4] Even in "serious cases," however,
the state did not routinely assume responsibility for prosecution.

Within London, the City seems to have expanded the prosecutorial man-
date of its City solicitor by midcentury. Where the records that survive for
the first three decades of the nineteenth century show a familiar mix of cases,
with various individuals being prosecuted for assaulting the City's constables, stealing the City's property, and keeping bawdy houses, by the late
1840s habitual offenders were clearly being targeted, and particularly preva-
lent crimes might also prompt the City's involvement. Violent theft continued to attract the City's attention, sexual offenses are prominent among
the cases prosecuted in the late 1840s, and the City intervened in family
disputes to prosecute men accused of domestic violence where the victims
themselves were unwilling to press charges. It also intervened to prosecute attempts to pervert the course of justice. Finally, the City prosecuted
counterfeiters, even in cases in which the Mint itself had declined to proceed.[5] In terms of numbers, however, this initiative was of small import. The

vast majority of cases tried at the Central Criminal Court originated outside the jurisdiction of the City of London.

In the absence of both a system of public prosecution and legal aid for defendants many—perhaps most—felony trials in mid-nineteenth-century London continued to take place without counsel, or with counsel engaged on only one side.[6] But while full implementation of adversarial procedure had by no means been achieved by 1850, a criminal bar was well established. Here too the politics of reform are conspicuous by their absence. While their activities altered the dynamic of the traditional felony trial, Old Bailey counsel in the eighteenth and early nineteenth century were not radicals. Many of them were not even liberals. Nor were they motivated by any new interest in prisoners' rights. With the possible exception of Basil Montagu, counsel were drawn to the Old Bailey and other criminal courts by pragmatic professional concerns. That in late-eighteenth-century London barristers appeared more frequently for the defense than for the prosecution was a reflection of client behavior rather than the political inclination of the counsel in question: institutional prosecutors like the Bank of England provided work for a small number of barristers, but the majority of private prosecutors chose to forgo the added expense of hiring counsel.

By 1850 the parameters of the Old Bailey barristers' broader legal practice were shifting slightly.[7] There were some continuities. The clear leader in practice at the Central Criminal Court was William Ballantine, and in a number of ways his practice was consistent with that of his eighteenth-century predecessors. When called to the bar in 1834 Ballantine had joined first the Middlesex sessions, making his professional debut at the Clerkenwell Sessions House and then proceeding to the Central Criminal Court. "Almost as a consequence" of these decisions he chose to travel the Home circuit.[8] Poor law cases at the metropolitan sessions still comprised a substantial portion of business. Ballantine can thus be seen as following directly in the footsteps of barristers like Fielding, Adolphus, and Alley.[9] But the City connections evident from the days of John Silvester were loosening, and the metropolitan practice described in Chapter 3 was altered in the wake of various reforms.

One of the last barristers to combine attendance at the London, Middlesex, and Westminster sessions with a purchased monopoly of practice in the various petty courts of the metropolis was John Locke. His career differs from those of his predecessors in that Locke, called to the bar in 1833, did not immediately attach himself to the Old Bailey. He traveled the Home circuit—Ballantine remembered him as "the very soul of the circuit table," whose speeches "solicited roars of laughter"[10]—and quickly established a

lead in business at the Surrey sessions.[11] Not until 1850 did the *Law List*
note his presence at the metropolitan sessions and the Central Criminal
Court. From 1843 Locke was one of the four counsel attached to the Palace
Court, and in 1845 he was appointed a City pleader. Overlap between Old
Bailey counsel and the Borough Court of Southwark likewise continued: in
1850 the recorder, who presided as judge in this court, appointed Locke,
Payne, Carrington, and Ryland as four of the court's eight counsel.[12] But
Locke's association with the Palace Court ended abruptly when the Court
of the Marshalsea of the Queen's House and the Court of the Queen's
Palace of Westminster were abolished by statute in 1849.[13] Purchased mo-
nopolies of business had long since fallen out of public favor,[14] and the
Palace Court had attracted criticism within the bar from the 1830s.[15] At the
Lord Mayor's and Sheriffs' Courts only one of Locke's co-pleaders, Archer
Ryland, combined the pleadership with an Old Bailey practice. And unlike
his eighteenth-century predecessors Locke won his office by election rather
than purchase;[16] moreover, it did not grant him any exclusive right to practice. In the City courts too, monopoly had come under attack. *The Times*
had condemned the pleaders' monopoly from the 1820s,[17] and the City conceded in 1842 that it was "injurious to the interests of the suitors" that the
common pleaders should hold, or seem to hold, an exclusive right to practice in any of the City's courts.[18] From that date candidates for the office
were required to provide the City with a letter pledging their willingness to
forgo the monopoly of practice which had earlier been the pleaders' right.[19]
While Locke retained his common pleadership until 1857, by which time he
had largely ceased to practice law,[20] it never carried the same advantages enjoyed by Silvester and his contemporaries. Nor would Locke "rotate" to the
office of recorder of London.

   If they were not reformers, and regardless of their (not unnatural) interest in earning a living, members of London's nascent criminal bar were, on
the whole, principled men rather than thugs and bullies who gloried in perversions of justice. (The only barrister whose behavior was truly reprehensible was Leonard MacNally, and his misconduct appears to postdate his Old
Bailey practice.)[21] They believed in that tenet of modern professionalism,
that the lawyer's duty is to his client. It was this belief that impelled Charles
Phillips, against his personal inclinations, to continue with Courvoisier's defense. They also believed in justice, and for all the criticism with respect
to their rough manners, Old Bailey counsel unquestionably made a genuine
contribution in this regard. Garrow and his contemporaries succeeded in
many cases in exposing false or malicious prosecutions and perjured testimony. Phillips had every right, as well as a professional duty, to point out

discrepancies in the evidence against his client and what were clearly fabrications by the police. Professional obligations to the client undoubtedly meant that in some cases counsel secured acquittals for the guilty, but the English had long believed "that it is better that ten guilty persons escape, than that one innocent suffer."[22]

The bar's practical contributions to justice notwithstanding, the legal profession did not engage theoretically with the adversarial criminal trial until the 1840s, and that engagement thus postdated significant developments in its history. This should come as no surprise: the "traditional image" of a lawyer is someone concerned with "the administration of the law, and not with the direction it takes."[23] The bar had resisted the changes instigated by the Prisoners' Counsel Act, but once that act was in place, it derived a means of working within the new parameters established. In the process a distinction between "truth" and "justice" was articulated.

Truth and justice had of course long been distinguished in the English courtroom. A distinction, that is, had been made between moral and legal guilt before lawyers became involved in criminal proceedings: witness the rule according to which a defendant was entitled to an acquittal if there was a flaw in the indictment. In the 1820s and 1830s the issues of truth and justice had seemed to converge in parliamentary debates over prisoners' counsel, a convergence made possible by the reduction in the scope of capital punishment. In the professional debate of the 1840s, however, "justice" rather than truth per se became the focus of attention. As described in Chapter 7, although the issue of procedural fairness had certainly been raised in the debates over prisoners' counsel, the relationship between advocacy and truth had predominated. The issues raised in the *Courvoisier* trial diverted professional attention. Even if one believes that the truth is best revealed by means of a contest between professional advocates, that contest potentially places one party in an awkward position, forcing him to advocate what he knows or suspects is not true. The barrister's personal relationship to the truth is thus compromised—hence the bar's insistence that a barrister is merely the "mouthpiece" of his client and assumes no moral responsibility for the defense. But in ensuring that a morally guilty client receives a fair trial and that the evidence against him is fully tested and proved in the courtroom, the barrister promotes justice.

Belief in procedural fairness had always been integral to English conceptions of the criminal trial; what had changed by the middle of the nineteenth century were ideas about what, precisely, constituted a fair trial. Acquittal by virtue of a flaw in the indictment was under attack from the late eighteenth century; Peel made minor changes in the law in 1826, and by the 1840s "there were calls for root and branch reform."[24] Denying an accused the right to make his full defense by counsel, however, had come to be viewed as wholly unfair. And where professional opinion with respect to the contribution of advocacy and adversarialism to a determination of the truth remains divided,[25] given the long-standing English suspicion of the state, the emphasis on procedural fairness and the necessity of defense counsel in particular could not but be strengthened and increased by the development of both a national police force and public prosecution in the second half of the nineteenth century.

When the furor over the *Courvoisier* trial, and the "licence of counsel" controversy more generally, died down, a number of important developments in adversarial procedure lay in the future: the establishment of the Director of Public Prosecutions in 1878 and the subsequent evolution of that office; the effects of the Criminal Evidence Act of 1898, which granted defendants the right to testify under oath; institution of an appeals procedure; and state provision of legal aid. If the felony trial in England had not assumed its modern form by 1850, however, a fundamental reconceptualization of that trial had been effected. The "amateur altercation" typical of earlier centuries had not been wholly eclipsed, but the practice of employing counsel for both the prosecution and the defense had become widely accepted. Where employed, the participation of defense counsel in particular had altered the structure of the hearing. Defense counsel effectively silenced the accused and "recenter[ed] the trial on the prosecution rather than on the defendant."[26] This focus, and the presumption of innocence underpinning it, was a product of the eighteenth century and was accepted as a given by the nineteenth. Changes would be made in the style of advocacy, and both the improved character of the bench in the second half of the nineteenth century and the institution of a bar mess at the Old Bailey in 1891 no doubt contributed to a decline in obstreperous behavior and the "legal fracas" of earlier days.[27] But advocacy and adversarial procedure in the criminal courts, the utility of which had once been queried by the criminal bar itself, ceased to be questioned.

Counsel at the Old Bailey,
1783–1850

Counsel who attached themselves (however briefly) to the London, Middlesex, and Westminster sessions (LM&W) or, after 1834, to the Central Criminal Court (CCC), from the 1780s through 1850 are listed below (biographical information for counsel who practiced at the Old Bailey pre-1780 is contained in the notes to Chapter 1). All entries draw upon the admission registers (printed and manuscript) of the Inns of Court; those registers are listed in the Bibliography. James Whishaw, *A Synopsis of the Members of the English Bar* (London, 1835) was also consulted. Any additional sources are specified at the conclusion of the individual entries. Information about parentage, marriage(s), and children has not been included: the entries deal solely with the barristers' professional careers.

Identification of the counsel named reflects the combined evidence of the OBSP and the annual *Law List*. In identifying practitioners for the period 1783–93 I have had to rely solely on the OBSP. From 1793 the evidence of the Sessions Papers was corroborated and supplemented by Browne's and subsequent *Law List*s, which, as of that date, printed a list of counsel who attended the London, Middlesex, and Westminster sessions and, after 1834, at the Central Criminal Court. While the OBSP make possible the identification of leaders at the Old Bailey—their evidence in this respect is confirmed by the legal periodical press—they are not as revealing about barristers whose practice in that court was on a more modest scale. The *Law List* permits the firm identification of practitioners who, despite a regular attendance at the Old Bailey, were infrequently named in the OBSP. It was also enormously useful when, in the nineteenth century, the OBSP curtailed information about the presence of counsel. Henry Beard, for example, was included in the list of barristers attending the sessions from 1812 to 1816; I did not find his name in the OBSP at all, but this period happens to coincide with that of the worst reporting of counsel in the Sessions Papers. The *Law List* was equally useful in weeding out those barristers named in the OBSP who did not regularly attend at that court: these included barristers eager for briefs of any sort; those who, like Erskine, made irregular appearances in high-profile cases; and those who routinely appeared in the prosecution of particular kinds of offenses, such as forgery or theft from the mails. Archibald Cullen falls into the latter category. Cullen's name appeared in the OBSP throughout the 1790s in numbers which, if not high enough to place him among the leaders of the Old Bailey bar, suggest that he might have habitually attended at that court. But Cullen was never recorded by the *Law List* as attending the metropolitan sessions, and closer examination of the trials in which he was named reveals that in almost every instance he prosecuted for the Mint, from whom he obviously held a retainer.

Like the obsp the *Law List* is an imperfect source. Its dating of attachments is often slightly inaccurate: a barrister may have practiced in London's criminal courts for a year or two before his attendance is recorded in the directory; similarly, a few names continued to be published after the practitioners in question had left practice, died, or emigrated. In quite a few instances barristers' names were included only sporadically in the *Law List* while a steady attendance was recorded by the obsp. Charles Hilgrove Hammond and Thomas Platt never appeared under the separate list of counsel attending the sessions, although their attendance was noted in their entries in the main list of counsel and they were named in the obsp over eighteen- and fourteen-year periods, respectively. John Vaillant's attendance at the Old Bailey was recorded in neither the main nor separate lists although he appeared in the obsp for more than fifteen years. Richard Peatt's name floated in and out of the *Law List*, although he was consistently named in the obsp. Thomas Challenor was first named in the obsp in 1811, but he was not included by the *Law List* until 1817, by which time he had already been mentioned in twenty-five cases. After appearing in eleven more cases in 1817, Challenor dropped out of sight in the Sessions Papers but continued to appear in the *Law List* until 1821.

Dates reflecting tenure of criminal practice are positioned at the end of each entry. Discrepancies between the evidence of the *Law List* and the obsp have also been noted.

Abbreviations

adm.	admitted
AG	Attorney General
Al. Cant.	John Venn, *Alumni Cantabrigiensis: A Biographical List of All Known Students, Graduates, and Holders of Office at the University of Cambridge from the Earliest Times to 1900*, pt. 2, 6 vols. (Cambridge, 1922–59)
Al. Ox.	Joseph Foster, *Alumni Oxoniensis: the members of the University of Oxford, [1500–1886]: their parentage, birthplace and year of birth, with a record of their degrees, 1715–1886*, 4 vols. (Oxford, 1888)
ap.	appendix
AR	*Annual Register*
asst.	assistant
B. Ex.	Baron of the Exchequer Court
BL	British Library
Bt.	Baronet
CCC	Central Criminal Court
CCP	City Common Pleader
ChC	Chester circuit
CJ	Chief Justice
CLRO	Corporation of London Record Office

Co.	Company
Co. Ct. Circ.	County Court Circuit
comm.	commissioner
conv.	conveyancer
Co. Pal. Durham	County Palatine of Durham
Co. Pal. Lancs.	County Palatine of Lancaster
corp.	corporation
CP	Court of Common Pleas
CS	Common Serjeant
dep.	deputy
DL	Deputy Lieutenant
DLB	*Dictionary of Legal Biography*
DNB	*Dictionary of National Biography*
ED	Equity Draftsman
Exch.	Exchequer
GAR	[Lincoln's Inn] General Admissions Register
GI	Gray's Inn
GL	Guildhall Library, London
GM	*Gentleman's Magazine*
HC	Home circuit
incorp.	incorporated
IT	Inner Temple
J.	Judge
JCP	Justice, Common Pleas
JKB	Justice, King's Bench
JOR	Journals, Common Council of London
JP	Justice of the Peace
KB	Court of King's Bench
KC	King's Counsel
Knt.	Knight
KSL	King's Serjeant-at-Law
LC	Lord Chancellor
LI	Lincoln's Inn
LJ	*Law Journal*
LL	*Law List*
LM	*Law Magazine*
LM&W	London, Middlesex, and Westminster sessions
LO	*Legal Observer*
LR	*Law Review*
LT	*Law Times*
MA	Master of Arts
mag.	magistrate
MC	Midland circuit

MM	*Monthly Magazine*
MP	Member of Parliament
Msex.	Middlesex
MT	Middle Temple
NC	Northern circuit
NMT	John Hutchison, *A Catalogue of Notable Middle Templars with Brief Biographical Notices* (London, 1902)
NorfC	Norfolk circuit
NWC	North Wales circuit
OB	Old Bailey
OBSP	Old Bailey Sessions Papers
OC	Oxford circuit
PC	Privy Council
PRO	Public Record Office, London
PWAG	Prince of Wales's Attorney General
PWSG	Prince of Wales's Solicitor General
QB	Court of Queen's Bench
QC	Queen's Counsel
QS	Quarter Sessions
readm.	readmitted
reapp.	reappointed
SC	Supreme Court
SG	Solicitor General
SL	Serjeant-at-Law
SP	Special Pleader
SW	South Wales
UCL	University College, London
VC	Vice-Chancellor
WC	Western circuit

Adolphus, John (1768–1845). Adm. IT 2 Nov. 1802, called 20 Nov. 1807. (Attorney, 1790). HC. Kent sessions. Also a historian; for publications see *DNB*. LM&W 1808–45. CCC 1835–45. Leading OB counsel. *Additional sources*: *DNB*; *GM* (1845); *Fraser's Magazine* 65 (1862): 606–9, 66 (1862): 49–53; Henderson, *Recollections*; Hardcastle, *Life of Campbell*, 1:142; Ballantine, *Experiences*, 57–58; B. C. Robinson, *Bench and Bar*, 66; Farington, *Diary* (multiple entries; see index); *LM* 35 (1846): 54–67; *LT* 5 (1845): 381–82.

Agar, James (?1757–1838). Adm. LI 29 Apr. 1779, called 28 June 1784. HC. LM&W 1793–1838. *Additional sources*: *GM* (1838); *LO* 17 (1838): 328.

Alley, John Hovenden (?1783–?1843). Adm. LI 22 May 1810, called 25 Nov. 1815. SP. HC. Police mag. 1822. LM&W 1824–38. Named in OBSP from 1816. CCC 1835–38.

Alley, Peter (1770–1834). Adm. MT 21 Jan. 1790, called 27 Nov. 1793. Leading OB counsel. LM&W 1797–1834. Named in OBSP from 1794. *Additional sources*: *The Times*, 14, 18, 19 Oct., 19 Nov. 1816; Ballantine, *Experiences*, 56–57; Farington, *Diary*, 14:4915, 4927, 4951, 4981; *LM* 35 (1846): 59–60; *LO* 9 (1834): 66–67.

Andrews, Thomas (?1775–1845). Adm. GI 18 Dec. 1798, called 4 Feb. 1803. HC. Kent sessions. SL 1827. LM&W 1803–27. *Additional sources*: [Grant], *Bench and Bar*, 2:201–4; Farington, *Diary*, 14:5062; *LM* 35 (1846): 60; *LT* 4 (1845): ap. 27.

Arabin, William St. Julien (?1775–1841). Adm. IT 18 Jan. 1793, called 8 May 1801. WC/HC. Wiltshire sessions. CCP 1807–22. Sheriffs' Court J. 1822. SL 1824. Commissioner (third civic judge at the OB) 1824. Deputy Judge Advocate, army 1824. Judge Advocate General 1838–39. LM&W 1804–25. *Additional sources*: Ballantine, *Experiences*, 55; B. C. Robinson, *Bench and Bar*, 43–48; [Churchill], *Arabiniana*; *LO* 23 (1841–42): 349–50, 446.

Baker, Thomas Barwick Lloyd (?1808–1886). Adm. LI 17 May 1828, no call date recorded, name removed from books 23 May 1836. ED and conv. Kent sessions. JP, High Sheriff, DL Gloucs. LM&W 1832–40.

Ball, Henry. Adm. GI 8 Feb. 1825, called 12 May 1830. SP. ED and conv. WC. Wilts. sessions. Named in OBSP 1831–32. Last entry in *Law List* 1855.

Ballantine, William (1812–1887). Adm. IT, called 6 June 1834. Revising barrister 1839–43. SL 1856. Patent of precedence 1863. Treasurer, Serjeant's Inn 1872–77. Counsel for prosecution of Franz Muller, 1864, of Madame Rachel, 1868; counsel for Tichborne claimant, 1871. Purported to be the original of Trollope's fictional barrister, Chaffanbrass. Leading OB counsel. CCC 1842–56. *Additional sources*: *DLB*; Ballantine, *Experiences*; Clarke, *Story of My Life*, 81; B. C. Robinson, *Bench and Bar*, 68–75; Williams, *Leaves of a Life*, 49–56, 309; Kelly, *Famous Advocates*; *LJ* (1887): 34, 48; *LT* 82 (1887): 198–99.

Barry, Henry (d. 1834). Adm. LI 18 Sept. 1818, called 26 May 1824, name removed from books 1832. Insolvent Debtors' Court. Southwark sessions. LM&W 1825–34.

Barry, R[obert?] (d. ?1821). SP. LM&W 1805–21. A "Barry" is named in the OBSP from 1804. Entry in LI copy of the 1822 *Law List* stroked through in pen, with annotation, "dead."

Bayley, John (1763–1841). Adm. GI 12 Nov. 1783, called 22 June 1792, adm. MT Nov. 1796. HC. SL 1799. Recorder of Maidstone (?1801). Knt., JKB 1808, B. Ex. 1830. For publications see *DNB*. LM&W 1793–97. *Additional sources*: *DNB*; *NMT*; Foss, *Judges*; *GM* (1841); *AR* (1841); *LO* 7 (1834): 305–6, 23 (1842): 177–79.

Bazett, William Young (d. 1842). Adm. MT 14 Apr. 1826, called 6 May 1831. HC. Herts., Essex sessions. CCC 1835–42. *Additional sources*: *LO* 26 (1843): 309.

Beard, Henry. Adm. IT 30 June 1800, called 22 Nov. 1805. NC. SP. President, Courts of Criminal and Civil Justice, Berbice. LM&W 1807–16.

Bell, John (1764–1836). Adm. MT 10 Nov. 1787, GI 8 Nov. 1790, called 1 Feb. 1792. Bencher 1813. Treasurer 1818–19, 1834–35. BA 1786, MA 1789 (Camb.). ED. NC. KC 1816. Extensive Chancery practice; author, *Thoughts on the proposed Alterations in the Court of Chancery* (1830). LM&W 1795. *Additional sources*: *DNB*; *Al. Cant.*; *NMT*; [Grant], *Bench and Bar*, 2:16–21; *The Bar*, 60–61; *LO* (1836): 265–66.

Beville, Robert (d. 1824). Adm. IT 5 Nov. 1792, called 17 Nov. 1797. NorfC, assizes for Isle of Ely. Lynn & Swassum sessions. Registrar, Bedford Level Corp. 1812–24. Author, *On the Law of Homicide and Larceny* (1799). LM&W 1799–1803. *Additional sources*: *DNB*.

Bird, Charles (?1784–1858). Adm. LI 5 May 1806, IT 17 Nov. 1809, called 17 May 1811.

SP. WC. Dorset & Portsmouth/Devon & Plymouth sessions. VC, Co. Pal. Lancs. LM&W 1812–18. *Additional sources*: *LT* 31 (1858): 146.

Birnie, Richard (?1808–?1888). Adm. IT 9 Jan. 1828, called 7 May 1833. BA 1830, MA 1837 (Camb.). SP. Bankruptcy & Insolvent Debtors' Courts. Borough Court of Southwark 1851–60. Emigrated to Australia ca. 1863; address in *Law List* from that date Ballarat, Victoria, then Melbourne (1873). Practiced before SC, Melbourne. LM&W 1850–59. CCC 1850–59. *Additional sources*: *Al. Cant.*

Bodkin, Sir William Henry (1791–1874). Adm. GI 9 Nov. 1821, called 15 Nov. 1826. HC. Kent and Dover sessions. Honorary counsel to Mendicity Society. Recorder of Dover 1832. MP Rochester 1841–47. Asst. J. Msex. sessions 1859. Counsel to the Treasury. DL Msex. Chairman, Metro Assessment Sessions. Knt. 1867. For publications see *DNB*. LM&W 1828–59. CCC 1835–59. *Additional sources*: *DNB*; B. C. Robinson, *Bench and Bar*, 75, 257–58; *LJ* (1874): 195; *LT* 56 (1873–74): 406.

Bolland, Sir William (1772–1840). Adm. MT 25 Jan. 1792, called 24 Apr. 1801. Bencher 1829. BA 1794, MA 1797 (Camb.). HC. Kent sessions. CCP 1804–29. Recorder of Reading 1817–29. B. Ex. 1829–39. LM&W 1802–29. *Additional sources*: *DNB*; *Al. Cant.*; Foss, *Judges*; *NMT*; *GM* (1840); *LM* 25 (1841): 155–58, 35 (1846): 61.

Brodrick, William (1784–1830). Adm. LI 14 Apr. 1807, called 7 Feb. 1814. BA 1807, MA 1810. HC. Essex, Herts. sessions. LM&W 1818–30. *Additional sources*: *Al. Ox.*; *LO* 1 (1830): 21–22; *LM* 4 (1830): 517, 35 (1846): 60.

Buckle, John (?1800–1891). Adm. IT 2 Feb. 1827, called 12 Feb. 1830. BA 1823, MA 1827 (Camb.). HC. Municipal corp. comm. 1833. Recorder of Worcester 1836–65. Recorder of Ludlow 1838–50. Name withdrawn from LI 4 July 1869. LM&W 1832–41. Not listed under CCC. *Additional sources*: *Al. Cant.*

Bullock, Edward (d. 1856). Adm. IT 9 Jan. 1818, called 26 Nov. 1824. HC. Essex and Herts. sessions. CCP 1829–47. Sheriffs' Court J. 1847–50. CS London 1850–55. CCC 1835–42. Named in OBSP from 1830. *Additional sources*: *LT* 31 (1858): 123.

Burney, Martin Charles. Adm. IT 28 Apr. 1813, called 20 June 1828. SP. HC. LM&W 1829–41. Last entry in *Law List* 1879.

Caarten, John Marinus Bicker (1814–1875). Adm. MT 25 Feb. 1833, called 25 Nov. 1836. SP. LM&W 1843–74. CCC 1843–74. *Additional sources*: *LT* 59 (1875): 427.

Carr, Thomas William (d. 1837). Adm. GI 10 Nov. 1792, called 24 June 1801. NC. Bankruptcy comm. Secretary of Lunatics 1825. Solicitor of Excise. LM&W 1802–6. *Additional sources*: *GM* (1837); *LO* 15 (1837): 331.

Carrington, Frederick Augustus (1801–1860). Adm. LI 5 Jan. 1818, called 7 Feb. 1823. SP. OC. Berks. sessions. Recorder of Wokingham 1838. DL Berks. JP Wilts. Author, *A Supplement to all the Treatises on the Criminal Law* (1826). LM&W 1825–32. CCC 1835–42. *Additional sources*: *GM* (1860); *LT* 35 (1860): 246.

Carter, Samuel (1814–1903). Adm. MT 25 Oct. 1844, called 5 Nov. 1847. SP. WC. Msex., Hampshire & Devonshire sessions; Devon, Devonport, Exeter & Plymouth sessions from 1860. MP Tavistock Apr. 1852–Feb. 1853. Revising barrister 1879–84. CCC 1849–57. *Additional sources*: Foster, *Men at the Bar*; [Foote], *"Pie Powder,"* 49–54; *LJ* (1904): 28; *LT* 116 (1903–4): 220.

Challenor, Thomas. Adm. LI 22 Aug. 1800, called 22 Nov. 1810, readm. 1811. SP. OC. LM&W 1817–20. Named in OBSP 1811–17.

Chambers, Montagu (1799–1885). Adm. LI 11 Feb. 1818, called 8 Feb. 1828. Bencher 1845. Treasurer 1868. SP. HC. Surrey sessions. Revising barrister to 1839. QC 1845. MP Greenwich 1852–57, Davenport 1868–74. CCC 1835–42. Named in OBSP 1830. *Additional sources*: *Al. Cant.*; Williams, *Leaves of a Life*; *LJ* (1885): 563; *LT* 79 (1885): 358–59.

Charnock, Richard (1799–1864). Adm. IT, called 12 June 1840. SP. HC. Borough Court of Southwark. Considerable Surrey sessions practice. Author of various legal tracts (see *LT* for list). CCC 1842–62. *Additional sources*: *LT* 39 (1864): 407.

Chetwood, John. Adm. MT 27 Nov. 1745, called 23 Nov. 1750. Marshalsea and Palace Court counsel. Named in OBSP 1783–89. *Additional sources*: PRO: PALA 9/5/2.

Churchill, John Henry Blencowe (?1801–1880). Adm. IT 10 Feb. 1821, called 9 Feb. 1827, incorp. GI 22 Jan. 1846. OC and sessions. LM&W 1828–31. Named in OBSP from 1827. CCC 1835–42. *Additional sources*: *Al. Cant.*; *LJ* (1880): 406.

Claridge, Sir John Thomas (1792–1868). Adm. MT 14 Nov. 1810, called 6 Feb. 1818. BA 1813, MA 1818 (Camb.). SP. HC. Kent sessions. Recorder, Prince of Wales's Island 1825–32. Knt. 1825. LM&W 1822–27. *Additional sources*: *Al. Cant.*; *LT* 45 (1868): 231.

Clarkson, William (d. 1856). Adm. IT 13 Nov. 1817, called 7 Feb. 1823. Kent and Rochester sessions. Recorder of Faversham 1842–56. LM&W 1824–56. CCC 1835–56. *Additional sources*: Ballantine, *Experiences*, 29, 35, 67–68; B. C. Robinson, *Bench and Bar*, 75–84; *LT* 28 (1856): 74.

Clifton, Thomas (d. 1814). Adm. GI 8 July 1794, called 29 Jan. 1800. NC. West Riding, Yorks. sessions. LM&W 1802–8. Named in OBSP from 1800. *Additional sources*: *GM* (1814).

Cockle, James (1819–1895). Adm. MT 12 Apr. 1838, called 6 Nov. 1846. BA 1842, MA 1845 (Camb.). SP. MC. First CJ Queensland 1863–79. Knt. 1869. Mathematician. CCC 1849–50. *Additional sources*: *Al. Cant.*; *LJ* (1895): 86; *LT* 98 (1895): 337.

Comyn, Samuel (d. 1835). Adm. MT 16 Nov. 1792, called 7 Feb. 1800. SP. HC. Surrey and Herts. sessions. Recorder of Rochester 1827–35. LM&W 1802–8. *Additional sources*: *LO* 11 (1840): 338; *GM* (1835).

Const, Francis (1751–1839). Adm. MT 20 Jan. 1778, IT 3 Feb. 1783, called 7 Feb. 1783. HC. Borough of Hertford sessions. Chairman, Msex. mags. 1819–32, and of Westminster sessions until 1839. Edited various editions of J. T. Pratt's *Laws Relating to the Poor*. LM&W 1793–1816. Named in OBSP from 1790. *Additional sources*: *DNB*; *NMT*; *GM* (1840); *LO* 19 (1840): 444.

Cooper, William (d. 1877). Adm. LI, called 10 June 1831. SP. NorfC. Beccles, Norwich, and Norfolk sessions. Recorder of Ipswich 1874–77. CCC and Msex. sessions 1847–77. *Additional sources*: *LJ* (1877): 553; *LT* 64 (1877): 52.

Courthope, George (1767–1835). Adm. MT 11 May 1791, called 10 June 1796. BA 1791, MA 1795 (Camb.). HC. Sussex sessions. LM&W 1801. Named in OBSP 1802. *Additional sources*: *Al. Cant.*; *GM* (1835).

Cowper, Charles (b. ?1766). Adm. MT 11 Dec. 1779, called 28 Nov. 1788. WC. Wilts. sessions. Bankruptcy comm. LM&W 1795. *Additional sources*: *Al. Ox.*

Cresswell, Robert Nathaniel. Adm. IT 22 Jan. 1817, called 21 June 1822. MC. Southwark sessions. Insolvent Debtors' Court. LM&W 1825–42. CCC 1835–42. Named in OBSP from 1822. Last entry in *Law List* 1859.

Crouch, Daniel Newton (b. ?1800). Adm. GI 9 June 1838, called 9 June 1841. HC. London, Msex., and Kent sessions. LM&W 1842–59. CCC 1846–59. Last entry in *Law List* 1871.

Curwood, John (d. 1847). Adm. MT 18 Jan. 1790, called 10 June 1796. HC. Kent sessions. LM&W 1797–1823 (continued to be named in OBSP through 1834). CCC 1835–42. *Additional sources*: [Grant], *Bench and Bar*, 2:147–51; B. C. Robinson, *Bench and Bar*, 66–68; *LO* 34 (1847); *LT* 9 (1847): 46.

Daly, D. Bingham (d. 1869). Adm. MT 1 May 1844, called 23 Nov. 1849. SP. HC. LM&W 1850–56. CCC 1850–56. *Additional sources*: *LT* 48 (1869): 2.

Dasent, John Bury (1806–1888). Adm. MT 18 Oct. 1823, called 1833. LLB 1830 (Camb.). SP. NorfC. J., Bow and Shoreditch Co. Cts. 1854–84. CCC 1835–42. *Additional sources*: *Al. Cant.*; *LJ* (1888): 216; *LT* 84 (1888): 449.

Dawson, Charles James (d. 1870). Adm. IT, called 5 May 1848. OC. Hereford and Gloucester sessions. Emigrated to Australia (Melbourne, Victoria) 1854. CCC 1850–54. *Additional sources*: *Al. Ox.*; *LT* 49 (1870): 59.

Deedes, John (1803–1885). Adm. IT 24 Apr. 1826, called 1829. Bencher 1863. Treasurer 1877. BA 1826, MA 1830 (Camb.). HC. Kent sessions. Recorder of Queensborough 1834–82, of Canterbury, Sandwich and Deal 1845–72. Revising barrister. Steward to Corporation of Faversham. Assessor to Liberty of Romney 1858. CCC 1835–42. *Additional sources*: *Al. Cant.*; *LJ* (1885): 57, 74; *LT* 68 (1885): 218.

Doane, Richard (d. 1848). Adm. IT 6 Feb. 1824, called 12 Feb. 1830. NC. CCC 1835–47. Named in OBSP from 1829. *Additional sources*: *LO* 36 (1848): 502.

Dower, Robert. Adm. MT 9 Aug. 1782, called 23 Nov. 1787. LM&W 1795. Named in OBSP 1788. Last listing in *Law List* 1795.

Dowling, Alfred Septimus (1804–1868). Adm. GI 12 Feb. 1823, called 18 June 1828. SP. HC. Hertford and Chelmsford sessions. SL 1842. J. Co. Ct. Circ. No. 15, 1849–68. LM&W 1831–42. CCC 1835–42. Named in OBSP from 1829. *Additional sources*: *LJ* (1868): 202.

Dowling, Sir James (1787–1844). Adm. MT 21 Apr. 1810, called 5 May 1815. Editor, *King's Bench Reports* 1822–27, *Magistrates Practice* 1822–27. Puisne J., New South Wales 1827; CJ 1837. Knt. 1837. LM&W 1818–27. Named in OBSP 1816. *Additional sources*: *NMT*; *LT* 4 (1844): ap. 83.

Dunbar. Listed in *Law List* under CCC without a Christian name, 1835–37. Never in main list of counsel.

Espinasse, Isaac (d. 1834). Adm. GI 19 Dec. 1780, called 10 Feb. 1787. HC. Hertford and Kent sessions. LM&W 1795. *Additional sources*: *LO* 9 (1834): 358.

Espinasse, James (1798–1867). Adm. GI 11 Feb. 1812, called 27 June 1827. BA 1820 (Ox.). SP. HC. Kent sessions. Recorder of Rochester 1842–67. J. Co. Ct. Circ. No. 49, 1847–67. Asst. chairman, West Kent QS. JP Kent. CCC 1835–46. *Additional sources*: *DLB*; *Al. Ox.*; *LJ* (1867): 158; *LT* 42 (1867): 397, 412.

Evans, George. Adm. GI 4 Dec. 1820, called 21 Nov. 1827. SP. Kent sessions. LM&W 1827–46. (He was never listed in the *Law List* as attached to the CCC.) Last entry in *Law List* 1879.

Ewart, Francis. Adm. MT 25 Nov. 1837, called 15 Jan. 1841. SP. NC. Durham, Newcastle & Northumberland sessions. Msex. sessions. CCC 1849–57. Last entry in *Law List* 1857.

Eykyn, William Pitt. Adm. MT 18 Oct. 1815, called 10 Nov. 1820. SP. OC. Ox. & Gloucs. sessions. LM&W 1823–27. Named in OBSP 1821.

Fielding, William (1748–1820). Adm. MT 5 May 1770, called 22 Nov. 1776. SP. HC. Mag., Queen's Square, Westminster 1809–20. LM&W 1793–1808. Named in OBSP from 1783. *Additional sources: DNB* (entry for father, Henry); *GM* (1820); Farington, *Diary* (multiple entries; see index).

Fish, Samuel Charles Cross (d. 1880). Adm IT 14 Nov. 1816, called 26 Nov. 1824. SP. HC. Hertford, Essex, and St. Albans sessions. LM&W 1825–42. *Additional sources: LJ* (1880): 554.

France, John (b. 1762). Adm. IT 14 Nov. 1782, called 30 May 1788. NC. West Riding, Yorks. sessions. Bankruptcy comm. LM&W 1795. Last entry in *Law List* 1819.

Fraser, John Simon Frederick (1765–1803). Adm. LI 14 Dec. 1780, called 12 Nov. 1789, ad eundem IT 17 Apr. 1793. HC. MP Inverness-shire 1796–1802. LM&W 1795. *Additional sources:* Thorne, *History of Parliament; Al. Ox.*

French, Pingston Arundel (?1764–1836). Adm. IT 19 May 1786, called 12 Nov. 1789. BA 1786, MA 1789 (Ox.). Perpetual Curate of Hawkhurst, Kent; Rector of Odcombe and Thorne Falcon, Somerset, 1803. LM&W 1793. *Additional sources: Westminster School Register.*

Garde, Richard. Adm. MT 4 Nov. 1825, called 28 Nov 1828. HC. Surrey sessions. CCC 1842–48. Last entry in *Law List* 1865.

Gardner, Richard. Adm. MT 25 June 1784, called 9 Nov. 1787. BA, MA 1786 (Ox.). Conv. LM&W 1793–97. Last entry in *Law List* 1797. *Additional sources: Al. Ox.*

Garrow, William (1760–1840). Adm. LI 27 Nov. 1778, called 26 Nov. 1783. HC. KC, Bencher 1793. Treasurer 1801. PWSG 1805–6. AG 1806–12, May 1813–May 1817. SG June 1812–May 1813. CJ Chester 1814–17. Puisne B. Ex. 1817–32. PC 22 Feb. 1832. Leading OB counsel, 1784–92 (OBSP). *Additional sources: DNB;* Thorne, *History of Parliament;* Foss, *Judges; GM* (1840); *Monthly Magazine* 9 (1840): 106–16; *LO* 3 (1832): 253–56; *LR* 1 (1844): 318–28; *LT* 4 (1844): 445–47.

Gleede, John. Adm. IT 9 May 1794, called 11 May 1798. OC and ChC. Gloucs. sessions. LM&W 1800. Named in OBSP 1800–1812. Last entry in *Law List* 1818; address given as "Edinburgh."

Glover, William (d. 1870). Adm. MT 1 June 1825, called 23 Jan. 1829. SP. HC. Surrey sessions / OC. Berks. and Staffs. sessions. SL 1840, expelled 1856. LM&W 1830–31.

Gurney, John (1768–1845). Adm. IT 10 Apr. 1788, called 3 May 1793. Bencher 1816. HC. Surrey and Kent sessions. Recorder of Bridport. KC 1816. Knt., Puisne B. Ex. 1832. LM&W 1799–1816. Named in OBSP from 1793. *Additional sources: DNB;* Foss, *Judges; The Times,* 4 Mar. 1845; *LM* 33 (1845): 274–79; *LT* 4 (1845): 447–48.

Gurney, Russell (1804–1878). Adm. IT 20 June 1822, called 21 Nov. 1828. Bencher 1845. BA 1826 (Camb.). SP. CCP 1829–45. HC. QC 1845. Sheriffs' Court J. 1850–55. CS London 1855–56. Recorder of London 1856–78. MP Southampton 1865–78. PC 1866. CCC 1835–42. *Additional sources: DNB; Al. Cant.; LJ* (1878): 345, 357; *LT* 65 (1878): 145.

Hall, Edward Crompton Lloyd. Adm. IT 5 Apr. 1826, called 29 Apr. 1831. SP. SW and ChC. Cardiganshire & Carmarthen sessions. LM&W 1832–40. Last entry in *Law List* 1855.

Hammond, Charles-Hilgrove (b. ?1770). Adm. LI 22 Aug. 1789, called 4 July 1797. BA

1792, MA 1795 (Ox.). HC. Recorder of Southampton. LM&W 1799–1810. *Additional sources: Al. Ox.* Last printed entry in *Law List* 1811; Hammond's name inked in in LI copy for 1816 (address given: 1 New Court).

Hance, Charles (d. 1873). Adm. IT 2 Nov. 1826, called 22 Nov. 1833. SP. HC. LM&W 1834–42. Never listed under CCC.

Harrison, William (d. 1841). Adm. IT 10 Feb. 1783, called 27 June 1800. SP. HC. KC 1816, reapp. 1830, 1837. Bencher 1816. Counsel to the Treasury and to the War Office. AG, Duchy of Cornwall. LM&W 1801–8. *Additional sources: GM* (1841).

Hart, Benjamin (surname changed to *Thorold*, London *Gazette*, Feb. 1820) (d. 1836). Adm. LI 6 June 1792, called 11 July 1797. SP. OC/NorfC. Gloucs. sessions. LM&W 1801–27.

Heaton, Charles H. Adm. MT 11 Mar. 1823, called 6 June 1828. SP. NC. West Riding, Yorks. sessions. LM&W 1829–33. Named in OBSP through 1834. CCC 1835–40. Last entry in *Law List* 1871.

Hill, William Alfred (b. ?1817). Adm. GI 21 Jan. 1837, called 22 Apr. 1840. BA 1841, MA 1842 (Ox.). SP. OC. Worcester and Stafford sessions. CCC 1847. Withdrew from bar 1847. Vicar from 1857, multiple posts. *Additional sources: Al. Ox.;* Foster, *Men at the Bar.*

Holt, Francis Ludlow (1780–1844). Adm. MT 11 Dec. 1801, called 27 Jan. 1809, adm. IT 1829. Bencher 1831. Treasurer 1840. SP. MC/NC. Warwick & Northampton/Liverpool & Manchester sessions. KC 1831. Treasurer 1840. VC Co. Pal. Lancs. 1826–44. Exch. bill loan comm. For publications see *DNB.* LM&W 1812–18. *Additional sources: DNB; NMT; Al. Ox.; GM* (1844); *LT* 4 (1844): 48.

Hone, Joseph Terry (b. ?1782). Adm. GI 2 Mar. 1806, called 30 June 1813. ED and conv. MC. Nottingham, Leicester, and Northampton sessions. OC. Gloucs. sessions. Union Hall mag. Master in the Superior Court; Common Court of Requests; chairman, Court of Quarter Sessions, Van Dieman's Land. Not listed as LM&W counsel but named in OBSP 1820–22. Last entry in *Law List* 1831.

Hosty, Henry. Adm. GI 17 Nov. 1781, called 27 June 1787. LM&W 1793. Named in OBSP from 1791. Last entry in *Law List* 1793, inked through in LI copy.

Hovell, James. Adm. IT 9 Nov. 1792, called 17 Nov. 1797. SP. HC. Borough of Hertford and Surrey sessions. LM&W 1799–1808. Named in OBSP from 1798. Last entry in *Law List* 1808.

Huddlestone, John Walter (1815–1890). Adm. GI 18 Apr. 1836, called 7 May 1839. Bencher 1857. Treasurer 1859, 1868. OC. Worcester and Stafford sessions. QC 1857. MP Canterbury 1865–68, Norwich 1874–75. Counsel to Admiralty. Judge-Advocate of the Fleet 1865–75. SL, JCP, Knt., B. Ex. 1875. JQB 1880–90. CCC 1842–57. *Additional sources: DNB; DLB;* B. C. Robinson, *Bench and Bar,* 41–42, 76; Ballantine, *Experiences,* 29; *LJ* (1890): 730; (1891): 600; *LT* 90 (1890): 127.

Hughes, Samuel (1801–1887). Adm. IT 18 June 1824, called 28 Jan. 1831. SP. HC. Sussex sessions. LM&W 1834–42. Not listed under CCC. *Additional sources: LJ* (1887): 672; *LT* 84 (1887): 162.

Hurlestone, Edwin Tyrell (1806–1881). Adm. IT 28 Jan. 1829, called 31 Jan. 1834. HC. LM&W 1834–41. Not listed under CCC. *Additional sources: LJ* (1881): 461.

Jackson, Randle (1757–1837). Adm. MT 1 Jan. 1785, called 9 Feb. 1793, ad eundem IT

24 May 1805. Created MA 1793. Bencher 1828. Reader, autumn 1834. HC. Surrey sessions. Parliamentary counsel to East India Co. Surrey mag. LM&W 1793–1803. *Additional sources: Al. Ox.; NMT; LO* 15 (1837): 330.

?Jackson, William (1770–1841). Adm. GI 29 Jan. 1793. Call date unknown. LLB 1795 (Camb.). LM&W 1812–16. "Jackson" named in OBSP 1806, 1810. *Additional sources: Al. Cant.*

Jerningham, Charles William Edward. Adm. IT, called 12 Feb. 1830. HC. Kent sessions. CCC 1842–46. Last entry in *Law List* 1899. *Additional sources:* Ballantine, *Experiences*, 74–75.

Jessop, John Sympson (?1780–1851). Adm. LI 24 Nov. 1796, called 27 Nov. 1801. HC. Essex, Herts. & Southwark sessions. JP Essex, Msex. & Herts. DL Essex. LM&W 1807–8, 1819–40. *Additional sources: Al. Ox.; GM* (1851); PRO: HO/47/73; *LO* 43 (1851): 197.

Johnston, Patrick Francis. Adm. MT 23 Jan. 1827, called 25 Nov. 1831. HC. CCC 1842–46. Last entry in *Law List* 1861.

Jones, Charles Chadwicke (1800–1852). Adm. MT 16 June 1825, called 25 June 1830. SP. HC. SL 1844. LM&W 1832–44. CCC 1835–44. *Additional sources: DLB.*

Keating, Robert. Adm. MT 25 June 1785, called 22 June 1792. WC. LM&W 1795. Last entry in *Law List* 1813.

Keneally, Edward (1819–1880). Adm. GI 13 Jan. 1838, called to Irish bar 1840, called to English bar 1 May 1847. Bencher 1868. BA 1840, LLB 1846, LLD 1850 (Dublin). SP. OC. Shrewsbury and Staffs. sessions. QC 1868. MP Stoke-upon-Trent 1874–80. Expelled from OC, dispatented by LC, disbenched and disbarred by GI 1874 for conduct in Tichborne case. CCC 1849–59. *Additional sources: DNB;* Kelly, *Famous Advocates; LJ* (1880): 213, 224, 233; *LT* 68 (1880): 460.

Kerr, James. Adm. IT 1 Sept. 1785, called 8 July 1791. Puisne J., Vice-Admiralty Court. President, Provincial Court of Appeals, Quebec. LM&W 1793.

Keys, Philip. Adm. LI 21 Mar. 1763, called 13 May 1768. HC. Borough Court of Southwark, Court of Record at Whitechapel. Conv. LM&W 1793–95. Named in OBSP 1783–90.

Kirwan, Andrew Valentine (1804–1870). Adm. GI 9 Feb. 1821, called 14 May 1828. SP. OC. Oxford sessions. Regular contributor to newspaper and professional press. Ceased to practice law 1850. CCC 1843–45. *Additional sources: LT* 49 (1870): 459.

Knapp, Jerome William (1762–1815). Adm. MT 24 Oct. 1776, called 23 Nov. 1787. BCL 1783, DCL 1787 (Ox.). Dep. clerk of arraigns, HC. LM&W 1793–1815. Named in OBSP from 1787. *Additional sources:* C. J. Robinson, *Merchant Taylors' School Register; Al. Ox.; GM* (1815); Grimaldi, "Memorial of the Knapp Family"; GL: MS 11,926; O. G. Knapp, *History.*

Knowlys, Newman (1758–1836). Adm. MT 22 Jan. 1774, called 8 Feb. 1782. Bencher 1817. Reader, Lent 1819. Treasurer 1826. CCP. HC. Steward, Borough Court of Southwark. CS London 1803–22. Recorder of London 1822–33. LM&W 1793–1803. Named in OBSP from 1784. *Additional sources: Al. Cant.; GM* (1836); *LO* 13 (1836): 345.

Knox, Vicesimus (d. 1855). Adm. IT 14 Jan. 1796, called 3 Feb. 1804. Bencher 1848. HC. Kent and Essex sessions. Dep. recorder, Saffron Walden. LM&W 1824–28. *Additional sources: LO* 49 (1855): 281.

Kyd, Stewart (d. 1811). Adm. MT 15 June 1782, called 22 June 1787. ED and conv. Essex and St. Albans sessions. For publications see *DNB*. LM&W 1793. *Additional sources*: *DNB*; *NMT*; *GM* (1811).

Law, Charles Ewan (1792–1850). Adm. IT 16 Jan. 1813, called 7 Feb. 1817. Bencher 1829. MA 1812, LLD 1847 (Camb.). Clerk of Nisi Prius, London and Msex., KB. HC. CCP 1823–27. Sheriffs' Court J. 1827–30. KC 1829. CS London 1830–33. Recorder of London 1833–50. MP Cambridge 1835–50. LM&W 1822–29. Named in OBSP from 1820. *Additional sources*: *DNB*; *GM* (1850); Ballantine, *Experiences*, 8, 55; B. C. Robinson, *Bench and Bar*, 49–50; *LO* 41 (1850): 236; *LT* 15 (1850): 467.

Leach, Thomas (1746–1818). Adm. MT 8 July 1778, called 25 June 1784. HC. Police mag., Hatton Garden 1790–1818. Chairman, Holborn Court of Requests. Publications include three editions of *Cases in Crown Law* (1789–1815). LM&W 1793–1803. Named in OBSP from 1786. *Additional sources*: *DNB*; *NMT*.

Lee, Francis Valentine (?1804–1846). Adm. LI 5 Dec. 1823, called 6 Feb. 1829. OC. SP. Worcester, Stratford, and Southwark sessions. LM&W 1820–40. CCC 1835–40. *Additional sources*: *LO* 32 (1846): 625; *LT* 8 (1846): 45.

Leigh, Patrick Brady (d. 1839). Adm. GI 24 Jan. 1824 (as *Lee*), called 8 June 1831. SP. WC. Wiltshire, Somerset sessions. CCC 1835–39. *Additional sources*: *LO* 19 (1839): 443.

Lewin, Thomas. Adm. IT 14 June 1804, called 22 Nov. 1811. BA 1808, MA 1832 (Ox.). HC. Kent sessions. LM&W 1813–16. Last entry in *Law List* 1819. *Additional sources*: *Al. Ox.*

Locke, John (1805–1880). Adm. IT 27 Jan. 1826, called 3 May 1833. Bencher 1857. BA 1829, MA 1832 (Camb.). HC. Surrey sessions. CCP 1845–57. QC 1857. Recorder of Brighton 1861–79. MP Southwark 1857–80. Publications include *Treatise on the Game Laws* (1849) and *The Doctrine and Practice of Foreign Attachment in the Lord Mayor's Court* (1853). Introduced bill which became 24 & 25 Vict., c. 66, allowing affirmations in criminal cases. CCC 1850–53. *Additional sources*: *DNB*; *Al. Cant.*; *The Times*, 30 Jan. 1880; *AR* (1880); Ballantine, *Experiences*, 66; *LJ* (1880): 52, 64; *LT* 58 (1880): 286.

Long, George (?1780–1868). Adm. GI 6 Feb. 1806, called 11 Jan. 1811. HC. Sussex sessions. Municipal corp. comm. Dep. steward, Marshalsea Court 1825. Recorder of Coventry 1837. Police mag., Marylebone 1840. For his publications see *LT*. LM&W 1816–17. *Additional sources*: *LT* 45 (1868): 250.

Lovett, Henry William (d. 1842). Adm. GI 3 Apr. 1809, called 3 June 1818. HC. LM&W 1822–28. Named in OBSP from 1819. *Additional sources*: *GM* (1842); *LO* 26 (1842): 309.

MacNally, Leonard (1752–1820). Adm. MT 8 June 1774, called to Irish bar 1776, called to English bar 30 May 1783. Gov't informer from ca. 1790. Named in OBSP 1784–89. *Additional sources*: *DNB*; *NMT*; Fitzpatrick, *Secret Service under Pitt*, chap. 14.

Maguire, George (1809–1851). Adm. MT 12 June 1827, called 3 May 1833. SP. NC. Kent sessions. CCC 1835–42. *Additional sources*: *Al. Cant.*; *LO* 43 (1851): 197.

Mahon, James Nicolas. Adm. MT 14 Jan. 1822, called 25 May 1827. Surrey sessions. CCC 1835–42. Last entry in *Law List* 1899.

Marshall, George Clough (d. 1830). Adm. IT 10 Nov. 1807, called 17 May 1811. BA 1808, MA 1810, Fellow to 1830 (Ox.). HC. Sussex sessions. SP and conv. LM&W 1812–20. *Additional sources*: *Al. Ox.*

Marsham, Robert Bullock (1786–1880). Adm. LI 12 Dec. 1807, called 1813. BA 1807, MA 1814, DCL 1826, Fellow 1812–16, Dean 1824, Warden, Merton College 1826–80 (Ox.). HC. Kent sessions. LM&W 1816. Named in OBSP to 1819. *Additional sources: Al. Ox.; LT* 70 (1880): 161.

Matthews, William (1769–1801). Adm. MT 9 Nov. 1793, called 11 Nov. 1796. HC. BA 1791, MA 1794. "Wordsworth's most intimate friend at Cambridge" (*Al. Cant.*). Died in Tobago. LM&W 1797–1801. *Additional sources:* C. J. Robinson, *Merchant Taylors' School Register; Al. Cant.; GM* (1801).

Meller, Henry James (1808–1881). Adm. MT 29 Apr. 1837, called 8 May 1840. SP. HC. Kent, Msex. sessions. J., District Court, and police mag., D'Urban, Port Natal 1852. Crown prosecutor, D'Urban, Port Natal, ?1856. CCC 1847–51. *Additional sources: LJ* (1881): 462.

Meteyard, Horace William (1808–1851). Adm. MT 7 Nov. 1829, called 3 May 1833. LLB 1833 (Camb.). SP. OC. Shrewsbury and Staffordshire sessions. CCC 1835–40. *Additional sources: Al. Cant.; LO* 43 (1851): 197.

Miller, Robert (d. 1876). Adm. MT 28 June 1821, called 10 Nov. 1826. BA 1822, MA 1827 (Dublin). MC. Coventry, Warwick & Northampton sessions. SL 1850. J. Co. Ct. Circ. No. 20, 1856–76. LM&W 1827–28. Named in OBSP to 1832. *Additional sources: LJ* (1876): 472, 489–90; *LT* 61 (1876): 289.

Minshull, George Rowland (d. 1840). Adm. GI 9 May 1786, IT 7 May 1789, called 18 Nov. 1791. Bencher 1831. HC. SP. Police mag., Bow Street 1821–40. Receiver General, Co. Bucks. LM&W 1793–95. *Additional sources: GM* (1840); *LO* 21 (1840): 394.

Mirehouse, John (1789–1850). Adm. LI 15 Sept. 1809, called 13 May 1817. BA 1812, MA 1817 (Camb.). HC. Essex and Carmarthen sessions. CCP 1823–31. Sheriffs' Court J. 1831. JP, DL Pembs. & Msex. CS London 1833–50. LM&W 1830–33. *Additional sources: Al. Cant.; GM* (1850); *The Times,* 25 Dec. 1838, 2 Jan. 1839; B. C. Robinson, *Bench and Bar,* 50–52; *LT* 14 (1850): 480.

Montagu, Basil (1770–1851). Adm. GI 30 Jan. 1789, called 19 May 1798. BA 1790, MA 1793 (Camb.) ED. NorfC. Bankruptcy comm. 1806. Accountant General in Bankruptcy 1835. KC 1835. Campaigner for reform of criminal and bankruptcy law. For publications see *DNB.* LM&W 1801. Named in OBSP to 1802. *Additional sources: DNB; Al. Cant.; LT* 18 (1851): 237; Farington, *Diary* (multiple entries; see index).

Montagu, Charles Parr (b. 1806). Adm. LI 16 May 1829, called 10 June 1834 (Trinity Term 1836 in GAR). "Died young" (*Al. Cant.*). CCC 1835–40. *Additional sources: Al. Cant.*

Moore, Charles. Adm. LI 12 Nov. 1792, called 22 Nov. 1793, left 20 Nov. 1809. SP. HC. Surrey sessions. Bankruptcy comm. LM&W 1795. Last entry in *Law List* 1810.

Myers, John (1767–1821). Adm. GI 8 July 1788, called 26 Nov. 1796. BA 1791, MA 1794 (Camb.). NC. A cousin of Wordsworth. LM&W 1806. Named in OBSP to 1811. *Additional sources: Al. Cant.*

O'Brien, Michael (1813–1873). Adm. LI 8 Nov. 1838, called 5 May 1842. BA 1835, MA 1842 (Dublin). MC. Msex., Leicester, Warwick & Birmingham sessions (leader of Birmingham sessions bar). SL 1862. Revising barrister 1854. Recorder of Lincoln 1872–73. CCC 1845–56. *Additional sources: DLB; LJ* (1873): 360; *LT* 55 (1873): 209.

Orde, William (?1772–1842). Adm. LI 2 Feb. 1793, called 8 Feb. 1799. NC. LM&W 1801–8. *Additional sources: LO* 26 (1842): 310.

Parker, Henry Walter. Adm. GI 15 June 1827, called 15 June 1832. SP. HC. Asst. Poor Law
  comm., Somerset House 1842. CCC 1835–42. Named in OBSP from 1832. Penciled
  note in LI copy of *Law List*, 1850, crosses name out: "Gone to Australia in Jany 1849."

Parry, John Humffreys (1816–1880). Adm. MT 28 Apr. 1838, called 9 June 1843. Bencher
  1878. SP. HC. Msex. sessions. CCC 1847–56. SL 1856. *Additional sources*: *DNB*; *NMT*;
  Kelly, *Famous Advocates*; [Foote], *"Pie Powder,"* 80–81; B. C. Robinson, *Bench and Bar*,
  91–93; Williams, *Leaves of a Life*, 141–42; *LJ* (1880): 25, 33; *LT* 58 (1880): 211.

Payne, Joseph (?1798–1870). Adm. LI 30 May 1820, called 14 June 1825, adm. MT 15 June
  1843. Dep. asst. J., Msex. sessions 1858. LM&W 1830–58. Named in OBSP from 1825.
  CCC 1835–58. *Additional sources*: *Al. Ox.*; B. C. Robinson, *Bench and Bar*, 258–63; *LJ*
  (1870): 196; *LT* 48 (1870): 427, 440, 460.

Payne, William John (1823–1884). Adm. LI 13 Feb. 1838, called 7 June 1844. NorfC.
  Counsel (1853–72), later J. (1873–84), Southwark Court of Record. SL 1859. Recorder
  of Buckingham 1866–84. Coroner, Duchy of Lancaster 1869. Coroner of London
  1873–84. LM&W 1849–72. CCC 1849–72. *Additional sources*: *LJ* (1884): 253, 256.

Peatt, Richard. Adm. IT 10 June 1771, called 7 Feb. 1777, adm. LI 2 Jan. 1786. HC.
  LM&W 1795. Named in OBSP 1784–1808.

Percy, Bernard Elliot (?1785–1871). Adm. LI 19 Nov. 1802, called 24 Nov. 1807, left
  29 Nov. 1813, readm. 18 Feb. 1822, "now Revd." BA 1805. HC. LM&W 1821–23. *Additional sources*: *Al. Ox.*

Phillips, Charles (1787–1859). Adm. MT 30 Oct. 1807, called to Irish bar 1812, called
  to English bar 9 Feb. 1821. BA 1806 (Dublin). Connaught circuit. OC. Bankruptcy
  comm., Liverpool 1842. Comm., Insolvent Debtors' Court 1848. For publications
  see *DNB*. Leader of OB 1825–42. LM&W 1828–42. Named in OBSP from 1821.
  Additional sources: *DNB*; UCL, Brougham Papers; *GM* (1859); *European Magazine*
  70:387–89; *AR* (1859): 468–69; Ballantine, *Experiences*, 58–59; B. C. Robinson, *Bench
  and Bar*, 53–56, 64–66; Kelly, *Famous Advocates*; *LT* 33 (1859): 19, 55–56.

Platt, Edward. Adm. IT 1 Nov. 1827, called 22 Nov. 1839. SP. WC. CCC 1844–80. *Additional sources*: Foster, *Men at the Bar*.

Platt, Thomas Joshua (?1790–1862). Adm. IT 24 Jan. 1806, called 9 Feb. 1816. BA 1810,
  MA 1814 (Camb.). SP. HC. Hertford and Essex sessions. KC 1834. Knt. 1845. B. Ex.
  1845–56. LM&W 1817–28. Named in OBSP to 1830. *Additional sources*: *DNB*; Foss,
  Judges; Ballantine, *Experiences*, 46, 47; *LT* 4 (1845): 364–65.

Plumptre, Charles John (1818–1887). Adm. GI 23 May 1838, called 5 June 1844. SP. WC.
  Exeter sessions (from 1851), Devon, Exeter, Plymouth & Devonport sessions (from
  1853). Subsequently lecturer on professional elocution at Oxford. CCC 1850–62.
  Additional sources: Foster, *Men at the Bar*; *LJ* (1887): 372; *LT* 83 (1887): 212.

Pooley, Robert (d. ?1816). Adm. IT 13 Apr. 1785, called 7 May 1790. HC. Essex sessions (from 1811). LM&W 1793–1816. (Name stroked through in LI copy of the 1816
  Law List).

Poulden, George (1802–1868). Adm. IT, called 12 Feb. 1830. SP. WC. Hampshire sessions. Counsel to the Post Office; junior counsel to the Admiralty, the War Dept., and
  the Mint. Revising barrister. Recorder of Portsmouth 1866. CCC 1835–42. *Additional
  sources*: *LT* 45 (1868): 171.

Prendergast, Michael (1795–1859). Adm. LI 14 May 1816, called 20 Nov. 1820. Bencher

1850–59. LLB 1821 (Ox.). SP. NorfC. Southwark and Suffolk sessions. Recorder of Bedford 1846–48. Recorder of Norwich 1848–59. QC 1850. Revising barrister 1856. Sheriffs' Court J. 1856–59. LM&W 1825–51. Named in OBSP from 1820. CCC 1835–50. *Additional sources*: C. J. Robinson, *Merchant Taylors' School Register*; *Al. Ox.*; *GM* (1859); Ballantine, *Experiences*, 30; *LT* 33 (1859): 19, 45, 78.

Prendergast, Michael, Jr. (b. 1822). Adm. MT 24 Nov. 1843, called 23 Nov. 1849. LLB 1850 (Camb.). SP. NorfC. Aylsbury and Ipswich sessions. Emigrated to Australia ?1853, New Zealand 1862. LM&W 1850–53. CCC 1850–53. *Additional sources*: *Al. Cant.*

Quin, Michael Joseph. Adm. LI 26 Jan. 1818, called 12 June 1823. NC. LM&W 1825. Named in OBSP to 1828.

Radford, Thomas. Adm. IT 1 Feb. 1823, called 8 Feb. 1828, name withdrawn 6 Nov. 1840. MC. Coventry & Warwick/Nottinghamshire sessions. Bankruptcy comm. for Coventry and district. LM&W 1828–32.

Raine, Jonathan (1763–1831). Adm. LI 18 Nov. 1785, called 26 May 1791. Bencher 1816. Treasurer 1821. BA 1787, Fellow 1789, MA 1790 (Camb.). NC. CCP. KC 1816. SG, Co. Pal. Durham, 1821–23. CJ NWC Mar. 1823–Aug. 1830. MP St. Ives 1802–6, Wareham 1806–7, Launceston 1812, Newport 1812–May 1831. LM&W 1793–1803. *Additional sources*: Thorne, *History of Parliament*; *Eton College Register*; *Al. Cant.*; *The Bar*, 128–29; *GM* (1831); *LM* 6 (1831): 244; *LO* 2 (1831): 58.

Randall, William. Inn of call unknown. HC. Bankruptcy comm. LM&W 1806.

Rawlings, Joseph. Adm. IT 25 Apr. 1828, called 6 June 1834. HC. LM&W 1836. Surrey sessions from 1837. CCC 1836–47.

Reynolds, Henry-Revell (1775–1854). Adm. LI 24 Oct. 1792, called 19 May 1798. BA 1796, MA 1799 (Camb.). SP. HC/MC. Warwick and Coventry sessions. CCP. Bankruptcy comm. 1806–20. Dep. steward, Marshalsea and Palace Court 1815. Chief comm., Insolvent Debtors' Court 1820–53. Publications: *Reports of cases in the Court for Relief of Insolvent Debtors* (1830), *Considerations on the state of the Law regarding Marriage with a Deceased Wife's Sister* (1840). LM&W 1800–1820. *Additional sources*: *Al. Cant.*; *GM* (1854); *LO* 48 (1854): 408.

Ribton, William (1815–1889). Adm. LI 12 Jan. 1839, called 3 May 1849. BA 1837 (Dublin). HC. Kent sessions. Revising barrister. CCC 1850–89. *Additional sources*: Foster, *Men at the Bar*; *LJ* (1889): 428, 435; *LT* 87 (1889): 230.

Roberts, William (1767–1849). Adm. MT 2 Nov. 1793, called 28 Nov. 1806. SP. HC. Surrey sessions. Editor, *British Review* 1811–22. Bankruptcy comm. 1812–31. Secretary to Ecclesiastical Commission 1831–35. For legal publications see *NMT*. Not listed under LM&W. Named in OBSP 1825–26. *Additional sources*: *NMT*.

Roe, William Thomas (?1777–1834). Adm. LI 6 Oct. 1794, called 24 May 1800. BA 1798, MA 1801 (Ox.). HC. Sussex sessions. Bankruptcy comm. 1804. Comm. of Customs 1819. KC for Duchy of Lancs. LM&W 1807–22. Named in OBSP from 1806. *Additional sources*: *Al. Ox.*

Rough, William (1772–1838). Adm. GI 9 Feb. 1796, IT 18 June 1801, called 19 June 1801. BA 1796, MA 1799 (Camb.) MC. Nottingham, Leicester, and Northampton sessions. SL 1808. President, Court of Justice for United Colony of Demerara and Essequibo (afterwards British Guyana) 1816–21. Puisne J. Ceylon 1830–36. CJ Ceylon 1836–38.

Knt. 1837. For publications see *DNB*. LM&W 1802–8. *Additional sources*: *DNB*; *Al. Cant.*; *LO* 49 (1838): 313–14.

Rowe, William Carpenter (?1801–1859). Adm. IT, called 12 Feb. 1830. BA 1823, MA 1827 (Ox.). WC. Exeter sessions. Recorder of Plymouth 1838. QC 1850. Knt. 1856. CJ Ceylon 1856. CCC 1835–40. *Additional sources*: *Al. Ox.*; *LT* 34 (1859/60): 174, 185.

Rowlatt, William Henry (1775–1863). Adm. IT 16 May 1794, called 4 May 1804. BA 1798, MA 1814 (Camb.). SP. HC. Kent sessions. Ordained deacon 27 Mar. 1814, priest 25 Sept. 1816. Curate of Rickmansworth, Herts., and Harefield, Msex. 1814–18. Librarian, IT 1818–56. Reader, Temple Church 1820–56. LM&W 1807–16. *Additional sources*: *Al. Cant.*

Ryland, Archer (?1791–1857). Adm. GI 30 June 1810, called 3 June 1818. Bencher 1841. BCL 1817 (Ox.). SP. HC. Herts., Essex, and Surrey sessions. CCP 1830–57. LM&W 1833–57. Named in OBSP from 1828. CCC 1835–42. *Additional sources*: *Al. Ox.*; B. C. Robinson, *Bench and Bar*, 172.

Sandford, Edward (b. ?1801). Adm. LI 9 June 1823, called 29 Jan. 1833. SP. MC. Coventry, Warwick, and Northampton sessions. Insolvent Debtors' Court. CCC 1835–42. Named in OBSP from 1833. Last entry in *Law List* 1848.

Schoen, George Lethieullier (1756–1829). Adm. LI 10 Jan. 1777, called 26 Nov. 1784, name removed from books 8 Apr. 1818. BCL 1784, DCL 1788 (Ox.). Rector, Crick, Northants. 1801–29. LM&W 1793–95. Named in OBSP from 1786. *Additional sources*: C. J. Robinson, *Merchant Taylors' School Register*; *Al. Ox.*; *GM* (1829).

Scott, William. Adm. IT, called 1797. ED. NC/WC/HC. LM&W 1801–8. *Additional sources*: *Al. Ox.*

Sedgwick, James (1775–1851). Adm. MT 25 Aug. 1795, called 23 Jan. 1801. HC. Comm. of Excise, Edinburgh 1809, chairman of the board 1811. Examiner of droits of admiralty accounts 1815. Chairman, Board of Stamps 1817–26. For publications see *DNB*. LM&W 1801–9. *Additional sources*: *DNB*; *Al. Ox.*; *GM* (1851); *The Times*, 30 Jan. 1851; *LO* 43 (1851): 253.

Sellon, John Baker (1762–1835). Adm. LI 15 Aug. 1781, IT 19 Nov. 1788, called 10 Feb. 1792. BCL 1785 (Ox.). SP. NorfC. SL 1798. Police mag., Union Hall 1814, Hatton Garden 1819–34. For publications see *DNB*. LM&W 1793–97. *Additional sources*: *DNB*; C. J. Robinson, *Merchant Taylors' School Register*; *Al. Ox.*; Woolrych, *Serjeants-at-Law*; *LO* 11 (1835–36): 338.

Shaw, William (b. ?1798). Adm. IT 20 June 1828, called 22 Nov. 1833. SP. HC. Msex. sessions. CCC 1835–42. Last entry in *Law List* 1899. *Additional sources*: *Al. Ox.*; Foster, *Men at the Bar*.

Shermer, John Joseph. Adm. LI 14 Oct. 1790, called 29 Apr. 1796. SP. HC. Surrey sessions. LM&W 1797. Last entry in *Law List* 1799.

Silvester, Sir John (1745–1822). Adm. MT 19 Apr. 1766, called 8 Feb. 1771. Bencher 1803. Reader, Lent 1807. Treasurer 1814. BCL 1771, DCL 1818. HC. CCP 1774–90. CS London 1790–1803. Steward, Borough Court of Southwark and Court of Record at Whitechapel. Recorder of London 1803–22. Bt. 20 May 1815. OBSP 1783–90. *Additional sources*: *New DNB*; GL: MS 7067; BL: Add MS 47466, Eg MS 3710; C. J. Robinson, *Merchant Taylors' School Register*; *Al. Ox.*; Fortin, *City Biography*, 116–17; *European Magazine* (Nov. 1815): 387–88; *GM* (1822); [Polson], *Law and Lawyers*, 98.

Smith, John. Adm GI 17 Jan. 1822 *or* 7 May 1823, called 7 Feb. 1827. NorfC. Bedford and Cambridge sessions. LM&W 1828–41. Named in OBSP from 1827. CCC 1836–42. Last entry in *Law List* 1844.

Smith, John Prince (?1774–1822). Adm. GI 25 Nov. 1794, called 6 May 1801. SP. ED. HC. Surrey sessions (from 1812). Second Fiscal, Demerara and Essequibo 1817. For publications see *DNB.* LM&W 1802–10. Named in OBSP from 1801. *Additional sources: DNB.*

Stammers, Joseph (1800–1885). Adm. GI 20 Feb. 1828, called 1 May 1833. SP. NC. CCC 1835. Named in OBSP 1833–34. *Additional sources: LJ* (1885): 318.

Steel, David. Adm. IT 10 Feb. 1786, called 11 Feb. 1791. SP. HC. LM&W 1793. Named in OBSP 1792–93. Last entry in *Law List* 1793.

Stirling, Thomas Henry (1789–1864). Adm. MT 28 Apr. 1804, called 23 Nov. 1810. LLB 1812. HC. Avocat à l'administration des relations universelles, Rue de la Micholdière, no. 4, Paris 1830. Puisne J. Ceylon 1856. LM&W 1823–42. Named in OBSP from 1820. CCC 1835–42. *Additional sources: Al. Cant.; GM* (1864).

Sturgeon, Charles. Adm. IT 6 June 1823, called 12 Feb. 1830. WC. Hampshire sessions. Court of Review. North and South-western Insolvency Circuit 1843–50. CCC 1835–42. Named in OBSP from 1830. Last entry in *Law List* 1872.

Symmonds, Thomas. Adm. IT 16 Nov. 1789, called 8 May 1795. ED. HC. LM&W 1801–10. Last entry in *Law List* 1811.

Taddy, William (1773–1845). Adm. IT 5 Nov. 1790, called 3 Feb. 1797. BA 1794 (Camb.). SP. HC. Kent sessions. SL 1818. KSL 1827. Queen's AG 1832–37, AG to Queen Dowager 1837–45. LM&W 1804–8. *Additional sources: Al. Cant.; GM* (1845).

Talbot, Robert (?1777–1843). Adm. MT 25 Apr. 1800, called 29 Apr. 1803. BA 1801, MA 1802 (Ox.). SP. HC. Kent sessions. LM&W 1807–8. *Additional sources: Al. Ox.*

Taunton, William Leonard Thomas Pyle (?1780–1851). Adm. MT 12 July 1796, called 27 Jan. 1804. SP and conv. WC. Somerset sessions from 1809. LM&W 1807–8. *Additional sources: Al. Ox.*

Thomas, Ralph (1803–1862). Adm. MT 6 May 1826, called 6 May 1831. SP. OC. SL 1852. Junior counsel in defense of Chartists 1839–40. LM&W 1842–52. CCC 1842–52. *Additional sources: DLB.*

Tooke, Charles (*Chevall-Tooke* by royal license, 1859) (1808–90). Adm. MT 21 Jan. 1826, called 30 Jan. 1833. HC. Hertford and Chelmsford sessions. JP Sussex 1847. CCC 1835–42. *Additional sources:* Foster, *Men at the Bar; LT* 90 (1890): 32.

Trebeck, James (?1767–1849). Adm. LI 2 Apr. 1785, called 4 Feb. 1793. BA 1787, MA 1791 (Camb.). HC. CCP 1793–1800. Bankruptcy comm. 1798. LM&W 1797–1803. Named in OBSP from 1793. *Additional sources: Al. Cant.*

Trevelyan, Raleigh (1781–1865). Adm LI 11 Nov. 1801, called 20 May 1812. BA 1804, MA 1807 (Camb.). SP. NC. North Riding, Yorks. & Northumberland sessions. Succeeded to family estate and relinquished legal practice 1818. For publications see *Al. Cant.* LM&W 1814–18. *Additional sources: Al. Cant.*

Turner, John. Adm. IT 23 Jan. 1792, called 3 Feb. 1797. HC. LM&W 1801–3.

Vaillant, John (d. 1827). Adm. IT 18 Oct. 1785, called 14 Nov. 1788. Bencher 1825. HC. CCP 1792–1807. Sheriffs' Court J. 1807–27. Steward, Court of Record at Whitechapel 1825. Not listed under LM&W. Named in OBSP 1793–1807.

Venner, John. Adm. IT 2 Nov. 1773, called 6 Feb. 1784. HC. Maidstone and Canterbury sessions. LM&W 1793–95. Last entry in *Law List* 1797. *Additional sources*: *Al. Cant.*

Wainwright, Reader. Adm. LI 25 Jan. 1788, called 11 May 1793. SP. ED and conv. HC. LM&W 1804–8.

Walesby, Francis Pearson (d. 1858). Adm. GI 15 Nov. 1821, called 26 Apr. 1826. BA 1820, MA 1824, BCL 1827 (Ox.). Bursar, Lincoln College 1828. Rawlinson Professor of Anglo-Saxon 1829–34. ED and conv. OC and sessions. Recorder of Woodstock from 1839. CCC 1835–42. Named in OBSP from 1832. *Additional sources*: *LT* 32 (1858): 79–80.

Walford, Joseph Green (1778–1851). Adm. LI 26 Jan. 1797, called 29 June 1805. BA 1800, Fellow 1802, MA 1803 (Camb.). SP. ED. HC. Essex sessions (and Hertford sessions from 1812). Solicitor to the Customs 1823–51. Recorder of Maldon 1829–51. LM&W 1807–23. *Additional sources*: *Al. Cant.*

Walsh, Frances (b. ?1799). Adm. IT, called 26 Nov. 1824. BA 1822 (Camb.). HC. Kent sessions. CCC 1835–42. Last entry in *Law List* 1882.

Ward, Charles Fielding (?1769–1799). Adm. GI 24 Apr. 1784, called 16 May 1794. BA 1789, MA 1791, BCL 1795 (Ox.). NC. LM&W 1797–99. Named in OBSP from 1795. *Additional sources*: *Al. Ox.*

Warren, Charles (1764–1829). Adm. LI 30 Jan. 1781, called 3 Feb. 1790. Bencher 1816, Treasurer 1821, Librarian 1822. BA 1785, MA 1788, Fellow 1786–1813 (Camb.). SP. HC. Surrey sessions. Bankruptcy comm. 1790–1816. Chancellor, diocese of Bangor 1797–1829. KC 1816. PWAG 1819–Jan. 1820. CJ Chester 1819–29. MP Dorchester 1819–26. LM&W 1804–6. *Additional sources*: *Al. Cant.*; Thorne, *History of Parliament*.

Warren, John Willing (b. ?1771). Adm. GI 26 Mar. 1785, IT 5 Feb. 1790, called 22 June 1798. BA 1789, MA 1792 (Ox.). SP. HC. Charity comm. LM&W 1804–16. *Additional sources*: *Al. Ox.*

Watlington, George (?1769–1848). Adm. IT 3 Oct. 1789, called 21 Nov. 1794. LLB 1796 (Camb.). SP. HC. Herts. sessions. Prothonotary, Common Pleas. Recorder of St. Albans 1811. Master, Common Pleas. LM&W 1801–3. *Additional sources*: *Al. Cant.*; *LO* 39 (1849): 122.

Watson, William (d. 1818). Adm. LI 13 Nov. 1789, called 21 Nov. 1794. SP. Conv. HC. Hertford sessions. CCP ?1797–1818. LM&W 1797–1810. *Additional sources*: *Al. Cant.*

Wentworth, John (1768–1816). Adm. IT 11 Feb. 1785, called 7 May 1790. SP. WC. Exeter sessions. LM&W 1795–97. Named in OBSP from 1793.

Whately, Joseph (surname changed to *Halsey* 1805) (1774–1818). Adm. IT 12 June 1795, called 27 June 1800. BA 1797, MA 1800 (Camb.), DCL 1810 (Ox.). HC. Hertford and Chelmsford sessions. MP St. Albans 1807–18. LM&W 1804–6. *Additional sources*: *Al. Cant.*; Thorne, *History of Parliament*.

Wilde, Henry Sedgwick (1810–1902). Adm. IT 6 May 1834, called 17 Nov. 1837. SP. NC. Bankruptcy court. Registrar, Court of Bankruptcy, Leeds 1851–65. LM&W 1845–51. CCC 1845–51. *Additional sources*: Foster, *Men at the Bar*; *LJ* (1902): 128; *LT* 102 (1902): 417.

Williams, Edward. Adm. LI 12 June 1792, called 22 June 1797. SP. OC. Herts. and Brecon sessions. Marshalsea and Palace Court counsel to 30 June 1802. LM&W 1801. Address only in *Law List* from 1805; name inked through in LI copy for 1810. *Additional sources*: PRO: PALA 9/5/3.

Windeyer, Richard (d. 1847). Adm. MT 15 May 1829, called 23 May 1834. CCC 1835–38 (but son's obituary records that Windeyer emigrated to Australia in 1835). *Additional sources*: LT 103 (1897): 460.

Notes

Abbreviations

CLRO   Corporation of London Records Office
DNB   *Dictionary of National Biography*
GL   Guildhall Library, London
JOR   Common Council Journals, Corporation of London Records Office
OBSP   Old Bailey Sessions Papers
Parl. Deb.   *Parliamentary Debates*
PRO   Public Record Office, London
St. Tr.   *A Complete Collection of State Trials and Proceedings for High Treason and Other Crimes and Misdemeanors*, compiled by T. B. Howell, 33 vols. (London, 1809–26)
UCL   University College Library, London, Manuscript Division

Introduction

1. Langbein, *The Origins of Adversary Criminal Trial*, 181.

2. See Langbein, "The Criminal Trial before the Lawyers," "Shaping the Eighteenth-Century Criminal Trial," "Prosecutorial Origins of Defence Counsel," and *The Origins of Adversary Criminal Trial*.

3. The phrase is Langbein's. See "The Criminal Trial before the Lawyers," 307.

4. Lewis, *The Victorian Bar*, 24; Cocks, *Foundations of the Modern Bar*, 22; Bentley, *English Criminal Justice*, 56; Cairns, *Advocacy and the Making of the Adversarial Criminal Trial*, 48.

5. See Langbein, *The Origins of Adversary Criminal Trial*.

6. See Beattie, "Scales of Justice," and Cairns, *Advocacy and the Making of the Adversarial Criminal Trial*.

Chapter One

1. The Roman city was itself predated by a late-Neolithic Celtic settlement. See, e.g., Ackroyd, *London*, chap. 1.

2. Marshall, *Dr. Johnson's London*, 4. For the history of the growth of London see ibid., chap. 1; George, *London Life*, chap. 2; Rudé, *Hanoverian London*, chap. 1; and Porter, *London*, chap. 5.

3. For contemporary accounts of eighteenth-century London see, e.g., Grosley, *A tour to London*, or Stow, *A survey of the cities of London and Westminster*.

4. See Summerson, *Georgian London*, chap. 4.

5. William Cowper, *The Task*, bk. I, "The Sofa," ll. 721–22.

6. Rudé, *Hanoverian London*, 6.

7. Porter, *London*, 131.

8. Quoted in Andrew and McGowen, *The Perreaus and Mrs. Rudd*, 87.

9. See ibid., esp. chaps. 4 and 5.

10. Rudé, *Hanoverian London*, 7–8.

11. Ibid., 41–42.

12. Admittance to chambers was a prerequisite to call to the bar, although frequently, no vacant chambers being available, a fine was paid to the Inn in lieu of the requirement. For lawyers' chambers see Lemmings, *Professors of the Law*, 49–50, and May, "Old Bailey Bar," 65–71.

13. Old Bailey counsel William Garrow (no. 25), Jerome William Knapp (no. 13) (his professional address was 13 Brick Court), Henry Revell Reynolds (no. 8), and Jonathan Raine (no. 33) all lived in Bedford Row at some point. *Law List*; GL MS 11,926 (Knapp Family Papers). These houses had been built in the 1720s.

14. By the 1860s "only old-fashioned barristers resided in Lower Bedford Place, Guilford Street, and Doughty Street" (Lewis, *The Victorian Bar*, 31), but in the early nineteenth century "it was as much a matter of course for a judge to reside in or about Bloomsbury as for a barrister to have chambers in an Inn of Court." "The Judges of England," *Fraser's Magazine* 60 (1864): 89–105 at 89. Ellenborough was said to be the first judge to move to the West End; his son Charles Ewan Law, whose legal career centered on the Old Bailey (see below, Chapters 2 and 6), eventually bought a house in Belgrave Square: no. 72, Eaton Place. Campbell, *Lives of the Chief Justices*, 3:246; *DNB* (Charles Ewan Law).

15. See Lewis, *The Victorian Bar*, 32–38, and Norton, *Mother Clap's Molly House*.

16. *Boswell's Life of Johnson*, 1:422.

17. Ibid., 2:337.

18. Daniel Defoe, *The Review*, 25 June 1709, quoted in Rudé, *Hanoverian London*, 37. For the plight of the poor in London generally see George, *London Life*, chap. 6, and Rudé, *Hanoverian London*, chap. 5.

19. William Blake, "London" (1794).

20. George, *London Life*, 82.

21. Ibid., 81–84; quotations at 83 and 84.

22. Quoted in ibid., 12.

23. Ibid., 269.

24. See Schwarz, *London in the Age of Industrialisation*, chap. 2, for employment in London, as well as George, *London Life*, chap. 4, and Rudé, *Hanoverian London*, 83–90.

25. See George, *London Life*, chap. 4; Schwarz, *London in the Age of Industrialisation*, chap. 4.

26. *Commons Journals*, 16 Jan. 1749/50, quoted in George, *London Life*, 343 n. 11.

27. George, *London Life*, 171.

28. See Innes, "Managing the Metropolis," 62–63.

29. See Chapter 3 below. In a few extreme cases paupers did not survive the process: in 1787 *The Times* reported the story of a pregnant woman driven from parish to parish who gave birth on a footpath and died. *The Times*, 20 Oct. 1787.

30. Both are quoted in Beattie, *Crime and the Courts*, 219. For public anxiety about crime in eighteenth-century London see also ibid., 220–22, and Devereaux, "Convicts and the State," 236–39. Such fears persisted into the nineteenth century. In 1829 the essayist William Hazlitt bought a pair of pistols to protect himself and his son when traveling on foot to visit friends on the Oxford Road (now Bayswater Road but then a length of country lane). Grayling, *Quarrel of the Age*, 338.

31. Fielding, *Enquiry into the Causes of the Late Increase of Robbers*, 349. Bow Street, from the mid-eighteenth century, was the site of Middlesex's principal magistrates' court. See below.

32. For the history of policing in eighteenth-century London see Beattie, *Policing and Punishment*; Reynolds, *Before the Bobbies*; Philips, "'A New Engine of Power and Authority'"; Paley, "The Middlesex Justices Act" and "An Imperfect, Inadequate and Wretched System?"; Styles, "The Emergence of the Police"; Andrew T. Harris, "Policing the City"; Palmer, *Police and Protest in England and Ireland*; and Emsley, *The English Police*. See also Radzinowicz, *History of the English Criminal Law*, vols. 2 and 3; Reith, *A New Study of Police History*; Critchley, *A History of Police in England and Wales*; and Tobias, *Crime and Police in England*.

33. Fielding, *Enquiry into the Causes of the Late Increase of Robbers*, 352, 350.

34. Ibid., 358. On eighteenth-century gin consumption see Warner, *Craze: Gin and Debauchery*.

35. Beattie, *Crime and the Courts*, 215; see also Beattie, *Policing and Punishment*, 46–48. On the relationship generally between crime rates, war, and peace see Beattie, *Crime and the Courts*, 213–35; Hay, "War, Dearth, and Theft"; and King, *Crime, Justice, and Discretion*, 161–68. King argues that only "massive demobilization" made a significant impact on indictment levels (166).

36. "An Act for better preventing the horrid crime of Murder," for instance, was passed in 1752 (25 Geo. II, c. 37), ordering that execution of a convicted murderer be carried out two days after conviction—unless it were a Sunday, in which case the execution would take place on the following day—and that the murderer's body subsequently be delivered to the surgeons for dissection if the judge had not ordered the alternative of having it hung in chains.

37. For the operation of discretion in the criminal justice system see King, "Decision-Makers and Decision-Making" and *Crime, Justice, and Discretion* (alternatives to prosecution are outlined in chap. 2); Beattie, *Crime and the Courts*, chap. 8.

38. See Beattie, *Crime and the Courts*, 400–406. In London the grand jury consisted of seventeen men.

39. See King, *Crime, Justice, and Discretion*, 231–36, and Beattie, *Crime and the Courts*, 419–30.

40. The origins of this practice lay in the medieval period, when clerics gained the

right to be tried for certain types of felonies by the ecclesiastical rather than the royal courts. "Benefit of clergy" was subsequently extended to convicted laymen, providing they could pass a literacy test, and in the seventeenth century to women as well. The literacy test also became a mere formality, allowing the judge a further exercise of discretion. Clergy had been removed, however, from the majority of the more serious older offenses—including murder, rape, highway and other forms of robbery, burglary and housebreaking, horse theft, and picking pockets—over the course of the sixteenth century, while the capital statutes enacted in the eighteenth century were made nonclergyable. Benefit of clergy was not entirely abolished until 1827. See Holdsworth, *History of English Law*, 3:294-302, and Beattie, *Crime and the Courts*, 141-45.

41. CLRO: Misc. MSS 5.10, "Inventory of Furniture—Sessions House" (1781).

42. For the operation of the pardon system see Beattie, "The Royal Pardon and Criminal Procedure"; Beattie, *Crime and the Courts*, 430-49; Devereaux, "Convicts and the State," chap. 6.

43. This system was unique to London. See Beattie, *Policing and Punishment*, 450-52, for the origins of the process. Elsewhere in the country, judges could recommend capital convicts to pardon.

44. For the history and significance of transportation to the administration of criminal justice see Beattie, *Crime and the Courts*, esp. 470-519. See also Innes, "The Role of Transportation"; Devereaux, "Convicts and the State," chaps. 3 and 5; Devereaux, "In Place of Death."

45. See Hay, "Property, Authority, and the Criminal Law," 49.

46. For a discussion of these courts see Chapter 3.

47. The distinction between felony and misdemeanor had consequences in English law until 1967. See Baker, *Introduction to English Legal History*, 572-73.

48. See Beattie, *Policing and Punishment*, 91-113, and Langbein, "Shaping the Eighteenth-Century Criminal Trial," 76-81, for the history of the City's magistracy. For the City's government more generally see [London. Corporation], *The Corporation of London*, esp. 1-56; Pulling, *Practical Treatise*.

49. The commissions were separate; it was possible, that is, to be a magistrate for Westminster and not for the county.

50. See Philips, "'A New Engine of Power and Authority,'" and Landau, *The Justices of the Peace*. Middlesex magistrates consistently attracted censure from *The Times*.

51. See Radzinowicz, *History of the English Criminal Law*, vol. 3, chaps. 1 and 2, and Philips, "'A New Engine of Power and Authority.'"

52. On market days, it was claimed by the 1770s, no one could approach the building "without imminent danger of personal mischief from the Horned Cattle." Greater London Record Office: MA/S/269, 270. So long as livestock entered the metropolis on foot the potential for harm was very real. Eighteenth-century newspapers are replete with accounts of fatal gorings.

53. See Greater London Record Office: MA/S/269, 270 for petitions for a new sessions house; MA/S/327, 373 for plans; and MA/S/369 for an insurance policy.

54. Beattie, *Policing and Punishment*, 12.

55. "The City Courts of Law. III—Central Criminal Court," *Law Journal* 93 (1943): 316-17 at 316. Published proceedings of the Old Bailey were dated according to mayoral year.

56. See Beattie, *Policing and Punishment*, 14. I am unsure when this practice ceased.

57. For the extension of the City's authority in this regard see Chapter 6 below.

58. Beattie, *Policing and Punishment*, 12–13.

59. See ibid., 13–14. The aldermen strenuously resisted the attempts of Middlesex magistrates to acquire equal treatment.

60. For a detailed account of the interrelationship of the sessions of the peace and gaol delivery sessions see Beattie, *Policing and Punishment*, 11–17.

61. Ibid., 15–16. For operation of the system in the early nineteenth century see UCL: Brougham Papers, 13,396.

62. Quoted in Crew, *The Old Bailey*, 8.

63. This print is reproduced in Langbein, *The Origins of Adversary Criminal Trial*, 50.

64. John Strype (1720), quoted in Gordon, *The Old Bailey and Newgate*, 327–29.

65. Dance's father, Dance the Elder, was responsible for the design of numerous City buildings, including Mansion House (the home of the lord mayor), the arcaded Fleet market, and the new Corn Exchange.

66. See Reginald Sharpe, *Memorials*, 14–15.

67. See Chapter 6 below.

68. CLRO: "Inventory of Furniture." A brief discussion of Dance's plans for the new sessions house may be found in Stroud, *George Dance*, 100–103; a rough sketch is housed in the Soane Museum, Dance Drawings, Slider IV, Set 4.

69. Sharpe, *Memorials*, 15.

70. Admission charges, like the City's dinners, became a source of frequent complaint in the nineteenth century. See, e.g., "Letters to the Editor," *Legal Examiner* 3 (1832–33): 17–19; "Admission to the Old Bailey," *Law Times* 3 (1844): 106–7. In 1834 the Court of Common Council reconsidered a report of 6 Dec. 1832 on the office of sword-bearer and the issue of whether fees for admission to the public galleries at the Old Bailey should be continued. Consultations were held with the lord mayor and sheriffs and "several of the counsel practising" in that court, and it was determined that discontinuing fees would not be "expedient." CLRO: *Common Council Minutes and Reports, Printed*, 1834.

71. CLRO: "Inventory of Furniture."

72. Elizabeth Piggot resigned the office of housekeeper in 1822; she had been paid £35 a year for her services. Thomas Edward Townsend and his wife assumed the housekeeper's duties, and in 1825 Townsend's appointment was made official. He was paid £50 per annum and granted an expense allowance of £100 to cover the costs of stationery, cleaning materials, etc. From 1830 an election was held in the Court of Common Council for the office when it fell vacant; there were three petitioners in that year, eight applicants for the job in 1842, and four in 1846. The housekeeper's allowance was increased by £50 in 1836 in recognition of an increase in duties (the Central Criminal Court Act of 1834 had expanded the jurisdictional boundaries of the court; see Chapter 6 below). CLRO: *Common Council Minutes and Reports, Printed*, 8 Dec. 1825; 23 Sept. 1830; 20 May 1836; 13 Oct., 7 Nov. 1842; and Report No. 8, 20 Mar. 1846.

73. T. Pennant, *Account of London* (1793), quoted in Gordon, *The Old Bailey and Newgate*, 332. See also Foster, *Crown Law*, 74–75.

74. For the early modern English criminal trial see Langbein, "The Criminal Trial before the Lawyers," "Shaping the Eighteenth-Century Criminal Trial," "Prosecutorial

Origins of Defence Counsel," and *The Origins of Adversary Criminal Trial*; Beattie, "Crime and the Courts in Surrey," *Crime and the Courts*, chap. 7, "Scales of Justice," and *Policing and Punishment*, chap. 6 and 384–401; Cockburn and Green, *Twelve Good Men and True*; Green, *Verdict According to Conscience*; Landsman, "The Rise of the Contentious Spirit"; King, *Crime, Justice, and Discretion*, 222–31.

75. See Hunnisett, *Wiltshire Coroner's Bills*, introduction, and Forbes, "Crowner's Quest."

76. Langbein, "Prosecutorial Origins of Defence Counsel," 314 n. 3.

77. For the English system of prosecution see Stephen, *History of the Criminal Law of England*, 1:493–503, and Hay, "Controlling the English Prosecutor," 175–76.

78. In 1750 prosecution counsel were employed in only 3 of the 563 cases tried at the Old Bailey; in the period 1740–75 the appearance of counsel for the prosecution was reported in between 0.5 and 3.1 percent of felony trials. Beattie, "Scales of Justice," 227, table 1.

79. The date of the Criminal Evidence Act, 61 & 62 Vict., c. 36.

80. Hawkins, *Pleas of the Crown*, 2:400. In practice, "this exception had little scope." Langbein, "Prosecutorial Origins of Defence Counsel," 316.

81. Ferdinando Pulton, *De Pace Regnis et Regni*, 193, quoted in Langbein, *The Origins of Adversary Criminal Trial*, 35; see also Hawkins, *Pleas of the Crown*, 2:400. The consequences of the participation of defense counsel for "the truth" in the criminal trial would become a crucial issue in the parliamentary debates on prisoners' counsel in the 1820s and 1830s. See Chapter 7 below.

82. Hawkins, *Pleas of the Crown*, 2:400.

83. Coke, *Institutes*, 29. For the logic underlying the prohibition of defense counsel and the way in which the judge functioned as "counsel" for the prisoner see Beattie, "Scales of Justice," 221, 223; Langbein, "Historical Origins of the Privilege against Self-Incrimination," 1050–52, and *The Origins of Adversary Criminal Trial*, 28–33.

84. See Beattie, "Scales of Justice," 223.

85. This was the word employed by a sixteenth-century commentator to describe the contest. Thomas Smith, *De Republica Anglorum*, bk. 2, chap. 23 at 114, quoted in Langbein, *The Origins of Adversary Criminal Trial*, 13.

86. Langbein, *The Origins of Adversary Criminal Trial*, 109.

87. The full title in the eighteenth century was *The Proceedings on the King's Commission of the Peace, Oyer and Terminer, and Gaol Delivery . . . in the Old Bailey*, with the appropriate dates and the name of the current lord mayor supplied. They were referred to by contemporaries as the Sessions Papers and are now commonly known as the Old Bailey Sessions Papers, or OBSP. For the history of this publication see Chapters 2 and 3 below.

88. OBSP, Jan. 1751, no. 179, 74–75.

89. For the "old" form of trial generally, see Beattie, *Crime and the Courts*, chap. 7, and *Policing and Punishment*, chap. 6; Langbein, "The Criminal Trial before the Lawyers" and *The Origins of Adversary Criminal Trial*, chap. 1.

90. See Alexander H. Shapiro, "Political Theory and the Growth of Defensive Safeguards"; Phifer, "Law, Politics, and Violence"; Reznek, "The Statute of 1696"; and Langbein, *The Origins of Adversary Criminal Trial*, chap. 2.

91. See Beattie, "Scales of Justice," 224. Judicial independence was not secured until the Act of Settlement, 12 & 13 Will. III, c. 2, s. 3 (1701). See Langbein, "Criminal Trial before the Lawyers," 310, and "Prosecutorial Origins of Defence Counsel," 317 n. 18.

92. Langbein, "The Criminal Trial before the Lawyers," 308. On the discrepancy in procedure among trials for treason, felony, and misdemeanor see also Langbein, *The Origins of Adversary Criminal Trial*, 36–40.

93. See Chapter 3 below.

94. For this development see Langbein, "Prosecutorial Origins of Defence Counsel" (quotation at 360) and *The Origins of Adversary Criminal Trial*, chap. 3.

95. The profession of solicitor was still in flux in the early eighteenth century. An act "for the better regulation of attorneys and solicitors" passed in 1729 (2 Geo. II, c. 23) made registration with one of the central courts mandatory to practice, providing a regulatory base for professional development. The distinction between solicitors and attorneys was ill-defined. The appellation of "attorney" predated that of "solicitor," but both terms were in use until the nineteenth century. "Solicitor" more usually applied to those individuals whose practice lay within the Court of Chancery. Such a practice had the greatest prestige, and the pejorative adjective "pettifogging" was less likely to be attached to it; "solicitor" would thus become the preferred term for members of the lower branch of the English legal profession, regardless of the court in which they practiced. England's corporate institutions, when they hired their own law officers, without exception gave them the title of solicitor, and contemptuous references to "Newgate solicitors"—the disreputable and often unqualified individuals who haunted Newgate prison in search of business—were deliberately ironic. For the history of attorneys and solicitors see Holdsworth, *History of English Law*, 6:453–57; Brooks, *Pettyfoggers and Vipers*; Kirk, *Portrait of a Profession*; and Robson, *The Attorney in Eighteenth-Century England*. The only historian to consider the criminal practice of solicitors, however, is John Langbein. See *The Origins of Adversary Criminal Trial*, 111–45.

96. Langbein, *The Origins of Adversary Criminal Trial*, 113–20.

97. Forgery of the Bank's seal, of sealed Bank bills, or of any Bank note of any sort whatsoever became a capital offense in 1697. See McGowen, "From Pillory to Gallows."

98. See Langbein, *The Origins of Adversary Criminal Trial*, 119 n. 52.

99. See Beattie, *Policing and Punishment*, chap. 8, "Crime and the State, 1714–1750." On prosecution by the executive see also Langbein, *The Origins of Adversary Criminal Trial*, 120–23.

100. Beattie, *Policing and Punishment*, 385.

101. OBSP, Apr. 1723, 1, cited in Langbein, *The Origins of Adversary Criminal Trial*, 120.

102. Ibid.

103. Beattie, *Policing and Punishment*, 389.

104. Ibid., 393.

105. Langbein, *The Origins of Adversary Criminal Trial*, 121.

106. CLRO: "Report of the Committee appointed to enquire into the nature and duties of the City Solicitor," PAR Book 13, 1. Holders of the office of City solicitor in the late eighteenth and early nineteenth centuries were James Roberts (1766), Phillip

Wyatt Crowther (1785), Joseph Bushnan (1797), William Lewis Newman (1803), and Robert Finch Newman (1834).

107. See Beattie, *Policing and Punishment*, 392, for the City solicitor's involvement in prosecution prior to 1750.

108. See Chapter 4 below.

109. See Langbein, *The Origins of Adversary Criminal Trial*, 129–31, esp. n. 119.

110. See Brooks, *Pettyfoggers and Vipers*, 190; the practice may have continued to a limited extent into the nineteenth century.

111. *R. v. Edward Arnold*, 16 St. Tr. 695; see Langbein, *The Origins of Adversary Criminal Trial*, 173–74.

112. Few eighteenth-century briefs, for either the prosecution or the defense, survive. Prosecuting counsel had little incentive to preserve these documents once the trial had been heard, while defense counsel may have, like a famous nineteenth-century solicitor, been inclined to destroy them. See Langbein, *The Origins of Adversary Criminal Trial*, 113; Beattie, *Policing and Punishment*, 392; and Chapter 4 below.

113. The dating of this development owes to the pioneering research of John Langbein and J. M. Beattie, the first legal historians to examine the records of ordinary trials of felony rather than the exceptional cases reported in the *State Trials*. See Beattie, "Crime and the Courts in Surrey," and Langbein, "The Criminal Trial before the Lawyers."

114. See Chapter 7 below.

115. A few exceptions to this prohibition have been identified: in one instance the accused was ill and the judge allowed his counsel to state his defense to the jury; in another the judge allowed defense counsel to state the facts as the accused was a foreigner. *R. v. Davis*, OBSP, Dec. 1771, no. 40; *R. v. Charles Bairns*, OBSP, Feb. 1783, no. 197. See Langbein, *The Origins of Adversary Criminal Trial*, 176.

116. Langbein, *The Origins of Adversary Criminal Trial*, 36.

117. Ibid., 170.

118. Stephen, *History of the Criminal Law of England*, 1:424. Working from the evidence of the *State Trials*, Stephen mistakenly believed the change did not occur before the second half of the eighteenth century.

119. *R. v. Samuel Goodere*, reported in 17 St. Tr. 1003 at 1022 and quoted in Langbein, *The Origins of Adversary Criminal Trial*, 174–75.

120. *Annesly & Redding*, OBSP, July 1742, supp. pamphlet, 19, quoted in Langbein, *The Origins of Adversary Criminal Trial*, 176 n. 334.

121. On forgery see McGowen, "From Pillory to Gallows," "Knowing the Hand," and "Forgery Discovered."

122. See, e.g., Langbein, *The Origins of Adversary Criminal Trial*, 171–72.

123. Beattie, *Crime and the Courts*, 51. On the reward system see ibid., 50–55; Beattie, *Policing and Punishment*, chap. 8; Radzinowicz, *History of the English Criminal Law*, 2:57–137, 326–46; Langbein, "Shaping the Eighteenth-Century Criminal Trial," 106–14, and *The Origins of Adversary Criminal Trial*, 148–58; Paley, "Thief-takers in London."

124. For Wild's career see Howson, *Thief-Taker General*, and Beattie, *Policing and Punishment*, 380–82.

125. On Waller see Langbein, *The Origins of Adversary Criminal Trial*, 152–58, and

the contemporary pamphlet, *The Life & Action of John Waller*. Waller was an "individual intrepeneur" where thief-taking was concerned, operating on his own rather than with a gang.

126. For the Macdaniel gang see Langbein, "Shaping the Eighteenth-Century Criminal Trial," 105–14, and *The Origins of Adversary Criminal Trial*, 155 n. 237; Paley, "Thief-takers in London"; Beattie, *Policing and Punishment*, 414–15. For a contemporary account of the gang's activities see Joseph Cox, *A Faithful Narrative*.

127. Langbein, "Shaping the Eighteenth-Century Criminal Trial," 114.

128. See Radzinowicz, *History of the English Criminal Law*, 2:80. The statute which repealed parliamentary rewards ("Bennet's Act," 58 Geo. III, c. 70) also contained a provision authorizing, at the court's discretion, the payment of an award to anyone who assisted in apprehending persons accused of specified offenses, regardless of whether the accused were convicted at trial. When Bennet's Act was repealed by 7 Geo. IV, c. 64 (1826) the courts retained their discretionary power to "remunerate" with "Conviction moneys" persons who assisted in the apprehension of certain suspected felons. Ibid., 81–82.

129. Landsman, "The Rise of the Contentious Spirit," 580.

130. *The Times*, 26 Nov. 1785.

131. Ibid., 12 Oct. 1785. Convicted after a trial lasting seven hours, Harvey was sentenced to three years' imprisonment in Newgate, in the course of which he was to be pilloried twice in the Old Bailey yard.

132. Ibid., 10 Aug. 1786. *The Times* returned to the issue of perjury, in civil as well as the criminal courts, repeatedly throughout the remainder of the decade. See, e.g., 28 Apr., 30 Aug., 7, 15, 21 Nov. 1786, 19 Nov. 1789.

133. Ibid., 28 Apr. 1786.

134. Langbein, *The Origins of Adversary Criminal Trial*, 157.

135. See ibid., 158–65.

136. Add Ms 9828, fol. 35, quoted in James Oldham, *The Mansfield Manuscripts*, 137.

137. Beattie, "Scales of Justice," 227, table 1; Landsman, "The Rise of the Contentious Spirit," 607. Sample years chosen and methods of identifying the presence of counsel vary between the two historians.

138. Lemmings, *Professors of the Law*, 59. For the history of the eighteenth-century bar see also Duman, "The English Bar in the Georgian Era" and "Pathway to Professionalism," and Lemmings, *Gentleman and Barristers*; for the earlier history of the English bar see Brand, *The Origins of the English Legal Profession*; Ives, *The Common Lawyers*; and Prest, *The Rise of the Barristers*.

139. Lemmings, *Professors of the Law*, 62–63; see table 3.1.

140. Ibid., 73. As Lemmings acknowledges, his counting exercise "represents those men involved in the most public and prestigious species of barristers' work" (ibid.).

141. See ibid., 210.

142. See, e.g., OBSP, Oct. 1758, no. 328, 348–62; Jan. 1769, nos. 108–9, 66–100; Dec. 1775, no. 1, 1–31; no. 33, 46–58; and CLRO: Sessions Papers, Box 35 (1759–60), Box 44 (1775–76). Lucas's Christian name may have been William, although on one brief the initial appears to be "R."

143. Lemmings, *Professors of the Law*, 210.

144. Serjeants Glynn and Davy, Graham, Howorth, and Bearcroft, together with James Wallace and James Adair, were named in 1843 as some of "the ablest lawyers of the past generation" who had been "schooled" at the Old Bailey. "Trial of Daniel M'Naughten," *Fraser's Magazine* 27 (1843): 444–54 at 446.

145. For Glynn see Baker, *The Order of Serjeants at Law*, 514. For Graham see *DNB*; "A Memoir of the Right Hon. Sir Robert Graham," *Legal Observer* 12 (1836): 489–90; Foss, *Judges*, 9:22–23.

146. See *Gentleman's Magazine* (1796): 972, and Thorne, *History of Parliament*, 1:70. Bearcroft (1737–1796) was subsequently MP for Hindon, 1784–90, and Saltash, 1790–96.

147. *Annual Register* (1783): 205.

148. O'Keefe, *Recollections*, 1:389.

149. Born ca. 1746, Howorth was admitted to Lincoln's Inn in 1764 and called to the bar in 1769. For Rudd's trial see Andrew and McGowen, *The Perreaus and Mrs. Rudd*; for Dodd see Howson, *The Macaroni Parson*.

150. *Gentleman's Magazine* (1783): 453.

151. Howorth's professional income, cited at 7,600 guineas in the year preceding his death, suggests that the bulk of his practice lay in the superior courts. Lemmings, *Professors of the Law*, 212 n. 33.

152. See Namier, *History of Parliament*, 2:650–51, for a brief biographical notice. See also *Gentleman's Magazine* (1783): 453; *Annual Register* (1783): 205–6; *Morning Chronicle*, 16 May 1783; PRO: PROB 11/1103. David Lemmings found Howorth to be among the leaders in practice on the Crown side of King's Bench in 1770, though he trailed far behind John Dunning (*Professors of the Law*, app. C, 347).

153. O'Keefe, *Recollections*, 1:389.

154. [Roscoe], *Westminster Hall*, 1:202.

155. For Davy's career see *DNB*; Woolrych, *Serjeants-at-Law*, 2:605–33; *Annual Register* (1773): 191; *Gentleman's Magazine* (1780): 591; Lemmings, *Professors of the Law*, 210 n. 25.

156. *DNB*.

157. Woolrych, *Serjeants-at-Law*, 2:605.

158. Called to the bar of Lincoln's Inn in 1756, Impey had an active practice on the Crown side of the Court of King's Bench. See Lemmings, *Professors of the Law*, app. C, 347.

159. *Balse and Quirk*, OBSP, Jan. 1769, nos. 108–9, 66–100 at 69–70.

160. Woolrych, *Serjeants-at-Law*, 2:625–26.

161. Henry Crabb Robinson, *Diary*, 1:472.

162. Freshfield, *Records of the Society of Gentlemen Practisers*, 114–15, quoted in Lemmings, *Professors of the Law*, 28 n. 13.

163. Forsyth, *Hortensius*, 316, 314, 312, 317.

164. "Bar Oratory," *New Monthly Magazine and Literary Journal* 14 (1825, pt. 2): 167–74; quotations at 167, 173.

165. "Mr. Serjeant Davy," *Law Times* 26 (1856): 212.

Chapter Two

1. "Notes Upon Circuit, No. III. The Crown Courts Bar," *Law Times* 1 (1843): 611.

2. Ibid.

3. A list of the counsel identified in the *Law List* as attached to the London, Middlesex, and Westminster sessions (and from 1835 to the Central Criminal Court) is found in the Appendix, below. To this list has been added those counsel whose regular attendance is traceable via the OBSP. As described in the sample years (1795 and 1830) analyzed in this chapter, the attachment of many of these barristers was of short duration. The leaders in practice are discussed within the main text.

4. *The Jurist* 9 (1845): 248.

5. For the publishing history of the OBSP see Langbein, "The Criminal Trial before the Lawyers," 267–72, "Shaping the Eighteenth-Century Criminal Trial," 3–26, and *The Origins of Adversary Criminal Trial*, 180–90; McKenzie, "Lives of the Most Notorious Criminals," 234–50; Michael Harris, "Trials and Criminal Biographies," 1–36; Devereaux, "The City and the Sessions Paper" and "The Fall of the Sessions Paper"; and Beattie, *Policing and Punishment*, 2–3.

6. See Browne, *Browne's General Law List* (1775–1801); Hughes, *The New Law List* (1798–1802); and W. Clarke, *Clarke's New Law List* (1803–40).

7. For a discussion of that press, see Chapter 5 below.

8. See the Appendix for the process of identifying the bar at the Old Bailey.

9. See, e.g., [Adolphus], "Memoir of Sir John Gurney," *Law Magazine* 33 (1845): 274–79 at 276.

10. Beattie, "Scales of Justice," 227, table 1.

11. See Lemmings, *Professors of the Law*, 213–14 and table 6.3, "Social Status and Occupations of Parties Represented by Counsel at the Old Bailey, 1740, 1770, and 1790."

12. May, "The Old Bailey Bar"; Lemmings, *Professors of the Law*, 205–25.

13. For the eighteenth-century bar see Duman, "Pathway to Professionalism" and "The English Bar in the Georgian Era," and Lemmings, *Professors of the Law* (size is discussed in chap. 3). On Lemmings's evidence, the "total number of barristers active all over the country probably did not exceed six hundred at any time" (ibid., 59), and the Westminster courts "provided work for between 250 and 400 barristers over the course of any one year" (ibid., 73).

14. Lemmings, *Professors of the Law*, 73.

15. In the 1830s the total bar as recorded in the *Law List* was well over the thousand mark; by 1840, 1,835 barristers were listed.

16. Garrow's career at the Old Bailey was first explored by J. M. Beattie in "Scales of Justice" and "Garrow for the Defence." Beattie is also the author of Garrow's entry in the *New DNB*. See as well Lemmings, *Professors of the Law*, 211–12.

17. Silvester's reputation as recorder is an unenviable one, and in many ways he did much to bring the office into public disrepute. See Chapter 6 below.

18. "Some Account of Sir John Silvester, Bart.," *European Magazine and London Review* (November 1815): 387–88.

19. The eighteenth century was a difficult period in which to establish a successful legal practice, as the central courts witnessed a decline in litigation and contraction of

business. The "litigation drought" is a central theme of Lemmings, *Professors of the Law* (see esp. 75–95). Although there had been some recovery in the Court of King's Bench after midcentury, competition for work must have been intense.

20. GL: MS 7067. The purchase price of the office itself was £950, paid to the previous incumbent, with a further £50 paid as an alienation fee to the Common Council of the City of London. See, e.g., JOR 69 ff. 363b–364b (1786); JOR 82, ff. 107–8 (1804).

21. See Morris, *Select Cases of the Mayor's Court*, 3–4. For "mercantilist impatience" with Westminster Hall see Lemmings, *Professors of the Law*, 11–12 and 85–95. The extent to which these courts were resorted to will unfortunately remain something of a mystery, given that few records of their work survive. See note 25 below.

22. By W. Brandon, quoted in "The City Courts of Law. II. — The Mayor's and Sheriffs' Courts," *Law Journal* 93 (1943): 301–3 at 302. For the history of the Sheriffs' Court see that article generally and Morris, *Select Cases of the Mayor's Court*, 7; for its workings in the eighteenth and nineteenth centuries see JOR 85, 19 Jan. 1809, ff. 14–14b, and CLRO: MS 116.1, Minutes for the Committee for Unrepealed By-laws, 1822–23, 25 May 1822.

23. Technically, appeal from the Sheriffs' Court lay to another ancient institution, the Court of Husting, but this court was moribund by the nineteenth century, and its jurisdiction was eventually abolished by the London City Small Debts Extension Act, 1852. See "The City Courts of Law. I. — The Court of Husting," *Law Journal* 93 (1943): 285–86.

24. See the Mayor's Court Procedure Act of 1857 for changes in procedure after that date.

25. For the medieval origins of the Mayor's Court see Thomas, *Calendar of Early Mayor's Court Rolls*, x, xvi et seq.; "The City Courts of Law. II," at 301; and CLRO: MS 69.4 (1828). For the eighteenth and nineteenth centuries see Emerson, *A Concise Treatise of the Courts of Law*, and Pulling, *A Practical Treatise*. Most of the eighteenth-century records of the court's business have unfortunately been destroyed. Two manuscript notebooks containing digests of a fraction of the cases tried survive: pleader John Vaillant's "Report" covers eighty-eight trials heard between 1794 and 1806 (GL: MS 97, [1831]); deputy registrar Joseph Keech's compilation contains digests of seventy-eight cases from the period 1791–1801 (CLRO, 1828). While I found no count of total cases for the periods in question, 379 causes were tried before the recorder between 1780 and 1788 and 257 in the period between 25 Nov. 1803 and 13 July 1804 (Appendix to John Silvester's "Report on the Duties of the Recorder of London," JOR 82, 25 Jan. 1805, ff. 139–139b).

26. CLRO: Solicitor's Papers, Briefs &c for prosecutions at the Sessions, &c (1786–1833), Boxes 1, 2; the cases cited were prosecuted in 1792 and 1803, respectively.

27. See, e.g., CLRO: Solicitor's Papers, Briefs &c in cases at the Old Bailey, Guildhall Sessions, Mayor's Court & other courts, c. 1802–1851, Bdles. 0051–59.

28. The pleaders in question were Newman Knowlys, John Vaillant, James Trebeck, and William Watson. The OBSP indicate that these counsel appeared for the defense as well as the prosecution, although Knowlys alone acquired any real success.

29. In 1790 Silvester was named in the OBSP as appearing for the prosecution in twenty cases and for the defense only twice.

30. Fortin, *City Biography*, 116–17.

31. Garrow claimed to have attended the Old Bailey for eight years prior to his call. OBSP, Jan. 1785, no. 224, 272, quoted in Beattie, "Scales of Justice," 262 n. 42.

32. See Beattie, "Scales of Justice," 263, n. 45, in which he quotes the *General Advertiser*, 28 Feb. 1785, as referring to "Counsellor Garrow, the famous orator of Coachmaker's Hall."

33. Erskine (1750–1823) acquired fame as the leading orator of his day; his reputation rested particularly with his defense of libel and treason cases. See Lovat-Fraser, *Erskine*; Stryker, *For the Defense*. Some of his speeches are reproduced in Erskine, *Speeches of the Right Hon. Lord Erskine*.

34. "Judicial Characters. No. V. Sir William Garrow," *Legal Observer* 3 (1832): 253–56 at 254.

35. See Chapter 3 below.

36. Aickles was indicted for stealing a bill of exchange, which he had obtained on a promise to get it discounted but then converted to his own use. Garrow argued that this was no felony, and although the jury convicted Aickles on the facts, the twelve judges to whom the case was referred agreed with Garrow on the point of law. OBSP, Jan. 1784, no. 266.

37. The figure of 182 is taken from Beattie, "Scales of Justice," 227, table 1; the count of 116 is my own. The source for both is the OBSP.

38. Beattie, "Scales of Justice," 264 n. 54.

39. Called to the bar in 1806, Campbell (1779–1861) was eventually made lord chief justice and lord chancellor; he was also a legal biographer. See *DNB*.

40. Hardcastle, *Life of John, Lord Campbell*, 1:198.

41. Called to the bar in 1809, Brougham (1778–1868) served as lord chancellor from 1830 to 1834. For an outline of his career see the *DNB* and Stewart, *Henry Brougham*. He was a proponent of a variety of law reforms, including prisoners' counsel (see Chapter 7 below), and author of one of the most controversial statements of an advocate's duty to his client (see Chapter 8).

42. "Memoir of Mr. Baron Garrow," *Law Review* 1 (1844–45): 318–28 at 319 (reprinted in *Law Times* 4 (1844–45): 445–47).

43. Farington, *Diary*, 11:4017 and 14:4769; see also 2:614: "[I]n *his profession* [Garrow] is as impudent as any of his brethren, in private is modest & reserved." John Adolphus too commented on Garrow's "peculiarly reserved and retiring disposition" (Henderson, *Recollections*, 103), as did Brougham ("Memoir of Mr. Baron Garrow," at 328).

44. "Memoir of Mr. Baron Garrow," 320.

45. See Chapter 5 below.

46. "Memoir of Mr. Baron Garrow," 321.

47. Fortin, *City Biography*, 116–17.

48. Ibid.

49. James Scarlett, quoted in Thorne, *History of Parliament*, 4:6.

50. See, e.g., *R. v. Burrows*, OBSP, Sept. 1790, no. 677, at 862–63 (Garrow's request that his acquitted client be granted a copy of the indictment so that he might pursue a prosecution for perjury).

51. "Memoir of Mr. Baron Garrow," 322; "The Court of Exchequer and its Judges," *Legal Observer* 2 (1831): 305–7 at 306. Billingsgate was London's chief fish market.

52. Hardcastle, *Life of John, Lord Campbell*, 1:198.

53. [Polson], *Law and Lawyers*, 1:218.

54. "Memoir of Mr. Baron Garrow," 320.

55. *Morning Chronicle*, 27 Sept. 1785.

56. Farington, *Diary*, 8:2956.

57. Charles J. Robinson, *Merchant Taylors' School Register*, 2:129; *Gentleman's Magazine* (1829): 378. Pingston Arundel French and William Henry Rowlatt likewise relinquished Old Bailey practice for holy orders. After nine years at the bar, in the first of which (1793) he was named by the *Law List* as attending London's criminal courts, French took up the positions of perpetual curate of Hawkshurst, Kent, and rector of Odcombe and Thorne Falcon, Somerset (Barker, *Westminster School Register*, 86). The history of Rowlatt's employment reveals a man scrambling to find a financial foothold. Called to the bar in 1804, he, like French, was never named in the OBSP. From 1810 Rowlatt tried farming but met with an equal lack of success. Ordained a priest in 1814, he held successive curacies, and his combined professional qualifications enabled him eventually to assume the positions of librarian of the Middle Temple and reader at the Temple church (Venn, *Alumni Cantabrigiensis*). Bernard Percy was unique in returning to practice at the Old Bailey in 1821 after a roughly ten-year stint as a curate in Surrey (Joseph Foster, *Alumni Oxoniensis*; *Law List*).

58. See Chapter 3 below.

59. In 1800, for instance, *The Times* reported that Garrow had been engaged to defend Joshua Palmer, a "Saffron-Hill Bank Note dealer" and "the first *Fence*" in London, indicted for receiving stolen goods valued at £200,000. Garrow's fee—and he was only one of several counsel—was rumored to be 200 guineas. *The Times*, 23 Jan. 1800.

60. Bayley, Bell, Fraser, and Leach can all be found in the *DNB*.

61. These dates reflect the combined evidence of the OBSP and the annual *Law Lists*. Dower appears in the latter in 1795 but was named in the Sessions Papers in 1788; he may therefore have attended from the earlier date but if so enjoyed little professional success.

62. GL: MS 421, Duties of the Common Serjeant, as described in Report to the Common Council, Chamber of the Guildhall of the City of London, on Thursday, 15 July 1790: "Your committee are . . . of opinion, that the Common Serjeant should not be permitted to practice as a barrister under these Commissions [oyer and terminer and gaol delivery], as there will be great impropriety in his so doing." The impropriety arose from the same committee's decision that owing to an increase in business the common serjeant should regularly serve on the bench at the Old Bailey. See also "Report of Officers' and Clerks' Committee on the Office of Common Serjeant," CLRO: *Common Council Minutes and Reports, Printed*, 25 Nov. 1830: the common serjeant was "[t]o attend the Guildhall Sessions whenever the Corporation have any business there, but not otherwise to practise as an Advocate in that, or in any other inferior Court of Criminal Jurisdiction."

63. See Chapter 3 below.

64. Raine was MP for St. Ives, 1802–6; Wareham, 1806–7; Launceston, 1812; and

Newport, 1812–31. Like Silvester, Raine was a City common pleader as well as Old Bailey barrister; he was made a KC in 1816, solicitor general for the County Palatinate of Durham (1812–23), and chief justice of the north Wales circuit (1823–30). See Thorne, *History of Parliament*, 5:2–4. On his death the *Law Magazine* drew attention to Raine's "management of horse-cases, in which he was confessedly without a rival, being perfectly at home in the slang, and thoroughly conversant with the whole science of jockeyship" (*Law Magazine* 6 [1831]: 244). He was also remembered as being "blessed or cursed with stentorian powers of speech" ([Polson], *Law and Lawyers*, 1:138). *The Bar . . . A Poem, with Notes* likewise commented, "Well-natured RAINE, whose strong stentorian lungs / Would furnish bellows for a hundred tongues, / In warfare, like the giant runs his course, / And gives the war-whoop with a giant's force, / Strikes the crest fallen foe with wild affright, / And wins the victory by sheer main and might" (128–29).

65. See Hutchinson, *Notable Middle Templars*, 132; *Legal Observer* 15 (1837): 330.

66. See *DNB*.

67. Ibid.; *Law List*.

68. For the evolution of this career path see Chapter 6 below.

69. See Chapter 6.

70. This was a plot by a group of radicals, led by Arthur Thistlewood, to murder members of Lord Liverpool's Tory cabinet while they dined and then to seize London. The conspirators were arrested in Cato Street, off the Edgware Road. Five were hanged, and five transported for life. See *The Trials of Arthur Thistlewood, J. Inge, J. T. Brunt, W. Davidson and R. Tidd*; Wilkinson, *An Authentic History of the Cato-Street Conspiracy*; and Stanhope, *The Cato Street Conspiracy*.

71. See *DNB*.

72. See Chapter 6.

73. The results of Stacey Grimaldi's research were published privately for the family in 1828, under the title "Memorial of the Knapp Family"; the text is included in volume 3 of Grimaldi's *Miscellaneous Writings*. A manuscript version and his rough notes are in the Guildhall Library (MS 11,926). See also Knapp, *History*.

74. Roughly 45 percent of the 145 counsel who practiced at the Old Bailey for a year or more between 1783 and the creation of the Central Criminal Court in 1834 were born in metropolitan London, and the vast majority of the leaders in practice (Silvester, Garrow, Knowlys, Knapp, Bolland, Adolphus, Andrews, and Arabin) were Londoners.

75. See Grimaldi, "Memorial of the Knapp Family," and Knapp, *History*. The circumstances of Garrow's marriage were somewhat unusual, in that he and his wife, Sarah Dawe, over whom he was reputed to have fought a duel, had lived together for some ten years before they married. John Silvester acted as a witness at the wedding. Parish register, St. George the Martyr, Queen Square, Holborn, 17 Mar. 1793. I am grateful to John Beattie for this information.

A biographer of the saturnine, surly barrister Vicary Gibbs, remarking on Gibbs's great affection for his wife, claimed that "there are few characters more thoroughly domestic than your hardworking lawyers," and the private life of Knapp, who requested in his will that he be buried as close to his mother as possible, supports this contention. "Life of Sir Vicary Gibbs," *Law Magazine* 14 (1835): 58–97 at 95 (the sour, crabbed, "Vinegar" Gibbs, who became chief justice of the Court of Common Pleas, was not an Old Bailey counsel); PROB 11/1576/31 (1814). Fierce in court, Old Bailey barristers were typically tame at home. Although their wives are largely invisible to posterity, the affection and esteem in which they were held is not. See, e.g., Henderson, *Recollections*, 253 (John Adolphus); PROB 11/2193/487 (will of Henry Revell Reynolds, 1851); PROB 11/2045/813 (will of Francis Valentine Lee, 1840); PROB 11/1776/588 (will of William Brodrick, 1829); PROB 11/1834/448 (will of Peter Alley, 1831). Recent revelations of George Carman's domestic life suggest that the phenomenon may not extend into the twentieth century.

76. Knapp virtually died in harness, suffering a heart attack in court in 1815 and dying at home, aged fifty-two, at four o'clock the following morning. GL: MS 11,926.

77. See *DNB* and Henderson, *Recollections*.

78. [Grant], *The Bench and the Bar*, 2:201–4. Serjeant Andrews committed suicide in 1844: "The melancholy depression of spirits produced by long study in the legal profession, is the only cause assignable for the rash act," reported the *Law Times*. *Law Times* 4 (1844–45): ap. 27.

79. For Bolland's career see *DNB*.

80. "Mr. Adolphus and his Contemporaries at the Old Bailey," *Law Magazine* 34 (1846): 54–67 at 61.

81. Foss's *Judges*, 9:147–49 at 148.

82. *The Times*, 4 Mar. 1845.

83. *Legal Observer* 21 (1841): 164; Foss's *Judges*, 9:147–49 at 148.

84. "Biographical Sketch of the Late Mr. Brodrick," *Legal Observer* 1 (1830): 21–22 at 22.

85. See Chapter 5 below.

86. Ballantine, *Experiences*, 57.

87. Hardcastle, *Life of John, Lord Campbell*, 1:142.

88. *Gentleman's Magazine* (1845), 1:315.

89. *Law Times* 5 (1845): 381–82 at 382.

90. "Mr. Adolphus and his Contemporaries at the Old Bailey," 65.

91. *Fraser's Magazine* 65 (1862): 606–9 at 608.

92. "Mr. Adolphus and his Contemporaries at the Old Bailey," 63.

93. Reproduced in the *Law Times* 5 (1845): 381–82; quotation at 382.

94. "Memoir of the Late Mr. Alley," *Legal Observer* 9 (1834): 66–67.

95. "Mr. Adolphus and his Contemporaries at the Old Bailey," 59.

96. For Law's career see Chapter 6 below.

97. See *DNB* and Chapter 8 below for an account of Phillips's career.

98. PRO 30/22/2C, Russell Papers, ff. 31–37, Henry Brougham to Lord John Russell (1835).

99. Coleridge, *Notebooks*, 5:5872.

100. See, e.g., Phillips, *The Speeches of Charles Phillips*.

101. Farington, *Diary*, 14:5034.

102. See *Quarterly Review* 16 (1817): 28–37; quotations at 28.

103. Farington, *Diary*, 15:5170.

104. "Editors and Newspaper Writers of the Last Generation," *Fraser's Magazine* 65 (1862): 606–9 at 608.

105. *The Bar . . . A Poem, with Notes,* 44–52 at 51.

106. Benjamin Coulson Robinson, *Bench and Bar,* 53.

107. See Chapter 6 below.

108. Macintosh (1765–1832) was called to the bar in 1795. See the *DNB* for an outline of his career.

109. *DNB.*

110. Hardcastle, *Life of John, Lord Campbell,* 1:252.

111. Robinson, *Bench and Bar,* 53.

112. Ballantine, *Experiences,* 58.

113. Their correspondence is preserved among the Brougham papers held at University College Library, Manuscript Division, London. It was not a friendship among equals, but Brougham did consult with Phillips on matters related to the criminal trial in London.

114. [Grant], *The Bench and the Bar,* 2:147–51; quotation at 147. Grant frequently provided physical descriptions of barristers. Curwood, like Leo McKern, the actor who played the fictional Old Bailey barrister Horace Rumpole, had a false eye. His was said to have impaired "the agreeable expression of his face." Grant continued that, at age fifty-five, "[h]is complexion is very dark, and his face rough. His features are otherwise regular, and his face is round. He is . . . of a firm, compact make" (2:151).

115. *Law Times* 9 (1847): 46. Curwood's home life appears to have been less than happy; he was said to have envied Adolphus when he became a widower (Robinson, *Bench and Bar,* 66).

116. By 1830 he had "attained to a high rank on the home circuit," was standing counsel to the London Bankers' Committee, and attended the Old Bailey only on special retainers. "Events of the Quarter," *Law Magazine* 4 (1830): 517.

117. Henderson, *Recollections,* 289.

118. "Sudden Death of Mr. Valentine Lee," *Law Times* 8 (1846): 45.

119. Again, the various tenures identified are based on the combined evidence of the OBSP and the *Law List.*

120. See Chapter 6 below.

121. Robinson, *Bench and Bar,* 258.

122. Ibid., 259, 258. See also *Law Times* 48 (1870): 427, 440, 460. "The unwearied patron of all institutions that promoted the well-being of the poor" (ibid., 427), Payne inspired great affection.

123. See, e.g., [Grant], *The Bench and the Bar,* 2:320; Williams, *Leaves of a Life,* 56.

124. Bodkin was made assistant judge in 1859. He was also secretary of the Society for the Suppression of Mendicity, and his statute making the irremoveable poor chargeable to the common fund of unions, originally passed for a single year, became the foundation of the system of poor relief of the later nineteenth century. *DNB.*

125. Robinson, *Bench and Bar,* 75.

126. Ibid., 258. "[M]en of solid, substantial, utilitarian instincts furnish very little matter for such chroniclers as myself," Robinson reported with some regret. Ibid.

127. Ballantine, *Experiences,* 30. William Ballantine was himself a successful Old Bailey counsel—see Chapter 6 below.

128. Venn, *Alumni Cantabrigiensis; Law Times* 33 (1859): 45.

129. In the first half of the 1830s Phillips was named in the OBSP between 200 and 300 times per year, Clarkson just over 100 times annually.

130. Robinson, *Bench and Bar*, 84.

131. Ibid., 75.

132. Ibid., 84.

133. Ballantine, *Experiences*, 68.

134. Beattie, "Scales of Justice," 230.

135. Lemmings, *Professors of the Law*, 216–17.

136. In his report on the office of recorder, John Silvester said that at the Old Bailey he tried "felonies of every kind or Description . . . and every sort of Misdemeanour under the Commission of Oyer and Terminer . . . [the recorder] sits and tries unassisted many Hours in each day of every Sessions." JOR 82, 25 Jan. 1805, f. 135b.

137. Holmes and Speck, *The Divided Society*, 58, quoted in Lemmings, *Gentlemen and Barristers*, 214.

138. Lemmings, *Gentlemen and Barristers*, 230.

139. Lucas, "A Collective Biography," 242; Lemmings, *Professors of the Law*, quotation at 312.

140. Pue, "Lawyers and Political Liberalism," 183. Paine was prosecuted in 1792 for seditious libel arising from the publication of his *Rights of Man*. Hardy, Horne Tooke, and Thelwall were indicted for high treason in 1794: as members of societies promoting parliamentary reform they were accused of conspiring to subvert the law and the constitution, thereby threatening the king.

141. Beattie, "Scales of Justice," 238.

142. Pue, "Lawyers and Western Political Liberalism," 184.

143. Lemmings, *Professors of the Law*, 318.

144. Beattie, "Scales of Justice," 238.

145. [Adolphus], "Memoir of Sir John Gurney," 275–76.

146. Ballantine, *Experiences*, 174. Gurney was eventually made a baron of the Exchequer, and by the time he reached the bench "high Church and State doctrines had taken firm root in his mind." Ballantine reported that he had "earned the reputation of being a very pitiless judge. . . . [H]is manner at times was almost brutal." Ibid.

147. Like many of his generation—although perhaps not so spectacularly as the poets Wordsworth and Coleridge—Garrow would later leave opposition politics behind: in the 1820s he opposed Romilly's attempts to reform the criminal law, spoke against Brougham's bill for liberty of the press, voted against Catholic relief, criticized the abuse of petitions for parliamentary reform, and defended the seditious meetings bill. Thorne, *History of Parliament*, 4:5–7.

148. See Chapter 6 below. Both Silvester and Knowlys clearly owed their promotion to higher City office to their political conservatism.

149. "Memoir of the Late Mr. Alley," 66.

150. Adolphus, *History of England*, ix.

151. "Mr. Adolphus and his Contemporaries at the Old Bailey," 56–57.

152. [Adolphus], "Memoir of Sir John Gurney," 275–76.

153. Henderson, *Recollections*, 110.

154. Law represented the University of Cambridge from 1835 until his death in 1850.

In his conservatism Law followed in the footsteps of his father, Lord Ellenborough, who "manifested an instinctive and unrestrained partiality for the establishment in church and state against reformers and radicals. . . . In the Lords he consistently resisted amelioration of the criminal law and (in 1803) was the author of legislation which created more capital offences." Lemmings, *Professors of the Law*, 89.

155. See Chapters 6 and 7 below.

156. Phillips received a national testimonial and the public thanks of the Catholic Board in 1813. The Irish barrister frequently had to defend his countrymen, but his attempts to excuse some of the behavior of the Irish peasants on the ground that their provocations "were too great for the endurance of human nature" were dismissed brusquely by Adolphus: "*Human nature*, Sir, don't talk such stuff—there's no such thing as *human nature* in Ireland." UCL: Brougham Papers, 26,361.

157. Phillips tried hard to win O'Connell the attorney generalship and wrote emphatically to Brougham that "the conciliation of that man is a thing which your well-wishers can never press too much." O'Connell, he said, lived "in Ireland's heart" and could "guide her wild energies." Ibid., 28,449.

158. Eighteen convicts were executed in January 1787. *The Times*, 10 Jan. 1787.

159. Their respective promotions to the bench of the Old Bailey are discussed in Chapter 6 below.

160. For the influence of City officials on penal policy generally see Devereaux, "Convicts and the State," 235.

161. The quotations are taken from a document Frankland presented to the House of Commons consisting of a list of questions posed by the solicitor general, Sir Thomas Plumer, to the City judges, together with their replies. This document is reproduced in *Parl. Deb.*, 1st ser., 19 (1811): 643–45; Radzinowicz, *History of the English Criminal Law*, 1:515–16; and Montagu, *Tracts on the Punishment of Death*, 53–58.

162. Garrow was appointed solicitor general in Liverpool's administration in 1812; in May 1813 he succeeded Plumer as attorney general, and he held that office until May 1817. Thorne, *History of Parliament*, 4:5–7.

163. *Parl. Deb.*, 1st ser., 24 (1813): 567–72.

164. Ibid., 570.

165. Ibid., 569.

166. Ibid., 572.

167. *Hanging, Not Punishment Enough* had advocated the institution of aggravated forms of the death penalty rather than its withdrawal from the statute book. Cesare Beccaria's *Of Crimes and Punishments* (English ed., 1767) famously argued for proportionate punishment.

168. Montagu, *The Debate in the House of Commons, April 15, 1813*, 15.

169. Ibid., 15–16.

170. In 1793 Montagu was living in chambers at Lincoln's Inn, where he had been admitted as a student in 1789, and he was struggling to bring up a young son (his wife had died a few days after giving birth) while studying for the bar. Although in later life he was known for a spartan lifestyle, in which early rising and long hours of work were combined with avoidance of alcohol and a virtually vegetarian diet, his behavior at this time was said, understandably, to be somewhat erratic, and he was drinking

heavily. Wordsworth took Montagu's child into his own household at Racedown Lodge in Dorset. Montagu would later offer similar assistance to Coleridge's sons, taking in Hartley when he lost his fellowship at Oriel in 1820 (although he threw him out roughly a year later) and contributing financially to Derwent's education. In literary history Montagu is remembered chiefly for instigating a breach between Coleridge and Wordsworth that was never entirely healed. His third wife was particularly keen to encourage the connection between her husband and the literary lions of their day, and in 1810 the Montagus invited Coleridge, estranged from his wife and in need of asylum, to live with them in London. Wordsworth, who had ample experience of Coleridge as a guest, intervened to warn Montagu of the extent of their friend's abuse of alcohol and opium. Montagu "then perceived that it would be better for Coleridge to have lodgings near him." He also famously told Coleridge that Wordsworth "had no Hope of him" and considered him an utter nuisance and "rotten drunkard." Richard Holmes, *Coleridge: Darker Reflections*, 211–13.

171. See ibid., 239.

172. Hardcastle, *Life of John, Lord Campbell*, 1:306.

173. See his entry in the *DNB* for details.

174. Holcroft, *Memoirs of Thomas Holcroft*, 265.

175. See Radzinowicz, *History of the English Criminal Law*, 1:348–50.

176. Montagu's publications include the following: *The Opinions of Different Authors upon the Punishment of Death* (1809; 2d ed. 1816); *An Examination of Some Observations made in the House of Commons upon a Passage in Dr. Paley's Moral Philosophy on the Punishment of Death* (1810); *An Account of the Origin and Object of the Society for the Diffusion of Knowledge upon the Punishment of Death and the Improvement of Prison Discipline* (1812); *An Enquiry into the Aspersions upon the late Ordinary of Newgate (B. Forde) with some Observations upon Newgate and upon the Punishment of Death* (1815); *Some Inquiries respecting the Punishment of Death for Crimes without Violence* (1818); *Thoughts upon the Abolition of the Punishment of Death, in cases of Bankruptcy* (1821); *The Rise and Progress of the Mitigation of the Punishment of Death, 1520–1687* (1822); *Thoughts on the Punishment of Death for Forgery* (1830). Montagu also published *Debates in the year 1810, upon Sir Samuel Romilly's Bills for Abolishing the Punishment of Death, etc.* (1810); *The Debates in the House of Commons during the year 1811 upon Certain Bills for Abolishing the Punishment of Death* (1811); *The Debate in the House of Commons, April 15, 1813, upon Sir Samuel Romilly's Bill on the Punishment of High Treason* (1813); *Debate in the House of Commons on Sir Samuel Romilly's Bill for taking away Corruption of Blood in Attainder of Felony and Treason, etc.* (1814).

177. The quotation is taken from *Thoughts on the Punishment of Death for Forgery*, xiv.

178. For the Ratcliffe Highway murders see De Quincey, *On Murder Considered as One of the Fine Arts*, and James and Critchley, *The Maul and the Pear Tree*.

179. Montagu, *The Debate in the House of Commons, April 15, 1813*, 14–16; quotations at 16 and 14. Montagu's account of the interment was picked up from the *Morning Chronicle*, 1 Jan. 1812.

180. Montagu, *Thoughts on the Punishment of Death for Forgery*, i–ii.

181. Ibid., vii.

182. Mackintosh, *Memoirs*, 1:155–56.

183. See Radzinowicz, *History of the English Criminal Law*, 1:567–95.

184. One Old Bailey barrister, in his later incarnation as a Surrey magistrate, proposed in 1828 the "permanent removal" of "convicts in general, including minor offenders as well as felons to parts beyond the seas, except in cases of extreme youth." In enumerating the causes of increased and increasing levels of crime, Randle Jackson, who had practiced at the Old Bailey between 1793 and 1802 (and who lost to Newman Knowlys in the election for common serjeant of London in 1803), demonstrated no faith in imprisonment. Jackson was a member of a committee formed by order of the general quarter sessions of the peace to consider the state of policing in Surrey and advise as to whether it would be expedient to establish a local preventative police force in the county, and it fell to him to write the committee's report. In assessing the causes of crime he predictably drew attention to the "almost unchecked parading of streets by notoriously dissolute and abandoned of both sexes," a multitude of gin shops, unlicensed wine shops, and "flash houses which provided places of resort for thieves and loose women." But he concluded that "above all, the constant and daily addition of expert and hardened criminals, who are in a state of continual return from short transportations, from the Hulks, the Penitentiaries, and from gaols and Houses of Correction" was responsible for the unprecedented level of crime. Jackson, *Considerations on the Increase of Crime*, 11–12.

185. Phillips, *Vacation Thoughts on Capital Punishment*, 110–15.

186. For partial verdicts see Chapter 4 below.

187. Phillips, *Vacation Thoughts on Capital Punishment*, 13.

188. Ibid., 16–17.

189. For changing religious views on punishment see McGowen, " 'He Beareth Not the Sword in Vain' " and "The Changing Face of God's Justice."

190. Phillips, *Vacation Thoughts on Capital Punishment*, 94–95.

191. Ibid., 152.

192. Ibid.

193. The legal practice of London's criminal bar outside the Old Bailey is discussed in Chapter 3.

194. Twiss, *Life of Lord Chancellor Eldon*, 1:105 (emphasis added).

195. Mackintosh, *Memoirs*, 1:145.

196. Hardcastle, *Life of John, Lord Campbell*, 1:160.

197. Ibid., 1:283, 294.

198. Ibid., 1:356.

Chapter Three

1. See Lemmings, *Professors of the Law*, 150–64, on the trials and tribulations inherent in embarking on a legal career in the eighteenth century.

2. Brydges, *Autobiography*, 192–93.

3. See Chapter 5 below.

4. In the eighteenth century the chief requirement for a call to the bar was seven years' (five after 1762) enrollment at one of the Inns of Court. The student had also to eat dinners in the hall of his Inn for twelve terms. See Duman, "The English Bar in the Georgian Era," and Lemmings, *Gentlemen and Barristers*, 22–23.

5. For the eighteenth-century circuits see Lemmings, *Professors of the Law*, 50–56; for their earlier history see Cockburn, *A History of English Assizes*, chap. 2.

6. In 1800 the *Law List* reported fifty-eight barristers as traveling the Home circuit. But fifty-five were named as following the Oxford circuit, and fifty-one were attached to the Northern circuit. Thirty-nine traveled the Western circuit, twenty-five the Midland circuit, and nineteen the Norfolk circuit.

7. On his first circuit John Campbell, the future lord chancellor, traveled through four counties (Essex, Kent, Sussex, and Surrey), which cost him £20. Hardcastle, *Life of John, Lord Campbell*, 1:209.

8. See Prest, *The Rise of the Barristers*, 25–26; Lemmings, *Professors of the Law*, 51.

9. These included John Bell, Thomas Clifton, John France, Charles Heaton, John Myers, William Orde, Jonathan Raine, William Scott, Raleigh Trevelyan, and Charles Fielding Ward. See the Appendix.

10. Hardcastle, *Life of John, Lord Campbell*, 1:198 (Garrow) and 197 (Fielding); [Adolphus], "Memoir of Sir John Gurney," *Law Magazine* 23 (1845): 275–79; Woolrych, *Serjeants-at-Law*, 2:808, and *Gentleman's Magazine* (1845) (Andrews).

11. A barrister who had acquired a good practice and whose reputation was unblemished could apply to the lord chancellor to be made a King's Counsel. The rank was in part recognition of past achievements (although politics too played a role), but it also promoted future success, as King's Counsel enjoyed the professional advantages of precedence in the court and preaudience. In the eighteenth century barristers were generally promoted ca. fifteen years after their call, although a few (including Garrow) received earlier promotion. Until 1830 KCs were granted a token salary of £40 per year plus an annual allowance of paper, pens, and purple bags (the forerunner of the modern "briefcase"). Patents of precedence granted the right of preaudience in the courts specific to a barrister's colleagues: either after King's Counsel generally, after the attorney general, or after a particular King's Counsel. See Holdsworth, "The Rise of the Order of King's Counsel," and Edwards, *Law Officers of the Crown*, 275–79, for the historical background to King's Counsel and patents of precedence; see also Lemmings, *Professors of the Law*, 264–70. For serjeants-at-law, an ancient order attached to the Court of Common Pleas, see Baker, *The Order of Serjeants at Law*.

12. See Ruggles, *The Barrister*, 158, and [Polson], *Law and Lawyers*, 1:158.

13. Some also attended borough sessions outside of London, again, chiefly within the Home counties.

14. See [Polson], *Law and Lawyers*, 1:158; Ballantine, *Experiences*, 29; Scarlett, *Memoir*, 49, 61–62.

15. Ruggles, *The Barrister*, 213.

16. Ballantine, *Experiences*, 29.

17. In the City at least, paupers were almost invariably "she," consisting largely of widows, abandoned wives, single mothers and their illegitimate children, or abandoned illegitimate infants. For further examples, see the Sessions Papers, Box 45, 1778 "Settlement," 1779 "Settlement," 1780 "Settlement."

18. CLRO: Sessions Papers, Boxes 45–57 (1777–1833).

19. Ballantine, *Experiences*, 31. Houses used for dancing or other public entertainment in London and Westminster or within twenty miles were required by the Act for

Regulating Places of Public Entertainment (25 Geo. II, c. 36 [1752]) to have a license from a justice of the quarter sessions.

20. The Licensing Act, 1753 (26 Geo. II, c. 31) largely repeated the provisions of the Alehouse Act, 1552 (5 & 6 Edw. VI, c. 25), which stipulated that no one could sell beer or ale without the consent of the local justices of the peace, given either at the full sessions of the peace or before two justices. Under the 1753 act, new licenses were to be granted only to persons producing certificates of good character signed by the ministers and churchwardens of the parish. General annual licensing meetings were established by 9 Geo. IV, c. 61 (1828). In Middlesex these meetings were held in March. Four to eight special sessions were held annually for the transfer of existing licenses.

21. CLRO: Solicitor's Papers, Briefs &c for prosecutions at the Sessions &c, Box 1 (1786–99), *In the matter of William Brown, a licensed victualler* (1799).

22. *The Times*, 1 Sept. 1787.

23. In the eighteenth century the Court of Chancery also sat at Lincoln's Inn.

24. Lemmings has described the Westminster bar as marked by an "essential division" into a "small privileged elite and a larger body of men awaiting their retirement." *Professors of the Law*, 103.

25. In using this method of determining the level of practice I follow David Lemmings. See *Gentlemen and Barristers*, app. 2, 264–66.

26. For the distribution of work and leadership in the Westminster courts in the eighteenth century see Lemmings, *Professors of the Law*, 164–89 and app. C.

27. "Sir Samuel Shepherd," *Law Magazine* 25 (1841): 289–310 at 291.

28. See Lemmings, *Professors of the Law*, 184–86.

29. "Memoir of John Bell," *Legal Observer* 11 (1836): 265–66.

30. For Davy see Chapter 1; for Ballantine, Chapter 6.

31. For the level of business in the eighteenth-century Court of Common Pleas see Lemmings, *Professors of the Law*, 172–75.

32. For the history of the serjeants see Baker, *The Order of Serjeants at Law*; for their eighteenth-century decline see Lemmings, *Professors of the Law*, 263.

33. For Arabin's promotion to the bench at the Old Bailey see Chapter 6 below.

34. For levels of Exchequer business see Lemmings, *Professors of the Law*, 175–81.

35. PRO: E15/(1790); E15/4, 5 (1815); and E15/19, 20 (1830). For 1790 see also Lemmings, *Professors of the Law*, app. C.

36. "Sir Samuel Shepherd," 291.

37. For business in the King's Bench see Lemmings, *Professors of the Law*, 168–72.

38. Hardcastle, *Life of John, Lord Campbell*, 1:195.

39. Marriage could of course provide a barrister with additional income or useful connections. William Clarkson was said to have derived considerable professional advantage through "connection by marriage with a respectable firm of solicitors" (Ballantine, *Experiences*, 67), while John Silvester married well from a financial point of view. At least one of his wives (he married widows in each instance) was wealthy, and he was sneered at for having "married a fortune" and acquiring "far more by the apron than by the gown" (Fortin, *City Biography*, 116). Neither Silvester's nor Newman Knowlys's wills demonstrate any of the tender affection evident in those of many of their colleagues.

40. PRO: KB125/174 (1789).

41. Hardcastle, *Life of John, Lord Campbell*, 1:142.

42. "Mr. Adolphus and his Contemporaries at the Old Bailey," *Law Magazine* 34 (1846): 54–67 at 60.

43. See PRO: KB21/45 (1789). For Bearcroft and Erskine see Chapters 1 and 2. James Mingay, KC, MP (1752–1812), was considered second only to Erskine in practice in the King's Bench. William Baldwin (?1737–1813) acquired a substantial King's Bench practice but relinquished it in favor of a political career in 1795. (In 1789, named in more than 800 motions in the rule book for the plea side of the King's Bench, he appears to have been the undisputed leader.)

44. For Scarlett see *DNB* and Scarlett, *Memoir*.

45. PRO: KB21/50 (1815).

46. PRO: KB21/56, 57 (1830).

47. See the *Law List* (1801), 1–3 for City courts, 3–7 for the remainder of the metropolitan courts.

48. See the Appendix for the dates of their attachments.

49. See Chapter 6 below.

50. *Law List* (1815), 230.

51. The court was held under a charter of Edward VI. "Southwark Corporate Court of Record," *Legal Observer* 37 (1848–49): 41–42 at 41.

52. *Second Report of the Commissioners Appointed to Inquire into the Municipal Corporations in England and Wales, 1837*, 12, 45, and 132.

53. *Law List*.

54. See Blackstone, *Commentaries*, 3:76–77; the 1795 edition of the *Law List*, 191–92; Holdsworth, *History of English Law*, 1:208–9; and Beattie, *The English Court in the Reign of George I*, 77–78.

55. *Law List* (1815), 222. This sum was increased to £20 in 1827.

56. PRO: PALA 9/9, Account Book of Fees Received by Counsel, 1815 Jan.–1817 Mar.

57. Watlington, listed as a metropolitan sessions counsel from 1801 to 1803, was attached to the Palace Court from March 1798 through March 1800; Beville, who practiced at the Old Bailey from 1799 to 1803, was Palace Court counsel from May 1801 through March 1803; French's tenure at the Palace Court was again just over two years' duration (June 1790 through November 1792); Jessop's tenure was even briefer: October 1803 through November 1804. PRO: PALA 9/5/2 and 3.

58. *Gentleman's Magazine* (1792); GL: MS 11,926.

59. For bankruptcy law in the eighteenth century see Holdsworth, *History of English Law*, 11:445–47; commissioners, specifically, are dealt with in 1:471–72 and 8:238–41. See also Hoppit, *Risk and Failure*, 35–41, and Lester, *Victorian Insolvency*, 12–39. For legislative changes to 1850 see Holdsworth, *History of English Law*, 13:376–77 and 15:97–99.

60. This description is based upon Montagu, *Digest of the Bankruptcy Laws*, vol. 3.

61. An Act to Prevent the Committing of Frauds by Bankrupts, 5 Geo II, c. 30 (1732).

62. Holdsworth, *History of English Law*, 1:471.

63. Ibid., 472.

64. His *Enquiry Respecting the Mode of Issuing Commissions in Bankruptcy* (1810) pro-

tested the practice of initiating bankruptcy proceedings by secret commissions. Montagu also published *An Enquiry Respecting the Expediency of Limiting the Creditor's Power to Refuse a Bankrupt's Certificate* (1809) and *Enquiries Respecting the Administration of Bankrupts' Estates by Assignees* (1811).

65. Hardcastle, *Life of John, Lord Campbell*, 1:179–80. Holdsworth's estimate of potential fees per annum was even higher: £300 (*History of English Law*, 1:472).

66. *Law List* (1779–1832). Other Old Bailey barristers who held commissions were Thomas Carr, Charles Cowper, John France, Charles Moore, Thomas Radford, William Randall, William Roe, and Charles Warren.

67. For the history of imprisonment for debt see Holdsworth, *History of English Law*, 8:230–36, and Lester, *Victorian Insolvency*. By the 1830s ca. 10,000 debtors were imprisoned annually, a quarter of them on mesne process, which allowed the creditor to have the debtor arrested or detained before the cause came to court (Cornish and Clark, *Law and Society in England*, 228–29).

68. See Holdsworth, *History of English Law*, 11:597–60; 48 Geo. III, c. 123.

69. Dickens, *Pickwick Papers*, 692–93.

70. See Prest, *The Inns of Court* and *The Rise of the Barristers*, for the decline of the old system of legal education; for the "do-it-yourself type of legal education" that prevailed in the eighteenth century see Lemmings, *Professors of the Law*, chap. 4. See also Bush and Wijffels, *Learning the Law*.

71. "Study of the Law—Part II, Method, etc.," *Lawyer's Magazine* 1 (1761): 249–56, 278–95 at 253.

72. See A. W. B. Simpson, "Rise and Fall of the Legal Treatise." For the evolution of legal publishing as it relates to the criminal law generally see Holdsworth, *A History of English Law*, 12:361–67, 13:463–68.

73. Ruggles, *The Barrister*, 187.

74. Ibid., 187, 190. For a modern analysis of the impact of Blackstone see Lieberman, *The Province of Legislation Determined*.

75. See Langbein, "Historical Foundations of the Law of Evidence."

76. The *Monthly Review* dismissed the work as completely unnecessary given the existence of Hale and Hawkins and complained bitterly of "the useless multiplication of law-books" (*Monthly Review* 29 [1799]: 86–87).

77. *R. v. Jarvis*, OBSP, Jan. 1800, no. 90, 80; Hardcastle, *Life of John, Lord Campbell*, 1:305 (1814). For the history of medical evidence see Clark and Crawford, *Legal Medicine in History*; on insanity see Eigen, *Witnessing Insanity*.

78. See Baker, *Introduction to English Legal History*, 211.

79. See, e.g., volume 40 (1763–64).

80. See Beattie, "Scales of Justice," 262 n. 44, and Langbein, *The Origins of Adversary Criminal Trial*, 188–89.

81. Henderson, *Recollections*, 26–27.

82. CLRO: Journal of the Committee for Rebuilding Newgate, 1767–85, 246.

83. Reginald Sharpe, *Memorials*, 15.

84. CLRO: Surveyor's Justice Plans, no. 242.

85. For the history of debating societies see Fawcett, "Eighteenth Century Debating Societies"; Thale, "London Debating Societies in the 1790s"; and Andrew, *London De-*

bating Societies. For their role in legal education see Lemmings, *Professors of the Law,* 142–43.

86. Henderson, *Recollections,* 63.

87. Hardcastle, *Life of John, Lord Campbell,* 1:142.

88. *Law Times* 5 (1845): 381–82 at 381.

89. Henderson, *Recollections,* 64, 101.

90. The separation occurred in the sixteenth and seventeenth centuries. See Robson, *The Attorney in Eighteenth-Century England,* 1–3; Kirk, *Portrait of a Profession,* 17–19; Lemmings, *Professors of the Law,* 26–29.

91. "The English Bar," *Law Magazine and Review* 23 (1867): 126–45 at 135. By 1850 this exception appeared to have judicial sanction. Campbell LCJ: "[I]n criminal cases it is conceded that the practice of a barrister not to plead unless instructed by an attorney does not prevail." *Doe d. Bennett v. Hale,* quoted in Bentley, *English Criminal Justice,* 117; see generally the discussion at 116–22. Similarly, in 1851 the chairman of the Middlesex sessions, Serjeant Adams, stated that "he wished it to be distinctly understood that there was no necessity whatever for the intervention of a third person between counsel and prisoners. Every barrister, not only in the Criminal Courts of the metropolis, but on the Circuits, who was not otherwise engaged, was bound to take up a case if called upon by the prisoner in the dock, and also to receive the fee from him. There was not the slightest necessity for the interference of any attorney or of any person who went about in the character of an attorney's clerk; and he wished it to be distinctly understood that counsel could be instructed by prisoners themselves" (*Law Review* 15 [1851–52]: 441).

92. OBSP, Feb. 1790, no. 311, 322–23 at 322.

93. *R. v. Pharoe et al.,* OBSP, Apr. 1790, 367–79 at 369.

94. *R. v. Phillis,* OBSP, Apr. 1782, no. 315, 339–42 at 340.

95. For this debate see *Legal Observer* 26 (1843): 217; 28 (1844): 75, 427–28, 458–59; 29 (1844–45): 1–2; 34 (1847): 541; 37 (1848–49): 61–62, 145; 40 (1850): 44–45; 41 (1851): 454; *Law Times* 3 (1844): 150, 252, 500, 501–2; 4 (1844–45): 79, 164.

96. *R. v. de la Motte,* OBSP, 1780, 258–324; *The Times,* 17 Jan. 1786, *R. v. Jaques;* 24 July 1786, *R. v. Martin.*

97. For Harmer's career see the *DNB.*

98. *Second Report on the Criminal Law,* app. 3 at 108.

99. Ballantine, *Experiences,* 69.

100. UCL: Brougham Papers, 28,365.

101. Juxon, *Lewis and Lewis,* 17–20.

102. UCL: Brougham Papers, 36,816.

103. Juxon, *Lewis and Lewis,* 20. Written in 1860, *Great Expectations* was set in the time of Dickens's childhood (1810–ca. 1830). It contains a wonderful description of the knots of clients who wait anxiously outside the attorney's office, comforting each other with "Jaggers would do it if it were to be done" and "Jaggers is for him. . . . [W]hat more *could* you have?" One particularly agitated man performs a jig, chanting to himself "Oh Jaggerth, Jaggerth, Jaggerth! All otherth ith Cag-maggerth, give me Jaggerth!" (190). "Cag-maggers" sold scraps of bad meat and refuse. Jaggers could hardly be described as the "poor man's lawyer," however, since his examinations of his clients always included the question of whether they had paid his clerk.

A far less flattering portrait of an early-nineteenth-century criminal attorney was painted by Thomas Gaspey in *The History of George Godfrey* (1828). "Mr. Scampo" 's sole interest is money, and he visits in Newgate the clients "to whom he had contributed, by defending, to convict" (183) to see whether they had a guinea left to employ him to assemble a petition to the throne. By the end of the novel he has been struck off the rolls for publishing "books about love" (228).

104. See Juxon, *Lewis and Lewis*.

105. Ballantine, *Experiences*, 70.

106. [Wontner], *Old Bailey Experience*. Wontner's chief criticisms of Old Bailey practice were aimed at the City judges (see Chapter 6 below), but he also condemned both "low" and "sham" attorneys who absconded with their clients' fees and barristers who, after receiving both brief and fee, failed to appear in court (66–68).

107. UCL: Brougham Papers, 28,466.

108. Ibid., 28,465.

109. Ibid., 28,463.

110. See *Morning Chronicle*, 23 Sept. 1841. Greater efforts, the paper reported, were being made by the sheriffs and undersheriffs to prevent unauthorized persons from gaining access to the gaols by posing as attorneys. But see *Law Times* 4 (1844): 164 for a slightly different twist to this scenario, in which a man named Henson impersonated not a solicitor but the clerk of Charles Phillips in order to obtain money from a relative of an accused. Elizabeth Street, whose son had been charged with an assault, sought Phillips in the George Public House across from the Old Bailey on 22 May 1841. Henson intercepted Street and told her that Phillips was out of town but he would help her himself, and over the following two weeks or so he took from her in installments £4 she could obviously ill afford. Street never saw Henson again after the 14th of June, and her son was tried and convicted on the 19th. The City of London subsequently prosecuted this particular imposter for fraud. CLRO: Solicitor's Papers, Briefs &c in cases at the Old Bailey, Guildhall Sessions, Mayor's Court & other courts, c. 1802–1851, Bdle. 0051 (1841).

111. "The Central Criminal Court," *Law Times* 3 (1844): 252. A regulation intended "to prevent frauds upon prisoners confined in her Majesty's gaol of Newgate, by unqualified persons acting as their legal advisers" ordered that year that "no person shall hereafter be permitted to see any prisoner confined in the gaol of Newgate, as the legal adviser of such prisoner, except such person shall be a certificated attorney, or solicitor, or his authorised clerk; and every person claiming admission as such attorney or solicitor, or authorised clerk, shall, for the verification thereof, before his admission to see any prisoner, sign his name, address, and the name of the prisoner by whom such attorney or solicitor is retained or employed, in a book to be kept for that purpose." Reproduced in the *Legal Observer* 28 (1844): 75. Three years later a "rule relating to prisoners committed for trial, or for examination" was approved by the home secretary, Sir George Grey, for the government of the prisons of the county of Middlesex:

Prisoners for trial shall be permitted to see their relations and friends on any weekday without any order, between the hours of 11 and 2 o'clock in the afternoon, and at any other time on a week-day by an order in writing from a visiting or com-

enjoyment, he never will" (269). Peter Alley, however, practiced at the Old Bailey for forty-four years, Adolphus for thirty-eight.

Chapter Four

1. See Beattie, *Crime and the Courts*, 270–71.

2. See Beattie, *Policing and Punishment*, chap. 2, for the history of the magistrate's court in the City of London. On the "increasingly lawyer-dominated pretrial" see also Langbein, *The Origins of Adversary Criminal Trial*, 109–45; quotation at 145.

3. For the history of Bow Street see Radzinowicz, *History of the English Criminal Law*, 2:26ff., 177ff., 3:29–62; Styles, "Sir John Fielding and the Problem of Criminal Investigation"; and Langbein, "Shaping the Eighteenth-Century Criminal Trial," 55–76.

4. See *The Times*, 5, 10, 23, 29, 30 Dec. 1785; 2 Jan., 9 Feb. 1786, for the Burgess and Addington affair. Despite its anxiety about high crime rates, the paper remained highly suspicious of the activities of Westminster magistrates, claiming that whereas the City's magistrates acted from "principles of the constitution and the law" and always consulted the recorder, Westminster magistrates based decisions on their own knowledge and encouraged "those pests to society, informers," thereby increasing litigation, multiplying offenders, and rendering the magistracy "contemptible." See "A Comparison; or, London versus Westminster," *The Times*, 14 Jan. 1786.

5. Carrington, *A Supplement*, 9.

6. *Cox v. Coleridge*, 2 D. & R. 86, quoted in Carrington, *A Supplement*, 9.

7. See Bentley, *English Criminal Justice*, 31–32.

8. The same impression is given by the French judge Cottu, who described criminal practice on the Northern circuit for the summer assizes of 1819; see *On the Administration of Criminal Justice*, 34.

9. "If anybody, of whatsoever degree, said a word that he didn't approve of, he instantly required to have it 'taken down.' If anyone wouldn't make an admission, he said, 'I'll have it out of you!' and if anybody made an admission, he said, 'Now I have got you!' The magistrates shivered under a single bite of his finger. Thieves and thief takers hung in dread rapture on his words and shrank when a hair of his eyebrows turned in their direction." Dickens, *Great Expectations*, 225.

10. *Morning Chronicle*, 1 Jan. 1778.

11. *The Times*, 5 June 1786.

12. See, e.g., *The Times*, 3 and 7 Aug., 29 Nov., 4 Dec. 1815.

13. Harmer, for example, reported that he had been excluded from the final examination of a woman charged with forging banknotes, at the request of the solicitor for the prosecution. His client was unable to tell him what had been sworn against her, and he was thus unable to advise her. Harmer, *Murder of Mr. Steele*, 65.

14. *The Times*, 4 Dec. 1815.

15. *R. v. Stevenson*, OBSP, Sept. 1784, no. 843, 1164–78.

16. Montagu, *Thoughts on the Punishment of Death for Forgery*, ii. For the unwritten rule prohibiting barristers from visiting or interviewing their clients in gaol see also Benjamin Coulson Robinson, *Bench and Bar* (1889), 60: "I never heard in modern times

of counsel interviewing a criminal in his cell. . . . I have always understood that it is quite contrary to the etiquette of the profession. There can be no reason or necessity for it, since the attorney can always communicate to counsel all that it is essential for him to know in the interests of the accused."

17. Juxon, *Lewis and Lewis*, 11.

18. Langbein, *The Origins of Adversary Criminal Trial*, 113.

19. A few of the City solicitor's briefs also survive from the earlier eighteenth century: see Beattie, *Policing and Punishment*, 392 and notes therein.

20. [Wontner], *Old Bailey Experience*, 67.

21. CLRO: Solicitor's Papers, Briefs &c for prosecutions at the Sessions &c, Box 4 (1809–11).

22. Ibid., Box 11 (1826–27).

23. For eighteenth-century briefs see also Langbein, *The Origins of Adversary Criminal Trial*, 146–47.

24. CLRO: Solicitor's Papers, Briefs &c for prosecutions, Box 7. At trial, however, two surgeons were called to testify that the cause of death could not be determined, and Reynolds, counsel for the prosecution, declined to prosecute any further. OBSP, Feb. 1817, no. 392, 155.

25. A brief prepared by the solicitor to the Bank of England in 1719 for the prosecution of Robert Minor for presenting a forged bill of exchange takes the same form. See Langbein, *The Origin of Adversary Criminal Trial*, 147.

26. CLRO: Solicitor's Papers, Briefs &c for prosecutions, Box 1 (1786–99).

27. See Bentley, *English Criminal Justice*, 39–40 and notes therein. The right to a copy of the indictment was granted by the Indictments Act, 1915, schedule r 13(1).

28. The OBSP reveal that it did. See OBSP, Apr. 1809, no. 380, 242–43.

29. Harmer, *Murder of Mr. Steele*, 65.

30. See Bentley, *English Criminal Justice*, 34–39. A literate accused, as Bentley suggests, could make his own notes at the hearing, but the number who actually did so must have been small.

31. OBSP, Apr. 1809, no. 380, at 243.

32. CLRO: Solicitor's Papers, Briefs &c for prosecutions, Box 11 (1826–27).

33. OBSP, Dec. 1826, no. 1, 3.

34. [Wontner], *Old Bailey Experience*, 68.

35. Harmer, *Murder of Mr. Steele*, 61.

36. Ibid., 62.

37. OBSP, Feb. 1789, no. 182, 214–37; quotation at 230.

38. Ibid., Feb. 1775, no. 175, 99–121 at 110.

39. Cottu reported in 1820 that while it was "the general case" for the accused to have counsel in the country, it was "very rare" in London (*On the Administration of Criminal Justice*, 88). Langbein suggests that junior barristers on circuit were likely to have undertaken such work without pay, for purposes of professional advancement. Langbein, *The Origins of Adversary Criminal Trial*, 256–57, 256 n. 16.

40. CLRO: Sessions Papers, Box 35 (1759–60).

41. Henderson, *Recollections*, 167. See also Beattie, *Crime and the Courts*, 376–78.

42. Ballantine, *Experiences*, 69–70.

43. "Mr. Adolphus and his Contemporaries at the Old Bailey," *Law Magazine* 34 (1846): 54–67 at 60 n.

44. For the eighteenth-century figures see Beattie, "Scales of Justice," 227, table 1; the nineteenth-century counts are my own.

45. See, e.g., *R. v. Evans*, reported in *The Times*, 21 Feb. 1818. The trial took nine hours, two of which were occupied by the judge's summing up of the evidence, and the jury retired for an hour to reach its decision.

46. [Wontner], *Old Bailey Experience*, 59.

47. "*Old Bailey Experience* (Review)," *Westminster Review* 20 (1834), 142–51 at 147.

48. UCL: Brougham Papers, 28,364. Complaints about undue haste continued throughout the 1830s. See Chapter 6 below.

49. See Beattie, "Scales of Justice," 228.

50. See Devereaux, "The City and the Sessions Paper."

51. JOR 99, fol. 214 (1807); 106, ff. 152–53 (1815); 107, ff. 228–29 (1816); 108, ff. 52–53 (1816); quotations at JOR 107, ff. 228–29 (1816). I am grateful to Simon Devereaux for these references.

52. JOR 97, fol. 145, 19 Nov. 1805. Again I thank Simon Devereaux for the reference.

53. For instance, between 1800 and 1805 Peter Alley was named in the OBSP roughly a hundred times per year; in 1806 the number of his appearances dropped to the sixties, and in 1816 he was named only sixteen times. Totals for Jerome William Knapp and John Gurney, who shared the lead in practice with Alley during this period, follow a similar pattern. In 1815 no barrister was named more than twenty times. Once Butler was replaced by Henry Buckler in November 1816, the totals increased again.

54. *R. v. M'Kenrott*, OBSP, Jan. 1816, no. 211, 63–70 at 70; *R. v. Hume*, OBSP, Apr. 1816, no. 388, 222; *R. v. Phillips*, OBSP, July 1816, no. 751, 342–43 at 343.

55. See, e.g., *R. v. M'Kenrott*, 68.

56. See, e.g., Charles Phillips's cross-examination of a witness in *R. v. Barns*, OBSP, May 1830, no. 1226, 538–40 at 539. There were occasional exceptions: Phillips's cross-examination of a witness in *R. v. Liepman*, OBSP, Apr. 1825, no. 825, 333–35 at 334 appears to have been reproduced in its entirety.

57. This concern is evident from the late 1780s. See, e.g., *The Times*, 22 Feb. 1787, which reported that, at a meeting of the Court of Aldermen convened to investigate the recorder's report, the recorder (James Adair) "expatiated very fully on the evils arising to the public, by the present mode of publishing trials of persons for burglary and other felonies, the evidence of accomplices, and the arguments of counsel, together with the points wherein the defect of evidence is frequently the occasion of the prisoners being acquitted. These publications, he said, tended to establish a system, by which persons of evil minds" were instructed "in what particular points, when on their trial, they should rest a defence."

Simon Devereaux suggests that by the 1820s production of the OBSP was driven chiefly by its role in the pardon process. From the 1810s capital convictions were reported together at the front of the publication; from 1821 the recorder provided the relevant OBSP page numbers beside the names of capital convicts whose cases were to be considered at the next report, and there was a clear hierarchy in the scope of cases reported. Reports of noncapital cases are generally half the length of those of capital cases. This pattern, Devereaux argues, is too consistent to be an accident. (Unpublished.)

58. See, for example, *R. v. O'Callaghan, Newbolt, and Phelan*, reported in *The Times* on 17 Jan. 1818. The prisoners, accused of murder (the result of a fatal duel) were represented by Nolan and Arabin. Only the answers to their cross-examinations are reported. Eighteenth-century newspaper reports likewise tended on the whole not to reproduce cross-examinations in full. See, e.g., *The Times*'s report of the trial of Robert Bond for forgery: "Mr. Garrow was very diffuse and pointed in his cross-examination of Mr. Weller, which took up near two hours; in the course of which several circumstances came from the Witness which very much weakened the force of the prosecution." *The Times*, 19 Dec. 1787.

59. *The Times*, 6 Oct. 1789. See also the discussion of the newspaper press in Chapter 5 below.

60. *Second Report on the Criminal Law*, 61, 10.

61. *Prisoners' Defence Bill—Lords' Evidence*, 4.

62. "Mr. Adolphus and his Contemporaries at the Old Bailey," 61.

63. OBSP, Jan. 1796, no. 84, 128–36 at 128.

64. Ibid., Apr. 1789, no. 422, 508–15 at 508.

65. Ibid., Dec. 1790, no. 28, 32–39 at 34–35. See also *R. v. Platt and Roberts*, OBSP, Dec. 1790, no. 35, 60–73 at 63.

66. *R. v. Platt and Roberts*, 60–61.

67. OBSP, July 1786, no. 572, 840–49 at 841.

68. See, e.g., *R. v. Woolridge*, OBSP, Feb. 1784, no. 358, 485–91 at 486; *R. v. Patmore*, OBSP, Feb. 1789, no. 182, 214–37 at 217.

69. Dickenson and Talfourd, *Practical Guide to the Quarter Sessions*.

70. OBSP, Jan. 1784, no. 192, 227–33 at 229. See also *R. v. Pringle*, OBSP, Jan. 1787, no. 155, 196–206 at 200.

71. OBSP, Sept. 1791, no. 312, 468–84; quotations at 470, 470–71.

72. *R. v. Stevenson*, OBSP, Sept. 1784, no. 843, 1164–78 at 1165 n. 14.

73. *R. v. Curtis*, OBSP, Sept. 1784, no. 925, 1221–23 at 1222.

74. For this trial see *The Trial of R. Patch*.

75. See, e.g., *Parl. Deb.*, 2d ser., 11 (1824): 195, 210, and *Second Report on the Criminal Law*, 10: "Occasionally, even on trials for Murder, the whole skill of an expert advocate has been allowed to be exerted in his opening statement. We may cite as an instance the celebrated speech of Mr. Garrow, on his opening the case against Patch on an indictment for Murder." See also Cairns, *Advocacy and the Making of the Adversarial Criminal Trial*, 41–44.

76. The problem again relates to sources. Extending to trials of misdemeanor the kind of statistical analysis of representation undertaken by Langbein, Beattie, and Landsman for trials of felony would, in metropolitan London, have to encompass not only the misdemeanors tried at the Old Bailey but those heard at Clerkenwell, the Guildhall, and Westminster Hall. No formal record of the participation of counsel exists for these jurisdictions. There is no equivalent of the OBSP, and while newspapers shed occasional light on the subject, misdemeanors were not reported systematically.

77. Dickenson and Talfourd, *Practical Guide to the Quarter Sessions*, 350.

78. OBSP, Oct. 1791, no. 443, 613–17 at 614; July 1790, no. 537, 613–61 at 619.

79. Ibid., Apr. 1787, no. 448, 580–623 at 581, 587.

80. GL: MS 420.

81. *The Times*, 11 Jan. 1790.

82. British Library: Add MS 47466; Eg MS 3710.

83. OBSP, Dec. 1784, no. 4, 35–57 at 48–51.

84. Letter to the editor, *Legal Observer* 12 (1836): 419.

85. OBSP, July 1786, no. 572, 840–49 at 848.

86. Ibid., Sept. 1791, no. 358, 532–39 at 336.

87. Ibid., July 1790, no. 537, 613–61; quotations at 649 and 650.

88. Ibid., Oct. 1777, no. 615, 360–78 at 374.

89. See, e.g., *The Times*'s report of the trial at the Old Bailey of a man named Parkins, accused of bigamy. *The Times*, 30 Apr. 1789.

90. See, e.g., *R. v. Lucasey & Wood*, OBSP, Feb. 1825, no. 384, 159–60 at 160 (joint written defense for a charge of burglary); *R. v. Seckerson*, *The Times*, 19 Jan. 1818.

91. *R. v. Ripley*, *The Times*, 10 Apr. 1815. Ripley was the butler of Frederick Robinson, MP. An anti–Corn Law mob had attacked his master's house, and Ripley had fired on the crowd.

92. *Second Report on the Criminal Law*, "Defence of Prisoners by Counsel," app. 1, 85.

93. OBSP, Jan. 1787, no. 158, 212–29 at 221.

94. See *R. v. Annesley & Redding*, OBSP, Jul. 1742 (separate pamphlet), and *R. v. Askew*, OBSP, Apr. 1746, no. 167, cited in Langbein, *The Origins of Adversary Criminal Trial*, 299 nn. 233, 234. Langbein concludes that these instances of nonenforcement of the usual rule prohibiting defense counsel from addressing the jury "were sufficiently isolated that counsel ordinarily had to reckon with the rule being enforced" (299).

95. OBSP, Jan. 1787, no. 158, 212–29 at 218. For examples of counsel arguing for a flaw in the indictment see the following cases reported in OBSP in 1788: *R. v. Bishop*, Feb., no. 246, 326–37 at 335; *R. v. Clary and Gombert*, Apr., no. 270, 367–99 at 367; *R. v. Slack*, Apr., no. 386, 501–26 at 517; *R. v. Collard and Andrews*, Oct., no. 619, 834–39 at 835.

96. OBSP, Jan. 1794, no. 126, 320–26 at 326.

97. Ibid., Jan. 1784, no. 203, 241–47; quotations at 246–47.

98. See, e.g., *R. v. England*, OBSP, Dec. 1788, no. 93, 74–84; *R. v. Bates et al.*, OBSP, June 1791, no. 246, 359–64; *R. v. Rebus*, OBSP, Sept. 1794, no. 473, 1010–16.

99. OBSP, Jan. 1788, no. 148, 203–6; quotation at 206.

100. Ibid., Apr. 1796, no. 265, 443–46; quotation at 444.

101. Ibid., Jan. 1811, no. 274, 158–59; quotation at 149.

102. Ibid., Oct. 1830, no. 1855, 823.

103. Ibid., Dec. 1792, no. 84, 121–23; quotations at 121–22.

104. Ibid., Feb. 1812, no. 311, 174–82.

105. *R. v. Oliver*, OBSP, Oct. 1791, no. 443, 613–17 at 615.

106. See, e.g., *R. v. Wood & Brown*, OBSP, Dec. 1784, no. 4, 35–56.

107. *R. v. Parr*, OBSP, Jan. 1787, no. 158, 212–29 at 225; *R. v. Slack*, OBSP, Apr. 1788, no. 386, 501–26 at 526. *R. v. Long*, OBSP, Oct. 1830, no. 1952, 856–62. The facts of this case were so gruesome and Long such a notorious quack that the trial was reported in much greater detail than was usual for this period. John Adolphus, retained by Long, became a patient himself "and not only survived, but believed himself cured by him." "Mr. Adolphus and his Contemporaries at the Old Bailey," 65 n.

108. Langbein found that in Dudley Ryder's mid-eighteenth-century trial notes

(Ryder was chief justice of the Court of King's Bench, 1754–56) the predominant evidentiary concern with respect to witness testimony was competency. Langbein, "Historical Foundations of the Law of Evidence," 1181.

109. Langbein, *The Origins of Adversary Criminal Trial*, 243.

110. OBSP, Dec. 1783, no. 35, 67–70 at 68.

111. Ibid., Apr. 1788, no. 270, 367–99 at 391.

112. Ibid., July 1797, no. 465, 454–56 at 455.

113. Ibid., Sept. 1784, no. 784, 1079–84 at 1082.

114. Ibid., Feb. 1786, no. 217, 370–73 at 371.

115. *The Times*, 16 Oct. 1789.

116. For the history of the hearsay rule see Langbein, "Criminal Trial before the Lawyers," 301–2, and "Historical Foundations of the Law of Evidence," 1174–76, 1186–90; Gallanis, "Rise of Modern Evidence Law," esp. 530–37; Bentley, *English Criminal Justice*, chap. 20.

117. Leach, *Cases in Crown Law*; Foster, *Crown Law*.

118. OBSP, Jan. 1791, no. 99, 164–70; quotations at 167 and 169.

119. Ibid., Apr. 1790, no. 430, 474–88 at 481.

120. Ibid., May 1788, no. 365, 464–70. For the history of the confession rule see Langbein, "Shaping the Eighteenth-Century Criminal Trial," 103–5; "Historical Foundations of the Law of Evidence," 1198 n. 147; and *The Origins of Adversary Criminal Trial*, 218–33. For its application in the early nineteenth century see Bentley, *English Criminal Justice*, 221–29.

121. OBSP, Feb. 1784, no. 357, 480–85 at 484.

122. *R. v. Hurt*, OBSP, Jan. 1785, no. 255, at 312, quoted in Langbein, *The Origins of Adversary Criminal Trial*, 304.

123. OBSP, Feb. 1786, no. 216, 361–70; quotations at 367–68.

124. Here too, of course, counsel could evade the restriction against addressing the jury. For examples see Langbein, *The Origins of Adversary Criminal Trial*, 296–300.

125. Langbein, "Historical Foundation of the Law of Evidence," 1199; Bentham, *Rational of Judicial Evidence*, 212 n, quoted in ibid. at 1199–1200. See also Landsman, "From Gilbert to Bentham," 1180–82.

126. See Twining, "The Rationalist Tradition of Evidence Scholarship," for a discussion of writers on evidence from Gilbert in the eighteenth century to Thomas Peake, William David Evans, and S. M. Phillips in the nineteenth; and Landsman, "From Gilbert to Bentham." See also Beattie, "Scales of Justice," and Langbein, *The Origins of Adversary Criminal Trial*, chap. 4, for a discussion of shifting perspectives on what constituted proof in criminal trials.

127. OBSP, July 1794, no. 444, 925–28 at 926.

128. [Wontner], *Old Bailey Experience*, 326.

129. See Hay, "Prosecution and Power."

130. OBSP, Sept. 1789, no. 674, 796–98.

131. Ibid., Dec. 1787, no. 17, 31–33 at 33.

132. For the history of the corroboration rule see Langbein, "Shaping the Eighteenth-Century Criminal Trial," 96–103, and *The Origins of Adversary Criminal Trial*, 203–17. The rule, although it did not become precedent until 1788 (*R. v. Atwood & Rob-*

bins, 168 Eng. Rep. 334), stretches back at least to the middle of the eighteenth century. Langbein argues that both the corroboration and the confession rules, "the two distinctively criminal rules of evidence," were, like the toleration of defense counsel, the product of judicial concern about the dangers of perjury occasioned by the reward and Crown witness systems (*The Origins of Adversary Criminal Trial*, 202). For the operation of the rule in the early nineteenth century see Bentley, *English Criminal Justice*, 252–59.

133. *R. v. Durham & Crowther*, OBSP, Dec. 1787, no. 38, 52–57 at 52–53.

134. *R. v. Jacques*, OBSP, Jan. 1786, no. 182, 268–83 at 270.

135. OBSP, Jan. 1788, no. 137, 177–84 at 183. See also *R. v. Jervais et al.*, OBSP, Feb. 1788, no. 186, 287–88 at 288.

136. On this issue see also Langbein, *The Origins of Adversary Criminal Trial*, 292–94.

137. *The Times*, 29 Apr. 1786.

138. Ibid., 27 Aug. 1789. For dismissal of the metropolitan magistrates' offices as "warrant shops" see, e.g., 14 Jan., 29 July, 24 Oct. 1786.

139. Ibid., 29 and 30 Aug. 1786.

140. OBSP, Dec. 1787, no. 84, 95–103; Dec. 1792, no. 6, 11–14.

141. This designation was coined by Langbein in "Shaping the Eighteenth-Century Criminal Trial" at 15. The accused, the charge, the verdict, the jury, and the judge were indicated in squib reports, but no details of the trial were provided.

142. OBSP, Sept. 1790, no. 677, 862–63.

143. Scarlett, *Memoir*, 87.

144. Langbein argues more strongly that "[o]nly a small fraction of eighteenth-century criminal trials were genuinely contested inquiries into guilt or innocence. In many cases, perhaps most, the accused had been caught in the act or with the stolen goods or otherwise had no credible defense. To the extent that trial had a function in such cases beyond formalizing the inevitable conclusion of guilt, it was to decide the sanction." *The Origins of Adversary Criminal Trial*, 59.

145. The phrase is Blackstone's: *Commentaries*, 4:239. On the practice of partial verdicts see Beattie, *Crime and the Courts*, 424–30; Langbein, *The Origins of Adversary Criminal Trial*, 57–60.

146. OBSP, Oct. 1790, no. 708, 925–96 at 926.

147. Ibid., Jan. 1795, no. [66], 223.

Chapter Five

1. For the history of the eighteenth-century newspaper see Werkmeister, *The London Daily Press*; Rea, *The English Press in Politics*; Lutnick, *The American Revolution and the British Press*; Black, *The English Press in the Eighteenth Century*; Barker, *Newspapers, Politics, and Public Opinion*; Bob Harris, *Politics and the Rise of the Press*; and Andrew and McGowen, *The Perreaus and Mrs. Rudd*, chap. 3.

2. London, by virtue of its size and its high levels of literacy, would dominate British print culture until well into the nineteenth century.

3. Black, *The English Press in the Eighteenth Century*, 14.

4. Barker, *Newspapers, Politics, and Public Opinion*, 22–33.

5. Bob Harris, *Politics and the Rise of the Press*, 27.

6. Ibid., 10.

7. See Andrew and McGowen, *The Perreaus and Mrs. Rudd*, 54–67.

8. See Michael Harris, "Trials and Criminal Biographies: A Case Study in Distribution"; Faller, *Turned to Account*; McKenzie, "Lives of the Most Notorious Criminals" and "Making Crime Pay"; Linebaugh, "The Ordinary of Newgate and His *Account*"; Langbein, "The Criminal Trial before the Lawyers" and "Shaping the Eighteenth-Century Criminal Trial"; and Devereaux, "The City and the Sessions Paper" and "The Fall of the Sessions Paper" for the relationship between crime and the press in the eighteenth century.

9. See Andrew and McGowen, *The Perreaus and Mrs. Rudd*, chap. 3.

10. See, e.g., *Gazeteer and London Daily Advertiser*, 16 Jan. 1756; *Morning Chronicle*, 16 Jan. 1775; *London Evening Post*, 13 Jan. 1778.

11. See, e.g., *Morning Herald*, 12 Jan. 1786; *Morning Post*, 21 Feb. 1793.

12. See *Gazetter and London Daily Advertiser*, 8, 17, 20 July 1762.

13. Habermas, *The Structural Transformation of the Public Sphere*. De Krey, *Fractured Society*, likewise argues for a "communications revolution" in 1695 in which the press assumed a critical role in London politics. But see Achinstein, *Milton and the Revolutionary Reader*, and Halasz, *Marketplace of Print*.

14. Black, *The English Press in the Eighteenth Century*, 293.

15. On transportation see Chapter 1, note 44, above.

16. *The Times*, 13 Jan. 1785.

17. *St. James Chronicle*, 1–3 Feb. 1785.

18. *The Times*, 31 Jan. 1785. Given the interest in execution in the capital, the recorder's report on capital convicts, made to the king in cabinet at the close of each Old Bailey sessions, was also the subject of press attention. Some papers merely reported the fact of its being made (see, e.g., *Morning Herald*, 1 Feb. 1786); others printed a detailed list of those reprieved and those ordered for execution (see, e.g., *St. James Chronicle*, 27–29 Jan. 1785). A letter lamenting delays in that report was printed in the *Morning Chronicle* in 1787 (12 Jan.).

19. The criminal law had become "so very sanguinary, as to make it indispensably necessary to have a revision of the whole." *The Times*, 16 Jan. 1787.

20. *The Times*, 31 Jan., 29 Apr., 20 Sept. 1785; 24 Feb. 1787.

21. Ibid., 13 May 1785.

22. Ibid., 29 Apr. 1785. The *Morning Chronicle* reported a more practical complaint made to the Guildhall by the parish of St. Sepulchre to the effect that executions at the Old Bailey constituted "a great nuisance to the inhabitants," who were disturbed at night by the sounds of scaffolding being put up and then obliged the next day to keep their shops closed, due to the size of the assembled crowd and the heightened danger of pickpockets. *Morning Chronicle*, 11 Jan. 1787.

23. *The Times*, 23 Feb. 1786.

24. Ibid., 6 Oct. 1786. For various perspectives on the establishment of Botany Bay see Martin, "The Foundation of Botany Bay"; Gillen, "The Botany Bay Decision"; Frost and Gillen, "Botany Bay"; Wilfrid Oldham, *Britain's Convicts to the Colonies*; Devereaux, "Convicts and the State," 289–310 and notes therein.

25. *The Times*, 4 Jan. 1785.

1603; chief justice of the Court of King's Bench, 1616); Thomas Coventry (recorder, 1616; Keeper of the Great Seal, 1625); Robert Heath (recorder, 1618; chief justice of the Court of Common Pleas, 1631; chief justice of the Court of King's Bench, 1643); Edward Littleton (recorder, 1631; chief justice of the Court of Common Pleas, 1639; Keeper of the Great Seal, 1640); George Jeffreys (recorder, 1678; chief justice of the Court of King's Bench, 1683; lord chancellor, 1685); John Holt (recorder, 1685; chief justice of the Court of King's Bench, 1689); Peter King (recorder, 1708; chief justice of the Court of Common Pleas, 1714; lord keeper, 1725); John Strange (recorder, 1739; master of the rolls, 1742). "Recorders of the City of London, 1298–1850."

34. *Morning Chronicle*, 12 Apr. 1822.

35. Beavan, *Aldermen of the City of London*, 2:145 n. 200; lviii.

36. See ibid., 2:203. Wood is described as a leader of the "advanced liberal party" in the City, Waithman as a leader of the City's "extreme Radical party." Both men voted in favor of Catholic relief and for parliamentary reform; see ibid., "Votes of Aldermen and Other Civic Personages in Parliament."

37. The three were John Atkins, William Heygate, and William Thompson. GL: "Corporation Pocketbooks: List of the Lord-Mayor, Recorder, Sheriffs, and Common-Councilmen, of the City of London: Together with the Committees and Standing Orders of the Court of Common-Council, for the Year 1822–23."

38. *DNB*. The statutes in question were 1 Geo. IV, cc. 115, 116, and 117 (1820).

39. See Chapter 2 above.

40. *Morning Chronicle*, 6 Mar. 1822. For Carlile, a "freethinker" repeatedly prosecuted for publishing the works of Thomas Paine and William Hone, among others, see the *DNB*.

41. *Morning Chronicle*, 6 Mar. 1822. Near the end of his recordership Knowlys resorted to similar courtroom tactics when Carlile himself appeared before him, charged with blasphemy. See below.

42. Ibid., 7, 11, 28 Mar. 1822.

43. Ibid., 1 Apr. 1822.

44. Ibid.

45. *The Times*, 18 Apr. 1822.

46. Ibid., 4 Apr. 1822.

47. In his youth Denman (1779–1854) had been a "strong Foxite" (*DNB*). He was called to the bar in 1806 and entered Parliament as a Whig in 1819. Denman was a staunch defender of a variety of reforms throughout his parliamentary career. *DNB*; Arnould, *Memoir of Lord Denman*.

48. George IV had tried to dissolve his marriage and deprive his estranged wife of her title by accusing her of adultery. For the "trial" of Queen Caroline, see Fulford, *The Trial of Queen Caroline*; E. A. Smith, *A Queen on Trial*; and Fraser, *The Unruly Queen*. John Adolphus also wrote a memoir, *The Royal Exile*.

49. *The Times*, 4 Apr. 1822.

50. Ibid., 3 Apr. 1822.

51. Ibid., 1 Apr. 1822.

52. "City Pleaders," *The Times*, 23 Apr. 1822.

53. Foss, *Judges*, 9:147–49; *Legal Observer* 21 (1841): 164.

26. *St. James Chronicle*, 1 Feb. 1785.

27. *The Times*, 24 Oct. 1786.

28. "Few men have made so rapid a progress in the legal business." Ibid., 26 Nov. 1785.

29. Ibid., 16 Mar. 1790.

30. Ibid., 5 Aug. 1790.

31. Ibid., 21 Aug. 1790.

32. Fielding, *Tom Jones*, 411.

33. See Andrew and McGowen, *The Perreaus and Mrs. Rudd*.

34. See ibid., 180–81.

35. *Morning Chronicle*, 17 Jan. 1781.

36. Unlike their counterparts in the City of London (the aldermen), Bow Street and other Middlesex magistrates routinely committed persons to prison solely by virtue of oaths sworn against them rather than conducting an immediate examination of the charges laid. Committal on oath dated from the Marian bail statutes; strictly speaking the magistrates were acting within their rights, but such practice was no longer considered acceptable. See Chapter 4 above.

37. *The Times*, 26 June 1786.

38. Ibid. Mainwaring was chairman of the Middlesex sessions.

39. Ibid., 9 July 1786. For the Metropolitan Police Bill of 1785 see Radzinowicz, *History of the English Criminal Law*, 3:108–21; Philips, "A New Engine of Power and Authority," 165–71; Paley, "Middlesex Justices Act," 221–26; Palmer, *Police and Protest*, 89–91; Reynolds, *Before the Bobbies*, 290–96; Devereaux, "Convicts and the State," 210–17.

40. *R. v. Holloway and Haggerty*, OBSP, Feb. 1807, no. 171, 143–44. At trial Holloway was represented by Thomas Andrews.

41. *The Times*, 6 May 1786.

42. Quoted in Lewis, *The Victorian Bar*, 53.

43. Henderson, *Recollections*, 158.

44. Ibid., 287.

45. Lemmings, *Professors of the Law*, 9.

46. For the reputation of lawyers generally in the eighteenth century see Lemmings, *Professors of the Law*, 9–23. For earlier periods see, inter alia, Ives, "Reputation of the Common Lawyers"; Prest, *The Rise of the Barristers*, 283–91; Tucker, *Intruder into Eden*. For the nineteenth century see Cocks, *Foundations of the Modern Bar*.

47. Prest, *The Rise of the Barristers*, 286.

48. Geoffrey Holmes, *Augustan England*, 116–17. For George Jeffreys (1648–1689) and William Scroggs (?1623–1683) see *DNB*. For their conduct in court see Langbein, *The Origins of Adversary Criminal Trial*, 79–80.

49. For the improved image of the bar see Holmes, *Augustan England*, 117, and Lemmings, *Gentlemen and Barristers*, 144–45. For the image of the lower branch of the legal profession in early modern England see Brooks, *Pettyfoggers and Vipers*, 179–81, and Lemmings, *Professors of the Law*, 15–17.

50. *Boswell's Life of Johnson*, 2:126.

51. *The Times*, 18 Oct. 1790.

52. *Directions for Prosecuting Thieves Without the Help of Those False Guides, the Newgate Sollicitors* (1728), quoted in Langbein, *The Origins of Adversary Criminal Trial*, 139.

53. See Langbein, *The Origins of Adversary Criminal Trial*, 124–40.

54. Fielding, *Tom Jones*, 704.

55. Ibid., 828.

56. Lemmings, *Professors of the Law*, 189.

57. *The Times*, 3 Nov. 1789.

58. "A Sharp between two Flats" and "A Flat between two Sharps," British Museum Catalogue (Prints) 3762, 3763, and 3764, reproduced in J. A. Sharpe, *Crime and the Law in English Satirical Prints*, 144, 146, and 148.

59. [Polson], *Law and Lawyers*, 1:124, quoted in Woolrych, *Serjeants-at-Law*, 2:631.

60. *Public Advertiser*, 9 Dec. 1775; *Morning Post*, 11 Dec. 1777, quoted in Andrew and McGowen, *The Perreaus and Mrs. Rudd*, 225.

61. *The Times*, 1 Nov. 1786.

62. Ibid., 28 July 1787.

63. Concannen, *Letter to William Garrow*, 18 (emphasis in original).

64. Hague, *A Letter to William Garrow*.

65. Ibid., 3, 6.

66. Lewis, *The Victorian Bar*, 23.

67. *The Times*, 12 July 1790.

68. As the *Legal Examiner & Law Chronicle* reported, "[T]he reporters are on the watch for horrors and vulgarities." The paper also claimed, however, that only lawyers could fully appreciate the absurdities found at the Old Bailey. "Scenes and Decisions in our Criminal Courts," *Legal Examiner & Law Chronicle* 3 (1834): 263–67 at 263.

69. [Sydney Smith], "Counsel for Prisoners," *Edinburgh Review* 65 (1826–27): 74–95 at 87.

70. Swift, *Gulliver's Travels*, 291.

71. Robert Southey, "All for Love, or a Sinner Saved."

72. *The Times*, 24 Aug. 1790.

73. Ibid., 28 Dec. 1789.

74. British Museum Catalogue (Prints) 7593 [Dent] [?1789].

75. Knapp and Baldwin, *Newgate Calendar*, 2:109–10.

76. Hazlitt, "Illustrations of *The Times* Newspaper," in *Selected Writings*, 4:129–35 at 130–31.

77. Mill, "The Influence of Lawyers" [30 Mar. 1827?], in *Collected Works*, 26:389–90.

78. See Chapter 7 below.

79. "Memoir of Sir William Garrow," *Monthly Magazine* 9 (1840): 106–16 at 109.

80. Cocks, *Foundations of the Modern Bar*, 22.

81. Simpson, *Reflections*, 46, quoted in Langbein, *The Origins of Adversary Criminal Trial*, 307 and n. 280.

82. Ruggles, *The Barrister*, 210–11.

83. Ibid., 213.

84. Ballantine, *Experiences*, 54.

85. "Central Criminal Court," *Westminster Review* 22 (1835): 195–212 at 200.

86. Duman, *The English and Colonial Bars*, 41.

87. Proceedings of the Midland circuit mess in the 1780s and 1790s are discussed in Lemmings, *Professors of the Law*, 302. For the changing character of the circuit mess in

the early nineteenth century see Cocks, "The Bar at the Assizes." Cocks characterized the bar mess of the Norfolk circuit in the period 1818–36 as an informal group of dining companions with little interest in rules and regulations.

88. See "The English Bar," *Law Magazine and Review* 23 (1867): 126–45 at 143. See also Duman, *The English and Colonial Bars*, 38–39, and Cocks, *Foundations of the Modern Bar*, 15–19.

89. Duman, *The English and Colonial Bars*, 37.

90. "Mr. Adolphus and his Contemporaries at the Old Bailey," *Law Magazine* 34 (1846): 54–67 at 62.

91. See Daintree, "The Legal Periodical," chap. 3, for the late-eighteenth-century legal periodical press.

92. *The Templar* 1 (1789): 239. The editor of this periodical has not been identified.

93. The journals in question are listed in Daintree, "The Legal Periodical," at the beginning of chap. 4.

94. The *Jurist* was edited by Henry Roscoe; the *Legal Observer*, described as "the direct antecedent" of the *Solicitor's Journal*, was owned and edited by Robert Maugham, the founder of the Law Institution and its successor, the Law Society. The editor(s) of the various incarnations of the *Legal Examiner* have not been identified. Hines, "The Development of Legal Periodical Publishing," 35. For the nineteenth-century legal press generally see ibid., chap. 3; Daintree, "The Legal Periodical," chaps. 4 and 5; Cocks, *Foundations of the Modern Bar*, 64–77; and Holdsworth, *History of English Law*, 13:426–27, 15:250. I thank Guy Holborn and Doug Hay for alerting me to these various histories.

95. Daintree, "The Legal Periodical," 91.

96. "Trial of Frederic Kendall, Esq. A.B. for setting fire to Sydney College," *Legal Review* 1 (1812–13): 593–98 at 594.

97. Ibid., 595, 594.

98. Ibid., 597.

99. See Chapter 8 below.

100. "Bounds of Old Bailey Decorum," *Legal Examiner* 1 (1831–32): 25–26.

101. OBSP, Sept. 1796, no. 463, 767. See also the pamphlet *Quack, Quack! I have done the baker out of his ducks*.

102. OBSP, Sept. 1796, no. 463, at 770–71.

103. Beattie, "Scales of Justice," 245–46.

104. For the history of Arabin's judgeship at the Old Bailey see Chapter 6 below.

105. *R. v. Harris*, 18 May 1834, in *Arabiniana*, a collection of ludicrous pronouncements made between 1830 and 1839 and privately published in 1843 by an Old Bailey barrister, Henry Blencowe Churchill. Churchill collected most of the material himself, although some items were provided by other members of the bar, including Ballantine and Charles Phillips. The majority of the examples date from 1832 and 1833. An American edition of *Arabiniana* was published in 1846, and the collection was reproduced (with some errors) in Ernest Bowan-Rowlands's biography of Harry Poland, *Seventy-two Years at the Bar*, and reprinted in 1969, under the title *Arabinesque-at-law*, by Sir Robert Megarry.

106. British Library: Add MS 33112, ff. 187–88, 15 July 1803. I am grateful to Simon Devereaux for this reference.

107. The Alley/Adolphus duel was one of eight documented duels fought in England in 1816 (Anthony Simpson, "Dandelions on the Field of Honor," 106, table 1). Formerly the prerogative of the aristocracy, dueling underwent a revival in early-nineteenth-century England as it enjoyed a brief popularity among the middle classes. Cecilia Morgan has suggested that the democratization of dueling occurred as the definition of honor expanded to embrace "the defence of professional behaviour and standards" (" 'In Search of the Phantom Misnamed Honour,' " 531). Morgan found that lawyers "made up the majority" of the participants of duels in Upper Canada and cites an 1812 duel in which the circumstances are similar to those described here. Lawyer William Warren Baldwin challenged Attorney General John McDonnell to a duel when McDonnell refused to apologize for or explain "wanton and ungentlemanly words" employed in an exchange with Baldwin (ibid., 545–46). Morgan argues that dueling in this period was an accepted alternative to legal action and supplemented the legal process; it is difficult to disagree when the duelists themselves are lawyers.

108. "The Late John Adolphus," *Fraser's Magazine* 66 (1862): 49–53 at 53.

109. Pue, "Guild-Training vs. Professional Education," 243.

110. Lemmings, *Professors of the Law*, 309.

111. Ibid., 146.

112. Ibid., 301.

113. Inner Temple, *Calendar of Inner Temple Records*, 5:iii–iv.

114. Ruggles, *The Barrister*, 29, 30.

115. "The English Bar," *Law Magazine and Review* 23 (1867): 126–45 at 133.

116. Pue, "Guild-Training vs. Professional Education."

117. Ibid., 244.

118. Quoted in ibid. at 255.

119. Ruggles, *The Barrister*, xv–xvi.

120. Campbell, *Lives of the Chief Justices*, 3:238.

121. "Biographical Sketch of the Late Mr. Brodrick," *Legal Observer* 1 (1830): 21–22 at 22.

122. "Mr. Adolphus and his Contemporaries at the Bar," 60. Brodrick is one of the few leaders of the Old Bailey whose manners were not criticized; rather, he was "marked by that high sense of honour, and correctness of feeling, which ought at all times to be inseparable from an English advocate" and "[d]istinguished for those courtesies which mark the gentleman" ("Biographical Sketch of the Late Mr. Brodrick," 22). It is worth noting that the barrister who drew the least criticism from his peers was also a gentleman in the sense that he was a man of independent means. Brodrick had not originally intended to practice in his profession at all; not pressed financially, he did not have to pursue the example of the wolf in the fable. In short, he could afford manners.

123. "The Central Criminal Court," *Legal Observer* 9 (1834): 17–18 at 18.

124. "Central Criminal Court," *Westminster Review* 22 (1835): 195–212, at 200.

125. Farington, *Diary*, 14:5062.

126. British Museum Catalogue (Prints) 12916.

127. Benjamin Coulson Robinson, *Bench and Bar*, 41.

128. Lemmings, *Professors of the Law*, 307.

129. This gentleman's bland and respectable world consists of men who "got up at

eight, shaved close at a quarter-past, breakfasted at nine, went to the City at ten, came home at half-past five, and dined at seven." Dickens, *Our Mutual Friend*, 131–32.

130. Chaffanbrass, who defends Alaric Tudor in *The Three Clerks* (1858), Lady Mason in *Orley Farm* (1861–62), and Phineas Finn in *Phineas Redux* (1873–74), amplifies the portrait of defense counsel Trollope had painted earlier in *The New Zealander*, a collection of social, political, and cultural essays written in 1855–56 but not published in his lifetime. (The manuscript, housed in the Robert H. Taylor Collection at Princeton, was published in the twentieth century: Trollope, *The New Zealander*, ed. H. John Hall.) In the chapter on the law (4) Trollope had used "Mr. Allewinde" to demonstrate the evils inherent in an adversarial justice system. Allewinde browbeats and confuses witnesses and boasts of his ability to make them perjure themselves; his efforts deliberately obscure rather than reveal the truth. In chapters 40 and 41 of *The Three Clerks* Trollope similarly reproduces criticisms made of Old Bailey counsel from the 1780s. Chaffanbrass is rude to opposing counsel and to the bench. He "bullies" and tortures witnesses for sport, as "a labour of love," and his abusive cross-examinations do not further the truth (481, 499). He is ignorant of the law: "As a lawyer, in the broad and high sense of the word, it may be presumed that Mr. Chaffanbrass knows little or nothing. . . . His business is to perplex a witness and bamboozle a jury" (481). This "cock" of the Old Bailey "dunghill" is physically repulsive, a dirty, ugly old man (482). More important, he is morally bankrupt: "Give him a case in which he has all the world against him; Justice with her sword raised high to strike; Truth with open mouth and speaking eyes to tell the bloody tale; outraged humanity shrieking for punishment; a case from which Mercy herself, with averted eyes, has loathing turned and bade her sterner sister do her work; give him such a case as this, and then you will see Mr. Chaffanbrass in his glory. Let him, by the use of his high art, rescue from the gallows and turn loose upon the world the wretch whose hands are reeking with the blood of father, mother, wife, and brother, and you may see Mr. Chaffanbrass, elated with conscious worth, rub his happy hands with infinite complacency. Then will his ambition be satisfied, and he will feel that in the verdict of the jury he has received the honour due to his genius. He will have succeeded in turning black into white, . . . in dressing in the fair robe of innocence the foulest, filthiest wretch of his day" (ibid.). The description is replete with centuries-old suspicion of paid advocacy. These prejudices are rehearsed again in *Orley Farm*, in which Old Bailey counsel are described as "the very scum of the gaols, men who live by rescuing felons from the punishment they deserve" (1:97, 2:153), and who devote their lives to "the propagation of untruth" (2:165).

Chaffanbrass was said to be mirrored on William Ballantine (see Ballantine's obituary in the *Law Times* 82 (1886–87): 198–99 at 199), but the portrait seems more of a composite. His slovenly dress and physical appearance call to mind Michael Prendergast Sr.; his manners are those not of Ballantine but of William Clarkson.

131. *The Times*, 4 Nov. 1834.

Chapter Six

1. The common serjeant's name had been included in the commission of oyer and terminer and gaol delivery from the late seventeenth century, and Common Serjeant Thomas Nugent had tried cases at the Old Bailey during the recordership of John Glynn

(1772–79), but he had considered his attendance on the Old Bailey bench as a favor rather than a duty. That attendance became a requirement of the job in 1790. "The City Courts of Law. III—Central Criminal Court," *Law Journal* 93 (1943): 316–17; GL: MS 421, "Duties of the Common Serjeant" (1790).

2. Reginald Sharpe, *Memorials*, 23. For a plan of the second courtroom see CLRO: Surveyor's Justice Plans, No. 242, Charles Smith's proposed alterations, Apr. 1823. Counsel occupied a table located below the bench and facing the dock. To their left was the jury box, to their right the witness stand. Immediately behind the witness stand was an enclosure for prosecutors and witnesses waiting to be heard. To the left and right of the prisoner were benches for students and jurors in waiting, respectively. The public gallery was above the dock. This second court seems to be the one depicted in a print of 1827, "Court of the Old Bailey Sessions House," reproduced in Hooper, *History of Newgate and the Old Bailey*. For a plan of the Old Court, as it existed in the late 1840s, see below.

3. CLRO: *Common Council Minutes and Reports, Printed*, 11 July 1822.

4. Ibid., 10 Mar. 1825.

5. 4 & 5 Will. IV, c. 36. The parishes affected are specified individually in sec. 2. Over the course of the nineteenth century the jurisdiction of the Central Criminal Court would continue to expand. In 1856 an act was passed that allowed indictments for felony or misdemeanor, even if committed outside the jurisdiction of the court, to be tried there if the Court of King's Bench believed the transfer to be in the interests of justice. In 1862 the King's Bench was empowered to order the trial of anyone subject to military or naval law to be transferred to the Central Criminal Court, and under the Judicature Act of 1873 that court became a branch of the High Court of Justice. In the early twentieth century the Criminal Justice Act of 1925 again instructed that cases originating from outside the Central Criminal Court's jurisdiction could be tried at that court in "certain circumstances of emergency." 25 & 26 Vict., c. 65; 36 & 37 Vict., c. 66. See [London. Corporation], *The Corporation of London*, 71.

6. *The Times*, 3 Nov. 1834.

7. Ibid., 7 Nov. 1834.

8. Ibid.

9. Ibid., 10 Nov. 1834.

10. But Phillips himself may have forwarded to the lord chancellor a copy of the earlier sketch: among Brougham's papers is a letter from Phillips referring to "*the old Recorder's draft* of a Bill (*Sylvesters*) with annotations by Mr. Shelton" (emphasis in the original); if the draft was enclosed, it did not remain with the letter. UCL: Brougham Papers, 46,711.

11. "Central Criminal Court," *Westminster Review* 22 (1835): 195–212 at 197.

12. Ibid., 197–98.

13. UCL: Brougham Papers, 26,409. Rotch was a short-lived chairman; he appears to have succeeded Francis Const in the office in 1833 and was himself succeeded (1836) by Serjeant Adams. *Law List*.

14. UCL: Brougham Papers, 26,359. This concern with curbing the jurisdiction of the Middlesex magistrates is evident in the introduction of the bill to the House of Lords. See *Parl. Deb.*, 3d ser., 22 (1834): 666–73.

15. "Central Criminal Court," 198.

16. Ibid., 210.

17. UCL: Brougham Papers, 26,364, 28,465.

18. "Old Bailey Experience," *Law Magazine* 10 (1833): 259–95 at 277, 278.

19. "Central Criminal Court," 210.

20. "Old Bailey Experience," 278.

21. UCL: Brougham Papers, 13,396.

22. Ballantine, *Experiences*, 54.

23. John Tremayn (recorder, 1390–92), Robert Danvers (recorder, 1442–50), Robert Broke (recorder, 1545–53), and Sir George Jeffreys (recorder, 1678–80). CLRO: *Common Council Minutes and Reports, Printed*, 1850, Report 19, "Recorders of the City of London 1298–1850."

24. Recorders William Shelley (1520–26), John Baker (1526–35), Ralph Cholmely (1553–63), Thomas Coventry (1616), Simon Urling (1742–46), and John Stracey (1746–48) had previously been judges of the Sheriffs' Court. Thomas Wilbraham (1568–71), Peter Pheasant (1643), Richard Adams (1748–53), James Eyre (1763–72), and John William Rose (1789–1803) had all been common pleaders. Ibid.

25. *Gentleman's Magazine* (1822): 371.

26. [Polson], *Law and Lawyers*, 2:164.

27. Farington, *Diary*, 12:4281 (1813).

28. British Museum Catalogue (Prints) 12208 (1814), 12817 (1816), 12814 (1816).

29. Jerdan, *Autobiography*, 1:131.

30. See Gatrell, *The Hanging Tree*, chap. 13, for what he calls "the beatification of Eliza Fenning." Charles Dickens is partially responsible for keeping the Fenning case in the public eye: in an article published in *All the Year Round* in 1867 he described Silvester as "a notorious hangman," inclined from the beginning against Fenning, and accused him of bias approaching criminality in his summing up. The article ended: "We reserve for our concluding paragraph, the statement that the Judge who tried this case was an Advocate against the girl, and was unfeeling and unfair." "Old Stories Re-Told. Eliza Fenning. (The Danger of Condemning to Death on Circumstantial Evidence Alone)," *All the Year Round*, 13 July 1867, 68–72; quotations at 69, 72. Fenning's entry in the *DNB* is more restrained; the case is cited for demonstrating the way in which "a consistent declaration of innocence on the part of a criminal tends to produce general belief in it," and the entry concludes by noting that "the evidence against her was very strong."

31. *Morning Chronicle*, 1 Apr. 1822.

32. *The Times*, 1 Apr. 1822.

33. Thomas Lodelow (recorder, 1353; chief baron of the Exchequer, 1366); John Cokeyn (recorder, 1394; chief baron of the Exchequer, 1401); John Fray (recorder, 1426; chief baron of the Exchequer, 1436); Thomas Billyng (recorder, 1450; chief justice of the Court of Common Pleas, 1469); Thomas Urswyck (recorder, 1454; chief baron of the Exchequer, 1472); Humphrey Sterky (recorder, 1471; chief baron of the Exchequer, 1484); Richard Broke (recorder, 1510; chief baron of the Exchequer, 1526); Roger Cholmely (recorder, 1535; chief baron of the Exchequer, 1546; chief justice of the Court of King's Bench, 1552); Robert Broke (recorder, 1545; chief justice of the Court of Common Pleas, 1554); Edward Coke (recorder, 1591; chief justice of the Court of Common Pleas, 1606; chief justice of the Court of King's Bench, 1613); Henry Montagu (recorder,

54. *The Times*, 24 Apr. 1822.

55. Arnould, *Memoir of Lord Denman*, 1:198.

56. *Morning Chronicle*, 27 Apr. 1822.

57. Bolland himself had nothing to do with the petition. Denman recorded privately that to his rival's "great honour" "his defeat, though an unexpected and severe blow after his long connection with the City with a view to that very object" had no effects on their subsequent relationship. In 1822 Bolland had been a common pleader for eighteen years. Arnould, *Memoir of Lord Denman*, 1:198.

58. *The Times*, 8 May 1822.

59. Arnould, *Memoir of Lord Denman*, 202.

60. PRO: HO 47.73/4 (Rudolph and Wilson's case), Aug. 1827, quoted in Gatrell, *The Hanging Tree*, 510. The king remained unimpressed: a false rumor of the death of Knowlys in 1824 prompted him to indicate that he "could never bring himself to signify his approbation of Mr. Denman's appointment" to the vacancy in the office of recorder; he trusted that the government would "exert themselves to prevent his being exposed to such a proposition and all the embarassment which it would occasion." Peel, then home secretary, responded that the recorder was not dead, but at any rate the election to the office lay with the Court of Aldermen, and he had "little doubt" but that they would elect Bolland "and not Mr. Denman." British Library: Add MS 40363, ff. 161-62. I am grateful to Simon Devereaux for this reference.

61. "The Hon. C. E. Law, Recorder of London," *Law Times* 15 (1850): 467.

62. The City had itself become unhappy with the sale of pleaderships. In 1804 it had attempted to take the offices back into its own hands and wrote to each pleader—John Vaillant, William Watson, Henry Revell Reynolds, and William Bolland—asking if he would consider giving the corporation the preference if and when he wished to part with the office. None were willing to do so at the time; the possibility seemed too remote, and Bolland also indicated that he had to consider his own interests. JOR 82, ff. 108a-108b. But in 1818 the City was able to regain control of one of the pleaderships when Watson died without having alienated the office, and in 1823 William Arabin sold his pleadership back to the Common Council on being appointed a judge of the Sheriffs' Court. John Mirehouse, Arthur Wilton, Law, and Archer Ryland petitioned to be allowed to fill the vacancies left by Arabin and George Norton (elected in 1818 to take Watson's place, Norton had resigned the office in December 1822 to take up an appointment in India). Law and Mirehouse were elected, receiving 147 and 145 ballots, respectively, to Wilton and Ryland's 103 and 62. CLRO: *Common Council Minutes and Reports, Printed*, 9 June, 6 July, 24, 28 Sept. 1818; 11 July, 19 Dec. 1822; 30 Jan. 1823.

63. CLRO: *Common Council Minutes and Reports, Printed*, 4 Oct. 1827.

64. Ballantine, *Experiences*, 8.

65. In both 1821 and 1822 Law was named in the OBSP between fifty and sixty times; for each of the years 1823-25 his total was roughly a hundred. Like most Old Bailey counsel, he was usually employed by the defense. Phillips's remarkable ascendancy, however, appears to have cut Law's share of business in half by 1826.

66. See *DNB*. One of the reforms Hill championed was prisoners' counsel (on which see Chapter 7), and his conviction of the necessity of allowing defense counsel to address the jury was said to be stimulated by the "shock he underwent in reading" of the

conviction of Eliza Fenning: "The poor girl's murder—for such it was, although no forms of law were violated—was due in no small degree to the inability of her counsel to address the jury; and to the removal of this cause of so terrible a miscarriage of justice, Mr. Hill, on entering Parliament, lost no time addressing himself." Davenport-Hill, *Memoir of Matthew Davenport-Hill*, 121–22.

67. CLRO: *Common Council Minutes and Reports, Printed*, 2 Dec. 1830. *The Times* reported a recount: the lord mayor had initially declared Hill the winner by five votes; when a cry was made for a division Hill was said to have lost by three; a ballot was then demanded, after which the paper claimed Hill was declared the loser by nineteen votes rather than eighteen. *The Times*, 3 July 1833.

68. *Parl. Deb.*, 3d ser., 5 (1831): 648–50. I am grateful to Simon Devereaux for this reference.

69. Ibid., 6 (1831): 546–47.

70. *The Times*, 25 June 1833.

71. Ibid.

72. *Morning Chronicle*, 1 July 1833.

73. *The Times*, 26 June 1833.

74. "Election of a Recorder," *The Times*, 3 July 1833.

75. CLRO: *Common Council Minutes and Reports, Printed*, 30 Jan. 1823, 10 Mar. 1831.

76. I found only a single mention of Mirehouse's name in the OBSP for 1830, whereas Phillips was named in 275 cases.

77. *The Times*, 6 July 1833.

78. Ibid., 1 July 1833.

79. Ibid., 6 July 1833.

80. *Morning Chronicle*, 4 July 1833.

81. Ibid., 28, 29 June 1833.

82. Benjamin Coulson Robinson, *Bench and Bar*, 43. Theodore Hook may have had Arabin in mind in the novel *Gilbert Gurney*: "[H]owever classical it may be to picture Justice blind, it is not, as a matter of convenience and utility, at all desirable that she should also be deaf" (186).

83. Ballantine, *Experiences*, 55. For examples of his "absurdities" see [Churchill], *Arabiniana*. For Arabin's reputation as a judge see also "On the Administration of the Central Criminal Court," *Monthly Law Magazine and Political Review* 1 (1838): 305–35 at 327.

84. *The Times*, 8 July 1833.

85. For Pearson, a philanthropist and "uncompromising radical" who was elected City solicitor in 1839, see Claus, "Languages of Citizenship," 28. I am grateful to Vivienne Aldous for this reference.

86. *The Times*, 8 July 1833. The author of a letter to the editor of *The Times* likewise contrasted the results of rotation—the promotion of "Little Jef" and "Black Jack" (Jeffreys and Silvester)—with its "glorious exception" in the election of the current chief justice (Denman) as common serjeant in 1822. Ibid., 25 July 1833.

87. "Report to the Court of Common Council from the Committee in Relation to Officers and Clerks, no. 4, Common Serjeant," CLRO: *Common Council Minutes and Reports, Printed*, 1833.

88. Treatise writing had by this date become an accepted way in which junior members of the bar supplemented their meager incomes, and inferior treatises abounded.

89. Appendix to "Report in Relation to Officers and Clerks." Mirehouse's letter to Judge Bayley opened with the aggrieved acknowledgment that he had been "represented as a person unknown in Westminster Hall and incompetent to discharge the duties of common serjeant" (ibid.). It is clear from the information he himself provided to the council that the first if not the second accusation was true.

90. Ibid.

91. "Election of a Common Serjeant," *The Times*, 26 July 1833; CLRO: *Common Council Minutes and Reports, Printed*, 25 July 1833.

92. *Morning Chronicle*, 1 July 1833.

93. *Second Report of the Commissioners Appointed to Inquire into the Municipal Corporations in England and Wales, 1837*, 37–39.

94. The judiciary at senior levels was likewise thoroughly politicized, and reformist lawyers were "largely excluded from the upper reaches of the judicial bench until after 1830." Lemmings, *Professors of the Law*, 288; see also 282.

95. *Gentleman's Magazine* (1786): 263–64.

96. See Chapter 7.

97. "Junius" was a pseudonym. The writer of these savage attacks on the government has never been identified.

98. *The Times*, 29 Apr. 1786, 26 Apr. 1787.

99. Fortin, *City Biography*, 146.

100. *DNB*.

101. Ballantine, *Experiences*, 55.

102. Robinson, *Bench and Bar*, 49.

103. [Grant], *The Great Metropolis*, 213–14.

104. Ballantine, *Experiences*, 55.

105. Ibid.

106. *The Times*, 25 Dec. 1838.

107. Robinson, *Bench and Bar*, 51–52.

108. Ibid., 51. Apart from the speed implied by this example, of course, what is immediately noticeable is the lack of counsel on either side. Mirehouse controlled the proceedings in the manner of an eighteenth-century judge.

109. *The Times*, 25 Dec. 1838.

110. Ibid., 2 Jan. 1839.

111. "Central Criminal Court," at 201.

112. House of Lords Papers 70 (1835), 37: 465.

113. "On the Administration of the Central Criminal Court," at 313–14.

114. "The Central Criminal Court," *Legal Observer* 9 (1834): 17–18.

115. *The Times*, 4 Nov. 1834.

116. Ibid., 3 Nov. 1834.

117. *Law List* (1835).

118. *The Times*, 4 Nov. 1834.

119. See the annual volumes of the *Law List*.

120. Quoted in Williams, *Leaves of a Life*, 56.

121. Sir Edward Clarke, *Story of My Life*, 81; Williams, *Leaves of a Life*, 49.

122. Robinson, *Bench and Bar*, 71.

123. Ibid., 70. Williams similarly claimed Ballantine's "opinion of men could never be relied upon, for he praised or blamed them from day to day, just as they happened to please or annoy him." *Leaves of a Life*, 49.

124. See *The Times*, 1 Nov. 1836, in which a grand juror wrote to complain of Clarkson's rudeness not merely to witnesses but to the bench.

125. "On the Administration of the Central Criminal Court," at 311.

126. Ibid., 326.

127. Ibid., 327.

128. Ibid., 329–33; quotations at 332–33.

129. See Madan, *Thoughts on Executive Justice*, 142–44, quoted in Langbein, *The Origins of Adversary Criminal Trial*, 25 n. 76.

130. *Parl. Deb.*, 3d ser., 5 (1831): 650.

131. Williams, *Leaves of a Life*, 162.

132. Ballantine, *Experiences*, 54.

133. Ibid.

134. "Mr. Adolphus and his Contemporaries at the Old Bailey," *Law Magazine* 34 (1846): 54–67 at 62–63. See also Williams, *Leaves of a Life*, 162, 222.

135. See Henderson, *Recollections*, 224; Ballantine, *Experiences*, chap. 9.

136. Hook, *Gilbert Gurney*, 189–90.

137. *Legal Examiner*, 12 Sept. 1832.

138. "On the Administration of the Central Criminal Court," 335.

139. Robinson, *Bench and Bar*, 46–47.

140. This threat prompted the *Monthly Law Magazine*, which in a previous article had likened the aldermen at the Old Bailey to self-important bantams ("On the Administration of the Central Criminal Court," 323), to launch an extended attack: the "deformed" hypocrisy of the aldermen disgraced the tribunal in which they sat, and until the "aldermanic commissioners" were removed from the Central Criminal Court and divested of an authority they did not know how to use, the administration of justice in metropolitan London could not appear respectable. "On the Administration of the Central Criminal Court," *Monthly Law Magazine and Political Review* 2 (1838): 193–215; quotation at 205.

141. By that date *Punch* too had turned its satirical eye to the subject of "Justice After Dinner," commenting on the speed at which it was dispatched after the cloth had been withdrawn and the bottle passed around. *Punch* 7 (1844): 218; cartoon at 219.

142. Robinson, *Bench and Bar*, 47.

143. Crew, *The Old Bailey*, 73. See also Williams, *Leaves of a Life*, 60.

144. Ballantine, *Experiences*, 304.

145. Mirehouse, the common serjeant, also died in 1850; his successor, Edward Bullock, "rotated" from lowlier City offices to replace him, but the appointment was of brief duration. The rotation was by this date routine: Bullock had become a City common pleader in 1829, combining his practice in the City courts with attendance at the Old Bailey, and he had been appointed a judge of the Sheriffs' Court in 1847. Ill health necessitated his retirement in 1855. *Law List* (1824–55); CLRO: *Common Council Minutes and Reports, Printed*, 20 Dec. 1855.

146. For Gurney's career see the *DNB*.

147. "The Late Mr. Russell Gurney," *Law Journal* (1878): 345. See also "The Right Hon. Russell Gurney, Q.C., M.P." *Law Times* 65 (1878): 145. Gurney was in turn succeeded as recorder by the common serjeant, Sir Thomas Chambers, who was similarly remembered as "an excellent criminal judge." Williams, *Leaves of a Life*, 60.

148. See *DNB*.

Chapter Seven

1. Based on my annual counts, the percentage appears to have declined from 12 to 6 between 1805 and 1830. The decrease may reflect less reliable reporting in the OBSP (see discussion in Chapter 4) rather than a real decrease in the number of counsel. Charles Phillips, however, commented on the general absence of counsel for the prosecution at the Central Criminal Court (see note 80 below); even if the decline is less than accurate we are probably safe to assume that the proportion of trials that took the form of a professional contest was very low.

2. *Parl. Deb.*, 2d ser., 11 (1824): 182. This solitary petition may in fact have been solicited by the reformers. See Beattie, "Scales of Justice," 255.

3. [Sydney Smith], "Counsel for Prisoners," *Edinburgh Review* 65 (1826–27): 74–95.

4. Gill, *Wordsworth*, 141.

5. For Martin see Lynum, *Humanity Dick*; his political career is summarized in Stenton, *Biographical Dictionary of the House of Commons*.

6. For the history of the parliamentary campaign for the Prisoners' Counsel Act see Beattie, "Scales of Justice," 250–58; Cairns, *Advocacy and the Making of the Adversarial Criminal Trial*, chap. 4; and Hostettler, *Politics of Criminal Law Reform*, chap. 4. For the debates themselves see *Parl. Deb.*, 2d ser., 4 (1821): 945–46, 1512–14; 11 (1824): 180–220; 15 (1826): 589–601; 3d ser., 18 (1833): 607–13; 24 (1834): 158–69, 822–26, 1098–99; 28 (1835): 628–34, 865–73; 31 (1836): 497, 1142–61. See also McGowen, "The Image of Justice," pt. 3, "The Meaning of the Trial," 117–22.

7. For Lushington see Waddams, *Law, Politics, and the Church of England*.

8. For Ewart see *DNB*; Stenton, *Biographical Dictionary of the House of Commons*.

9. *Parl. Deb.*, 3d ser., 24 (1834): 163.

10. Ibid., 2d ser., 11 (1824): 207–8; 3d ser., 34 (1836): 763.

11. Ibid., 3d ser., 34 (1836): 769.

12. Copley (1772–1863) was called to the bar in 1804 (Lincoln's Inn); made serjeant-at-law, 1813; king's serjeant and chief justice of Chester, 1818; solicitor general, 1819; attorney general, 1824; master of the rolls, 1826; and lord chancellor, 1827 (now Baron Lyndhurst). Copley had risen rapidly in his profession but owed his "first great start" to a criminal case tried at the Nottingham assizes in 1812. In that case he secured the acquittal of his client, the Luddite John Ingham, who was charged with the capital offense of riot and destruction of machinery, not by exposing the truth of the charges but via an "ingenious objection" to the indictment. His speech in defense of Dr. Watson and Thistlewood, tried for treason in 1817, was described as "one of the ablest and most effective ever delivered in a court of justice," and their subsequent acquittal was attributed to the eloquence of their counsel. Copley enjoyed a reputation for "tempered advocacy"; he was said to be scrupulous and dignified, an excellent speaker with a talent

for cross-examination, who never overstepped the bounds of courtesy. *DNB*; Martin, *Life of Lord Lyndhurst.*

13. *Parl. Deb.*, 2d ser., 11 (1824): 215–16.

14. Called to the bar in 1791, Scarlett (1769–1844) was made a King's Counsel in 1816 and lord chief baron of the Exchequer in 1834. He entered Parliament in 1819; although a Whig, he served as attorney general under both Canning and the Duke of Wellington. Never "a very ardent reformer," Scarlett opposed the Reform Act of 1832, and from 1832 he sat as a Tory. In 1835 he was created Baron Abinger and took his seat in the House of Lords. *DNB*; Scarlett, *Memoir.*

15. *Parl. Deb.*, 2d ser., 15 (1826): 622; 3d ser., 35 (1836): 182.

16. *Second Report on the Criminal Law*, 2.

17. See Beattie, "Scales of Justice," 256; Cairns, *Advocacy and the Making of the Adversarial Criminal Trial*, 69.

18. Reproduced in Fonblanque, *Life and Labours*, 353. For the history of the *Examiner* see Chapter 8 below.

19. Beattie, "Scales of Justice," 256–57; quotation at 257. Randall McGowen makes the same point: see "The Image of Justice and Reform," esp. 117–25.

20. For the influence of Beccaria see Radzinowicz, *History of the English Criminal Law*, 1:277–300.

21. For the history of the repeal of the death penalty see ibid., vol. 1, pt. 5; the capital statutes which remained on the books as of 1839 are listed in app. 5.

22. Beattie, "Scales of Justice," 256. For the operation of discretionary justice in the late eighteenth and early nineteenth centuries see King, *Crime, Justice, and Discretion.*

23. On this issue see also McGowen, "The Image of Justice and Reform."

24. For the history of the legal periodical press see Chapter 5 above.

25. "On the Prisoners' Counsel Bill," *Legal Observer* 8 (1834): 24.

26. "The Prisoners' Counsel Bill," *Legal Observer* 10 (1835): 225.

27. "Proposed Amendment of the Prisoners' Counsel Bill," *Legal Observer* 10 (1835): 278–79. The Prisoners' Counsel Act did not grant defendants this right.

28. "The Progress of Law Reform," *Legal Observer* 13 (1836): 1.

29. "Defence of Prisoners on Trial for Felony," *Legal Examiner* 1 (1831–32): 601–4; quotations at 601, 604.

30. "Events of the Quarter," *Law Magazine* 14 (1835): 238.

31. "The Prisoners' Counsel Bill," *Law Magazine* 15 (1836): 394–402 at 400. See also "Events of the Quarter," *Law Magazine* 16 (1836): 243 and 17 (1837): 224.

32. "The Prisoners' Counsel Bill," *Law Magazine* 15 (1836) at 398.

33. Ibid., at 395.

34. *Parl. Deb.*, 2d ser., 11 (1824): 182, 204.

35. *Second Report on the Criminal Law*, app. 1, 85; *Parl. Deb.*, 3d ser., 31 (1836): 497.

36. Hardcastle, *Life of John, Lord Campbell*, 2:106–7. Park did not make good on this threat.

37. Ibid.

38. *Legal Observer* 10 (1835): 225.

39. *Parl. Deb.*, 2d ser., 11 (1824): 204.

40. Bentham, "A Commentary on Mr. Humphreys' Real Property Code," in *Works*,

5:389; *Memoirs and Correspondence of Francis Horner, M.P.*, 2:380–81, quoted in Lemmings, *Professors of the Law*, 293.

41. Calvert, *Letter to the Right Hon. Lord Dacre.*

42. *Second Report on the Criminal Law*, app. 1, 60.

43. Ibid., 61.

44. For Spankie see, e.g., [Grant], *The Bench and the Bar*, 190–93.

45. *Second Report on the Criminal Law*, app. 2, 103–6.

46. [Wontner], *Old Bailey Experience*, 323–24.

47. Ibid., 325.

48. Ibid., 324.

49. Ibid., 325.

50. Ibid., 327.

51. Harmer, *The Case of Edward Harris* and *The Murder of Mr. Steele*; *Second Report on the Criminal Law*, app. 1.

52. Harmer, *The Murder of Mr. Steele*, 63.

53. *Second Report on the Criminal Law*, app. 1, 85.

54. This argument was cited by Daniel O'Connell, who dismissed it: *Parl. Deb.*, 3d ser., 28 (1835): 869–70.

55. *Prisoners' Defence Bill—Lords' Evidence*, 20.

56. Ibid., 18.

57. Ibid., 19.

58. Ibid., 21.

59. UCL: Brougham Papers, 28,481.

60. *The Trial of John Taylor*, 14–15, quoted in King, *Crime, Justice, and Discretion*, at 229.

61. UCL: Brougham Papers, 26,364.

62. Ibid.; see also 28,444. "Wilde" was Thomas Wilde, later Lord Truro (1782–1855). For an outline of his career see *DNB*; see also [Grant], *The Bench and the Bar*, 152–54.

63. UCL: Brougham Papers, 26,364.

64. *Prisoners' Defence Bill—Lords' Evidence*, 3.

65. Ibid., 6.

66. Ibid., 7.

67. Ibid., 9.

68. Ibid., 8.

69. Ibid. On *Patch*, see, e.g., *Second Report on the Criminal Law*, 10, and "Defence of Prisoners on Trial for Felony," 603. As discussed in Chapter 4, *Patch* was tried at the Surrey assizes in 1806; Garrow's "whole skill" as an advocate was exerted in his opening speech for the prosecution.

70. *Prisoners' Defence Bill—Lords' Evidence*, 9.

71. UCL: Brougham Papers, 28,444. Calvert, *Letter to the Right Hon. Lord Dacre*; "The Prisoners' Counsel Bill," *Law Magazine* 15 (1836): 394–402.

72. UCL: Brougham Papers, 28,444.

73. Ibid., uncatalogued.

74. Ibid., 28,446.

75. *Parl. Deb.*, 3d ser., 31 (1836): 497. Although O'Connell retracted his accusation almost immediately, his attack provoked a considerable uproar in the House. Phillips and O'Connell had been friends for many years, and the former had worked hard, albeit in vain, to persuade Brougham to appoint O'Connell attorney general.

76. Ibid., 1151.

77. UCL: Brougham Papers, 28,444.

78. Ibid., 5,768.

79. *Prisoners' Defence Bill—Lords' Evidence*, 8.

80. UCL: Brougham Papers, 26,364.

81. "R. v. Dighton," in [Churchill], *Arabiniana*.

82. UCL: Brougham Papers, 26,364.

83. One of the most interesting aspects of the debate over prisoners' counsel is the fact that both proponents of the legislation and those who opposed it possessed experience of criminal trials. Many of the Whig reformers were barristers and had been engaged in criminal trials on circuit. They based their arguments in favor of the Prisoners' Counsel Act on their personal acquaintance with practice in the criminal courts, just as those who opposed the act drew on their own professional experience. Opponents and supporters of prisoners' counsel did not merely argue over what form the felony trial ought to assume, they provided contradictory descriptions of contemporary practice, testifying to the diversity which prevailed in early-nineteenth-century courtrooms.

84. Kurland and Waters, "Public Prosecutions in England," 497.

85. See Bentham's "Draft Code for the Organisation of the Judicial Establishment in France," in *Works*, 4:385–92.

86. *Twenty-Eighth Report of Committee on Finance, etc.*, [1810] IV *PP* 415; Bentham, *Works*, 4:384–406, 9:570–77; Colquhoun, *Treatise on the Police of the Metropolis* (6th ed., 1800), 21, 26, 426–27, 430–32, 539, 615, 646; *Minutes of Evidence taken before the Committee on the State of the Police of the Metropolis* (1816); *Third Report from the Committee on the State of the Police of the Metropolis* [1818] VIII *PP* 32, all cited in Kurland and Waters, "Public Prosecutions in England," at 497–98.

87. Romilly, *Memoirs*, 1:xvi; 3:372 n. 1.

88. See [Denman], "Law of Evidence in Criminal Procedure," at 191; *Parl. Deb.*, 3d ser., 137 (1855): 961–62.

89. Quoted in "Events of the Quarter," *Law Magazine* 13 (1835): 281–82.

90. "Old Bailey Experience," *Law Magazine* 10 (1833): 259–95 at 283.

91. "On the Prisoners' Counsel Bill," *Legal Observer* 8 (1834): 24.

92. *Second Report on the Criminal Law*, app. 1, 53.

93. UCL: Brougham Papers, 28,437.

94. Ibid., 36,815.

95. Ibid., 28,437.

96. Ibid., 36,815.

97. Ibid., 26,364.

98. PRO 30/22/2C, Russell Papers, ff. 31–37. I am grateful to Simon Devereaux for this reference.

99. UCL: Brougham Papers, 305.

100. "Events of the Quarter," *Law Magazine* 12 (1834): 518.

101. "Events of the Quarter," *Law Magazine* 13 (1835): 281. The Whig ministry was dismissed by the king in November 1834; under the new Tory government Lord Lyndhurst succeeded Brougham as lord chancellor.

102. See the Conclusion for developments in public prosecution.

103. Brougham to Lyndhurst, 20 Dec. 1836, reproduced in Martin, *Life of Lord Lyndhurst*, 371–72.

104. "Proposed Practice under the Prisoners' Counsel Act," *Legal Observer* 12 (1836): 340–41; quotation at 340.

105. See his entry in the Appendix, below.

106. "Proposed Practice under the Prisoners' Counsel Act," 341.

107. "Practice under the Prisoners' Counsel Act," *Legal Observer* 12 (1836): 419–20. It was held in *R. v. Boucher* (1837), 8 C & P 141, and *R. v. Burrows* (1838), 2 M & Rob. 124, that the defense was entitled to address the jury only once. The defendant thus had to choose between speaking himself or having his counsel speak for him.

108. "Prisoners' Counsel—Practice. Memorandum," *Law Magazine* 17 (1837): 470. The memorandum is reproduced in Cairns, *Advocacy and the Making of the Adversarial Criminal Trial*, 182–83; see also discussion at 118, 120–21.

109. Cairns, *Advocacy and the Making of the Adversarial Criminal Trial*, 121.

110. "Prisoners' Counsel—Practice. Memorandum," 470.

111. "Practice under the Prisoners' Counsel Act," *Legal Observer* 12 (1836): 497–98.

112. Ibid.

113. *Law Times* 28 (1856): 74.

114. Bentley, *English Criminal Justice*, 108.

115. A brief experiment had been made a year before the passage of the Prisoners' Counsel Act, at the instigation of one of London's sheriffs, whereby a man was appointed to "attend daily at Newgate Prison" and take from prisoners, without charge, a written statement of their cases. (He was not to provide any legal advice as to what they should say and what they should omit.) Yorston, the man appointed, claimed the plan worked "remarkably well." Sheriff Salomans had also instructed Yorston to advise him of the names of any prisoners who appeared to be innocent and paid out of his own pocket the fees for counsel to defend them. This plan, however, was abandoned after a single session, "on the *complaint of the lawyers*." "The Poor Prisoner," *Law Times* 1 (1843): 607; see also Bentley, *English Criminal Justice*, 123. Charles Bird, who had been attached to the metropolitan sessions in the 1810s, attracted attention in the mid-1840s, by which time he was a "provincial barrister," based in Exeter and well known on the Western circuit, by making a lengthy speech at the Devon quarter sessions to the effect that he had been briefed by a prisoner without the intercession of an attorney and intended to pursue this course in the future. The prisoner had been poor and could not afford an attorney. Bird's "charity to the poor," however, was disputed by an attorney who pointed out that he did not waive his own fees. *Law Times* 5 (1845): 359, 379.

116. Bentley cites the following cases: *R. v. Plant, The Times*, 17 Dec. 1857; *R. v. Murray, The Times*, 2 Aug. 1858; *R. v. Jones, The Times*, 30 Mar. 1859; *R. v. Jones, The Times*, 21 Dec. 1861; *R. v. Hunnisett, The Times*, 4 Aug. 1862. *English Criminal Justice*, 112 n. 43. All of these cases appear to have been presided over by a judge (Martin B.) "more reluctant than others to assign" counsel (112). After 1860, Bentley argues, assign-

ment in murder cases "became an almost routine practice" (113). But on the evidence of *The Times*, nine people accused of murder went undefended in the period 1860–69, and six in the period 1870–79. After 1880 the accused in a murder trial was "invariably" assigned counsel if he could not afford to hire a barrister himself. Ibid.

117. See Phillips's *Vacation Thoughts on Capital Punishment.*

Chapter Eight

1. The criminal law commissioners had offered a simple, Broughamite articulation of the duty owed by the advocate: "It is the duty of the Advocate, by the most strenuous exertion of his powers, to urge his own view of the case, and by force of argument to compel the Jury to adopt it." *Second Report on the Criminal Law*, 8.

2. Forsyth, *Hortensius*, 281–83.

3. When a written set of rules appeared in 1915—in the Annual Statements of the Bar Council (created in 1895)—they echoed the conclusions reached by 1850. The Bar Council's principal rulings, together with authorities from other sources, were gathered together by Sir William Boulton in 1953 and published under the title *Conduct and Etiquette at the Bar.* Updated editions appeared between 1957 and 1975. The General Council of the Bar was replaced by the Senate of the Inns of Court and the Bar, which incorporated a restructured Bar Council. The wording of the standards which appear in the Bar Council's *Code of Conduct of the Bar of England and Wales* varies only slightly from that of the material which appeared in the first edition of Boulton; see app. H, "Written Standards for the Conduct of Professional Work—Standards Applicable to Criminal Cases."

4. *Parl. Deb.*, 3d ser., 15 (1826): 624.

5. Ibid., 35 (1836): 183. By 1836 Lyndhurst agreed—despite the fact that in 1824 he had claimed that counsel who chose not to speak in defense of a client pronounced by their silence a verdict of guilty. Ibid., 2d ser., 11 (1824): 207.

6. For Scarlett's own assessment of his style of advocacy see his *Memoir*, chap. 18.

7. Ballantine wrote in his memoirs: "I suppose few counsel have defended more accused persons than myself, and I must allow that innocence was not the characteristic feature of the majority of my clients," although he could not remember any case in which he "received an unqualified admission of guilt." *Experiences*, 64.

8. See "The English Bar," *Law Magazine and Review* 23 (1867): 126–45 at 143; Duman, *The English and Colonial Bars*, 38–41; and Cocks, *Foundations of the Modern Bar*, 15–19.

9. Brougham, *Speeches of Henry Lord Brougham*, 1:105.

10. Forsyth, *Hortensius* (2d ed.), 389 n, reproduced in Cairns, *Advocacy and the Making of the Adversarial Criminal Trial*, 139.

11. Quoted in [Polson], *Law and Lawyers*, 2:256.

12. Joseph Stammers, *The Case of The Queen v. D'Israeli* (1838), 11, quoted in Mellinkoff, *The Conscience of a Lawyer*, 189.

13. "The Barrister," *The Jurist, or Quarterly Journal of Jurisprudence and Legislation* 3 (1832): 94–100.

14. Ibid., 96.

15. Erskine, *Speeches of the Right Hon. Lord Erskine*, 1:90–91. Erskine was at the time

attorney general for the Prince of Wales, and Paine's *Rights of Man* (1791), a radical response to Edmund Burke's *Reflections on the Revolution in France* (1790)—it argued, inter alia, that the vote be granted to all men over the age of twenty-one, and for the abolition of the House of Lords—included an offensive attack on the royal family. The press and his friends had advised Erskine not to defend Paine; Erskine was convinced that he had to.

16. *Boswell's Life of Johnson*, 2:47.

17. Ibid., 5:26–27.

18. Sir John Davies, preface to *A Report of Cases*, 20. This passage was quoted by both Forsyth in *Hortensius* (384) (in a chapter [10] devoted to the subject of "forensic casuistry") and Mellinkoff, *Conscience of a Lawyer*, 146, in a section (145–49) considering the religious influence on the practice of advocacy. On the subject of the "good advocate" see also Lemmings, *Professors of the Law*, 17–18.

19. Fuller, *The Holy State*, bk. 2, chap. 1, 51.

20. Cook, *The Vindication of the Professors* (1646), 8, likewise quoted by both Forsyth (*Hortensius*, 384) and Mellinkoff (*Conscience of a Lawyer*, 147).

21. Mellinkoff, *Conscience of a Lawyer*, 147.

22. *Considerations on Various Grievances in the Practick Part of our Laws*, 29–30, quoted in Lemmings, *Professors of the Law*, 17.

23. Boswell's *Life of Johnson*, 1:47–48.

24. "The Barrister," *The Jurist, or Quarterly Journal* 2 (1828): 367–74 at 371.

25. Coleridge, *Table Talk*, 26 Oct. 1831, 251–52.

26. The English edition was not published until 1827.

27. See Bentham, "Rationale of Judicial Evidence," in *Works*, 7:473–79 at 474. The quotation is Denman's summary of Bentham's position, made in his review of the French edition. [Denman], "Law of Evidence—Criminal Procedure—Publicity," *Edinburgh Review* 40 (1824): 169–207 at 185.

28. [Denman], "Law of Evidence—Criminal Procedure—Publicity," 186. This position finds expression in the modern English rule with respect to the responsibility of defense counsel: "When defending a client on a criminal charge, a barrister must endeavour to protect his client from conviction except by a competent tribunal and upon legally admissible evidence sufficient to support a conviction for the offence charged." Bar Council, *Code of Conduct for the Bar of England and Wales*, app. H, subs. 12.1.

29. Dymond (1796–1828), a moralist, Quaker, and pacifist, died of consumption at the age of thirty-one; the work in question was published posthumously. See *DNB*.

30. Dymond, *Essays on the Principles of Morality*, 129.

31. Ibid., 129–30.

32. Paley, *Principles of Moral and Political Philosophy*, bk. 3, chap. 15, 1. For Paley (1743–1805), see *DNB*.

33. Thomas Gisbourne (1758–1846), author of *Principles of Moral Philosophy* (1789), advocated absolute right over the utilitarian morality espoused by Paley. He considered the legal profession in *An Inquiry into the Duties of Men in the Higher Ranks of the Middle Classes* (1794).

34. Dymond, *Essays on the Principles of Morality*, 138.

35. Ibid., 136.

36. Ibid., 134.

37. On the phenomenon of Newgate novels see Hollingsworth's classic *The New-gate Novel* (1963) and Juliet John's introduction to *Cult Criminals: The Newgate Novels, 1830–1847*, the 1998 Routledge reprint of Bulwer's *Paul Clifford, Eugene Aram, Lucretia,* and *Night and Morning* and Harrison Ainsworth's *Rookwood* and *Jack Sheppard.* These novels were frequently attacked for glamorizing the criminal world. On the reading public in the nineteenth century see Altick, *The English Common Reader*; on the treatment of topics of the day in nineteenth-century fiction see Altick, *The Presence of the Present.*

38. Turpin, Aram, Sheppard, and Wainewright can all be found in the *DNB.* England's poet laureate, Andrew Motion, recently published a fictional autobiography of Wainewright; *Wainewright the Poisoner*; see the afterword for a discussion of various nineteenth-century treatments of Wainewright's story.

39. Mellinkoff, *Conscience of a Lawyer*, 225. See also Albany Fonblanque's nineteenth-century conflation of "lawyer" and "liar," quoted below (at note 97).

40. Bulwer, *Paul Clifford*, 437–38 (emphasis added).

41. Negative stereotypes of counsel in nineteenth-century fiction are not limited to the Newgate novels. Dickens's "Stryver" in *A Tale of Two Cities* (1859), the barrister who defends Darnay on a charge of treason, is "stout, loud, red, bluff, and free from any drawback of delicacy," a man with "a pushing way of shouldering himself (morally and physically) into companies and conversations"; he is "glib" and "unscrupulous" as well as "ready" and "bold" in the conduct of his practice (93, 101–2). (Although the trial took place in the late eighteenth century, Stryver is rumored to have been based on the nineteenth-century barrister Edwin James [1812–1882], whom Dickens had met in 1858 or early in 1859 [487, note to p. 93].) Relatively little comment is made on Stryver's courtroom activities (see chaps. 2 and 3), but in *The Old Curiosity Shop* (1840–41), the barristers engaged for and against Kit, accused of theft, are devoid of principle (573–74). "Nobody knows the truth, everybody believes a falsehood" because of the "ingenuity" of counsel (575). In the preface to the "Cheap Edition" of the *Pickwick Papers* published in 1847, Dickens again commented on the "license of Counsel, and the degree to which Juries are ingeniously bewildered" (46). Similarly, "Bar" in *Little Dorrit* (1855–57) is described as possessing a "little insinuating Jury droop" and "persuasive double eye-glass"; having a "verdict to get . . . against the evidence," Bar "improve[s] the shining hours in setting snares for the gentlemen of the jury" (772–73). Elizabeth Gaskell, for her part, quietly condemns advocates not for deliberate perversion of the truth but for indifference to it, and for placing self-interest above truth and justice: see the trial of Jem for the murder of Henry Carson in *Mary Barton* (1848).

42. [Brougham], "Rights and Duties of Advocates," *Edinburgh Review* 64 (1836–37): 155–68 at 155.

43. Ibid., 156.

44. Ibid., 164.

45. Ibid., 166.

46. "A Barrister's Advocacy of his Client's Cause," *Legal Observer* 15 (1837): 216–17.

47. Quoted in Mellinkoff, *Conscience of a Lawyer*, 238.

48. Ibid.

49. Brougham had advised the queen since 1811; he is said not to have actually believed in her innocence. Denman apparently did, but neither man allowed his wife to call upon her. *DNB*.

50. In the *Age of Reason* (1794) Paine turned his attention from politics to religion and queried the truth of Christianity, claiming that the Gospels were rife with inaccuracy and contradiction.

51. See Mellinkoff, *Conscience of a Lawyer*, 240–47; quotation at 246.

52. Henry Crabb Robinson, *Diary and Correspondence*, 1:11.

53. The consequences of the *Courvoisier* trial for the history of advocacy were thoughtfully explored by Mellinkoff in *The Conscience of a Lawyer*, which also provides a detailed account of the murder and trial, summarizing and reproducing much of the press coverage, including the text of Phillips's three-hour speech for the defense (chap. 6). That speech is also reproduced in Cairns, *Advocacy and the Making of the Adversarial Criminal Trial*, app. 3, while the trial itself and the controversy over Phillips's behavior is discussed at 129–36.

54. The trial was reported by all of the major newspapers. *The Times*'s coverage, which was acknowledged to be the most reliable, began on 19 June; the *Courier*, an evening paper, was first in the field on 18 June, the day the trial opened, but it was unable to report the entire day's events owing to its press time. Coverage in *The Times*, the *Morning Chronicle*, the *Morning Herald*, and the *Post*, inter alia, ran from 19 to 22 June. A less detailed account appears in the OBSP, June 1840, 216–71. See also Townsend, *Modern State Trials*, 244–313; [Warren], "The Practice of Advocacy.—Mr. Charles Phillips, and his Defence of Courvoisier," *Law Review and Quarterly Journal* 11 (1849–50): 376–436; and Mellinkoff, *Conscience of a Lawyer*, chaps. 1–6.

55. *Ballantine, Experiences*, 61.

56. Ibid.

57. Henderson, *Recollections*, 204.

58. *The Times*, 22 June, 3 July 1840.

59. Serjeant Robinson brackets Flowers's name with those of Harmer and Steele in recalling criminal attorneys in the late 1830s and claims that the three were "the original of Quirk, Gammon, and Snap" in Samuel Warren's popular novel, *Ten Thousand a Year*. Benjamin Coulson Robinson, *Bench and Bar*, 38.

60. *The Times*, 19 June 1840.

61. "Correspondence between Samuel Warren and Charles Phillips," *The Times*, 20 Nov. 1849. Reprinted in Warren, *Correspondence Between Samuel Warren, Esq., Barrister-at-Law, and Charles Phillips, Esq., Relative to the Trial of Courvoisier*. Adolphus reported that Courvoisier was to have been dismissed by Russell, whom he had offended by removing a favorite watchdog from the bedroom door and placing him in the stable, and that the threat of dismissal had been the immediate cause of the murder. Henderson, *Recollections*, 155.

62. Bar Council, *Code of Conduct of the Bar of England and Wales*, app. H, "Written Standards for the Conduct of Professional Work—Standards Applicable to Criminal Cases," sec. 13, "Confessions of Guilt." The "mere fact that a person charged with a crime has confessed to his counsel that he did commit the offence charged is no bar to that barrister appearing or continuing to appear in his defence, nor indeed does such a

confession release the barrister from his imperative duty to do all that he honourably can for his client" (13.2). A confession of guilt does, however, impose "very strict limitations on the conduct of the defence." A barrister "must not assert as true that which he knows to be false" (13.3). Subsection 13.4 specifies that the barrister would be entitled to object to the competency of the court, the form of the indictment, the admissibility of evidence, or the evidence admitted, but he cannot suggest that someone else has committed the crime or call evidence he knows to be false: the barrister must not "set up an affirmative case inconsistent with the confession made to him." The rules acknowledge the difficulty of determining the limits within which the barrister can attack the evidence for the prosecution in either cross-examination or in the course of a speech and conclude, "No clearer rule can be laid down than this, that he is entitled to test the evidence given by each individual witness and to argue that the evidence taken as a whole is insufficient to amount to proof that the defendant is guilty of the offence charged. Further than this he ought not to go" (13.5).

63. "Correspondence between Samuel Warren and Charles Phillips."

64. "Courvoisier's Confession of Guilt," *The Times*, 22 June 1840.

65. Letter to the editor of the *Morning Chronicle*, 23 June 1840, reproduced in *The Letters of Charles Dickens*, 2:86–89. Quotations at 88–89.

66. *Morning Chronicle*, 26 June 1840; *Letters of Charles Dickens*, 2:90–91 at 90. In fact, some of the police evidence was patently untrue. See below.

67. *Morning Chronicle*, 30 June 1840.

68. *Parl. Deb.*, 5th ser., 55 (1840): 1401.

69. Ibid., 1402.

70. *The Times*, 25 June 1840.

71. Ibid., 26 June 1840.

72. *Morning Chronicle*, 25 June 1840. For the evolution of the standard of reasonable doubt see Barbara Shapiro, *"Beyond Reasonable Doubt" and "Probable Cause,"* and Langbein, *The Origins of Adversary Criminal Trial*, 261–66.

73. For locations of the text of Phillips's speech see notes 53 and 54, above.

74. As Mellinkoff comments, the first reaction to the news that Phillips had continued in the defense of a client who had privately confided his guilt came from the working press, "newspapermen who had seen Phillips in action before, veterans of the criminal trial," who were generally sympathetic to his predicament. *Conscience of a Lawyer*, 141.

75. *The Times*, 22 June 1840.

76. The *Herald*, 22 June 1840, quoted in Mellinkoff, *Conscience of a Lawyer*, 141.

77. *Examiner*, 16 Aug. 1845.

78. During their editorship the Hunt brothers had annoyed the government by their advertisement of the fact that half of the paper's price owed to government taxes, and in 1812 they had been convicted of libel (the result of an article which criticized the Prince of Wales) and sentenced to two years' imprisonment plus a fine of £500. A defiant Leigh Hunt had continued to edit the paper from prison. *DNB*.

79. [Grant], *The Great Metropolis*, 117; Fonblanque's entry in the *DNB*.

80. *DNB*.

81. [Grant], *The Great Metropolis*, 120, 119.

82. Reproduced in Fonblanque, *Life and Labours*, 326.

83. Ballantine, *Experiences*, 62.

84. *The Times*, 20 Nov. 1849.

85. Ibid., 23 June 1840.

86. *Courier*, 22 June 1840.

87. See the letter to the editor from "One in the Court" and the paper's reply, ibid., 22 June 1840.

88. Ballantine, *Experiences*, 63.

89. *The Times*, 22 June 1840.

90. [Samuel Warren], "The Practice of Advocacy.—Mr. Charles Phillips, and his Defence of Courvoisier," *Law Review and Quarterly Journal* 11 (1849–50): 376–436 at 433.

91. Ibid. (emphasis in the original).

92. See "Duties of Inquests and Licence of Counsel," *Examiner*, 12 July 1840: "An advocate might . . . feel bound by rule, even after a confession of guilt had been communicated to him, to go through a defence; but in this case we contend that the advocate should scrupulously refrain from any line of defence the effect of which would be to procure the acquittal of his client by criminating or destroying the characters of persons who had but borne true evidence against him."

93. Cosgrove, "Law," 17. The first series of the *Law Magazine or Quarterly Review* ran between 1828 and 1844, the second from 1844 to 1856. As Cosgrove notes, one of the objectives of the *Law Magazine* and its competitors was "to make the law a respectable, 'professional' career." Ibid.

94. "Events of the Quarter," *Law Magazine* 24 (1840): 238.

95. Reproduced in Fonblanque, *Life and Labours*, 327–28.

96. Ibid., 328–30.

97. "The Bar and the Press," *Examiner*, 16 Aug. 1845.

98. "War Between the Press and the Bar," *Punch* 9 (1845): 64–65. The first issue of *Punch*, the comic magazine launched by Mark Lemon and Henry Mayhew, appeared on 17 July 1841. Lemon and Mayhew were reforming Liberals and hoped to combine humor with political comment. During its first few years *Punch*, like the *Examiner*, championed various radical causes, attacking the high cost of the monarchy, campaigning against the 1834 poor law and the corn laws, and supporting "moral force" Chartism. When Mayhew left in 1845 the radical content of the magazine diminished, and by 1850 it was conservative in its opinions. For the history of *Punch* during the 1840s see Altick, *Punch*.

99. "What a Barrister May Do; and What He May Not Do," *Punch* 9 (1845): 113.

100. Ibid.

101. "On the Principle of Advocacy as Developed in the Practice of the Bar," *Law Magazine* 84 (1846): 1–34, reprinted in *Law Magazine and Review*, n.s., 20 (1854): 265–98. This article referred specifically to the attacks published in the *Examiner*. For Talfourd see "The Late Mr. Justice Talfourd," *Law Magazine* 51 (1854): 298; "The Life and Writings of the Late Mr. Justice Talfourd," *North British Review* 25 (1856): 47; and *DNB*. He had been a serjeant from 1833 and was made a judge of the Court of Common Pleas in 1849.

102. "On the Principle of Advocacy as Developed in the Practice of the Bar," *Law Magazine and Review*, 265–66.

103. Ibid., 288 (emphasis in original).

104. Ibid., 289.

105. "On the Profession of the Bar," *London Magazine*, n.s., 1 (1825): 323–38; quotations at 328, 329.

106. "On the Principle of Advocacy," *Law Magazine and Review*, 268.

107. For Cairns's discussion of Talfourd, see *Advocacy and the Making of the Adversarial Criminal Trial*, 143–49.

108. "On the Principle of Advocacy," *Law Magazine and Review*, 275–76.

109. Ibid., 291.

110. Ibid., 292.

111. For the trial see *The Times*, 22–24 Dec. 1847.

112. Ibid., 30 Dec. 1847.

113. Ibid.

114. *Examiner*, 30 Dec. 1847.

115. "Licence of Counsel," *Law Magazine* 39 (1848): 53–61 at 59.

116. The speeches of counsel were reported in *The Times*, 27 Oct. 1849.

117. *The Times*, 27 Oct. 1849.

118. See, e.g., the *Observer*, 29 Oct. 1849; the *Examiner*, 27 Oct., 3 Nov. 1849. Both Maria Manning (1821–49) and her husband were convicted and hanged on 13 November 1849. Maria, who like Courvoisier was Swiss, had demanded to be tried by a jury composed equally of Englishmen and foreigners, but it was determined that she had become a British subject on her marriage to Manning. She wore a black satin gown to her execution, rendering that material unpopular. *DNB*. See Borowitz, *The Woman Who Murdered Black Satin*; see also, e.g., Bowen-Rowlands, *Seventy-two Years at the Bar*, 30–35. The case continues to excite popular interest and was recently retold as a BBC Radio 4 afternoon play starring the late Charlotte Coleman.

119. *Examiner*, 3 Nov. 1849.

120. James A. Davies, *John Forster*, 222.

121. Forster became the paper's official editor in November 1847; Fonblanque retained his ownership until 1865. For Forster's career (he was, among other things, a friend and future biographer of Dickens), see Davies, *John Forster*.

122. In 1843, however, he decided to be called to the bar—in large part, it would seem, for social reasons: being able to describe himself as "barrister-at-law" on the title page of his biography of Oliver Goldsmith and to inscribe "John Forster of the Inner Temple" on his bookplates helped to assuage the sting of his critics' taunt, "J. Forster, the butcher-boy." Ibid., 81–83.

123. "I think it my duty," William Evans, sheriff of London and Middlesex, wrote in a letter to *The Times* in response to Ainsworth's denial of the connection between the novel and Courvoisier's crime, "to state distinctly, that Courvoisier did assert to me that 'the idea of murdering his master was first suggested to him by a perusal of the book called *Jack Sheppard*, and that the said book was lent to him by a valet of the Duke of Bedford.'" *The Times*, 9 July 1840.

124. *Examiner*, 3 Nov. 1839. The story of Jack Sheppard had also been dramatized.

Fonblanque wrote to Forster in 1839, "I really think we abdicate our critical duty in not attacking this disgusting sort of publication. If you don't, I must!" (Fonblanque, *Life and Labours*, 428 n. 1). John Adolphus, however, saw the play performed at the Adelphi Theatre "with undiminished pleasure and admiration" (Henderson, *Recollections*, 200).

125. See Davies, *John Forster*, 178–83.

126. Take, for example, Forster's reponse to the argument that the objectionable passages in Phillips's speech owed in part to the fact that they had been composed prior to Courvoisier's confession: "Mr. Phillips, as we need not say to such as are unhappily familiar with his effusions . . . has little change of dress for a change of occasion. He has had to furbish up a very scanty collection of tawdry rags and ornaments for his various public appearances; and we can easily conceive his inability to meet a sudden demand for inflated and bombastic epithets and sentences" "Mr. Charles Phillips and the *Examiner*," *Examiner*, 24 Nov. 1849.

127. UCL: Brougham Papers, 5768.

128. Both the *Examiner* (16 Aug.) and *Punch* ("War Between the Press and the Bar") had made this argument in 1845.

129. *The Times*, 20 Nov. 1849. The language—and course of action—employed by Phillips seems to have penetrated Dickens's subconscious; see the following passage from part 9 of *David Copperfield*, published in January 1850: "I never shall forget that night. I never shall forget how I turned and tumbled; how I wearied myself with thinking about Agnes and this creature; how I considered what I could do, and what I ought to do; how I could come to no other conclusion than that the best course for her peace was to do nothing, and to keep to myself what I had heard. If I went to sleep for a few moments, the image of Agnes with her tender eyes, and of her father looking fondly on her, as I had so often seen him look, arose before me with appealing faces, and filled me with vague terrors. When I awoke, the recollection that Uriah was lying in the next room, sat heavy on me like a waking nightmare; and oppressed me with a leaden dread, as if I had some meaner quality of devil for a lodger" (443).

130. *Examiner*, 24 Nov. 1849. Fonblanque would make similar sarcastic comment on the relation of fees and feeling in 1851; see *Life and Labours*, 340–41.

131. As discussed in Chapter 2, he also did not believe in capital punishment, even for murder. See Phillips, *Vacation Thoughts on Capital Punishment*.

132. *Morning Chronicle*, 22 June 1840.

133. UCL: Brougham Papers, 26,364.

134. *Prisoners' Defence Bill—Lords' Evidence*, 7.

135. Brougham, *Speeches of Henry Lord Brougham*, 1:105.

136. *The Times*, 20 Nov. 1849.

137. Warren, *Correspondence Between Samuel Warren, Esq., Barrister-at-Law, and Charles Phillips, Esq., Relative to the Trial of Courvoisier*.

138. *Examiner*, 8 Dec. 1849.

139. "Mr. Charles Phillips and the *Examiner*."

140. [Warren], "The Practice of Advocacy," 433.

141. UCL: Brougham Papers, undated and uncatalogued.

142. [Warren], "The Practice of Advocacy," 430.

143. *The Times*, 20 Nov. 1849.

144. "Mr. Charles Phillips, and His Defence of Courvoisier," *Legal Observer* 39 (1849–50): 137–38 at 137.

145. "Vindication of Mr. Phillips in Courvoisier's Case," "Mr. Charles Phillips, and his Defence of Courvoisier," and two further notices, both entitled "Mr. Charles Phillips' Defence of Courvoisier," 39 *Legal Observer* (1849–50): 62–63, 137–38, 276–78, 297–98.

146. "Vindication of Mr. Phillips," 63.

147. "Mr. Charles Phillips, and his Defence of Courvoisier," 138.

148. "The Defence of Courvoisier, and the Plea for it," *Law Magazine* 43 (1850): 26–36.

149. Ibid., 30.

150. *The Jurist* 13 (1849): 497–99.

151. Ibid. 4 (1840): 593–94. In fact, even this statement is open to doubt: as late as 1848 the *Legal Observer* was being questioned by a correspondent as to whether a barrister was at liberty to refuse a cause where he believed it to be wrong. "Can a Barrister Refuse a Brief?" *Legal Observer* 35 (1847–48): 501. And Forsyth argued in *Hortensius*: "It is *not* the true theory of an advocate's profession, that he is bound to undertake any and every cause which is offered to him, in utter disregard of its nature or merits" (381; emphasis in original). He cites a host of authorities from Cicero onward in support of his position, while acknowledging that it is at odds with the dicta of Lords Erskine and Brougham (see 381–89).

152. *The Jurist* 4 (1840): 593–94 at 593.

153. Ibid.

154. Ibid.

155. Ibid., at 594.

156. Ibid. 11 (1848): 537–38 at 537. The same point had been made some four years earlier; see 8 (1844): 237–38.

157. Ibid. 11 (1848): 537–38 at 537.

158. Ibid., at 538.

159. Ibid. 13 (1849): 469–70 at 469.

160. Ibid., 497–99 at 499.

161. Ibid., 469–70 at 469.

162. Ibid.

163. Ibid., at 470.

164. Ibid.

165. Ibid. (emphasis in original).

166. Ibid., 497–99. The same suggestion had been made by "A Barrister" in a letter published in *The Jurist* in 1848: "Much that is indefensible in the practice of the bar is occasioned by jury trial,—an ancient and once invaluable piece of armour, which we obstinately persist in wearing, although, by change of circumstances, it has become a nuisance of the first magnitude. The Old Bailey and Nis Prius arts, that shed a moral infection over every branch of practice, would cease to exist if the tribunal upon which alone they can be successfully exercised were abolished." 12 (1848): 24–25 at 25.

167. Mellinkoff, *Conscience of a Lawyer*, 7. By the early twentieth century it had become a commonplace among the legal profession that "possibility, and not truth, is the

essential element of a defence" ([Foote], *"Pie-Powder,"* 116). See also John Mortimer: "A British criminal trial is not primarily an investigation into the truth, although the truth may sometimes be disinterred by chance. A criminal trial is a test of the prosecution evidence, a procedure to discover if a case against an accused person can be proved beyond reasonable doubt." *Clinging to the Wreckage,* 213.

168. Mellinkoff, *Conscience of a Lawyer,* 157.

169. Ibid., 159.

170. Ibid., 158.

171. All of the commissioners have entries in the *DNB.* For a brief summary of their legal careers see Cairns, *Advocacy and the Making of the Adversarial Criminal Trial,* 73 n. 23. On the commission itself see Lobban, *The Common Law,* chap. 7.

172. Trollope, *Phineas Redux,* 177–78. Trollope's attitude toward his Old Bailey counsel in this, the third novel in which Chaffanbrass appears, seems to have mellowed somewhat (see Chapter 5, note 130, above). As one biographer notes, "[T]he simplicities of *The New Zealander*" have been abandoned (Hall, *Trollope,* 156). Whether he agreed with it or not, Trollope has in Chaffanbrass's words accurately reproduced the conceptualization of the criminal trial formulated by the bar over the course of the 1840s.

173. See Crew, *The Old Bailey,* 56–78, in which he compares the "turgid, bombastic eloquence" and "blustering," "theatrical" (76) advocacy typical until late in the century with the "quiet, dignified, and judicial" (78) behavior of late-nineteenth-century criminal barristers.

174. See note 18 above.

175. Sir John Davies, *A Report of Cases,* 20.

176. Forsyth, *Hortensius,* 326.

177. See Beattie, *Crime and the Courts,* 340–41.

178. Hannen, President, in *Smith v. Smith,* 7 P.D. 84 at 89, quoted in Mellinkoff, *Conscience of a Lawyer,* 219.

179. Forsyth, *Hortensius,* 409.

180. "Commissioner Phillips—Courvoisier—and the 'Examiner,'" *Punch* 17 (1849): 223–24. And as Mellinkoff points out, Phillips's entry in the *DNB* damns him, commenting that his conduct in the *Courvoisier* trial was "generally condemned" and repeating the accusation that "though fully aware of his client's guilt, he pledged his word that he was innocent, and sought to fasten the crime on another." See Mellinkoff, *Conscience of a Lawyer,* 220.

Conclusion

1. See *Law Times* 1 (1843): 590, 607, 635 (quotation at 590); 2 (1843–44): 281.

2. The Poor Prisoners Defence Act received royal assent on 14 August 1903 and came into effect on 1 January 1904. See Bentley, *English Criminal Justice,* chap. 12, for the various means by which a "poor prisoner" might have acquired the assistance of counsel before that date.

3. See, e.g., "Prosecutions," *Law Times* 1 (1843): 467–68, and the letter of "A Country Solicitor," reproduced in *Law Times* 4 (1844–45): 61–62, complaining of the absence of counsel for the prosecution and the impropriety of judges assuming this role.

In 1843 the *Legal Observer* called attention to a brief discussion in the House of Commons on the subject and invited professional debate; in 1848 it commented (negatively) on recommendations urged by the secretary of state. "The Appointment of a Public Prosecutor," *Legal Observer* 27 (1843): 502; "Conduct of Prosecutions by the Government," *Legal Observer* 35 (1847–48): 341. See also "A Public Prosecutor," *Law Magazine* 39 (1848): 197–201. For the parliamentary campaign see Kurland and Waters, "Public Prosecutions in England"; Edwards, *Law Officers of the Crown*, chap. 16. See also "A Public Prosecutor," *Law Magazine* 39 (1848): 197–201.

4. See Edwards, *Law Officers of the Crown*, chap. 13.

5. The records show that in 1849 it prosecuted two individuals for stealing City property and three for assaulting the City's constables. But it also prosecuted two people for keeping a bawdy house, five for theft, five for receiving stolen goods, three for uttering counterfeit coin, one for forgery, three for rape and another for assault with carnal intent, one for attempted murder, one for threatening to murder, and one for manslaughter. CLRO: Solicitor's Papers, Briefs &c in cases at the Old Bailey, Guildhall Sessions, Mayor's Court & other courts, c. 1802–1851, Bdles. 0055, 0056, 0059.

6. We still do not know the proportion of felony trials heard on circuit in which counsel were engaged on both sides.

7. The Victorian bar as a whole continued to expand dramatically. Samuel Warren believed that it almost doubled between 1835 and 1845, to include just over 2,300 barristers. Warren, *A Popular and Practical Introduction to Law Studies*, 2, cited in Cocks, *Foundations of the Modern Bar*, 57. For the Victorian bar see ibid. (chap. 3 for the 1840s); Lewis, *The Victorian Bar*; Pue, "Exorcising Professional Demons," "Guild-Training vs. Professional Education," "Lawyers and Political Liberalism," "Rebels at the Bar."

8. Ballantine, *Experiences*, 42.

9. He also shared Adolphus's love of the theater: "The Serjeant was a very great favourite with members of the theatrical profession, and, when he was in the zenith of his fame, there was scarcely ever a theatrical case heard without his being engaged on one side or the other." Williams, *Leaves of a Life*, 57.

10. Ballantine, *Experiences*, 45.

11. *DNB*.

12. "Borough of Southwark Court," *Legal Observer* 39 (1848–49): 465.

13. 12 & 13 Vict., c. 101.

14. The Palace Court monopoly irritated William Makepeace Thackeray, among others:

> The nature of this Court
> My hindignation riles
> A few fat legal spiders
> Here sit and spin their viles
> To rob the town theyr privilige is,
> In a hayrea of twelve miles
>
> . . . .
>
> Four counsel in this Court
> Misnamed of justice—sits;

These lawyers owes their places to
Their money, not their wits
And there's six attornies under them,
As here their living gits.

These lawyers, six and four,
Was a livin at their ease,
A sending of their writs about,
And droring in the fees.

Quoted in Christian, *A Short History of Solicitors*, 207. Christian commented that it was fortunate "that no novellist fell afoul of the Mayor's Court" (208).

15. See the various letters to the editor published in the *Legal Examiner* 3 (1832–33): 483; *Legal Observer* 6 (1833): 408, 37 (1848–49): 105–6; *Law Times* 1 (1843): 91, 127–28, 193. See also "The Palace Court Monopoly," *Legal Observer* 37 (1848–49): 64–65; "The Marshalsea and Palace Courts," *Legal Observer* 37 (1848–49): 345–46; *Law Times* 4 (1844): 42; 12 (1848): 160; *The Jurist* 13 (1849): 245–46.

16. It was his second attempt; Locke had competed unsuccessfully with Peter Laurie for an earlier vacancy in 1842.

17. See, e.g., *The Times*, 23 Apr. 1822.

18. CLRO: *Common Council Minutes and Reports, Printed*, 17 Mar. 1842.

19. Ibid., 27 Feb. 1845.

20. In 1853 he published a treatise on practice unique to London's customary court: *The Doctrine and Practice of Foreign Attachment in the Lord Mayor's Court.*

21. MacNally practiced at the Old Bailey from 1784 to 1789. He subsequently returned to Ireland and became a government informer, receiving an annual pension of £300 from the Secret Service fund. MacNally regularly betrayed his countrymen from perhaps as early as 1790. "It seems to have been his regular practice when taking a brief for the defence in a government prosecution to disclose its contents to the crown lawyers." *DNB.*

22. Blackstone, *Commentaries*, 4:352. Fortescue had similarly argued, three centuries earlier, "I should, indeed, prefer twenty guilty men to escape death through mercy, than one innocent be condemned unjustly." *De Laudibus Legum Angliae*, 65, quoted in Langbein, *The Origins of Adversary Criminal Trial*, 262 n. 38.

23. David Hare, *Murmuring Judges*, act 2, scene 8.

24. "The Glorious Uncertainty of the law was fully evinced by a circumstance which passed on Saturday at the Old Bailey. A woman was indicted for stealing a *lawn cap*. The evidence of the theft was quite clear, and the poor creature trembled for her fate, when lo! The cap turned out to be made of *muslins*; and the prisoner was acquitted," wrote *The Times*, 19 Apr. 1790. For the reforms implemented by Peel in 1826 and the Criminal Procedure Act of 1851, which restricted the practice of acquittal in cases of flawed indictments (while not wholly abolishing it), see Bentley, *English Criminal Justice*, 136–37; quotation at 136.

25. Compare, e.g., Langbein, *Origins of Adversary Criminal Trial* and Cairns, *Advocacy and the Making of the Adversarial Criminal Trial.*

26. Langbein, *The Origins of Adversary Criminal Trial*, 271.

27. Rumors that a bar mess would soon be instituted, "to which those only will be admitted who sternly resist whatever, in old customs of the Court and habits of its Bar, is opposed to that which, by the Bar in all other courts, is deemed unprofessional and unbecoming a gentleman," circulated as early as the 1840s. "Notes upon Circuit, No. V. The Central Criminal Court," *Law Times* 2 (1843–44): 46. Members of the bar practicing at the Central Criminal Court and the Middlesex sessions were reported to have held a meeting to "consider the state of practice" in those courts and appointed a committee of inquiry. *Law Times* 4 (1844): 180. Among that bar opinion was divided, however, and a bar mess was not instituted at the Central Criminal Court until much later.

Bibliography

Primary Sources

MANUSCRIPTS
British Library
   Add MSS 33112, 40363, 47466
   Eg MS 3710
Corporation of London Records Office
   Common Council Journals, 1780–1821
   Common Council Minutes and Reports, Printed, 1818–55
   Journal of the Committee for Rebuilding Newgate, 1767–85
   Misc. MSS 5.10, "Inventory of Furniture—Sessions House" (1781)
   MS 69.4
   MS 97
   MS 116.1
   "Report of the Committee appointed to enquire into the nature and duties of the
     City Solicitor," PAR Book 13
   Sessions Papers, Boxes 35–57 (1759–1833)
   Solicitor's Papers, Briefs &c for prosecutions at the Sessions &c, Boxes 1–13 (1786–
     1833)
   Solicitor's Papers, Briefs &c in cases at the Old Bailey, Guildhall Sessions, Mayor's
     Court & other courts, c. 1802–1851, Bdles. 0051–59
   Surveyor's Justice Plans
Greater London Record Office
   MA/S/269, 270, 327, 369, 373
   MJ/SP.1794, 1814
Guildhall Library
   MSS 420, 421, 7067, 7289, 9983, 11,926
Inns of Court
   Gray's Inn Admission Register
   Lincoln's Inn General Admissions Register
   Lincoln's Inn Red Books
Public Record Office
   E15/4, 5, 19, 20

KB21/45, 50, 56, 57
KB125/174, 192, 193, 197, 198, 202, 203, 211, 212, 213, 221, 222, 223, 231, 232, 233, 241, 242, 243
PALA 9
PRO 30/22/2C, Russell Papers
PROB6, 11
University College Library, London, Manuscript Division
    Brougham Papers

PARLIAMENTARY DEBATES
Parliamentary Debates, 1st ser., 1803–20 (41 vols.)
Parliamentary Debates, 2d ser., 1820–30 (25 vols.)
Parliamentary Debates, 3d ser., 1830–91 (356 vols.)

PARLIAMENTARY PAPERS
Prisoners' Defence Bill. Minutes of Evidence taken before the Select Committee of the House of Lords, etc. (1836) Lords' Papers 119.
Second Report of the Commissioners Appointed to Inquire into the Municipal Corporations in England and Wales. Parliamentary Papers (House of Commons), 1837.
Second Report of the Commissioners on the Criminal Law. Parliamentary Papers (House of Commons), 1836.

BOOKS AND PAMPHLETS
Adolphus, John. *History of England from the Accession of George III to the Conclusion of Peace in 1783*. London, 1802.
———. *Observations on the Vagrant Act and Some Other Statutes, and on the Powers and Duties of Justices of the Peace*. London, 1824.
———. *The Royal Exile; or, Memoirs of the Public and Private Life of Her Majesty, Caroline, Queen Consort of George*. London, 1821.
Archbold, J. F. *Pleading and Evidence in Criminal Cases*. London, 1822.
Arnould, Sir Joseph. *Memoir of Thomas, First Lord Denman*. 2 vols. London, 1873.
Ballantine, William. *Some Experiences of a Barrister's Life*. 8th ed. London, 1883.
The Bar, with Sketches of Eminent Judges, Barristers; etc., etc. A Poem, with Notes. London, 1825.
Barker, George Fisher Russell. *The Westminster School Register from 1764 to 1883*. London, 1892.
Bathurst, Henry. *Theory of Evidence*. London, 1761.
Beccaria, Cesare. *Of Crimes and Punishments*. London, 1767.
Bentham, Jeremy. *The Works of Jeremy Bentham*. Edited by John Bowring. 11 vols. Edinburgh, 1843.
Beville, Robert. *On the Law of Homicide and Larceny*. London, 1799.
Blackstone, Sir William. *Commentaries on the Law of England*. 4 vols. London, 1765–69.
Boswell, James. *Boswell's Life of Samuel Johnson, together with Boswell's Journal of a tour to the Hebrides, and Diary of a journey into North Wales*. Edited by George Birkbeck Hill. Revised by L. F. Powell. 6 vols. Oxford, 1964.

Bowen-Rowlands, Ernest. *Seventy-two Years at the Bar: A Memoir*. London, 1924.

Brougham, Henry. *Speeches of Henry Lord Brougham*. 4 vols. Edinburgh, 1838.

Browne, John, comp. *Browne's General Law List*. London, 1775–1801 (annual volumes).

Brydges, Sir Egerton. *The Autobiography, Times, Opinions and Contemporaries of Sir Egerton Brydges*. London, 1834.

Buller, Francis. *An Introduction to the Law Relative to Trials at Nisi Prius*. London, 1772.

Bulwer Lytton, Edward. *Paul Clifford*. 1830. Reprint, London, 1998.

Calvert, Frederick. *Letter to the Right Hon. Lord Dacre, Chairman of the Quarter Sessions of Hertfordshire, on the Prisoners' Counsel Bill*. London, 1836.

Campbell, John. *Lives of the Chief Justices of England*. 3 vols. London, 1845–57.

Carrington, F. A. *A Supplement to all the Treatises on the Criminal Law*. London, 1826.

Chitty, Joseph. *Practical Treatise on the Criminal Law*. 4 vols. London, 1816.

Christian, Edmund B. V. *A Short History of Solicitors*. London, 1896.

[Churchill, John Henry Blencowe]. *Arabiniana*. London, 1843.

Clarke, Sir Edward. *The Story of My Life*. London, 1918.

Clarke, W., comp. *Clarke's New Law List*. London, 1803–40.

Coke, Edward. *The Third Part of the Institutes of the Laws of England: Concerning High Treason and Other Pleas of the Crown, and Criminal Cases*. London, 1644.

Coleridge, Samuel Taylor. *The Notebooks of Samuel Taylor Coleridge*. Vol. 5, *1827–1834*. Edited by Kathleen Coburn and Anthony John Harding. Princeton, 2002.

Collier, John Payne. *Criticisms on the Bar: Including Strictures on the Principal Counsel Practising in the Courts of King's Bench, Common Pleas, Chancery and Exchequer*. London, 1819.

A Complete Collection of State Trials and Proceedings for High Treason and Other Crimes and Misdemeanors. Compiled by T. B. Howell. 33 vols. London, 1809–26.

Comyns, Sir John. *A Digest of the Laws of England*. London, 1762–67.

Concannen, Matthew. *Letter to William Garrow, Esquire, on the Subject of his Illiberal Behaviour to the Author, on the trial of a cause (Ford against Pedder and others)*. London, 1796.

Considerations on Various Grievances in the Practick Part of our Laws. With Some Observations on the Code Frederick, the Roman Law, and our own Courts of Equity. Dublin, 1756.

Cottu, Charles. *On the Administration of Criminal Justice in England and Wales; and the Spirit of English Government*. London, 1822.

Cox, E. W. *The Advocate*. London, 1852.

Cox, Joseph. *A Faithful Narrative of the most Wicked and Inhuman Transactions of that Bloody-Minded Gang of Thief-takers alias Thief-Makers Macdaniel, Berry, Salmon, Eagan alias Gahagen*. London, 1756.

Davenport-Hill, Rosamund and Florence. *A Memoir of Matthew Davenport-Hill; with selections from his correspondence*. London, 1878.

Davies, Sir John. *A Report of Cases*. London, 1615.

De Fonblanque, E. B. *The Life and Labours of Albany Fonblanque*. London, 1874.

De Quincey, Thomas. *On Murder Considered as One of the Fine Arts*. 1827. Reprint, London, 1980.

Dickens, Charles. *David Copperfield*. 1850. Reprint, Harmondsworth, Middlesex, 1985.

———. *Great Expectations*. 1860–61. Reprint, Harmondsworth, Middlesex, 1980.

————. *The Letters of Charles Dickens*. 12 vols. Oxford, 1969–2002.

————. *Little Dorrit*. 1855–57. Reprint, Harmondsworth, Middlesex, 1981.

————. *The Old Curiosity Shop*. 1841. Reprint, Harmondsworth, Middlesex, 1985.

————. *Our Mutual Friend*. 1864–65. Reprint, Harmondsworth, Middlesex, 1997.

————. *Pickwick Papers*. 1836–37. Reprint, Harmondsworth, Middlesex, 1986.

————. *A Tale of Two Cities*. 1859. Reprint, Harmondsworth, Middlesex, 1970.

Dickenson, W., and Thomas Noon Talfourd. *A Practical Guide to the Quarter Sessions and Other Sessions of the Peace, Adapted to the Use of Young Magistrates, and Professional Gentlemen, at the Commencement of their Practice*. 3d ed. London, 1829.

Dymond, Jonathan. *Essays on the Principles of Morality*. New York, 1839.

Eden, William. *Principles of Penal Law*. London, 1771.

Emerson, T. *A Concise Treatise of the Courts of Law of the City of London*. London, 1794.

Erskine, Thomas. *The Speeches of the Right Honorable Lord Erskine When at the Bar, with a Preparatory Memoir by the Right Hon. Lord Brougham*. Edited by James Ridgway. 4 vols. London, 1810.

Farington, Joseph. *The Diary of Joseph Farington*. Edited by Kenneth Garlick and Kenneth Mackintyre. 16 vols. New Haven and London, 1978–84.

Fielding, Henry. *An Enquiry into the Causes of the Late Increase of Robbers*. In *The Works of Henry Fielding*, 10:349–467. New York, 1903.

————. *A Proposal for Making an Effective Provision for the Poor*. London, 1753.

————. *Tom Jones*. 1749. Reprint, Harmondsworth, Middlesex, 1966.

Fitzpatrick, William John. *Secret Service under Pitt*. London, 1892.

Fonblanque, Albany. *Life and Labours*. London, 1874.

[Foote, J. A.]. *"Pie Powder": Being Dust from the Law Courts, Collected and Recollected on the Western Circuit*. London, 1911.

Forsyth, William. *Hortensius; or The Advocate*. London, 1849.

Fortin. *City Biography, containing Anecdotes and Memoirs of the Rise, Progress, Situation and Character of the Aldermen and Other Conspicuous Personages of the Corporation of the City of London*. 2d ed. London, 1800.

Foss, Edward. *The Judges of England with Sketches of their Lives*. 9 vols. London, 1848–64.

Foster, Joseph. *Alumni Oxonienses: the members of the University of Oxford, [1500–1886]: their parentage, birthplace and year of birth, with a record of their degrees*. 1715–1886. 4 vols. Oxford, 1888.

————. *Men at the Bar: A Biographical Handlist of the Members of Various Inns of Court including Her Majesty's Judges etc*. London, 1885.

Foster, Sir Michael. *A Report of Some Proceedings on the Commission of Oyer and Terminer and Gaol Delivery for the Trial of Roberts in the Year 1746 in the County of Surrey and of Other Crown Cases, to which are added Discourses upon a few Branches of the Crown Law*. Oxford, 1762.

Freshfield, E., ed. *Records of the Society of Gentlemen Practisers in the Courts of Law and Equity called the Law Society*. London, 1897.

Fuller, Thomas. *The Holy State and the Profane State*. Edited by Maximilian Graff Walten. 2 vols. 1642. Reprint, New York, 1938.

Gaskell, Elizabeth. *Mary Barton*. 1848. Reprint, Harmondsworth, Middlesex, 1970.

Gaspey, Thomas. *The History of George Godfrey*. London, 1828.

Gilbert, Geoffrey. *Law of Evidence*. London, 1754.

Gisbourne, Thomas. *An Inquiry into the Duties of Men in the Higher Ranks of the Middle Classes*. London, 1794.

———. *Principles of Moral Philosophy*. London, 1789.

[Grant, James]. *The Bench and the Bar*. 2d ed. 2 vols. London, 1838.

———. *The Great Metropolis*. 2 vols. London, 1837.

Grimaldi, Stacey. "Memorial of the Knapp Family, shewing likewise their kindred to Sir Thomas White, Founder of St. John's College, Oxford." In *Miscellaneous Writings*. London, 1874–81.

Grosley, M. Jean Pierre. *A tour to London, or, New Observations on England, and its Inhabitants*. London, 1772.

Hague, Thomas. *A Letter to William Garrow, Esquire, in which the Conduct of Counsel in the Cross-Examination of Witnesses and Commenting on their Testimony is fully discussed and the Licentiousness of the Bar Exposed*. London, 1808.

Hale, Sir Matthew. *History of the Pleas of the Crown*. London, 1736.

Hanging, Not Punishment Enough. 1701. Reprint, London, 1812.

Hardcastle, Mary, ed. *Life of John, Lord Campbell*. 2 vols. London, 1881.

Harmer, James. *The Case of Edward Harris*. London, 1825.

———. *The Murder of Mr. Steele*. London, 1807.

Hawkins, William. *A Treatise on the Pleas of the Crown*. 2 vols. London, 1716–21.

Hazlitt, William. "Illustrations of *The Times* Newspaper: On Modern Lawyers and Poets." In *Selected Writings*, edited by Duncan Wu, 4:129–35. London, 1998.

Henderson, Emily. *Recollections of the Public Career and Private Life of John Adolphus*. London, 1871.

Holcroft, Thomas. *Memoirs of Thomas Holcroft*. 1816. Reprint, Oxford, 1926.

Hook, Theodore E. *Gilbert Gurney*. 1836. Reprint, London, 1841.

Hughes, John, comp. *The New Law List*. London, 1798–1802.

Jackson, Randle. *Considerations on the Increase of Crime and the Degree of its Extent. The principle causes of such increase, and the most likely means for the prevention, or mitigation of this public calamity. Addressed to the Magistracy of the County of Surrey, in the form of a report, as originally drawn by Randle Jackson, Esq., a Magistrate of that County*. London, 1828.

Jerdan, William. *The Autobiography of William Jerdan*. 4 vols. London, 1852.

JPT. *An Extempore Essay on the Oratorical Style of Charles Phillips Esq*. London, 1821.

Kelly, Bernard W. *Famous Advocates and their Speeches: British Forensic Eloquence, From Lord Erskine to Lord Russell of Killowan, with an Historical Introduction*. London, 1921.

Knapp, Andrew, and William Baldwin. *Criminal Chronology; or, the Newgate Calendar*. 4 vols. London, 1809.

Leach, Thomas. *Cases in Crown Law, determined by the Twelve Judges; by the Court of King's Bench; and by the Commissions of Oyer and Terminer, and General Gaol Delivery*. London, 1815.

The Life & Action of John Waller, Who Made his Exit at the 7 Dials on 13 May 1732; Containing All the Villainies . . . Swearing Robberies Against Innocent People, To Take Away their Lives for the Sake of the Rewards. London, 1732.

Lincoln's Inn. *The Records of the Honorable Society of Lincoln's Inn. Admissions and Chapel Registers*. 4 vols. London, 1896.

————. *The Records of the Honorable Society of Lincoln's Inn. The Black Books*. 4 vols. London, 1897–1902.

Mackintosh, R. J., ed. *Memoirs of the Life of the Right Honourable Sir James Mackintosh*. 2d ed. 2 vols. London, 1836.

MacNally, Leonard. *The Rules of Evidence in Pleas of the Crown*. London, 1802.

Madan, Martin. *Thoughts on Executive Justice*. London, 1785.

Martin, Sir Theodore. *A Life of Lord Lyndhurst from Letters and Papers in Possession of his Family*. London, 1883.

Mill, John Stuart. "The Influence of Lawyers." In *Collected Works*, edited by John M. Robson. Vol. 26, *Journals and Debating Speeches*, 385–91. Toronto, 1998.

Montagu, Basil. *An Account of the Origin and Object of the Society for the Diffusion of Knowledge upon the Punishment of Death and the Improvement of Prison Discipline*. London, 1812.

————. *The Debate in the House of Commons, April 15, 1813, upon Sir Samuel Romilly's Bill on the Punishment of High Treason*. London, 1813.

————. *Debate in the House of Commons on Sir Samuel Romilly's Bill for taking away Corruption of Blood in Attainder of Felony and Treason, etc*. London, 1814.

————. *The Debates in the House of Commons during the year 1811 upon Certain Bills for Abolishing the Punishment of Death*. London, 1811.

————. *Debates in the year 1810, upon Sir Samuel Romilly's Bills for Abolishing the Punishment of Death, etc*. London, 1810.

————. *Digest of the Bankruptcy Laws*. 4 vols. London, 1807.

————. *Enquiries Respecting the Administration of Bankrupts' Estates by Assignees*. London, 1811.

————. *An Enquiry into the Aspersions upon the late Ordinary of Newgate (B. Forde) with some Observations upon Newgate and upon the Punishment of Death*. London, 1815.

————. *An Enquiry Respecting the Expediency of Limiting the Creditor's Power to Refuse a Bankrupt's Certificate*. London, 1809.

————. *Enquiry Respecting the Mode of Issuing Commissions in Bankruptcy*. London, 1810.

————. *An Examination of Some Observations made in the House of Commons upon a Passage in Dr. Paley's Moral Philosophy on the Punishment of Death*. London, 1810.

————. *The Opinions of Different Authors upon the Punishment of Death*. London, 1809; 2d ed., 1816.

————. *The Rise and Progress of the Mitigation of the Punishment of Death, 1520–1687*. London, 1822.

————. *Some Inquiries respecting the Punishment of Death for Crimes without Violence*. London, 1818.

————. *Thoughts on the Punishment of Death for Forgery*. London, 1830.

————. *Thoughts upon the Abolition of the Punishment of Death, in cases of Bankruptcy*. London, 1821.

————. *Tracts on the Punishment of Death: Debates in the House of Commons upon the Removal of Capital Punishment for Stealing in Bleaching Grounds*. London, 1811.

Morgan, John. *Essay on Evidence*. London, 1789.

O'Keefe, John. *Recollections of the Life of John O'Keefe, written by himself*. 2 vols. London, 1826.

Paley, William. *The Principles of Moral and Political Philosophy*. London, 1785.

Peake, Thomas. *Compendium of the Law of Evidence*. London, 1801.

Perkins, Augustus Thorndike. *A Sketch of the Life, and a List of Some of the Works of John Singleton Copley*. N.p., 1873

Phillips, Charles. *The Speeches of Charles Phillips*. 2d ed. London, 1822.

———. *Vacation Thoughts on Capital Punishment*. London, 1857.

Phillips, S. M. *A Treatise on the Law of Evidence*. London, 1814.

[Polson, Archer]. *Law and Lawyers: A Sketchbook of Legal Biography, Gossip, and Anecdote*. 2 vols. London, 1840.

Pulling, Alexander. *A Practical Treatise of the Laws, Customs, and Regulations of the City and Port of London*. London, 1842.

Quack! Quack! I have done the baker out of his ducks. London, 1796.

[Raithby, J.]. *The Study and Practice of the Law Considered in their Various relations to Society*. London, 1798.

Reeve, John. *Chart of Penal Law, Exhibiting an Historical View of Crimes and Punishments*. London, n.d.

Robinson, Benjamin Coulson. *Bench and Bar: Reminiscences of One of the Last of an Ancient Race*. London, 1889.

Robinson, Charles J. *A Register of the Scholars Admitted to the Merchant Taylors' School*. 2 vols. Lewes, 1882.

Robinson, Henry Crabb. *Diary, Reminiscences, and Correspondence*. Edited by Thomas Sadler. 3 vols. London, 1869.

Romilly, Sir Samuel. *Memoirs of the Life of Sir Samuel Romilly*. London, 1840.

[Roscoe, Henry]. *Westminster Hall: or Professional Relics and Anecdotes*. 3 vols. London, 1825.

Ruggles, Thomas [pseud.]. *The Barrister; or, Strictures on the Education Proper for the Bar*. Dublin, 1792.

Russell, W. O. *Treatise on Felonies and Misdemeanours*. London, 1819.

Scarlett, Peter Campbell. *A Memoir of the Right Honourable James, First Lord Abinger*. London, 1877.

Smith, Thomas. *De Republica Anglorum*. [1583]. Reprint, edited by Mary Dewar, London, 1982.

Starkie, Thomas. *Treatise on Criminal Pleading with Precedents of Indictments, Special Pleas, etc*. London, 1814.

Stephen, Sir James Fitzjames. *A History of the Criminal Law of England*. 3 vols. London, 1883.

Storer, T. and H. S., and T. Cromwell. *History of Clerkenwell*. London, 1828.

Stow, John. *A survey of the cities of London and Westminster, and the Borough of Southwark . . . corrected, improved, and very much enlarged, in the year 1720, by John Strype*. 6th ed. London, 1754–55.

Strange, Sir John. *Reports of Adjudged Cases in the Courts of Chancery, King's Bench, Common Pleas, and Exchequer*. London, 1745.

Swift, Jonathan. *Gulliver's Travels*. 1726. Reprint, Harmondsworth, Middlesex, 1985.

Townsend, William C. *Modern State Trials: Revised and illustrated with essays and notes*. London, 1850.

The Trial of R. Patch, for the Wilful Murder of I. Blight . . . Taken in short hand by J. Gurney and W. B. Gurney. London, 1806.

The Trials of Arthur Thistlewood, J. Inge, J. T. Brunt, W. Davidson and R. Tidd. London, [?1820].

Trollope, Anthony. *The New Zealander.* [1855–56]. Edited by H. John Hall. Oxford, 1972.

———. *Orley Farm.* 1861–62. Reprint, Oxford, 1985.

———. *Phineas Redux.* 1873–74. Reprint, Oxford, 1983.

———. *The Three Clerks.* 1858. Reprint, Oxford, 1943.

Twiss, Horace. *The Public and Private Life of Lord Chancellor Eldon.* 3 vols. London, 1844.

Viner, Charles. *General Abridgment of Law and Equity.* 23 vols. London, 1741–53.

Warren, Samuel. *Correspondence between Samuel Warren, Esq., Barrister-at-Law, and Charles Phillips, Esq., Relative to the Trial of Courvoisier.* London, 1849.

Whishaw, James. *A Synopsis of the Members of the English Bar.* London, 1835.

Wilkinson, George Theodore. *An Authentic History of the Cato-Street Conspiracy; with the trials at large of the conspirators.* 1820. Reprint, New York, 1972.

Williams, Montagu. *Leaves of a Life.* London, 1890.

[Wontner, Thomas]. *Old Bailey Experience: Criminal Jurisprudence and the Actual Working of our Penal Code.* London, 1833.

Woolrych, Humphrey William. *Lives of the Eminent Serjeants-at-Law of the English Bar.* 2 vols. London, 1869.

JOURNAL ARTICLES

"Absence of Counsel.—Audience of Attorneys." *Legal Observer* 35 (1847): 60.

"Admission to the Old Bailey." *Law Times* 3 (1844): 106–7.

[Adolphus, John]. "Memoir of Sir John Gurney." *Law Magazine* 23 (1845): 275–79.

Adolphus, John Leycester. "The Late John Adolphus." *Fraser's Magazine* 66 (1862): 58–97.

"Advocacy of Prisoners." *Legal Observer* 26 (1843): 217.

"Allowance of Counsel to Prisoners." *Legal Examiner and Law Chronicle* 3 (1834): 311.

"The Appointment of a Public Prosecutor." *Legal Observer* 27 (1843): 502.

"The Bar and the Central Criminal Court." *Law Times* 3 (1844): 501–2.

"The Bar and the Press—The State of the Profession." *Law Review* 3 (1845–46): 27–43.

"Bar Oratory." *New Monthly Magazine and Literary Journal* 14 (1825, pt. 2): 167–74.

"The Barrister." *The Jurist, or Quarterly Journal of Jurisprudence and Legislation* 2 (1828): 367–74; 3 (1832): 94–100, 213–19.

"A Barrister's Advocacy of his Client's Cause." *Legal Observer* 15 (1837): 216–17.

"Barristers Receiving Briefs from Suitors." *Legal Observer* 40 (1850): 44–45.

"Biographical Sketch of the Late Mr. Brodrick." *Legal Observer* 1 (1830): 21–22.

"Borough of Southwark Court." *Legal Observer* 39 (1849–50): 465.

"Bounds of Old Bailey Decorum." *Legal Examiner* 1 (1831–32): 25–26.

"Briefs to Counsel." *Law Times* 4 (1844–45): 79.

[Brougham, Henry]. "Rights and Duties of Advocates." *Edinburgh Review* 64 (1836–37): 155–68.

"Can a Barrister Refuse a Brief?" *Legal Observer* 35 (1847–48): 501.

"The Central Criminal Court." *Law Times* 3 (1844): 252.

"The Central Criminal Court." *Legal Observer* 9 (1834): 17–18.

"Central Criminal Court." *Westminster Review* 22 (1835): 195–212.

"Central Criminal Court Bar." *Legal Observer* 28 (1844): 458–59.

"Changes Made in the Law During the Last Session of Parliament, 1834. No. V. The Central Criminal Court Act." *Legal Observer* 8 (1834): 486–88.

"Commissioner Phillips—Courvoisier—and the 'Examiner.'" *Punch* 17 (1849): 223–24.

"Conduct of Prosecutions by the Government." *Legal Observer* 35 (1847–48): 341.

"The Corporation of London and Municipal Reform." *Westminster Review* 39 (1843): 499.

"Correspondence. License of Counsel." *The Jurist* 12 (1848): 24–25.

"A Country Solicitor." *Law Times* 4 (1844–45): 61–62.

"The Court of Exchequer and its Judges." *Legal Observer* 2 (1831): 305–7.

"The Criminal Courts of England." *Legal Observer* 4 (1832): 337–38.

"Criminal Trials." *Legal Observer* 4 (1832): 20–22.

"The Defence of Courvoisier, and the Plea for It." *Law Magazine* 43 (1850): 26–36.

"Defence of Prisoners on Trial for Felony." *Legal Examiner* 1 (1831–32): 601–4.

[Denman, Thomas]. "Law of Evidence—Criminal Procedure—Publicity." *Edinburgh Review* 40 (1824): 169–207.

"Editors and Newspaper Writers of the Last Generation." *Fraser's Magazine* 65 (1862): 606–9.

"The English Bar." *Law Magazine and Review* 23 (1867): 126–45.

"Events of the Quarter." *Law Magazine* 4 (1830): 517; 12 (1834): 518–19; 13 (1835): 281–82; 14 (1835): 238; 16 (1836): 243; 24 (1840): 238.

"Hearing Attorneys at Quarter Sessions." *Legal Observer* 30 (1845): 25–26.

"Hearing Attorneys at Quarter Sessions.—Pre-Audience of Counsel." *Legal Observer* 29 (1844–45): 136.

"Hints to Practitioners. No. II." *Legal Observer* 2 (1831): 53–55.

"The Hon. C. E. Law, Recorder of London." *Law Times* 15 (1850): 467.

"The Irish Bar, a Few Years after the Union." *Law Review* 7 (1847–48): 10–11.

"The Judges of England." *Fraser's Magazine* 60 (1864): 89–105.

"Judicial Characters. No. V. Sir William Garrow." *Legal Observer* 3 (1832): 253–56.

"The Late John Adolphus." *Fraser's Magazine* 66 (1862): 49–53.

"The Late Mr. Justice Talfourd." *Law Magazine* 51 (1854): 298.

"The Late Mr. Russell Gurney." *Law Journal* 13 (1878): 345.

"The Law of Advocacy in England." *Law Review* 13 (1850–51): 122–34.

"Legal Advisers of Prisoners." *Legal Observer* 28 (1844): 75.

"Legal Advisers of Prisoners." *Legal Observer* 34 (1847): 541.

"Legal Obituary—Mr. Commissioner Phillips." *Law Times* 33 (1859): 55–56.

"Letters to the Editor." *Legal Examiner* 3 (1832–33): 17–19.

"Letters to the Editor—Palace Court." *Legal Examiner* 3 (1832–33): 483–84.

"Licence of Counsel." *Law Magazine* 39 (1848): 53–61.

"License of Counsel and Criminal Procedure." *Law Magazine* 25 (1841): 143–55.

"The Life and Writings of the Late Mr. Justice Talfourd." *North British Review* 25 (1856): 47.

"Life of Sir Vicary Gibbs." *Law Magazine* 14 (1835): 58–97.

"The Lord Mayor's Court.—Monopoly of the Common Pleaders." *Legal Observer* 45 (1852–53): 431–32.

"Mal-practice in the Criminal Courts." *Legal Observer* 41 (1851): 454.

"The Marshalsea and Palace Courts." *Legal Observer* 37 (1848–49): 345–46.

"Memoir of John Bell." *Legal Observer* 11 (1836): 265–66.

"Memoir of Mr. Baron Garrow." *Law Review* 1 (1844–45): 318–28. Reprinted in *Law Times* 4 (1844–45): 445–47.

"Memoir of Sir William Garrow." *Monthly Magazine* 9 (1840): 106–16.

"Memoir of the Late Mr. Alley." *Legal Observer* 9 (1834): 66–67.

"A Memoir of the Right Hon. Sir Robert Graham." *Legal Observer* 12 (1836): 489–90.

"Middlesex Sessions.—August 12." *Legal Guide* 4 (1840): 285–86.

"Middlesex Sessions.—Dec. 19." *Legal Guide* 1 (1838–39): 154–56.

"Mr. Adolphus and his Contemporaries at the Old Bailey." *Law Magazine* 34 (1846): 54–67.

"Mr. Baron Garrow." *Law Review* 1 (1844): 18–28.

"Mr. Charles Phillips, and his Defence of Courvoisier." *Legal Observer* 39 (1849–50): 137–38.

"Mr. Charles Phillips and the *Examiner*." *Examiner*, 24 Nov. 1849.

"Mr. Charles Phillips' Defence of Courvoisier." *Legal Observer* 39 (1849–50): 276–78, 297–98.

"Mr. Serjeant Davy." *Law Times* 26 (1856): 212.

"The New Recorder of London." *Legal Observer* 40 (1850): 425.

"Notabilia—Chairman of the Middlesex Sessions." *Legal Examiner* 3 (1832–33): 164.

"Notes Upon Circuit, No. III. The Crown Courts Bar." *Law Times* 1 (1843): 611.

"Notes Upon Circuit, No. V. The Central Criminal Court." *Law Times* 2 (1843–44): 46.

"The Old Bailey, and its Practices." *Law Magazine and Review*, n.s., 1 (1872): 326–34.

"The Old Bailey Bar and Sir Peter Laurie." *Legal Observer* 37 (1848–49): 145.

"Old Bailey Experience." *Law Magazine* 10 (1833): 259–95.

"*Old Bailey Experience* (Review)." *Westminster Review* 20 (1834): 142–51.

"Old Bailey Practice.—Licence of Counsel." *Legal Observer* 38 (1849): 230.

"Old Stories Re-told. Eliza Fenning. (The Danger of Condemning to Death on Circumstantial Evidence Alone)." *All the Year Round* (13 July 1867): 68–72.

"On the Administration of the Central Criminal Court." *Monthly Law Magazine and Political Review* 1 (1838): 305–35; 2 (1838): 193–215.

"On the Mode of Taking the Examination and Committal for Trial of Persons Charged with Felony and Misdemeanour." *The Jurist* 4 (1840): 234–39.

"On the Principle of Advocacy as Developed in the Practice of the Bar." *Law Magazine* 84 (1846): 1–34. Reprinted in *Law Magazine and Review*, n.s., 20 (1854): 265–98.

"On the Prisoner's Counsel Bill." *Legal Observer* 8 (1834): 24.

"On the Profession of the Bar." *London Magazine*, n.s., 1 (1825): 323–38.

"Palace Court.—Counsel." *Legal Observer* 6 (1833): 408.

"The Palace Court Monopoly." *Legal Observer* 37 (1848–49): 64–65.

"Palace Court Practice." *Legal Observer* 37 (1848–49): 105–6.

"Parliamentary Notices.—The Prisoners' Counsel Bill." *Legal Observer* 10 (1835): 225.

"The Poor Prisoner." *Law Times* 1 (1843): 607.

"Poor Prisoners." *Law Times* 1 (1843): 635.

"Postscript." *Law Review* 15 (1851): 444.

"Postscript—Public Prosecutors." *Law Review* 16 (1852): 443-45.

"Practice at the Old Bailey Bar." *Legal Observer* 35 (1847-48): 2-4.

"Practice under the Prisoners' Counsel Act." *Legal Observer* 12 (1836): 419-20, 497-98.

"Pre-audience of the Bar at Quarter Sessions." *Legal Observer* 32 (1846): 275-76.

"The Prisoners' Counsel Bill." *Law Magazine* 15 (1836): 394-402.

"The Prisoners' Counsel Bill." *Legal Observer* 10 (1835): 225.

"Prisoners' Counsel—Practice. Memorandum." *Law Magazine* 17 (1837): 470.

"The Progress of Law Reform." *Legal Observer* 13 (1836): 1.

"Proposed Amendment of the Prisoners' Counsel Bill." *Legal Observer* 10 (1835): 278-79.

"Proposed Practice Under the Prisoners' Counsel Act." *Legal Observer* 12 (1836): 340-41.

"Prosecutions." *Law Times* 1 (1843): 467-68.

"The Province of the Bar in England." *Law Review* 9 (1848-49): 89-101.

"A Public Prosecutor." *Law Magazine* 39 (1848): 197-201.

"The Right Hon. Russell Gurney, Q.C., M.P." *Law Times* 65 (1878): 145.

"Scenes and Decisions in Our Criminal Courts." *Legal Examiner and Law Chronicle* 3 (1834): 263-67.

"Second Report on Criminal Law." *Law Magazine* 16 (1836): 368-96.

"Selections from Correspondence—Advocacy of Prisoners." *Legal Observer* 26 (1843): 217.

"Selections from Correspondence—Copies of Depositions." *Legal Observer* 16 (1838): 449-50.

"Selections from Correspondence—Prisoners' Counsel Act." *Legal Observer* 16 (1838): 313.

"The Sessions-bar, and Attorneys." *Legal Observer* 37 (1848-49): 61-63.

"Sir Samuel Shepherd." *Law Magazine* 25 (1841): 289-310.

"Sir William Garrow." *Legal Observer* 3 (1832): 253-56.

[Smith, Sydney]. "Counsel for Prisoners." *Edinburgh Review* 65 (1826-27): 74-95.

"Some Account of Sir John Silvester, Bart." *European Magazine and London Review* (Nov. 1815): 387-88.

"Soup System.—Prosecution by Magistrates." *Law Magazine* 41 (1849): 103-19.

"Southwark Corporate Court of Record." *Legal Observer* 37 (1848-49): 41-42.

"The State of the Bar." *Legal Observer* 28 (1844): 427-28.

"The State of the Profession." *Law Review* 10 (1849): 148-64.

"The State of the Profession." *Legal Observer* 29 (1844-45): 1-2.

[Stephen, James]. "The Morality of Advocacy." *Cornhill Magazine* 3 (1861): 447-59.

"Study of the Law—Part II, Method, etc." *Lawyer's Magazine* 1 (1761): 249-56, 278-95.

"Sudden Death of Mr. Valentine Lee." *Law Times* 8 (1846): 45.

Talfourd, Thomas N. "On the Profession of the Bar." *London Magazine*, n.s., 1 (1825): 323-38.

"Trial of Daniel M'Naughten, the Bar at the Central Criminal Court, and the Plea of Insanity." *Fraser's Magazine* 27 (1843): 444-54.

Index